DATE DUE

			PRINTED IN U.S.A.

SOMETHING ABOUT THE AUTHOR

ISSN 0276-816X

SOMETHING ABOUT THE AUTHOR

Facts and Pictures about Authors
and Illustrators of Books for Young People

EDITED BY
ANNE COMMIRE

VOLUME 54

Gale Research Inc.
Book Tower • Detroit, Michigan 48226

Editor: Anne Commire

Associate Editors: Agnes Garrett, Helga P. McCue

Senior Assistant Editor: Dianne H. Anderson

Assistant Editors: Eunice L. Petrini, Linda Shedd

Sketchwriters: Marguerite Feitlowitz, Mimi Hutson

Researcher: Catherine Ruello

Editorial Assistants: Catherine Coray, Joanne J. Ferraro, Marja T. Hiltunen,
Evelyn Johnson, June Lee, Dieter Miller, Karen Walker

Permissions Assistant: Susan Pfanner

Special acknowledgment is due to Elisa Ann Ferraro, Assistant Editor,
for her compilation of the Character Index
which appears in this volume.

In cooperation with the staff of *Something about the Author Autobiography Series*

Editor: Joyce Nakamura

Assistant Editors: Carolyn Chafetz, Motoko Fujishiro Huthwaite

Research Assistant: Shelly Andrews

Production Manager: Mary Beth Trimper

External Production Assistants: Linda Davis, Anthony J. Scolaro

Internal Production Associate: Louise Gagné

Layout Artist: Elizabeth Lewis Patryjak

Art Director: Arthur Chartow

Special acknowledgment is also due to the members of the *Contemporary Authors* staff
who assisted in the preparation of this volume.

Copyright © 1989 by Gale Research Inc. All rights reserved.

Library of Congress Catalog Card Number 72-27107

ISBN 0-8103-2264-1
ISSN 0276-816X

Computerized photocomposition by
Typographics, Incorporated
Kansas City, Missouri

Printed in the United States

Contents

Introduction ix   Acknowledgments xv

Character Index 183   Illustrations Index 275

Author Index 295

Contents

Introduction

As the only ongoing reference series that deals with the lives and works of authors and illustrators of children's books, *Something about the Author (SATA)* is a unique source of information. The *SATA* series includes not only well-known authors and illustrators whose books are most widely read, but also those less prominent people whose works are just coming to be recognized. *SATA* is often the only readily available information source for less well-known writers or artists. You'll find *SATA* informative and entertaining whether you are:

—a student in junior high school (or perhaps one to two grades higher or lower) who needs information for a book report or some other assignment for an English class;

—a children's librarian who is searching for the answer to yet another question from a young reader or collecting background material to use for a story hour;

—an English teacher who is drawing up an assignment for your students or gathering information for a book talk;

—a student in a college of education or library science who is studying children's literature and reference sources in the field;

—a parent who is looking for a new way to interest your child in reading something more than the school curriculum prescribes;

—an adult who enjoys children's literature for its own sake, knowing that a good children's book has no age limits.

Scope

In *SATA* you will find detailed information about authors and illustrators who span the full time range of children's literature, from early figures like John Newbery and L. Frank Baum to contemporary figures like Judy Blume and Richard Peck. Authors in the series represent primarily English-speaking countries, particularly the United States, Canada, and the United Kingdom. Also included, however, are authors from around the world whose works are available in English translation, for example: from France, Jean and Laurent De Brunhoff; from Italy, Emanuele Luzzati; from the Netherlands, Jaap ter Haar; from Germany, James Krüss; from Norway, Babbis Friis-Baastad; from Japan, Toshiko Kanzawa; from the Soviet Union, Kornei Chukovsky; from Switzerland, Alois Carigiet, to name only a few. Also appearing in *SATA* are Newbery medalists from Hendrik Van Loon (1922) to Russell Freedman (1988). The writings represented in *SATA* include those created intentionally for children and young adults as well as those written for a general audience and known to interest younger readers. These writings cover the spectrum from picture books, humor, folk and fairy tales, animal stories, mystery and adventure, science fiction and fantasy, historical fiction, poetry and nonsense verse, to drama, biography, and nonfiction.

Information Features

In *SATA* you will find full-length entries that are being presented in the series for the first time. This volume, for example, marks the first full-length appearance of Laurene Krasny Brown, Sandy Dengler, Thomas M. Disch, Tibor Gergely, Rachel Isadora, Suse MacDonald, and W. Somerset Maugham.

Obituaries have been included in *SATA* since Volume 20. An Obituary is intended not only as a death notice but also as a concise view of a person's life and work. Obituaries may appear for persons who have entries in earlier *SATA* volumes, as well as for people who have not yet appeared in the series. In this volume Obituaries mark the recent deaths of James Baldwin, Virginia Haviland, Clement Hurd, Arnold Lobel, Ben Stahl, Eloise Wilkin, and others.

Revised Entries

Since Volume 25, each *SATA* volume also includes newly revised and updated entries for a selection of *SATA* listees (usually four to six) who remain of interest to today's readers and who have been active enough to require extensive revision of their earlier biographies. For example, when Beverly Cleary first appeared in *SATA* Volume 2, she was the author of twenty-one books for children and young adults and the recipient of numerous awards. By the time her updated sketch appeared in Volume 43 (a span of fifteen years), this creator of the indefatigable Ramona Quimby and other memorable characters had produced a dozen new titles and garnered nearly fifty additional awards, including the 1984 Newbery Medal.

The entry for a given biographee may be revised as often as there is substantial new information to provide. In this volume, look for revised entries on Mollie Hunter, Fran Manushkin, Gary Paulsen, Peter Spier, Theodore Taylor, and P. L. Travers.

Illustrations

While the textual information in *SATA* is its primary reason for existing, photographs and illustrations not only enliven the text but are an integral part of the information that *SATA* provides. Illustrations and text are wedded in such a special way in children's literature that artists and their works naturally occupy a prominent place among *SATA*'s listees. The illustrators that you'll find in the series include such past masters of children's book illustration as Randolph Caldecott, Walter Crane, Arthur Rackham, and Ernest H. Shepard, as well as such noted contemporary artists as Maurice Sendak, Edward Gorey, Tomie de Paola, and Margot Zemach. There are Caldecott medalists from Dorothy Lathrop (the first recipient in 1938) to John Schoenherr (the latest winner in 1988); cartoonists like Charles Schulz ("Peanuts"), Walt Kelly ("Pogo"), Hank Ketcham ("Dennis the Menace"), and Georges Rémi ("Tintin"); photographers like Jill Krementz, Tana Hoban, Bruce McMillan, and Bruce Curtis; and filmmakers like Walt Disney, Alfred Hitchcock, and Steven Spielberg.

In more than a dozen years of recording the metamorphosis of children's literature from the printed page to other media, *SATA* has become something of a repository of photographs that are unique in themselves and exist nowhere else as a group, particularly many of the classics of motion picture and stage history and photographs that have been specially loaned to us from private collections.

Indexes

Each *SATA* volume provides a cumulative index in two parts: first, the Illustrations Index, arranged by the name of the illustrator, gives the number of the volume and page where the illustrator's work appears in the current volume as well as all preceding volumes in the series; second, the Author Index gives the number of the volume in which a person's biographical sketch, Brief Entry, or Obituary appears in the current volume as well as all preceding volumes in the series. These indexes also include references to authors and illustrators who appear in *Yesterday's Authors of Books for Children* (described in detail below). Beginning with Volume 36, the *SATA* Author Index provides cross-references to authors who are included in *Children's Literature Review*.

Starting with Volume 42, you will also find cross-references to authors who are included in the *Something about the Author Autobiography Series* (described in detail below).

Character Index

If you're like many readers, the names of fictional characters may pop more easily into your mind than the names of the authors or illustrators who created them: Snow White, Charlotte the Spider, the Cat in the Hat, Peter Pan, Mary Poppins, Winnie-the-Pooh, Brer Rabbit, Little Toot, Charlie Bucket, Lassie, Rip Van Winkle, Bartholomew Cubbins—the list could go on and on. But who invented them? Now these characters, and several thousand others, can lead you to the *SATA* and *YABC* entries on the lives and works of their creators.

First published in Volume 50, the Character Index provides a broad selection of characters from books and other media—movies, plays, comic strips, cartoons, etc.—created by listees who have appeared in all the published volumes of *SATA* and *YABC*. This index gives the character name, followed by a *"See"* reference indicating the name of the creator and the number of the *SATA* or *YABC* volume in which the creator's bio-bibliographical entry can be found. As new *SATA* volumes are prepared, additional characters are included in the cumulative Character Index and published annually in *SATA*. (The cumulative Illustrations and Author Indexes still appear in each *SATA* volume.)

It would be impossible for the Character Index to include every important character created by *SATA* and *YABC* listees. (Several hundred important characters might be taken from Dickens alone, for example.) Therefore, the *SATA* editors have selected those characters that are best known and thus most likely to interest *SATA* users. Realizing that some of your favorite characters may not appear in this index, the editors invite you to suggest additional names. With your help, the editors hope to make the Character Index a uniquely useful reference tool for you.

What a *SATA* Entry Provides

Whether you're already familiar with the *SATA* series or just getting acquainted, you will want to be aware of the kind of information that an entry provides. In every *SATA* entry the editors attempt to give as complete a picture of the person's life and work as possible. In some cases that full range of information may simply be unavailable, or a biographee may choose not to reveal complete personal details. The information that the editors attempt to provide in every entry is arranged in the following categories:

1. The "head" of the entry gives

    —the most complete form of the name,
    —any part of the name not commonly used, included in parentheses,
    —birth and death dates, if known; a (?) indicates a discrepancy in published sources,
    —pseudonyms or name variants under which the person has had books published or is publicly known, in parentheses in the second line.

2. "Personal" section gives

    —date and place of birth and death,
    —parents' names and occupations,
    —name of spouse, date of marriage, and names of children,
    —educational institutions attended, degrees received, and dates,
    —religious and political affiliations,
    —agent's name and address,
    —home and/or office address.

3. "Career" section gives

    —name of employer, position, and dates for each career post,
    —military service,
    —memberships,
    —awards and honors.

4. "Writings" section gives

    —title, first publisher and date of publication, and illustration information for each book written; revised editions and other significant editions for books with particularly long publishing histories; genre, when known.

5. "Adaptations" section gives

    —title, major performers, producer, and date of all known reworkings of an author's material in another medium, like movies, filmstrips, television, recordings, plays, etc.

6. "Sidelights" section gives

> —commentary on the life or work of the biographee either directly from the person (and often written specifically for the *SATA* entry), or gathered from biographies, diaries, letters, interviews, or other published sources.

7. "For More Information See" section gives

> —books, feature articles, films, plays, and reviews in which the biographee's life or work has been treated.

How a *SATA* Entry Is Compiled

A *SATA* entry progresses through a series of steps. If the biographee is living, the *SATA* editors try to secure information directly from him or her through a questionnaire. From the information that the biographee supplies, the editors prepare an entry, filling in any essential missing details with research. The author or illustrator is then sent a copy of the entry to check for accuracy and completeness.

If the biographee is deceased or cannot be reached by questionnaire, the *SATA* editors examine a wide variety of published sources to gather information for an entry. Biographical sources are searched with the aid of Gale's *Biography and Genealogy Master Index*. Bibliographic sources like the *National Union Catalog*, the *Cumulative Book Index*, *American Book Publishing Record*, and the *British Museum Catalogue* are consulted, as are book reviews, feature articles, published interviews, and material sometimes obtained from the biographee's family, publishers, agent, or other associates.

For each entry presented in *SATA*, the editors also attempt to locate a photograph of the biographee as well as representative illustrations from his or her books. After surveying the available books which the biographee has written and/or illustrated, and then making a selection of appropriate photographs and illustrations, the editors request permission of the current copyright holders to reprint the material. In the case of older books for which the copyright may have passed through several hands, even locating the current copyright holder is often a long and involved process.

We invite you to examine the entire *SATA* series, starting with this volume. Described below are some of the people in Volume 54 that you may find particularly interesting.

Highlights of This Volume

MOLLIE HUNTER......was raised in Lowland Scotland and nourished by the Scottish tales and ballads of that region. "The shadow of history fell over me every day," she says. The history of her village was in its people and in their speech, and Hunter spoke Doric "as fluently as the standard English required from me at school." There "the idea that I would be a writer was planted in my head" by a strong-minded—and prophetic—teacher. With the idea of becoming a writer firmly set, Hunter became a habitual reader and researcher—two activities essential to the development of her writing craft. Using the premise that "history is people," Hunter became a noted children's writer of historical fiction. "History is ordinary people shaped and shaken by the winds of their time, as we in our time are shaped and shaken by the wind of current events. To write about the people of any time, one must know them so well that it would be possible to go back and live undetected among them."

W. SOMERSET MAUGHAM......grew up "with many disabilities. I was small; I had endurance but little physical strength; I stammered; I was shy; I had poor health. I had no facility for games...and I had...an instinctive shrinking from my fellow men....I have loved individuals; I have never cared for men in the mass." Since it was unthinkable in nineteenth-century England for anyone from a respectable, upper-middle class family to become a writer, Maugham studied to be a doctor, although the medical profession did not interest him. His first novel was published the same year he received his physician's certificate. During World War I, the author and physician became a secret agent for British Intelligence. "The work appealed both to my sense of romance and my sense of the ridiculous." It also gave him a wealth of background material for future novels. Another activity that yielded creative material was travel. During his life Maugham journeyed throughout the world, settling in the United States during World War

II. He spent the remainder of his life (in which writing was "an essential part") at his villa on the French Riviera.

GAIL OWENS......was born in Detroit, Michigan, a city that had a profound influence on her artwork. "I can see how growing up here has everything to do with my becoming interested in drawing faces, and in portraying interaction between people, a compensation, I think, for the fact that there was no landscape to look at." Although she drew at an early age and worked as a free-lance artist at sixteen, Owens never thought she would become an artist. "I might have given up working in the field of art altogether had it not been for the hard, economic fact of having to support my two children." Since she couldn't "type or take dictation," Owens supported her family by working as a graphic designer, director, and layout person before becoming an illustrator of children's books. She feels, however, that illustration is not really art. "The illustrator's work is never seen in its original quality....There is a big difference between original artwork and final reproduction."

PETER SPIER......spent his childhood in Amsterdam "in an intellectual milieu. Books were very important." He also delighted in "making things, mostly in clay and plasticine." His formal art training included classes in drawing, etching, and graphics at the Royal Academy of Art in Amsterdam. While working for a large Dutch newspaper, Spier was sent on assignment to Houston, Texas ("cultural shock!"). After a year, he moved to New York City where he worked as a free- lance illustrator. "I illustrated about fifty books before I started writing my own." Spier believes that "writing and drawing are two of the same art forms. What you say in the text, you no longer have to say in the pictures and vice versa." Spier's picture book, *Noah's Ark,* won the Caldecott Medal in 1978. His success depends on the high standards he sets for each book. "A good book," says Spier, "is always child-like—a poor one, childish."

THEODORE TAYLOR......was never fond of school, preferring instead vacations where he "excelled in the practice of freedom," roaming through fields, creeks, and other interesting places around town. "I had remarkable freedom for a kid curious about most things," he remembers. A major influence on his future writing—aside from his explorations—was Nappy, a half-beagle, half-terrier dog. "Many of the books I've written have canine characters in them, notably the *Teetoncey* trilogy, with 'Boo Dog'; 'Tuck' in *The Trouble with Tuck*; 'Rufus' in *Walking up a Rainbow*." His formal writing career began at the age of thirteen as a cub reporter for the Portsmouth, Virginia *Evening Star.* Books and then screenplays and documentaries were the mainstay of his writing credits until he began writing for children. One of Taylor's most successful books was *The Cay,* which won over eleven literary awards, and launched his career as a writer of children's books. His books, he insists, are not creative, but are drawn from real life events and people. "I stress that I don't have a good imagination, I'm still basically a reporter, finding it easier to work from real-life models."

P. L. TRAVERS......wrote poems and stories "always in secret" during her childhood in Queensland, Australia. She also read books—penny books ("real paper books they were, little thin books"), her mother's novels, and Bible stories. As a teenager, she found employment first as an actress and only later as a writer. Eventually she saved enough money by writing and acting to go to England and then on to her father's homeland, Ireland. Major influences in her development as a writer were her friendship with the Irish poet and editor AE (George William Russell) and her acquaintance with yet another Irish author, William Butler Yeats. "These men...saw nothing shameful or silly in myths and fairy stories....They allowed for the unknown." Travers wrote her most famous book from an old thatched manor house while recovering from an illness. "The idea of Mary Poppins has been blowing in and out of me, like a curtain at a window, all my life." Travers insists that the book, as well as her other books, was not written directly for children. "I suppose if there is something in my books that appeals to children, it is the result of my not having to go *back* to my childhood; I can, as it were, turn *aside* and consult it."

These are only a few of the authors and illustrators that you'll find in this volume. We hope you find all the entries in *SATA* both interesting and useful.

Yesterday's Authors of Books for Children

In a two-volume companion set to *SATA, Yesterday's Authors of Books for Children (YABC)* focuses on early authors and illustrators, from the beginnings of children's literature through 1960, whose books are still being read by children today. Here you will find "old favorites" like Hans Christian Andersen, J. M. Barrie, Kenneth Grahame, Betty MacDonald, A. A. Milne, Beatrix Potter, Samuel Clemens, Kate Greenaway, Rudyard Kipling, Robert Louis Stevenson, and many more.

Similar in format to *SATA, YABC* features bio-bibliographical entries that are divided into information categories such as Personal, Career, Writings, and Sidelights. The entries are further enhanced by book illustrations, author photos, movie stills, and many rare old photographs.

In Volume 2 you will find cumulative indexes to the authors and to the illustrations that appear in *YABC*. These listings can also be located in the *SATA* cumulative indexes.

By exploring both volumes of *YABC,* you will discover a special group of more than seventy authors and illustrators who represent some of the best in children's literature—individuals whose timeless works continue to delight children and adults of all ages. Other authors and illustrators from early children's literature are listed in *SATA,* starting with Volume 15.

Something about the Author Autobiography Series

You can complement the information in *SATA* with the *Something about the Author Autobiography Series (SAAS),* which provides autobiographical essays written by important current authors and illustrators of books for children and young adults. In every volume of *SAAS* you will find about twenty specially commissioned autobiographies, each accompanied by a selection of personal photographs supplied by the authors. The wide range of contemporary writers and artists who describe their lives and interests in the *Autobiography Series* includes Joan Aiken, Betsy Byars, Leonard Everett Fisher, Milton Meltzer, Maia Wojciechowska, and Jane Yolen, among others. Though the information presented in the autobiographies is as varied and unique as the authors, you can learn about the people and events that influenced these writers' early lives, how they began their careers, what problems they faced in becoming established in their professions, what prompted them to write or illustrate particular books, what they now find most challenging or rewarding in their lives, and what advice they may have for young people interested in following in their footsteps, among many other subjects.

Autobiographies included in the *SATA Autobiography Series* can be located through both the *SATA* cumulative index and the *SAAS* cumulative index, which lists not only the authors' names but also the subjects mentioned in their essays, such as titles of works and geographical and personal names.

The *SATA Autobiography Series* gives you the opportunity to view "close up" some of the fascinating people who are included in the *SATA* parent series. The combined *SATA* series makes available to you an unequaled range of comprehensive and in-depth information about the authors and illustrators of young people's literature.

Please write and tell us if we can make *SATA* even more helpful to you.

Acknowledgments

Grateful acknowledgment is made to the following publishers, authors, and artists for their kind permission to reproduce copyrighted material.

AVON BOOKS. Cover illustration from *Battle in the English Channel* by Theodore Taylor. Text copyright © 1983 by Theodore Taylor. Illustrations copyright © 1983 by Andrew Glass. Reprinted by permission of Avon Books.

BRADBURY PRESS. Illustration by Suse MacDonald from *Alphabatics* by Suse MacDonald. Copyright © 1986 by Suse MacDonald./ Jacket illustration by Jon Weiman from *Sentries* by Gary Paulsen. Copyright © 1986 by Gary Paulsen. Jacket illustration copyright © 1986 by Bradbury Press./ Jacket illustration by John Weiman from *Dancing Carl* by Gary Paulsen. Copyright © 1983 by Gary Paulsen. Jacket illustration copyright © 1983 by Bradbury Press./ Jacket illustration by Neil Waldman from *Dogsong* by Gary Paulsen. Copyright © 1985 by Gary Paulsen. Jacket illustration copyright © 1985 by Bradbury Press./ Jacket illustration by Jon Weiman from *Tracker* by Gary Paulsen. Copyright © 1984 by Gary Paulsen. All printed by permission of Bradbury Press.

CAROLRHODA BOOKS, INC. Illustration Peter E. Hanson from *Buttons for General Washington* by Peter and Connie Roop. Copyright © 1986 by Carolrhoda Books, Inc./ Illustration by Peter E. Hanson from *Keep the Lights Burning, Abbie* by Peter and Connie Roop. Copyright © 1985 by Carolrhoda Books, Inc. Both reprinted by permission of Carolrhoda Books, Inc.

CHILDRENS PRESS. Illustration by Mike Venezia from *Sometimes I Worry...* by Alan Gross. Copyright © 1978 by Regensteiner Publishing Enterprises, Inc. Reprinted by permission of Childrens Press.

COWARD, McCANN & GEOGHEGAN. Illustration by Gail Owens from *The Paper Caper* by Caroline B. Cooney. Text copyright © 1981 by Caroline Cooney. Illustrations copyright © 1981 by Gail Owens./ Jacket illustration by Salem Krieger from *The Case of the Semi-Human Beans* by Jane Werner Watson. Copyright © 1979 by Jane Werner Watson. Both reprinted by permission of Coward, McCann & Geoghegan.

THOMAS Y. CROWELL, INC. Jacket illustration by Richard Cuffari from *Rebellion Town: Williamsburg, 1776* by Theodore Taylor. Copyright © 1973 by Theodore Taylor./ Illustration by Robert Andrew Parker from *Battle in the Arctic Seas: The Story of Convoy PQ 17* by Theodore Taylor. Copyright © 1976 by Theodore Taylor. Both reprinted by permission of Thomas Y. Crowell, Inc.

CROWN PUBLISHERS, INC. Illustration by Diane de Groat from *Little Rabbit's Baby Brother,* created by Lucy Bate. Story by Fran Manushkin. Text copyright © 1986 by Crown Publishers, Inc. Illustrations copyright © 1986 by Diane de Groat./ Illustration by Irene Trivas from *Sometimes I Get Angry* by Jane Werner Watson, Robert E. Switzer, M.D., and J. Cotter Hirschberg, M.D. Text copyright © 1986 by Jane Werner Watson, Robert E. Switzer, and J. Cotter Hirschberg. Illustrations copyright © 1986 by Irene Trivas. Both reprinted by permission of Crown Publishers, Inc.

DELACORTE PRESS. Illustration by Mary Shepard from *Mary Poppins in Cherry Tree Lane* by P.L. Travers. Text copyright © 1982 by P. L. Travers. Illustrations copyright by Mary Shepard. Reprinted by permission of Delacorte Press.

DELL PUBLISHING CO., INC. Cover illustration from *Summer at High Kingdom* by Louise Dickinson Rich. Copyright © 1975 by Louise Dickinson Rich. Reprinted by permission of Dell Publishing Co., Inc.

ANDRE DEUTSCH LTD. Illustration by Geoffrey Patterson from *A Pig's Tale* by Geoffrey Patterson. Copyright © 1983 by Geoffrey Patterson. Reprinted by permission of Andre Deutsch Ltd.

DILLON PRESS, INC. Illustration by Chris Wold Dyrud from *Slow as a Panda* by Rebecca Larsen. Copyright © 1986 by Dillon Press, Inc. Reprinted by permission of Dillon Press, Inc.

DOUBLEDAY & CO., INC. Illustration by Karen Schmidt from *The Brave Little Toaster: A Bedtime Story for Small Appliances* by Thomas M. Disch. Text copyright © 1980, 1986 by Thomas M. Disch. Illustrations copyright © 1986 by Karen Schmidt./ Sidelight excerpts from *The Summing Up* by W. Somerset Maugham. Copyright 1938 by Somerset Maugham./ Illustration by Peter Spier from *Oh, Were They Ever Happy!* by Peter Spier. Copyright © 1978 by Peter Spier./ Illustration by Peter Spier from *Rain* by Peter Spier. Illustrations copyright © 1982 by Peter Spier./ Illustration by Peter Spier from *The Fox Went Out on a Chilly Night: An Old Song.* From "The Fox," arranged by Burl Ives. Copyright 1945 by Leeds Music Corp. Copyright © 1961 by Peter Spier./ Illustration by Peter Spier from *Noah's Ark,* translated from the Dutch by Peter Spier. Illustrations and translation copyright © 1977 by Peter Spier./ Illustration by Peter Spier from *London Bridge Is Falling Down!* Copyright © 1967 by Peter Spier./ Illustration by Peter Spier from *Bored—Nothing to Do!* by Peter Spier. Copyright © 1978 by Peter Spier./ Jacket illustration by Milton Glaser from *The Cay* by Theodore Taylor. Copyright © 1969 by Theodore Taylor./ Jacket illustration by Charles Santore from *The Trouble with Tuck* by Theodore Taylor. Copyright © 1981 by Theodore Taylor./ Illustration by Richard Cuffari from *Teetoncey* by Theodore Taylor. Text copyright © 1974 by Theodore Taylor. Illustrations copyright © 1974 by Richard Cuffari./ Jacket illustration by Paul Lambert from *The Maldonado Miracle* by Theodore Taylor. Copyright © 1962 by McCall Corp. Copyright © 1973 by Theodore Taylor./ Jacket illustration by Richard Cuffari from *The Odyssey of Ben O'Neal* by Theodore Taylor. Text copyright © 1977 by Theodore Taylor./ Illustration by Peter Spier from *We the People: The Story of the U.S. Constitution* by Peter Spier. Copyright © 1987 by Peter Spier./ Illustration by Peter Spier from *Crash! Bang! Boom!* by Peter Spier. Copyright © 1972 by Peter Spier./ Illustration by Peter Spier from *The Star-Spangled Banner* by Peter Spier. Copyright © 1973 by Peter Spier./ Illustration by Peter Spier from *Dreams* by Peter Spier. Copyright © 1986 by Peter Spier./ Illustration by Peter Spier from *The Erie Canal* (folk songs). Illustrations copyright © 1970 by Peter Spier. All reprinted by permission of Doubleday & Co., Inc.

DOWN EAST BOOKS. Illustration from *We Took to the Woods* by Louise Dickinson Rich. Copyright 1942, renewed © 1970 by Louise Dickinson Rich. Reprinted by permission of Down East Books.

E. P. DUTTON, INC. Illustration by Gail Owens from *That Julia Redfern* by Eleanor Cameron. Text copyright © 1982 by Eleanor Cameron. Illustrations copyright © 1982 by E. P. Dutton, Inc./ Illustration by Gail Owens from *Ella of All of a Kind Family* by Sydney Taylor. Text copyright © 1978 by Sydney Taylor. Illustrations copyright © 1978 by Gail Owens./ Illustration by Gail Owens from *Julia and the Hand of God* by Eleanor Cameron. Text copyright © 1977 by Eleanor Cameron. Illustrations copyright © 1977 by Gail Owens./ Illustration by Gail Owens from *Julia's Magic* by Eleanor Cameron. Text copyright © 1984 by Eleanor Cameron. Illustrations copyright © 1984 by Gail Owens./ Illustration by Gail Owens from *Cassie Bowen Takes Witch Lessons* by Anna Grossnickle Hines. Text copyright © 1985 by Anna Grossnickle Hines. Illustrations copyright © 1985 by Gail Owens./ Jacket illustration by Andrew Rhodes from *Popcorn Days and Buttermilk Nights* by Gary Paulsen. Copyright © 1983 by Gary Paulsen. All reprinted by permission of E. P. Dutton, Inc.

GARRARD PUBLISHING CO. Photograph by Michael J. O'Neill from *The People's Republic of China: Red Star of the East* by Jane Werner Watson. Copyright © 1976 by Jane Werner Watson./ Photograph by René Burri, Magnum from *The Indus: South Asia's Highway of History* by Jane Werner Watson. Copyright © 1970 by Jane Werner Watson./ Illustration by June Goldsborough from *Tanya and the Geese* by Jane Werner Watson. Copyright © 1974 by Jane Werner Watson. All reprinted by permission of Garrard Publishing Co.

THE C. R. GIBSON CO. Illustration by Cara Marks from *Beware When Elephants Sneeze* by Alice Joyce Davidson. Text copyright © 1986 by Alice Joyce Davidson. Illustrations copyright © 1986 by Cara Marks. Reprinted by permission of The C. R. Gibson Co.

GREENWILLOW BOOKS. Illustration by Rachel Isadora from *The Potters' Kitchen* by Rachel Isadora. Copyright © 1977 by Rachel Isadora Hite. Reprinted by permission of Greenwillow Books.

HARCOURT BRACE JOVANOVICH, INC. Illustration by Mary Shepard from *Mary Poppins in the Park* by P. L. Travers. Copyright 1952 by P. L. Travers./ Illustration by Mary Shepard and Agnes Sims from *Mary Poppins Opens the Door* by P. L. Travers. Copyright 1943 by P. L. Travers./ Illustration by Mary Shepard from *Mary Poppins Comes Back* by P. L. Travers. Copyright 1935 by P. L. Travers./ Jacket illustration by Charles Keeping from *Friend Monkey* by P. L. Travers. Copyright © 1971 by P. L. Travers. All reprinted by permission of Harcourt Brace Jovanovich, Inc.

HARPER & ROW, PUBLISHERS, INC. Illustration by Gertrude Hermes from *I Go by Sea, I Go by Land* by P. L. Travers. Copyright 1941 by P. L. Travers./ Illustration by Tibor Gergely from *Wheel on the Chimney* by Margaret Wise Brown. Illustrations copyright © 1954 by Tibor Gergely./ Jacket illustration by Michael Nakai from *A Stranger Came Ashore* by Mollie Hunter. Copyright © 1975 by Maureen Mollie Hunter McIlwraith./ Jacket illustration by Stephen Gammell from *The Wicked One* by Mollie Hunter. Copyright © 1977 by Maureen Mollie Hunter McIlwraith./ Illustration by Stephen Gammell from *The Kelpie's Pearls* by Mollie Hunter. Text copyright © 1964 by Mollie Hunter McIlwraith. Illustrations copyright © 1976 by Stephen Gammell./ Jacket illustration by Laszlo Kubinyi from *The Haunted Mountain* by Mollie Hunter. Text copyright © 1972 by Maureen Mollie Hunter McIlwraith. Illustrations copyright © 1972 by Laszlo Kubinyi./ Jacket illustration by Robert Blake from *The Third Eye* by Mollie Hunter. Copyright © 1979 by Maureen Mollie Hunter McIlwraith./ Illustration from *You Never Knew Her as I Did!* by Mollie Hunter. Copyright © 1981 by Maureen Mollie Hunter McIlwraith./ Jacket illustration by Dave Holmes from *A Sound of Chariots* by Mollie Hunter. Copyright © 1972 by Maureen Mollie Hunter McIlwraith. Jacket illustration copyright © 1983 by Dave Holmes./ Jacket illustration by Stephen Seymour from *Cat, Herself* by Mollie Hunter. Copyright © 1985 by Maureen Mollie Hunter McIlwraith. Jacket illustration copyright © 1985 by Stephen Seymour. Jacket copyright © 1986 by Harper & Row, Publisher, Inc./ Sidelight excerpts from *Talent Is Not Enough: Mollie Hunter on Writing for Children* by Mollie Hunter./ Illustration by Dick Gackenbach from "The Monster in the Third Dresser Drawer" in *The Monster in the Third Dresser Drawer and Other Stories about Adam Joshua* by Janice Lee Smith. Text copyright © 1981 by Janice Lee Smith. Illustrations copyright © 1981 by Dick Gackenbach./ Illustration by Ronald Himler from *Baby Come Out!* by Fran Manushkin. Text copyright © 1972 by Frances Manushkin. Illustrations copyright © 1972 by Ronald Himler. All reprinted by permission of Harper & Row, Publishers, Inc.

THE HORN BOOK, INC. Sidelight excerpts from an article "If You Can Read" by Mollie Hunter, June, 1978 in *Horn Book*. Copyright © 1978 by The Horn Book, Inc. Reprinted by permission of The Horn Book, Inc.

HOUGHTON MIFFLIN CO. Illustration by Giulio Maestro from "Body Parts" in *Mad as a Wet Hen! And Other Funny Idioms* by Marvin Terban. Text copyright © 1987 by Marvin Terban. Illustrations copyright © 1987 by Giulio Maestro. Reprinted by permission of Houghton Mifflin Co.

KESTREL BOOKS. Sidelight excerpts from an article "The Last Lord of Redhouse Castle," by Mollie Hunter in *The Thorny Paradise: Writers on Writing for Children*, edited by Edward Blishen. Copyright © 1975 by Kestrel Books. Reprinted by permission of Kestrel Books.

J. B. LIPPINCOTT CO. Sidelight excerpts from *Innocence under the Elms* by Louise Dickinson Rich. Copyright 1945 by J. B. Lippincott Co./ Sidelight excerpts from "We Took to the Woods" in *The Forest Years* by Louise Dickinson Rich. Copyright © 1963 by J. B. Lippincott Co./ Photographs from *Happy the Land* by Louise Dickinson Rich. Copyright 1946 by Louise Dickinson Rich./ Illustration by Grattan Condon from *The Peninsula* by Louise Dickinson Rich. Copyright © 1958 by Louise Dickinson Rich. All reprinted by permission of J. B. Lippincott Co.

LITTLE, BROWN AND CO. Illustration by Robert Lawson from *Mr. Popper's Penguins* by Richard and Florence Atwater. Copyright © 1958 by Florence Atwater, Doris Atwater, and Carroll Atwater Bishop. Reprinted by permission of Little, Brown and Co.

MACMILLAN PUBLISHING CO. Illustration by Gail Owens from *Tac's Island* by Ruth Yaffe Radin. Text copyright © 1986 by Ruth Yaffe Radin. Illustrations copyright © 1986 by Gail Owens. Reprinted by permission of Macmillan Publishing Co.

McGRAW-HILL BOOK CO. Sidelight excerpts from *About Sleeping Beauty* by P. L. Travers. Reprinted by permission of McGraw-Hill Book Co.

MOODY PRESS. Cover illustration from *Path of the Promise-Keeper* by Muriel Leeson. Copyright © 1984 by Muriel Leeson. Reprinted by permission of Moody Press.

WILLIAM MORROW & CO., INC. Illustrations by Lisbeth Zwerger from *Thumbeline* by Hans Christian Andersen. Translated from the Danish by Richard and Clara Winston. English translation copyright © 1980 by Clara Winston. Copyright © 1980 by Verlag Neugebauer Press. Both reprinted by permission of William Morrow & Co., Inc.

THOMAS NELSON, INC. Jacket illustration by Richard Cuffari from *The Foxman* by Gary Paulsen. Copyright © 1977 by Gary Paulsen. Reprinted by permission of Thomas Nelson, Inc.

W. W. NORTON & CO., INC. Wood engraving by Thomas Bewick from *The Fox at the Manger* by P. L. Travers. Copyright © 1962 by John Lyndon Ltd. Reprinted by permission of W. W. Norton & Co., Inc.

PENGUIN BOOKS. Cover illustration "The Cafe" by Graham Bell from *Of Human Bondage* by W. Somerset Maugham. Copyright 1915 by George H. Doran Co./ Cover illustration "Martin Coleman" by Glyn Philpot from *The Razor's Edge* by W. Somerset Maugham. Copyright 1943, 1944 by W. Somerset Maugham. Both reprinted by permission of Penguin Books.

PHILOMEL BOOKS. Photograph from *Deserts of the World: Future Threat or Promise?* by Jane Werner Watson. Copyright © 1981 by Jane Werner Watson. Reprinted by permission of Philomel Books.

RAND McNALLY & CO. Sidelight excerpts from *Conversations* by Roy Newquist. Copyright © 1967 by Rand McNally & Co. Reprinted by permission of Rand McNally & Co.

RANDOM HOUSE, INC. Photograph by Photo Researchers, Inc. from *Wonder Women of Sports* by Betty Millsaps Jones. Copyright © 1981 by Random House, Inc./ Sidelight excerpts from *Pipers at the Gates of Dawn: The Wisdom of Children's Literature* by Jonathan Cott. Copyright © 1981, 1983 by Jonathan Cott. Both reprinted by permission of Random House, Inc.

REED PUBLISHING. Sidelight excerpts from an article "Reminiscing with P. L. Travers," by Michelle Field, March 21, 1986 in *Publishers Weekly*. Copyright © 1986 by Reed Publishing. Reprinted by permission of Reed Publishing.

REYNAL & HITCHCOCK. Sidelight excerpts from *Aunt Sass* by P. L. Travers. Copyright 1941 by Reynal and Hitchcock./ Illustration by Mary Shepard from *Mary Poppins* by P. L. Travers. Both reprinted by permission of Reynal & Hitchcock.

SCHOLASTIC, INC. Cover illustration by John Hyatt from *Mission of the Secret Spy Squad* by Ruth Glick and Eileen Buckholtz. Copyright © 1984 by Ruth Glick and Eileen Buckholtz./ Illustration by Bert Dodson from *Captain Kid and the Pirates* by Ruth Glick and Eileen Buckholtz. Copyright © 1985 by Parachute Press. Both reprinted by permission of Scholastic, Inc.

CHARLES SCRIBNER'S SONS. Illustration by Ronald Himler from *Allison's Grandfather* by Linda Peavy. Text copyright © 1981 by Linda Sellers Peavy. Illustrations copyright © 1981 by Ronald Himler./ Illustration by Gail Owens from *Ash Brooks: Super Ranger* by Wanda Vanhoy Smith. Text copyright © 1984 by Wanda Vanhoy Smith. Illustrations copyright © 1984 by Gail Owens. Both reprinted by permission of Charles Scribner's Sons.

VIKING PENGUIN, INC. Illustration by Gail Owens from *The Cybil War* by Betsy Byars. Text copyright © 1981 by Betsy Byars. Illustrations copyright © 1981 by Viking Penguin, Inc./ Illustration by Leo and Diane Dillon from "The Sandals of Ayaz" in *Two Pairs of Shoes,* retold by P. L. Travers. Text copyright © 1976 by P. L. Travers. Illustrations copyright © 1980 by Leo Dillon and Diane Dillon. Both reprinted by permission of Viking Penguin, Inc.

FRANKLIN WATTS, INC. Illustration by Victor Mays from *The First Book of Lumbering* by Louise Dickinson Rich. Copyright © 1967 by Louise Dickinson Rich./ Illustration by Gunvor Edwards from *Grandmother's Donkey* by Joan Smith. Text copyright © 1983 by Joan Smith. Illustrations copyright © 1983 by Gunvor Edwards. Both reprinted by permission of Franklin Watts, Inc.

WEIDENFELD PUBLISHERS LTD. Photographs from *Somerset Maugham* by Anthony Curtis. Copyright © 1977 by Anthony Curtis. Reprinted by permission of Weidenfeld Publishers Ltd.

WESTERN PUBLISHING CO., INC. Illustration by Tibor Gergely from *My Head-to-Toe Book* by Jean Tymms. Copyright © 1974 by Western Publishing Co., Inc. Reprinted by permission of Western Publishing Co., Inc.

Sidelight excerpts from an article "What Ever Happened to Geraldo Rivera? Who?," by Geraldo Rivera, April, 1986 in *Esquire*. Reprinted by permission of *Esquire*./ Sidelight excerpts from an article "Some Friends of Mary Poppins: Interview by Group of American Children," May, 1966 in *McCall's*. Reprinted by permission of *McCall's*./ Sidelight excerpts from an article "I Never Wrote for Children," by P. L. Travers, July 2, 1978 in *New York Times*

Magazine. Reprinted by permission of *New York Times Magazine.*/ Sidelight excerpts from an article "Where Did She Come From? Why Did She Go?," by P. L. Travers, November 7, 1964 in *The Saturday Evening Post.* Copyright © 1964 by The Curtis Publishing Co. Reprinted by permission of The Curtis Publishing Co./ Sidelight excerpts from an article "Only Connect," by P. L. Travers in *The Openhearted Audience: Ten Authors Talk about Writing for Children,* edited by Virginia Haviland. Reprinted by permission of P. L. Travers./ Sidelight excerpts from an article "The Art of Fiction LXXIII: P. L. Travers," winter, 1982 in *Paris Review.* Reprinted by permission of P. L. Travers.

PHOTOGRAPH CREDITS

Cheryl Walsh Bellville: Buzz Magnuson (staff photographer), St. Paul Pioneer Press Dispatch; Mollie Hunter: copyright © The Scotsman Publications Ltd.; Rebecca Larsen: Marian Little; Loreen Leedy: Virginia Leedy Catley; Suse MacDonald: Gisela Gamper; W. Somerset Maugham (portrait): Tate Gallery (London); Gary Paulsen: *Duluth (Minn.) News Tribune & Herald*; Janice Lee Smith: James F. Smith; Peter Spier: David Osika; Theodore Taylor: John Graves; P. L. Travers: Jerry Bauer.

SOMETHING ABOUT THE AUTHOR

AITKEN, Amy 1952-

PERSONAL: Born October 19, 1952; daughter of Gerard James (a physician) and Gloria (a physician; maiden name, Stone) Aitken. *Education:* Attended New College, Sarasota, Fla., 1970-72, and Parsons School of Design, 1973-76. *Home:* New York, N.Y.

CAREER: Author and illustrator.

WRITINGS—All self-illustrated: *Ruby!*, Bradbury, 1979; *Kate and Mona in the Jungle*, Bradbury, 1981; *Ruby, the Red Knight*, Bradbury, 1983; *Wanda's Circus*, Bradbury, 1985.

Illustrator: Bronnie Cunningham, *Best Book of Riddles, Puns, and Jokes*, Doubleday, 1979; Penelope Jones, *I'm Not Moving*, Bradbury, 1980; Judy Blume, *The One in the Middle Is a Green Kangaroo*, Bradbury, 1981.

AMY AITKEN

ASIMOV, Janet (Jeppson) 1926-
(J. O. Jeppson)

PERSONAL: Born August 6, 1926, in Ashland, Pa.; daughter of John Rufus (a physician) and Rae (a housewife; maiden name, Knudson) Jeppson; married Isaac Asimov (a writer), November 30, 1973. *Education:* Attended Wellesley College, 1944-46; Stanford University, B.A., 1948; New York University, College of Medicine, M.D., 1952; William A. White Psychoanalytic Institute, postdoctoral study, 1955-60. *Politics:* Liberal Democrat. *Religion:* "Ethical Culture." *Home and office:* 10 West 66th St., Apt. 33-A, New York, N.Y. 10023.

CAREER: Philadelphia General Hospital, Philadelphia, Pa., intern, 1952-53; Bellevue Hospital, New York City, psychiatric resident, 1953-56; private practice of medicine in New York City, 1956—; writer, 1966—; William A. White Psychoanalytic Institute, New York City, assistant director of clinical services, 1967-71, training and supervisory analyst, 1969—, director of training, 1974-82. *Member:* Authors League of America, Authors Guild, American Academy of Psychoanalysis, William Alanson White Society, New York State Medical Society, New York County Medical Society, New York Society for Ethical Culture, Phi Beta Kappa.

WRITINGS—"Norby Chronicles" series; with husband, Isaac Asimov; juvenile science fiction: *Norby, the Mixed-Up Robot*, Walker, 1983; *Norby's Other Secret*, Walker, 1984; *Norby and the Invaders*, Walker, 1985; *Norby and the Lost Princess*, Walker, 1985; *The Norby Chronicles*, Ace Books, 1986; *Norby and the Queen's Necklace*, Walker, 1986; *Norby Finds a Villain*, Walker, 1987; *Norby: Robot for Hire*, Ace Books, 1987.

Other: *Mind Transfer*, Walker, 1988.

Under name J. O. Jeppson: *The Second Experiment* (young adult science-fiction novel), Houghton, 1974; *The Last Immortal* (young adult science-fiction novel), Houghton, 1980; (editor with I. Asimov) *Laughing Space: Funny Science Fiction* (anthology), Houghton, 1982; *The Mysterious Cure and Other Stories of Pshrinks Anonymous* (science-fiction short

JANET ASIMOV

stories), Doubleday, 1985; (with I. Asimov) *How to Enjoy Writing: A Book of Aid and Comfort,* Walker, 1987.

Contributor of articles and short stories to periodicals. Associate editor of *Contemporary Psychoanalysis,* 1970—.

ADAPTATIONS: ''Norby, the Mixed-Up Robot'' (cassette), Caedmon, 1986.

WORK IN PROGRESS: Norby Down to Earth, with I. Asimov; *The Package in Hyperspace* for the seven- to twelve-year-old reader.

SIDELIGHTS: ''Like my husband, I read constantly in childhood—and still do. My first ambition was to be a writer of children's books, but the Great Depression and World War II years convinced me I ought to have a more financially secure career. I became a physician, specializing in psychiatry and psychoanalysis.

''In my thirties I started writing again (I'd written a lot in high school and college), and in 1966 my first published short story appeared in the *Saint Mystery* magazine. I didn't get going on children's books until Walker & Co. asked me to try. I roped Isaac in on final copy (and some of the ideas), and the ''Norby'' series began. I'm fond of Norby. He first appeared in a story I wrote back in the sixties, but I scrapped that. When he found Jeff, I knew I had a winning combination. Now I'm branching out with other science-fiction books for younger readers. All of my novels emphasize respect for life, preservation of ecology, and the importance of cooperation rather than destruc-

tiveness. Plus a little humor because books without it bore me.''

HOBBIES AND OTHER INTERESTS: Nature, geology, Zen.

FOR MORE INFORMATION SEE: Albany Sunday Times-Union, July 21, 1974; *Biographical Directory of the American Psychiatric Association,* Cattell, 1977; *Science Fiction and Fantasy Literature,* Volume 2, Gale, 1979.

ATWATER, Richard (Tupper)   1892-1948 (Riq)

PERSONAL: Born Frederick Mund Atwater on December 29, 1892, in Chicago, Ill.; name legally changed in 1913; died August 21, 1948, in Downey, Ill.; son of Clarence and Mae (maiden name, Marks) Atwater; married Florence Hasseltine Carroll (a writer), 1921; children: Doris, Carroll (daughter). *Education:* University of Chicago, A.A., 1909, B.A. (with honors), 1910, graduate study, until 1917. *Residence:* Chicago, Ill.

CAREER: Writer. Worked at various jobs, including professor at the University of Chicago, Ill., columnist for the *Evening Post,* in Chicago, Ill. and for the *Daily News,* Chicago, Ill. Also book editor and columnist for other newspapers. *Military service:* Served in the U.S. Army, 1918-1919. *Awards, honors:* Newbery Honor Book from the American Library Association, 1939, Young Reader's Choice Award from the Pacific Northwest Library Association, 1941, and Lewis Carroll Shelf Award, 1958, all for *Mr. Popper's Penguins.*

WRITINGS: (Under pseudonym Riq) *Rickety Rimes of Riq* (adult), Ballou, 1925; (translator) Procopius of Caesarea, *Secret History of Procopius,* Covici-Friede, 1927; *Doris and the Trolls* (juvenile; illustrated by John Gee), Rand McNally, 1931; (with wife, Florence Atwater) *Mr. Popper's Penguins* (juvenile; illustrated by Robert Lawson), Little, Brown, 1938.

Also author of operetta *The King Sneezes,* 1933, and of humor column under pseudonym, Riq, for the *Evening Post,* Chicago, Ill. and the Chicago *Daily News.* Contributor of column to Chicago *Tribune.*

ADAPTATIONS: ''Mr. Popper's Penguins'' (listening cassette; read-along cassette; record; filmstrip with cassette), Miller-Brody, 1975, (sound filmstrip), Pied Piper Productions, 1979, (videocassette), Random House, 1985, (film), Rhinoceros Presentations. *Mr. Popper's Penguins* is also available as a talking book and in braille.

SIDELIGHTS: Atwater's second and last children's book, *Mr. Popper's Penguins,* was a Newbery Honor Book in 1939. The story is about a house painter who receives penguins as a gift and keeps them in the family refrigerator. Elizabeth Rider Montgomery in *The Story behind Modern Books,* called it ''an amusing story. . . . Because of its very absurdity, the book is entrancing, and its matter-of-fact style adds to its charm. In fact, it is hard to tell whether the story owes its popularity more to the humor of its situation or to the simple way it is told.''

The idea for *Mr. Popper's Penguins* came to Atwater after attending a film of the first Byrd Antarctic Expedition with his wife and two daughters. Although he had great interest in his idea, his story did not satisfy him and he abandoned the manuscript in a desk drawer. His wife, Florence, found the

All that kept him from breaking down completely was the knowledge that what he was doing was best for them, too. ■ (From *Mr. Popper's Penguins* by Richard and Florence Atwater. Illustrated by Robert Lawson.)

manuscript a few years after Atwater had died of a cerebral hemorrhage. Thinking constantly about the half-finished story she had found and enjoyed, she decided to finish it herself. She rewrote the first few chapters leaving the middle chapters as they were and completing the final chapters. *Mr. Popper's Penguins* was published in 1938 and was an immediate success. It has been enjoyed by children and their parents ever since.

Atwater died of a cerebral hemorrhage at the V.A. Hospital in Downey, Illinois on August 21, 1948. He was fifty-six years old.

Mr. Popper's Penguins has been translated into Italian, Dutch, German, Catalan, Danish, French, Polish, Spanish, Swedish and Japanese-Korean.

FOR MORE INFORMATION SEE: New York Times, October 23, 1938; Elizabeth Rider Montgomery, *The Story behind Modern Books,* Dodd, 1949; Muriel Fuller, editor, *More Junior Authors,* H. W. Wilson, 1963; W. J. Burke and Will D. Howe, *American Authors and Books, 1640 to the Present Day,* 3rd revised edition, Crown, 1972; D. L. Kirkpatrick, editor, *Twentieth-Century Children's Writers,* St. Martin's, 1978, 2nd edition, 1983; Jim Robinski, compiler, *Newbery and Caldecott Medalists and Honor Book Winners,* Libraries Unlimited, 1982.

BAKER, Betty (Lou) 1928-1987

OBITUARY NOTICE—See sketch in *SATA* Volume 5: Born June 20, 1928, in Bloomsburg, Pa.; died November 6, 1987, in Tucson, Ariz. Author of books for young readers. Baker began her writing career in the early 1960s and subsequently produced numerous books about the legends, history, and culture of the southwestern United States and Mexico. Many of her works focus on the American Indian, such as *Killer-of-Death* and *And One Was a Wooden Indian,* both winners of the Western Heritage Award. Her later works included humorous fantasy like *Save Sirrushany!* Baker also served as editor for Western Writers of America's monthly magazine.

FOR MORE INFORMATION SEE: Contemporary Authors, New Revision Series, Volume 2, Gale, 1981; *Twentieth-Century Children's Writers,* 2nd edition, St. Martin's, 1983. Obituaries: *School Library Journal,* February, 1988.

BALDWIN, James (Arthur) 1924-1987

OBITUARY NOTICE—See sketch in *SATA* Volume 9: Born August 2, 1924, in New York, N.Y.; died of stomach cancer, December 1, 1987, in St. Paul de Vence, France; buried at Ferncliff Cemetery in Ardsley, N.Y. Preacher, laborer, and author. An eloquent and passionate critic of racial discrimination, Baldwin is considered one of the most important writers to appear since World War II. The child of a Harlem minister, he began his own preaching career in Harlem as a young teenager. After experiencing a religious crisis, Baldwin left the church and moved to New York City's bohemian Greenwich Village, where he worked at menial jobs and wrote articles for publications such as *Nation* and *Commentary.* By the late 1940s Baldwin had become disgusted with American bigotry, and before the decade ended he moved to France. He made his literary debut in 1953 with *Go Tell It on the Mountain,* a novel about an adolescent coming to terms with his own religious and social convictions in an oppressive environ-

ment. This work, derived from Baldwin's own childhood experiences, showed him to be an intense, talented writer.

Baldwin's next work, the nonfiction *Notes of a Native Son,* brought him even greater acclaim as an articulate critic of bigotry and social inequality. Two more nonfiction volumes, *Nobody Knows My Name* and *The Fire Next Time,* confirmed his status, and by the early 1960s he ranked as a leading figure in contemporary literature. During the middle years of that decade Baldwin returned to the United States, where he became involved in the civil rights movement. But following the assassination of leading activist Martin Luther King, Jr., Baldwin began making periodic trips to France, and in 1974 he once again settled there. Among his later works is the novel *Harlem Quartet*—about jazz clubs of the 1950s—which earned him the French-American Friendship Prize, one of his many literary awards.

FOR MORE INFORMATION SEE: Dictionary of Literary Biography, Gale, Volume 2, *American Novelists since World War II,* 1978, Volume 7, *Twentieth-Century American Dramatists,* two volumes, 1981, Volume 33, *Afro-American Writers after 1955,* 1984; *American Writers: A Collection of Literary Biographies,* Supplement 1, Scribner, 1979; *Contemporary Authors, New Revision Series,* Volume 3, Gale, 1981; *Contemporary Literary Criticism Series,* Gale, Volume 17, 1981, Volume 42, 1987; *Contemporary Authors Bibliography Series,* Volume 1, Gale, 1986. Obituaries: *Chicago Tribune,* December 2, 1987; *Los Angeles Times,* December 2, 1987; *New York Times,* December 2, 1987, December 9, 1987; *Times* (London), December 2, 1987; *Washington Post,* December 2, 1987; *USA Today,* December 2, 1987; *Facts on File,* December 4, 1987; *AB Bookman's Weekly,* January 1, 1988; *School Library Journal,* February, 1988.

BELLVILLE, Cheryl Walsh 1944-

PERSONAL: Born August 27, 1944, in Deming, N.M.; daughter of William Vincent (a horseman) and Elsie (a homemaker; maiden name, Lofback) Walsh; married Rod Bellville (a musician), July 28, 1972 (divorced, June, 1986); children: Luke Kyper, Katherine Anne. *Education:* Attended South Dakota State University, 1965; University of Minnesota, B.F.A., 1970. *Politics:* Liberal. *Home:* Minneapolis, Minn. *Office:* Cheryl Walsh Bellville Photography, 2823 Eighth St. S., Minneapolis, Minn. 55454.

CAREER: Cheryl Walsh Bellville Photography, Minneapolis, Minn., photographer, 1968—. Teacher of photography and art at schools for Native Americans in Minneapolis, 1969; public school teacher of photography for Minneapolis Urban Arts, 1970-71. Member of Sherlock Holmes Housing Cooperative, Minneapolis. *Exhibitions:* University of Minnesota Galleries; St. Paul Arts and Science Center, Minn.; Minneapolis Institute of Art, Minn.; Tenth Annual Minnesota Photographer's Exhibit. *Member:* Friends of Planned Parenthood, American Society of Magazine Photographers. *Awards, honors:* Outstanding Science Trade Book for Children from the National Science Teachers Association and the Children's Book Council, 1983, for *Large Animal Veterinarians; Rodeo* was selected one of Child Study Association of America's Children's Books of the Year, 1985, and *Theater Magic,* 1986; Notable Children's Trade Book in the Field of Social Studies from the National Council of Social Studies and the Children's Book Council, 1986, and Award from the Wisconsin Writer's Council, 1987, both for *Theater Magic;* Photography Award from the Organization of American States (Washington, D.C.), 1987, for photography in Mexico.

CHERYL WALSH BELLVILLE

WRITINGS—Juvenile; all self-illustrated with photographs: *Round-Up,* Carolrhoda, 1982; (with Rod Belleville) *Large Animal Veterinarians,* Carolrhoda, 1983; (with R. Bellville) *Stockyards,* Carolrhoda, 1983; *All Things Bright and Beautiful,* Winston Press, 1983; *Farming Today: Yesterday's Way,* Carolrhoda, 1984; *Rodeo* (Reading Rainbow selection), Carolrhoda, 1985; *Theater Magic: Behind the Scenes at a Children's Theater,* Carolrhoda, 1986.

WORK IN PROGRESS: A book on aircraft, tentative title, *Flying, the Dream That Came True.*

SIDELIGHTS: "My primary motivation is the desire to communicate the impact of the natural world in an aesthetic/visual sense. I try to provide a small bridge between the technical urban present and the fragile ecosystem.

"I have always loved reading, writing, drawing, and taking pictures. Still, as an adult I read as many books for young people as I do adult books. There are more wonderful books available now for children than when I was a little girl, and our house is always filled with new treasures from the library. This love of books is why I enjoy writing for children so much. I can hardly believe I am an author myself.

"When I talk to children about my books and other work I usually tell them that the reason the books have done well is that I write about and photograph things I am already interested in. One of my great loves is farming. Another is horses. I am familiar with these things and so I can take my camera into the country and work around farms and animals with a real and active involvement. I think this is fun, and the photos always show how much I like the people and events I encounter doing this kind of work.

"All of us have some special love, some special area of our world that we enjoy learning more about and working with. I always encourage people to follow that interest and see if there is some way it can be developed into a career or what is called an avocation, a job you may not be paid for, but which is a serious and ongoing interest. I tried many different jobs before I discovered photography. When, as an art student at the Uni-

versity of Minnesota, I took my first photography class I immediately recognized it as an area I wanted to work in. Not everyone is lucky enough to have this kind of instant recognition of something they want to do, but everyone encounters many things that hold the promise of an interesting future. Go for it when this happens. I had to work two jobs after school and add time to my education so I could study photography, but I have always been glad I did."

She brought her portfolio to an editor at Carolrhoda Books who asked her for book ideas. Bellville suggested a round-up. "I . . . got on a horse and shot some pictures. Then Susan [the editor] said I was going to write the book too. I told her I was not a writer, but she said, 'Take notes, explain and organize and I'll edit it.'

"I do not write for children. Sometimes I get a little heat from editors and readers for using words outside of the kids' age range. And I definitely don't illustrate for children. The photos in the books are the best I can do." [Mary Ann Grossmann, "Kids' Author Focuses on Adventure," *St. Paul Pioneer Press Dispatch* (Minn.), August 21, 1987.[1]]

When taking photographs, Bellville gets close to the action. While documenting a horse race, a horse broke through the fence. "I couldn't judge distance because of the (long) lens, and the horse was almost on me before I realized it wasn't on the track anymore. I tucked a camera under each armpit and rolled. He hit me head-on, but I instinctively saved my cameras.

"I've been smashed, bashed and taken falls off horses. Once I flew over the neck of a horse into a canyon. That's why I never take my Hasselblads on horseback. They're the Cadillacs of photography. Mostly I use Nikons; three of them hit the dust this year alone. My friendly camera repairman is like my family doctor.

"I just want to keep getting better in my work. But much as I love photography, I love my family more. Until the kids are on their own, photography takes a back seat."[1]

"Right now I am working on a book on aircraft. My father was a pilot, I lived on airbases as a child, and planes are marvelous machines. I am looking forward to spending most of my summer traveling to airshows and airbases doing photos for this book.

"Another project is on the people of Mexico. My children and I love Mexico and find the people remarkably friendly and hospitable. We are studying Spanish so we can talk to the Mexican people in their own language when we visit them. We aren't very good at speaking Spanish yet, but everyone is very kind about our efforts.

"At first I just took pictures of the ocean and the countryside because it was new to me and very beautiful. Little by little my pictures got closer and closer to the families and homes of Mexico, and now my favorite thing is taking portraits of the people we meet. Soon, I am sure, I will have an idea for a book, and then I will spend more time in Mexico and work on a particular project. This is how all the books began, with an interest, then with more involvement with the subject, then focusing on a particular aspect of that interest."

FOR MORE INFORMATION SEE: Mary Ann Grossmann, "Kids' Author Focuses on Adventure," *St. Paul Pioneer Press Dispatch* (Minn.), August 21, 1987.

BODECKER, N(iels) M(ogens) 1922-1988

OBITUARY NOTICE—See sketch in *SATA* Volume 8: Born January 13, 1922, in Copenhagen, Denmark; immigrated to the United States, 1952; died of cancer of the colon, February 1, 1988, in Hancock, N.H. Illustrator and author of children's books. Bodecker was perhaps best known as editor, illustrator, and translator of *It's Raining Said John Twaining,* a collection of Danish nursery rhymes that was named a notable book in 1973 by the American Library Association, the School Library Association, and the National Book League of the United Kingdom. Among Bodecker's other self-illustrated works are *Miss Jaster's Garden; Hurry, Hurry, Mary Dear! and Other Nonsense Poems;* and *A Person from Britain Whose Head Was the Shape of a Mitten, and Other Limericks.* Bodecker also illustrated children's books by other writers, including Edward Eager and Robert Kraus.

FOR MORE INFORMATION SEE: Contemporary Authors, New Revision Series, Volume 4, Gale, 1981; *Twentieth-Century Children's Writers,* 2nd edition, St. Martin's, 1983. Obituaries: *New York Times,* February 3, 1988; *Publishers Weekly,* February 26, 1988; *School Library Journal,* March, 1988.

BROWN, Laurene Krasny 1945-
(Laurene Krasny Meringoff)

PERSONAL: Born December 16, 1945, in New York, N.Y.; daughter of Morris (an accountant) and Helen (a teacher; maiden name, Meyer) Krasny; married Stephen Meringoff, August 27, 1967 (divorced September, 1974); married Marc Brown (an author and illustrator), September 11, 1983; children: Eliza Morgan; (stepchildren) Tucker Eliot, Tolon Adam. *Education:* Cornell University, B.S., 1966; Columbia University, M.A., 1967; Harvard University, Ed.D., 1978. *Religion:* Jewish. *Home and office:* 562 Main St., Hingham, Mass. 02043; Old South Rd., Gay Head, Mass. 02535 (summer). *Agent:* Phyllis Wender, 3 East 48th St., New York, N.Y. 10017.

CAREER: Federal Headstart Program, Boston, Mass., evaluator, 1967-68; Child Guidance Center, Cape Cod, Mass., staff psychologist, 1968-71; Gene Reilly Group (consumer research), Darien, Conn., senior research associate, 1972-74; Harvard University, Cambridge, Mass., researcher at Center for Research in Children's Television, 1975-76, research associate and co-director of Project Zero (researching cognitive development in the arts), 1978-83; consultant and expert witness for the Federal Trade Commission, 1978-79; consultant to the New York Council of Better Business Bureaus, 1979; writer and consultant on children's media, 1983—; Department of Education, Washington, D.C., consultant, 1986; consultant to CBS-TV in judging Television Worth Teaching, 1987. *Member:* American Film Institute, Society for Research in Child Development. *Awards, honors:* Grants from National Association of Broadcasters, 1976-77, and John and Mary R. Markle Foundation, 1977-83; *The Bionic Bunny Show* was selected a Notable Children's Book by the Association for Library Service to Children of the American Library Association, runner-up for *Redbook*'s Best Children's Book of the Year, and one of *School Library Journal*'s Best Books of the Year, all 1984.

WRITINGS—Juvenile; all illustrated by husband, Marc Brown: *The Bionic Bunny Show* (ALA Notable Book; "Reading Rainbow" selection), Atlantic/Little, Brown, 1984; *Visiting the Art Museum,* Dutton, 1986; *Dinosaurs Divorce: A Guide for Changing Families,* Atlantic/Little Brown, 1986; *Dinosaurs Travel,* Joy Street Books, 1988.

Other: *Take Advantage of Media: A Manual for Parents and Teachers,* Routledge & Kegan Paul, 1986. Contributor to periodicals, including *School Library Journal, Journal of Aesthetic Education, Language Arts,* and *Journal of Educational Psychology.*

Under Laurene Krasny Meringoff: (Contributor) R. Adler, editor, *Effects of TV Advertising on Children,* Lexington Books, 1980; (editor) *Children and Television: Annotated Bibliography,* Council of Better Business Bureaus, 1980; (contributor) J. Bryant and D. R. Anderson, editors, *Children's Understanding of TV,* Academic Press, 1983.

WORK IN PROGRESS: Dinosaurs Keep Well, illustrated by Marc Brown, to be published by Joy Street Books; *Baby Time* (working title), illustrated by M. Brown, to be published by Knopf; a preprimer text to be published by D. C. Heath.

SIDELIGHTS: "I was born and grew up in New York City, a wonderfully exciting place to explore, always changing, always surprising you with something new. I was fortunate to be accepted in the High School of Music and Art, where I studied piano and played violin in a student orchestra. Maybe I will become a concert pianist, I thought. But I wasn't passionate enough about that goal to practice several hours every day. Instead, I went to college and graduate school, studying child development, psychology and education.

"Since then, all my jobs have had something to do with children. I've sold toys, done counseling and intelligence testing, taught preschool, testified in Washington, D.C. about the effects on children of television advertising, investigated what children learn from radio, film, television and picture books, and evaluated commercials for toys, breakfast cereals, and other products promoted to children. I still give producers advice about the various videos, films or other media projects they hire me to look at.

"Somehow I gradually realized that I wanted to be the person writing the books or producing the videos—that is, I wanted to do the creating myself. Rather than finding out what children as audience members liked or disliked, I wanted to try making the materials for them to enjoy.

"The opportunity to work on picture books with my illustrator husband, Marc Brown, was simply too tempting to resist. Picture books are especially fun, because words and pictures can work together so well. You get to be involved in designing the whole book—with the publisher's help—and figuring out things like just how much to say in the text on each page and how much to show in the illustration.

"Now that we have a young daughter, I have more ideas for books, because I read to her so much and see what kinds of things interest her. Some time, I'm going to try drawing pictures too, so I might do some books myself."

HOBBIES AND OTHER INTERESTS: "I love reading books, especially ones that have pictures. I like reading stories aloud. Writing letters and adding little pictures is another favorite pastime. Cooking and baking quick little breads are fun. I enjoy listening to music, and play the piano a little. Being outdoors is a pleasure: walking, jogging, bicycling, and in summer tending a little vegetable and herb garden. I like to swim, though I'd like to be better at it.

"I'm not sure why yet, but I like collecting buttons, ribbons, and interesting scraps of paper and cloth."

FOR MORE INFORMATION SEE: New York Times Book Review, July 22, 1984.

BUCHAN, Stuart   1942-1987

OBITUARY NOTICE: Born August 30, 1942, in Sydney, New South Wales, Australia; died of pneumonia related to acquired immune deficiency syndrome (AIDS), October 15, 1987, in Pittsfield, Mass. Educator and author. From 1969 to 1972 Buchan taught childhood education and served as director of nursery schools, turning to full-time writing in 1973. Among his books for young adults are several titles in Dell's "Roots of Love" series as well as the novels *When We Lived with Pete* and *Guys Like Us*. He was also the author of short stories and produced an adult mystery entitled *Fleeced*.

FOR MORE INFORMATION SEE: Contemporary Authors, Volumes 57-60, Gale, 1976. Obituaries: *New York Times,* October 27, 1987.

BUCKHOLTZ, Eileen (Garber)   1949-
(Samantha Chase, Alyssa Howard, Amanda Lee, Rebecca York)

PERSONAL: Born February 1, 1949, in Atlanta, Ga.; daughter of Karl U. (a businessman) and Fannie (a businesswoman; maiden name, Davidson) Garber; married Howard Buckholtz (a director of computer operations), June 28, 1970; children: David Brian, Ryan Herschel. *Education:* Ohio State University, B.A., 1969; University of Maryland at College Park, M.S., 1973. *Home:* Sykesvlle, Md. *Agent:* Linda Hayes, Columbia Literary Associates, Inc., 7902 Nottingham Way, Ellicott City, Md. 21043.

CAREER: U.S. Department of Defense, Washington, D.C., systems analyst, 1970-75, senior systems analyst, 1975-80, manager of new technology branch, 1981-84, personal computer consultant, 1984-86, work force development manager, 1987—. *Member:* Association for Computing Machinery, Romance Writers of America, Washington Romance Writers. *Awards, honors:* Romantic Times Lifetime Achievement Award for Best Romantic Suspense Series, 1987; selected one of Maryland's Outstanding Women in Math and Science by Maryland's Commission on Women, 1988.

WRITINGS—Juvenile: (With JoAnn Settel) *The Kids Computer IQ Book,* Howard Sams, 1983; (with Ruth Glick) *Mission of the Secret Spy Squad,* Scholastic, 1984; (with R. Glick) *Space Attack,* Scholastic, 1984; (with husband, Howard Buckholtz) *ABPC: A Kid's Guide to the IBM Personal Computer,* Howard Sams, 1984; (with R. Glick) *Mindbenders,* Scholastic, 1984; (with R. Glick) *Doomstalker,* Scholastic, 1985; (with R. Glick) *Captain Kid and the Pirates* (illustrated by Bert Dodson), Scholastic, 1985; (with R. Glick) *The Cats of Castle Mountain,* Scholastic, 1985.

Creator with R. Glick; young adult romantic adventure series; all published by Pageant Books: *Saber Dance,* 1988; *Roller Coaster,* 1988.

Romance novels under pseudonym Alyssa Howard: *Love Is Elected,* Silhouette, 1982; *Southern Persuasion,* Silhouette, 1983.

Romance novels under pseudonym Amanda Lee: (With R. Glick) *End of Illusion,* Silhouette, 1984; (with Nancy Baggett) *Love in Good Measure,* Silhouette, 1984; (with R. Glick) *Logical Choice,* Silhouette, 1986; (with R. Glick) *Great Expectations,* Silhouette, 1987; (with R. Glick) *A Place in Your Heart,* Silhouette, 1988.

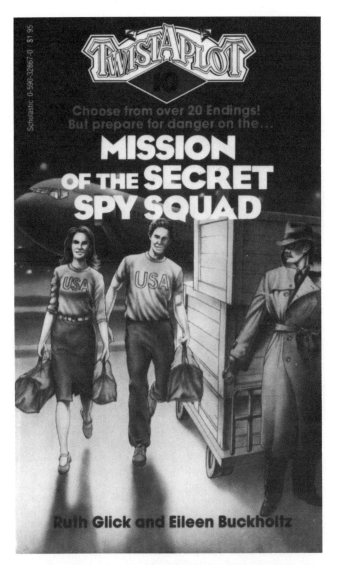

(Cover illustration by John Hyatt from *Mission of the Secret Spy Squad* by Ruth Glick and Eileen Buckholtz.)

Under pseudonym Rebecca York; all with R. Glick: *Talons of the Falcon* (romantic adventure novel), Dell, 1986; *In Search of the Dove* (romantic adventure novel), Dell, 1986; *Flight of the Raven,* Dell, 1986.

Under pseudonym Samantha Chase: (With R. Glick) *Postmark* (suspense novel), Tudor, 1988.

WORK IN PROGRESS: A contemporary romance novel, *Silver Creek Challenge;* a thirteen-book series for Pageant Books; another suspense novel.

SIDELIGHTS: "Since I enjoy both of my professions, author and computer analyst, I'm still trying to balance two careers. Sometimes I even have the opportunity to write fiction and program for the same project. This was the case with the 'Micro Adventure' and 'Magic Micro' series for Scholastic. Over the years I've found that discipline and persistence have been the key to getting published and meeting contract commitments.

"I've written many of my books in collaboration with other authors and found that team writing works well for me. Discipline is certainly easier to maintain, since we usually have

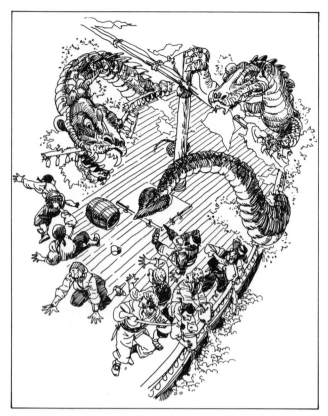

Then you hear a tearing sound. The other monster is shredding the sails. ■ (From *Captain Kid and the Pirates* by Ruth Glick and Eileen Buckholtz. Illustrated by Bert Dodson.)

a scheduled meeting time each day to work. Plotting, character development, dialogue, and editing all benefit from the joint venture. Feedback is vitally important to every author, and, here again, collaboration has the edge over writing alone. Of course, finding the right person to write with is critical to the success of any team writing project.

"One note on the mechanics of writing—take advantage of the technology in personal computers. Writing with a word processor can reduce the drudgery of the effort while giving you more time to be creative. We've found our personal computers have probably tripled our output, produced cleaner copy, and made complex revisions possible."

HOBBIES AND OTHER INTERESTS: Computer education, bridge, public speaking, watching sons play baseball, basketball and soccer.

BURSTEIN, John 1949-
(Slim Goodbody)

PERSONAL: Born December 25, 1949, in Mineola, N.Y.; son of Herbert (an attorney) and Beatrice (a state Supreme Court judge; maiden name, Sobel) Burstein; married June Beznover (a teacher), June 26, 1976. *Education:* Hofstra University, B.A. 1972.

CAREER: Entertainer, author and television personality. One-man health education musical performer in elementary schools in United States, under stage name Mr. Slim Goodbody, 1974—; author of books for children. Starred in "The Adventures of Slim Goodbody in Nutri-City," biweekly feature on "Captain

Kangaroo" program , CBS-TV. *Awards, honors:* New Jersey Authors Award from New Jersey Institute of Technology, 1978, for *Mr. Slim Goodbody Presents the Inside Story.*

WRITINGS: Mr. Slim Goodbody Presents the Inside Story (illustrated by Craigwood Phillips and with photographs by J. Paul Kirouac), McGraw, 1977; *Slim Goodbody: Your Body, Health and Feelings,* Society for Visual Education, 1978; *Slim Goodbody: What Can Go Wrong and How to Be Strong* (illustrated by J. P. Kirouac), McGraw, 1978; *Slim Goodbody's Healthy Days Diary: Activity Book,* Caedmon, 1983. Also author of and performer on "The Inside Story" record album, Macmillan, 1975.

Under name Slim Goodbody: *Lucky You!,* McGraw, 1980; *The Get-Well Hotel,* McGraw, 1980; *The Force Inside You* (illustrated with photographs by Bruce Curtis), Coward, 1983; *The Healthy Habits Handbook,* Coward, 1983.

ADAPTATIONS: "Slim Goodbody and Your Body" (filmstrip), Society for Visual Education, 1978; "Slim Goodbody: The Inside Story" (record or cassette), Caedmon, 1980; "Slim Goodbody's World of Animals and Plants" (filmstrip), Society for Visual Education, 1981; "Slim Goodbody: Inside Out" (cassette), Caedmon, 1982; "Slim Goodbody's World of Weather and Climate" (filmstrip), Society for Visual Education, 1983; "Slim Goodbody's Galactic Health Adventure" (record or cassette), Caedmon, 1983; "Slim Goodbody's Kid-fit: Body Builders" (record or cassette), Caedmon, 1984.

WORK IN PROGRESS: A book on health subjects.

SIDELIGHTS: Wearing a body suit with pictures of internal organs, muscles, and bones, Burstein performs his Mr. Goodbody's "The Inside Story" to help school children counter

John Burstein as Slim Goodbody.

anxieties and confusion about the workings of their bodies. "I believe it is vitally important that children learn to appreciate their bodies and love themselves. Our educational system has been based on learning facts about the world 'out-there' and it's time we learned to focus on each individual's creative potential and inner worth."

FOR MORE INFORMATION SEE: Newsweek, May 12, 1975; *Publishers Weekly,* May 2, 1977; *New York Times Book Review,* March 4, 1979.

DAVIDSON, Alice Joyce 1932-

PERSONAL: Born September 2, 1932, in Cincinnati, Ohio; daughter of David (a merchant) and Yetta (a merchant; maiden name, Hymon) Citron; married Marvin Davidson (in sales), September 6, 1953; children: Edward Lewis, Carol Sue Davidson Kessler. *Education:* Attended University of Cincinnati, 1951-53. *Home and office:* 2709 Mapletree Ct., Cincinnati, Ohio 45236. *Agent:* Mary Jane Ross, 85 Sunset La., Tenafly, N.J. 07670.

CAREER: Writer, 1962—; Gibson Greeting Cards, Cincinnati, Ohio, editor, 1963-65, editor, editorial director, and inspirational manager, 1972-81; free-lance writer for advertising agencies and greeting card companies, 1965-67; WXIX-TV, Cincinnati, continuity director, 1967-69; WCPO-TV, Cincinnati, promotion manager, 1969-72. *Awards, honors:* Angel Award for Excellence, 1988, for *Christmas Wrapped in Love.*

WRITINGS—Poems: *A Cat Called Cindy* (juvenile), A. Whitman, 1981; *Because I Love You* (self-illustrated), Fleming Revell, 1982; *Reflections of Love,* Fleming Revell, 1983; *Loving One Another,* Fleming Revell, 1984; *Beware When Elephants Sneeze* (juvenile; illustrated by Cara Marks), C. R. Gibson, 1986; *Monkeys Never Say Please* (juvenile; illustrated by C. Marks), C. R. Gibson, 1986.

"Alice in Bibleland" series; juvenile; all illustrated by Victoria Marshall; all published by C. R. Gibson: *The Story of Creation,* 1984; *The Story of Noah,* 1984; *The Story of Jonah,* 1984; *Psalms and Proverbs for You,* 1984; *The Story of David and Goliath,* 1985; *The Story of Baby Moses,* 1985; *The Story of the Loaves and Fishes,* 1985; *The Story of the Baby Jesus,* 1985; *The Story of Daniel and the Lions,* 1986; *Prayers and Graces,* 1986; *The Story of Easter,* 1988; *The Twenty-Third Psalm,* 1988; *The Story of Isaac's Wife,* 1989; *The Prodigal Son,* 1989; *The Story of the Tower of Babel,* 1989; *The Story of Esther,* 1989.

Other: *Christmas Wrapped in Love,* Abingdon, 1987.

Author of television stories for children. Creator of greeting cards, calendars, and gift books.

WORK IN PROGRESS: Additional books in the "Alice in Bibleland" series, for C. R. Gibson.

SIDELIGHTS: "My dearest prayer is that I may be an instrument, that I might make a contribution, that my life here on earth might have meaning." [Dorothy Nelson, "Alice Joyce Davidson: An Author Profile," *Bookstore Journal,* September, 1984.[1]]

A long-time friend and associate, Helen Steiner Rice, encouraged Davidson to pursue her writing talents. "I learned so much from Ms. Rice during those years we worked together

at the Gibson Card Company. She was the star of the inspirational lines, while I 'Twinkled' off and on in the humorous field. Yet, I find that nothing has ever given me more satisfaction than writing from the soul.

"When I began writing my first book of poetry, *Because I Love You,* Helen encouraged me with her interest and such generous praise as 'These three verses are terrific. You are getting better and better, so all your efforts have paid off in glory to God!' For the prologue of my book she wrote, 'She speaks from her heart in a special way, and in her special style she opens new doors to God.' This meant so much to me.

"We discussed the need for good Bible stories written in language that youngsters can understand. The thought came to me one day that the Bible itself is a wonderland. My name being Alice, why not 'Alice in Bibleland' for a title? The first book in the series, *The Story of Creation,* just flowed as I used the Bible closely as my guide. I couldn't wait to dig into Noah's story!

"My hope is that my books will reach all denominations, the unaffiliated as well as the affiliated, so I choose to write in rhyme with a touch of whimsey, a smile tucked into the reverence I feel.

"God's plan seems so evident in my life. Each piece of the puzzle has fallen into place so nicely—my working for the Gibson Card Company, writing TV shows for children, publishing poetry books. My work on the 'Alice in Bibleland' stories now seems to be the culmination of all these experiences. And in my own way, I am somehow carrying on the work of a dear friend I was privileged to know—Helen Steiner Rice. It's a humbling task, and I pray that the words I write will always show our world as a place of beauty—a proof of God's love."[1]

(From *Beware When Elephants Sneeze* by Alice Joyce Davidson. Illustrated by Cara Marks.)

"I feel writers have a responsibility to their readers. Our words can influence and help shape lives—and shape the world. In my poet's mind I visualize a world of peace, where the common denominator is love. By teaching our children moral values—the values taught in the Bible—perhaps the time will come when greed, fear, and hate are replaced by hope, love, and brotherhood."

HOBBIES AND OTHER INTERESTS: Sewing, gardening, painting.

FOR MORE INFORMATION SEE: Dorothy Nelson, "Alice Joyce Davidson: An Author Profile," *Bookstore Journal,* September, 1984.

DENGLER, Sandy 1939-

PERSONAL: Born June 8, 1939, in Newark, Ohio; daughter of Walter Stecker (a businessman) and Alyce (a telephone operator; maiden name, Kabrhel) Hance; married William F. Dengler (a National Park Service ranger), January 11, 1963; children: Alyce Ann, Mary Margaret. *Education:* Bowling Green State University, B.S., 1961; Arizona State University, M.S., 1967. *Religion:* "Non-sectarian Christian." *Home and office:* 112 Tahoma Woods, Star Route, Ashford, Wash. 98304. *Agent:* Ric McCue, Auburn, Calif. 95603.

CAREER: Writer, 1972—. Volunteer worker at Death Valley, Grand Canyon, Saguaro National Monument, Acadia National Park, Joshua Tree National Monument, Yosemite National Park,

SANDY DENGLER

and Mount Rainier National Park, 1965—; in charge of horses at children's summer camp, 1975-80; first aid instructor for American Red Cross. *Awards, honors:* Award for Best Traditional Romance Novel from the Romance Writers of America, 1986, for *Opal Fire;* Writer of the Year from the Warm Beach Writers Conference, 1986.

WRITINGS—Juvenile, except as noted; all published by Moody: *Fanny Crosby: Writer of Eight Thousand Songs,* 1985; *John Bunyan: Writer of Pilgrim's Progress,* 1986; *D. L. Moody: God's Salesman,* 1986; *Susanna Wesley: Servant of God* (young adult), 1987; *Florence Nightingale,* 1988.

"Pioneer Family Adventure" series; juvenile historical novels; all published by Moody: *Summer of the Wild Pig,* 1979; *The Horse Who Loved Picnics,* 1980; *Arizona Longhorn Adventure,* 1980; *The Melon Hound,* 1980; *Rescue in the Desert,* 1981; *Mystery at McGeehan Ranch,* 1982; *Three in One Pioneer Family Adventure Series,* 1985.

"Daniel Tremain Adventure" series; juvenile novels; all published by Moody: *Socorro Island Treasure,* 1983; *The Chain Five Mystery,* 1984.

Adult: *Getting into the Bible,* Moody, 1979; *Beasts of the Field* (puzzle book), Moody, 1979; *Yosemite's Marvelous Creatures,* Flying Spur Press, 1980; *Birds of the Air* (puzzle book), Moody, 1981; *Man and Beast Together* (puzzle book), Moody, 1982; *Song of the Nereids* (romance novel), Zondervan, 1984; *Summer Snow* (romance novel), Zondervan, 1984; *To Die in the Queen of Cities,* Nelson, 1986; *Opal Fire,* Zondervan, 1986; *This Rolling Land,* Zondervan, 1986; *Winterspring,* Zondervan, 1986; *Jungle Gold,* Zondervan, 1987.

WORK IN PROGRESS: From the Cosmos to the Carpenter, a new look at the creation/evolution controversy.

SIDELIGHTS: "I was a weird kid. Teenage girls in the fifties were supposed to primp and stick to feminine pursuits and win a man. While my girlfriends were doing all that, I was out riding my horse. In college I was the only girl in most of my biology field courses (if girls took biology at all, it was lab stuff). By grad school the world had convinced me that was no way to get a man, so I decided phooey on men. I'd stay single and enjoy it. Six months later I was married. So much for planning.

"The man who changed my phooey to whoopy so abruptly became a park service ranger. In the National Park Service you move a lot. We've lived in Saguaro National Monument, the Grand Canyon, Death Valley, Joshua Tree, Acadia, Yosemite and Mount Rainier. What a great way to raise our two girls! It's great for a writer, too. Wide travel is one of the very best tools a writer can have, for it exposes us not just to new people and places but new attitudes. It is far easier to write about a place you've been—about a different way of looking at things when you've seen it firsthand.

"National parks, though, are hardly ever near cities. So unless both man and wife work for the park (very, very rare), there's little job opportunity for the non-ranger. Most writers write at home, though—perfect for me. I had always enjoyed writing but never thought of it as a career. I was an unemployed biologist. I tried a few articles, got a lot of rejections and a couple of sales. My husband Bill said, 'If you're serious about this I'll send you to the Decision School of Christian Writing.' I was, he did, and that's what launched me.

"I must do a lot of research for every book I write, but it's not that hard. Our bookmobile comes by twice a month bearing stacks of splendid references. The county library has an 800 information number. And my personal library (about a ton of books, the mover said) contains references I need frequently—histories, costume and fashion, encyclopaedias (I use two), atlases, Bible study aids—even a reference book on horse-drawn vehicles and harness.

"The contemporary scene changes from moment to moment; a historical setting is frozen in place. Perhaps that's why I enjoy writing historical fiction (my children's novels and romance novels are all historical). Once I research a pretty good vision of a particular frozen moment, the moment itself suggests plot and situations. It shapes the characters. It seems more colorful and exciting than today's world (a curious thing, for the good old days weren't good in most respects). If it is presented well, that distant moment sharpens our perceptions of the present and shows us flaws in our attitudes—and some strong points as well.

"Now, twenty years later, I see that just about everything a writer does and studies in school helps. My background in biology/ecology lets me set scenes more vividly. A good setting can be made to move a story along. In *Jungle Gold* the Amazon is as much a character as are the soldier of fortune and the news reporter. Riding horses when I could have been flirting or primping taught me about horses, and horses are an integral part of most historical pieces. They become characters, too, like the sleek grey Nizhoni of *Summer Snow* and Roller, Daniel Tremain's wonderful little does-everything grulla gelding.

"But in the end, no writing is simply entertainment. Every book delivers a message whether it means to or not. The lousiest book says something, even if only 'life is dull.' And that's why I write—I have something to say and the best way to say a thing is to tell a story.

"For, you see, I know that a strong moral standard makes you feel good about yourself, not to mention that it keeps you out of trouble. In real life the hero does not always win the day; but if he remains true to his moral convictions he wins the greatest prize—his self-respect and dignity. I want to remind people how intensely important a strong moral code is, and how it shapes the way we see ourselves.

"Morality can't get me an eternity in heaven—only Jesus Christ can get me that—but it certainly gives my life value and meaning; I know it, and I want to tell the world."

HOBBIES AND OTHER INTERESTS: Miniatures—dollhouses and ship models mostly; needlework, including knitting, crochet, embroidery, sewing; gardening.

DISCH, Thomas M(ichael) 1940-
(Thom Demijohn, Leonie Hargrave, Cassandra Knye)

PERSONAL: Born February 2, 1940, in Des Moines, Iowa; son of Felix Henry (a salesman) and Helen (Gilbertson) Disch. *Education:* Attended New York University, 1959-62. *Agent:* Barney Karpfinger, 500 Fifth Ave., #2800, New York, N.Y. 10010.

CAREER: Doyle Dane Bernbach, Inc., New York, N.Y., copywriter, 1963-64; free-lance writer, 1964—. Lecturer at universities. *Member:* P.E.N., Writers Guild East, National Book Critics Circle (board member, 1988—). *Awards, hon-*

ors: O. Henry Prize, 1975, for story "Getting into Death," and 1979, for story "Xmas"; John W. Campbell Memorial Award, 1980, for *On Wings of Song;* British Science Fiction Award, 1981, for story "The Brave Little Toaster."

WRITINGS—Juvenile: *The Brave Little Toaster: A Bedtime Story for Small Appliances* (illustrated by Karen Lee Schmidt), Doubleday, 1986; *The Tale of Dan De Lion* (illustrated by Rhonda McClun), Coffee House Press, 1987; *The Brave Little Toaster Goes to Mars,* Doubleday, 1988.

Novels: *The Genocides,* Berkley, 1965; *Mankind under the Leash* (also see below), Ace Books, 1966 (published in England as *The Puppies of Terra,* Panther Books, 1978); (with John Sladek under joint pseudonym Cassandra Knye) *The House That Fear Built,* Paperback Library, 1966; *Echo 'Round His Bones,* Berkley, 1967; (with J. Sladek under joint pseudonym Thom Demijohn) *Black Alice,* Doubleday, 1968; *Camp Concentration,* Hart-Davis, 1968, Doubleday, 1969; *The Prisoner,* Ace Books, 1969; *334,* MacGibbon & Kee, 1972, Avon, 1974; (under pseudonym Leonie Hargrave) *Clara Reeve,* Knopf, 1975; *On Wings of Song,* St. Martin's, 1979; *Triplicity* (omnibus volume), Doubleday, 1980; (with Charles Naylor) *Neighboring Lives,* Scribner, 1981; *The Businessman: A Tale of Terror,* Harper, 1984; *Amnesia* (computer-interactive novel), Electronic Arts, 1985; *The Silver Pillow: A Tale of Witchcraft,* Mark Ziesing, 1988.

Story collections: *One Hundred and Two H-Bombs and Other Science Fiction Stories* (also see below), Compact Books, 1966, revised edition published as *One Hundred and Two H-Bombs,* Berkley, 1969 (published in England as *White Fang Goes Dingo and Other Funny S. F. Stories,* Arrow Books, 1971); *Under Compulsion,* Hart-Davis, 1968, published as *Fun with Your New Head,* Doubleday, 1969; *Getting into Death: The Best Short Stories of Thomas M. Disch,* Hart-Davis, 1973, revised edition, Knopf, 1976; *The Early Science Fiction Stories of Thomas M. Disch* (contains *Mankind under the Leash* and *One Hundred and Two H-Bombs and Other Science Fiction Stories*), Gregg, 1977; *Fundamental Disch,* G. K. Hall, 1977; *The Man Who Had No Idea,* Bantam, 1982.

Thomas M. Disch, age twelve.

Poetry: (With Marilyn Hacker and Charles Platt) *Highway Sandwiches,* privately printed, 1970; *The Right Way to Figure Plumbing,* Basilisk Press, 1972; *Haikus of a Pillow,* Bellevue Press, 1980; *ABCDEFG HIJKLM NOPQRST UVWXYZ,* Anvil Press Poetry, 1981; *Orders of the Retina,* Toothpaste Press, 1982; *Burn This,* Hutchinson, 1982; *Here I Am, There You Are, Where Were We,* Hutchinson, 1984; (with others) *Burning with a Vision: Poetry of Science and the Fantastic,* Owlswick Press, 1984.

Editor: (Ghost editor with Robert Arthur) *Alfred Hitchcock Presents: Stories That Scared Even Me,* Random House, 1967; *The Ruins of Earth: An Anthology of Stories of the Immediate Future,* Putnam, 1971; *Bad Moon Rising: An Anthology of Political Foreboding,* Harper, 1975; *The New Improved Sun: An Anthology of Utopian Science Fiction,* Harper, 1975; (with C. Naylor) *New Constellations: An Anthology of Tomorrow's Mythologies,* Harper, 1976; (with C. Naylor) *Strangeness: A Collection of Curious Tales,* Scribner, 1977; Richard Lupoff, *Stroka Prospekt,* Toothpaste Press, 1982.

Other: (Librettist) "The Fall of the House of Usher" (opera), first produced in New York, N.Y., by the Bel Canto Opera Company, 1979; (librettist) "Frankenstein" (opera), first produced in Greenvale, N.Y., at the C. W. Post Center of Long Island University, 1982; *Ringtime* (short story), Toothpaste Press, 1983; *Torturing Mr. Amberwell* (short story), Cheap Street, 1985.

Work appears in anthologies. Contributor to periodicals, including *Omni, Nation, Fantasy and Science Fiction, Poetry, Playboy,* and *New York Times Book Review.* Regular reviewer for *Washington Post Book World.*

ADAPTATIONS: "The Brave Little Toaster" (movie), Walt Disney Productions, 1988.

WORK IN PROGRESS: The M.D.: A Horror Story.

SIDELIGHTS: "From as far back as I can remember, I loved story-telling in any form it took. I practically lived at the library in Fairmont, Minnesota, but I also listened to all the after-school radio serials, and a good deal of what I earned on my paper route was spent on movie tickets. I started filling tablets with plots of stories somewhere around age twelve when I was bit by the sci-fi bug, but even back in second grade I would tell my friend Dennis White stories about Ronald Rabbit while we walked home from school. Later on, my best friend Bruce Burton and I would play story tag for days on end.

"As for how I came to write for children, that's an easy question for any sci-fi writer to answer, since a good part of science fiction has always been written for an audience of 'kids of all ages.' There's a saying in our field that the golden age of science-fiction is twelve—the age you start to read it.

"Children have one advantage over most grown-ups as readers. They still remember how to pretend. Whether it's a game of cops and robbers or managing all the imaginary lives in a doll house, kids give more active exercise to their imaginations than most grown-ups do—and that makes them ideal readers for a book like *The Brave Little Toaster.* They're willing to go along with the idea that toasters and radios and other appliances have lives of their own and can speak English just as well as cats or rabbits.

"As to what I want to get across to my audience, it's pretty much the same whether I'm writing for children or grown-ups. I want to share the fun and excitement of the story I'm

(From *The Brave Little Toaster: A Bedtime Story for Small Appliances* by Thomas M. Disch. Illustrated by Karen Schmidt.)

writing. Also, I guess I'm a typical older brother (I had three brothers and a sister, who were from five to ten years younger than me): I like to be an authority, explaining how the world works and the best way to get along in it. If I hadn't become a writer, I would probably have been a teacher.

"As a teacher, here and now, I'll give one piece of good advice about how to become a writer. Read. Read everything you can—newspapers, library books, magazines, comics, paperbacks, poetry, cereal boxes. Become an expert in whatever you're interested in—airplanes, dinosaurs, horses, the history of the Civil War—by reading the best books on the subject that you can get hold of. Books—reading matter of all sorts—are as necessary for learning to be a writer as water is for learning to swim."

FOR MORE INFORMATION SEE—Books: Samuel R. Delany, *The Jewel-Hinged Jaw: Notes on the Language of Science Fiction,* Dragon, 1977; Robert Scholes and Eric S. Rabkin, *Science Fiction: History, Science, Vision,* Oxford University Press, 1977; S. R. Delany, *The American Shore: Meditations on a Tale of Science Fiction by Thomas M. Disch,* Dragon, 1978; Charles Platt, *Dream Makers: The Uncommon People Who Write Science Fiction,* Berkley, 1980.

Periodicals: *Times Literary Supplement,* February 15, 1974, May 15, 1981, June 12, 1981, June 19, 1981, August 27, 1982, May 25, 1984; *New York Times Book Review,* July 27,

1975, March 21, 1976, October 28, 1979, March 22, 1981, August 26, 1984; *Time,* July 28, 1975, July 9, 1984; *Virginia Quarterly Review,* summer, 1976; *New Statesman,* June 22, 1979, May 22, 1981, July 13, 1984; *Observer,* June 24, 1979; *Magazine of Fantasy and Science Fiction,* February, 1980; *Village Voice,* August 27-September 2, 1980; *Washington Post Book World,* November 23, 1980, March 1, 1981, July 26, 1981, October 31, 1982, March 13, 1983; *Saturday Review,* February, 1981; *Los Angeles Times,* February 3, 1981; *Newsweek,* March 9, 1981, July 2, 1984; *Chicago Tribune Book World,* March 22, 1981; *Detroit News,* April 19, 1981; *Los Angeles Times Book Review,* November 21, 1982, July 13, 1984; *Washington Post,* July 3, 1984; *Minnesota Review,* fall, 1984; *San Francisco Review of Books,* November-December, 1984; *American Book Review,* July-August, 1985.

EPPENSTEIN, Louise (Kohn) 1892-1987

OBITUARY NOTICE: Born in 1892; died July 14, 1987, in Chicago, Ill. Journalist and author. A writer of children's books, Eppenstein also contributed to the "Observer" column in the *Chicago Tribune.* Her books include *Sally Goes Traveling Alone* and *Sally Goes to the Circus Alone.*

FOR MORE INFORMATION SEE: Chicago School Journal, May, 1951. Obituaries: *Chicago Tribune,* July 15, 1987.

FERN, Eugene A. 1919-1987

OBITUARY NOTICE—See sketch in *SATA* Volume 10: Born September 29, 1919, in Detroit, Mich.; died of an apparent heart attack, September 6, 1987, in East Hardwick, Vt. Artist, educator, and author. Fern taught art at New York City Community College (now New York City Technical College) for nearly thirty years while also working as a commercial illustrator and designer. Fern wrote and illustrated many children's books, including *Pepito's Story, The Most Frightened Hero, What's He Been Up To Now?* (winner of a *Parents' Magazine* award in 1961), *The King Who Was Too Busy, Birthday Presents,* and *Lorenzo and Angelina.*

FOR MORE INFORMATION SEE: Contemporary Authors, New Revision Series, Volume 16, Gale, 1986. Obituaries: *New York Times,* September 11, 1987; *School Library Journal,* November, 1987.

FOLEY, (Mary) Louise Munro 1933-

PERSONAL: Born October 22, 1933, in Toronto, Ontario, Canada; daughter of William Angus (a pharmacist) and Mary (a homemaker; maiden name, Nicholls) Munro; married Donald J. Foley, August 9, 1957 (divorced, 1984); married Rod C. Hulme (a broadcaster), September 11, 1987; children: (first marriage) Donald, William. *Education:* Attended University of Western Ontario, 1951-52, and Ryerson Institute of Technology, 1952-53; California State University at Sacramento, B.A. (with honors), 1976. *Politics:* Republican. *Religion:* Presbyterian. *Home and office:* 5010 Jennings Way, Sacramento, Calif. 95819. *Agent:* Ruth Cohen, P.O. Box 7626, Menlo Park, Calif. 94025.

CAREER: CHOK Radio, Sarnia, Ontario, copy editor, 1953-54; CJSP Radio, Leamington, Ontario, copy editor, 1954-56; KLIX-TV, Twin Falls, Idaho, copy editor, 1956-58; KGMS Radio, Sacramento, Calif., copy editor, 1958-60; copy chief

LOUISE MUNRO FOLEY

(retail) for Breuner's, Weinstock's, and Rhodes department stores, 1961-65; *News Argus,* Goldsboro, N.C., columnist, 1966; author, 1967—; California State University at Sacramento, Institute for Human Management, editor, 1975-80; Fremont Presbyterian Church, Sacramento, Calif., executive secretary, 1984—. *Member:* National League of American Penwomen, California Writer's Club. *Awards, honors:* Advertising Club of Sacramento Award, 1971, "for excellence in creative, effective advertising in the field of brochures."

WRITINGS: The Caper Club, Random House, 1969; *Somebody Stole Second,* Delacorte, 1972; *Sammy's Sister,* Bobbs-Merrill, 1974; *A Job for Joey,* Bobbs-Merrill, 1974; *No Talking,* Bobbs-Merrill, 1974; *Tackle 22* (illustrated by John Heinly), Delacorte, 1978.

"Choose Your Own Adventure" series; all published by Bantam: *The Lost Tribe,* 1984; *The Mystery of the Highland Crest,* 1984; *The Mystery of Echo Lodge,* 1984; *Danger at Anchor Mine* (illustrated by Leslie Morrill), 1985; *Forest of Fear,* 1985; *The Mardi Gras Mystery,* 1987; *Mystery of the Sacred Stones,* 1988.

"Twistaplot Books" series; all published by Scholastic: *The Train of Terror* (illustrated by David Febland), 1982; *The Sinister Studios of KESP-TV* (illustrated by D. Febland), 1983.

Editor: *Stand Close to the Door,* Institute for Human Service Management, 1976; *Women in Skilled Labor,* Institute for Human Service Management, 1978.

Contributor of humorous daily column, in collaboration with husband, appearing in *News-Argus* (Goldsboro, N.C.).

WORK IN PROGRESS: Australia, fiction for young readers, for McGraw-Hill.

SIDELIGHTS: Foley enjoys writing "'fun' fiction for kids—rather than moralistic stories—[I] believe kids need escapist reading just as much as adults."

HOBBIES AND OTHER INTERESTS: Music, art.

FOR MORE INFORMATION SEE—Collections: De Grummond Collection at the University of Southern Mississippi.

GASPERINI, Jim 1952-

PERSONAL: Born October 21, 1952, in Glen Cove, N.Y.; son of Edwin L. (an attorney) and Charlotte (a teacher; maiden name, Colburn) Gasperini. *Education:* Williams College, B.A., 1974. *Religion:* Unitarian. *Home:* 270 Riverside Dr., No. 12A, New York, N.Y. 10025. *Agent:* Victoria Pryor, Arcadia, Ltd., 221 West 82nd St., Suite 7D, New York, N.Y. 10024.

CAREER: Stichting Video Heads, Paris, France, technician, 1974-75; *Video,* Paris, video editor, 1976-77; Sterling Lord Agency, Inc., New York City, assistant, 1978-80; Byron Preiss Visual Publications, New York City, editor, 1981-82; Ballen Booksellers International, Commack, N.Y., regional manager, 1983-86; author, 1984—; Trans Fiction Systems, Inc., New York City, software developer, 1986—.

WRITINGS—Juvenile: *Secret of the Knights* (illustrated by Richard Hescox), Bantam, 1984; *Sail with Pirates* (illustrated by John Pierard and Alex Nino), Bantam, 1984; *The Mystery of Atlantis,* Bantam, 1985; (co-author with Ron Martinez and programmer) "Star Trek: The Promethean Prophecy" (computer software), Simon & Schuster, 1986.

WORK IN PROGRESS: "Astounding Adventures," computer software for Electronic Arts; "Verdict of History" series (a political simulation series); computer "encounter" software for Springboard, Publishers (Minn.): volume 1 about Central America entitled, "Hidden Agenda" and volume 2 about eastern Europe entitled "Perestroika."

SIDELIGHTS: "I am involved in creating computer fiction, interactive storytelling, which we hope to develop into a truly expressive medium. In its simplest form, interactive storytelling involves the sort of 'reader-active' branching of stories represented by the 'Time Machine' series I helped develop for Bantam. As the nine- to twelve-year-old reader works through the story, he or she is periodically offered a choice as to how the story will proceed and invited to turn ahead to one page or another to find alternate continuations. These are informed choices based on clues planted earlier in the story, common sense, or key facts about the history of the period in which the story is set (provided in the introductory material). The reader is challenged to find the unique ending: wrong choices will result eventually in a return to an earlier point in the story.

"The computer offers a much more supple environment for such interactive storytelling. I like to call what I write 'interactive screenplays,' because they seem to have more in common with drama than any other form of narrative. The computer provides an imaginary environment in text form, which the player reads about on a screen. The player becomes the main character in the story, and it is up to him or her to decide what to do and type in appropriate commands at the keyboard. The computer provides a series of linked 'stage sets,' 'props' in the form of imaginary objects the player can manipulate, 'actors' in the form of characters who come and go and can be questioned about what's going on, and even a sort of 'audience' and 'director' that react with disapproval if the player attempts to act out of character.

"Though this form of storytelling is still closer to games than it is to literature, we have high hopes for its future. Someday this may be remembered as the start of a new genre of narrative, much as we might look back on the early days of film. Whether it takes as long for this medium to develop as it took for cinema remains to be seen."

GATES, Doris 1901-1987

OBITUARY NOTICE—See sketch in *SATA* Volume 34: Born November 26, 1901, in Mountain View, Calif.; died September 3, 1987, in Carmel, Calif. Librarian, educator, and author. Gates served as director of the children's department of the Fresno County Library from 1930 to 1940. During this time, she broadcast weekly story hours on the radio and began writing books for children. She is best known for her 1941 Newbery Honor Book entitled *Blue Willow,* which was based on her work with children of migrant workers. It is considered by some critics to be one of the first in a new era of realistic children's novels about problems in America. Gates often wrote about horses, such as in *Little Vic,* noted for its use of a black central character and winner of the William Allen White Children's Book Award in 1954. Among her other works are several textbooks, six volumes of Greek mythology, and the autobiographical *Elderberry Bush.*

FOR MORE INFORMATION SEE: Contemporary Authors, New Revision Series, Volume 1, Gale, 1981; *Dictionary of Literary Biography,* Volume 22, *American Writers for Children,* Gale, 1983; *Twentieth-Century Children's Writers,* 2nd edition, St. Martin's, 1983; *Something about the Author Autobiography Series,* Volume 1, Gale, 1986. Obituaries: *School Library Journal,* December, 1987.

GERGELY, Tibor 1900-1978

PERSONAL: Born August 3, 1900, in Budapest, Hungary; came to United States in 1939; died January 13, 1978 (some sources say January 12), in New York, N.Y.; married Anna Lesznai (a poet and artist). *Education:* Attended art school in Vienna for six months. *Residence:* New York, N.Y.

JIM GASPERINI

TIBOR GERGELY

CAREER: Artist, illustrator, and stage designer. Caricaturist for Viennese newspapers, 1923-31. Helped to establish an art school in Budapest, Hungary, 1931. Work has been exhibited in Europe and the United States. *Awards, honors:* Caldecott Honor Book from American Library Association, 1955, for *Wheel on the Chimney; Busy Day, Busy People* was chosen one of Child Study Assoication of America's Children's Books of the Year, 1973, *Animals,* 1975, and *Wheel on the Chimney,* 1986.

WRITINGS—Self-illustrated juveniles: *The Great Big Fire Engine Book,* Simon & Schuster, 1950; (with Robert Leydenfrost) *Animal Talk: A Pop-up Alphabet Zoo,* Golden Press, 1960; *The Parrot Book: Parrots and Other Exotic Birds,* Golden Press, 1965; *Great Big Book of Bedtime Stories,* Golden Press, 1967, published as *Tibor Gergely's Bedtime Stories,* Western, 1972; *Emily's Moo,* Golden Press, 1969; *Baby Wild Animals from A to Z,* Golden Press, 1973, published in sign language (with Frank A. Paul) as *Baby Wild Animals from A to Z: In Sign Language,* translated by John Joyce, Joyce Media, 1977; *Busy Day, Busy People,* Random House, 1973; *Animals: A Picture Book of Facts and Figures,* McGraw, 1974.

Illustrator: Georges Duplaix, *Topsy Turvy Circus,* Harper, 1940; Dorothy Canfield, *Tell Me a Story,* University Publishing, 1940; Margaret Platt, *Talking Typewriter,* Lothrop, 1940; Jean Lilly, *A Hundred Tuftys,* Dutton, 1940; Frances M. Fox, *True Monkey Stories,* Lothrop, 1941; G. Duplaix, *The Merry Shipwreck,* Harper, 1941, reissued, Golden Press, 1971; Heinrich Hauser, *Folding Father,* translated by Barrows Mussey, Lothrop, 1942; Joseph Krumgold, *Sweeny's Adventure,* Random House, 1942; Jane Tompkins, *The Storks Fly Home,* Stokes, 1943; Walter D. Edmonds, *Two Logs Crossing: John Haskell's Story,* Dodd, 1943; Hendrik DeLeeuw, *Peewee the Mousedeer,* McKay, 1943; Lucy S. Mitchell, *Red, White and Blue Auto,* Scott, 1943; Janette S. Lowrey, *Day in the Jungle,* Simon & Schuster, 1943; Jane Werner (pseudonym of Jane W. Watson), *Noah's Ark,* Grosset, 1943, published as *Tibor Gergely's Noah's Ark Book,* Simon & Schuster, 1966; Margaret McConnell, *Bobo, the Barrage Balloon,* Lothrop, 1943; Maurice Dolbier, *Jenny: The Bus That Nobody Loved,* Random House, 1944; Helen Ferris, *''Watch Me!'' Said the Jeep,* Garden City, 1944; Ger-

trude Crampton, *Tootle,* Simon & Schuster, 1945, reissued, Golden Press, 1973; Jean Greene, *The Forgetful Elephant,* McKay, 1945.

G. Crampton, *Scuffy the Tugboat and His Adventures Down the River,* Simon & Schuster, 1946, reissued, Golden Press, 1986; L. S. Mitchell and others, *The Taxi That Hurried,* Simon & Schuster, 1946; Nancy B. Turner, *When It Rained Cats and Dogs,* Lippincott, 1946; Margaret W. Brown and Edith T. Hurd, *Five Little Firemen,* Simon & Schuster, 1948; Olga Cabral, *The Seven Sneezes,* Simon & Schuster, 1948; Marion Conger, *Circus Time,* Simon & Schuster, 1948; M. Dolbier, *The Magic Bus,* Wonder Books, 1948; L. S. Mitchell, *A Year in the City,* Simon & Schuster, 1948; Jane Werner, editor, *The Golden Book of Nursery Tales,* Simon & Schuster, 1948; Muriel Ward, *Little Pond in the Woods,* Simon & Schuster, 1948; Helen Palmer, *Bobby and His Airplanes,* Simon & Schuster, 1949; Robert Garfield (pseudonym of Kathryn Jackson and Byron Jackson) and Jessie Knittle, *Train Stories,* Simon & Schuster, 1949.

M. Conger, *A Day at the Zoo,* Simon & Schuster, 1950; K. Jackson and B. Jackson, *Little Yip Yip and His Bark,* Simon & Schuster, 1950; Annie North Bedford (pseudonym of Jane W. Watson), *The Jolly Barnyard,* Simon & Schuster, 1950; Miryam Yardumian, *The Happy Man and His Dump Truck,* Simon & Schuster, 1950; K. Jackson and B. Jackson, *Christopher and the Columbus,* Simon & Schuster, 1951; *Golden Grab Bag of Stories, Poems and Songs,* Simon & Schuster, 1951; Norman Corwin, *Dog in the Sky,* Simon & Schuster, 1952; M. W. Brown and E. T. Hurd, *Seven Little Postmen,*

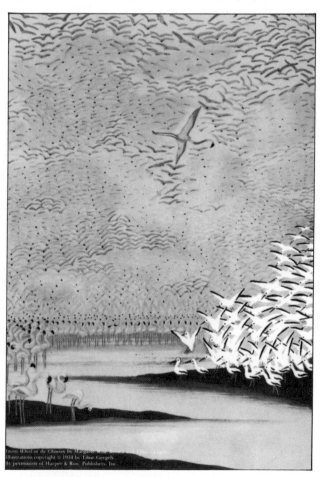

(From *Wheel on the Chimney* by Margaret Wise Brown. Illustrated by Tibor Gergely.)

Simon & Schuster, 1952; Nita Jonas, *Little Golden Book of Dogs,* Simon & Schuster, 1952; Marian Potter, *The Little Red Caboose,* Golden Press, 1953; Peter Archer (pseudonym of K. Jackson and B. Jackson), *Gergely's Golden Circus,* Simon & Schuster, 1954; Janet Frank, *Daddies,* Simon & Schuster, 1954; M. W. Brown, *Wheel on the Chimney* (ALA Notable Book), Lippincott, 1954, reissued, 1985; John P. Leventhal, *From Then to Now,* Simon & Schuster, 1954.

Elsa J. Werner (pseudonym of Jane W. Watson), *Houses,* Simon & Schuster, 1955; Rose Wyler, *My Little Golden Book about the Sky,* Simon & Schuster, 1956; Kathleen N. Daly, *My Little Golden Book about Travel,* Simon & Schuster, 1956; Beth G. Hoffman, *Animal Gym,* Simon & Schuster, 1956; K. N. Daly, *A Little Golden Book about the Seashore,* Simon & Schuster, 1957; K. N. Daly, *Giant Little Golden Book about Dogs,* Simon & Schuster, 1957; Georges Duplaix and others, *Giant Little Golden Book of Animal Stories,* Simon & Schuster, 1957; Horace Elmo, *Golden Books of Questions and Answers: Hundreds of Questions about People, Animals and Places, with Facts and Surprises for Children on Every Page,* Simon & Schuster, 1957; Ilo Orleans, *Animal Orchestra,* Simon & Schuster, 1958; Bertha M. Parker, *Deep Blue Sea,* Golden Books, 1958; R. Wyler, *Exploring Space,* Golden Books, 1958; Nancy Hulick, *Little Golden Picture Dictionary,* Golden Press, 1959; Horace Elmo and Nancy F. Hulick, *Quiz Fun: Hundreds of Questions and Answers,* Golden Press, 1959.

Ellen L. Buell, editor, *Treasury of Little Golden Books,* Golden Press, 1960; Carl Memling, *Rupert the Rhinoceros,* Golden Press, circa 1960; Caroline Emerson, *Make Way for the Thruway,* Golden Press, 1961 (also issued as *Make Way for the Highway*); George, *Jokes,* Golden Press, 1961; George [Wolf-

son], *My Little Golden Book of Jokes,* Golden Press, 1961; Rudyard Kipling, *Jungle Books,* Golden Press, 1963; Alice Lunt, *Little Gray Donkey,* Norton, circa 1964; Kathleen N. Daly, *Good Humor Man,* Golden Press, 1964; Peggy Parish, *Golden Calendar,* Western, 1965; Leone Arlandson, *Mister Puffer-Bill: Train Engineer,* Golden Press, 1965; John Peter, *Golden 1966 Calendar,* Golden Press, 1966; M. W. Brown, editor, *Great Big Book of Bedtime Stories,* Golden Press, 1967; Jane W. Watson and Kenneth Stafford Norris, *The Happy Little Whale,* Golden Press, 1968; Barbara S. Hazen, *Noah's Ark,* Golden Press, 1969; Kathe Recheis, *No Room for the Baker,* Four Winds, 1969; Patricia M. Scarry, *The Golden Story Book of River Bend,* Golden Press, 1969.

Joseph A. Davis, *Five Hundred Animals from A to Z,* American Heritage Press, 1970; Jean Tymms, *The Me Book,* Golden Press, 1974; J. Tymms, *My Head-to-Toe Book,* Golden Press, 1974. Also illustrator of *Lion Cub's Busy Day,* Golden Press; and Annemarie von Hill's *Mein grosses Vogel-Lexicon,* 1977.

Other: Anna Lesznai, *Eltevedt Litaniak,* Libelli, 1922; Bela Balazs, *Richtige Himmelblau, 3 Marchen,* Masken, 1925. Contributor of cartoons and drawings to Hungarian, Austrian, and German periodicals. Also illustrator of covers for *New Yorker.*

ADAPTATIONS: "Wheel on the Chimney" (sound filmstrip), Weston Woods, 1965; "Busy Day, Busy People" (cassette; filmstrip with cassette), Random House, 1971.

SIDELIGHTS: Tibor Gergely, much of whose life had been spent in Hungary, Austria, and Czechoslovakia, found the roots for his work in the peasant life of Yugoslavia, where he took

(From *My Head-to-Toe Book* by Jean Tymms. Illustrated by Tibor Gergely.)

part in the festivals, village dances, and country fairs, as well as in the quarrels and regional jealousies. With one parent a Yugoslavian and the other a Hungarian, he understood only too well the feeling of national pride so strong throughout the Balkans.

During his school years he helped train himself as an artist with the dubious occupation of caricaturing his teachers. He had not seriously considered a career in art, however, until he was twenty when he went to Vienna for the only formal art schooling he was to have. He followed that six-month stint with two years of stage decorating and puppet designing for an experimental marionette theater in Vienna.

From 1923-1931 Gergely worked as a caricaturist for Viennese newspapers. He returned to his native Budapest in 1931 to help establish and to teach in a new art school. He was entirely self-taught, his style of painting determined by the artistic achievement of the "Paris School" of Modern Art.

Gergely immigrated to the United States in 1939 because he "didn't like it over there," and settled permanently in New York City. Shortly after his arrival, he collaborated with author Georges Duplaix on two children's books, *Topsy Turvy Circus* and *The Merry Shipwreck*.

His association with Golden Books spanned from 1942 when Simon & Schuster began publishing the popular series of brightly illustrated, simply written, sturdy books until his death in 1978. In them he created worlds populated with baby wild animals and barnyards, fire engines, and taxis. The motivations for his illustrations sprang from the desire to draw what he would have wanted to see during his own childhood.

His fascination with animal life led him to collaborate with Joseph A. Davis in 1970 on *Five Hundred Animals from A to Z* and in 1974 to write the text and illustrate *Animals: A Picture Book of Facts and Figures*.

FOR MORE INFORMATION SEE: Bertha E. Mahony and others, compilers, *Illustrators of Children's Books: 1744-1945*, Horn Book, 1947; "Festival Poster Designed by Tibor Gergely—Order Now," *Herald Tribune Book News*, February 18, 1949; B. M. Miller and others, compilers, *Illustrators of Children's Books, 1946-1956*, Horn Book, 1958; Dorothy A. Marquardt and Martha E. Ward, *Illustrators of Books for Young People*, Scarecrow, 1975; Barbara Bader, *American Picture Books from Noah's Ark to the Beast Within*, Macmillan, 1976; Jim Roginski, compiler, *Newbery and Caldecott Medalists and Honor Book Winners*, Libraries Unlimited, 1982.

Obituaries: *Publishers Weekly*, January 30, 1978; *School Library Journal*, April, 1978.

Collections: De Grummond Collection at the University of Southern Mississippi; Kerlan Collection at the University of Minnesota; Ogle Collection at the University of Oregon Library; Special Collections at the University Research Library, University of California at Los Angeles; Rare Book and Manuscript Library at Columbia University.

GROSS, Alan   1947-

PERSONAL: Born June 29, 1947, in Chicago, Ill.; son of Melvin (a retailer) and Shirlee (Marks) Gross; married Norma Topa (an artist), June 26, 1978. *Education:* Attended University of Missouri, 1965-69. *Home and office:* Writer's Group, Inc., 1730 North Wells, Chicago, Ill. 60614.

What if my house gets hit by lightning, or carried off in a flood, or attacked by monsters? ■ (From *Sometimes I Worry...* by Alan Gross. Illustrated by Mike Venezia.)

CAREER: Writer, teacher, and actor. Worked as writer and creative director in advertising in Chicago, Ill., 1969-77; teacher for Chicago Public Library, Writer's Group, and Victory Gardens, all in Chicago, and Piven Theatre Workshop in Evanston, Ill., 1978-79; actor with "Second City" and theaters and workshops. *Member:* Dramatists Guild, Authors League. *Awards, honors:* Two Joseph Jefferson Awards, 1978, for play "Lunching"; finalist, O'Neill Festival National Playwrights Conference, 1978, for play "Phone Room."

WRITINGS—Juvenile: *Sometimes I Worry* (illustrated by Mike Venezia), Childrens Press, 1978; *What If the Teacher Calls on Me?* (illustrated by M. Venezia), Childrens Press, 1979; *I Don't Want to Go to School*, Childrens Press, 1982.

Plays: "Lunching" (two-act), first produced in Chicago, Ill., at Body Politic, December, 1977, produced on Broadway, October, 1979; "The Phone Room" (two-act), first produced in Chicago at Theatre Building, February, 1978; "The Man in 605" (two-act), first produced in Chicago at Theatre Building, June, 1979, produced on National Public Radio, fall, 1979.

Contributor to *Chicago* magazine.

WORK IN PROGRESS: How to Be a Native New Yorker, a satirical picture book; two plays, "Nora's Room" and "Soon to Be a Major Motion Picture"; and "film treatments."

SIDELIGHTS: "I want my life to be as simple and dull as possible. I spent years figuring creativity could wait until I got everything else straight, but as Abraham Maslow says, creativity is at the top of the hierarchy, and I realized you have to have it now, or it'll never happen. Making commercials is fine—I had a good living—but it'll never be literature. For years I wrote stories, which is the best preparation for a playwright. I want to be an old man who can look back on a string of plays and see my life in them and know it mattered."

FOR MORE INFORMATION SEE: Chicago Tribune, July 26, 1978.

Children have more need of models than of critics.
—Joseph Joubert

GEORGETTE GUAY

GUAY, Georgette (Marie Jeanne) 1952-

PERSONAL: Surname sounds like "gay"; born October 18, 1952, in Windsor, Ontario, Canada; daughter of George F. (a factory worker) and Suzanne (a homemaker; maiden name, Racicot) Guay; married second husband, Bob Simms; children: Nicole Marie, Adam George. *Education:* University of Windsor, B.A., 1974; University of Toronto, B.Ed., 1976. *Religion:* Christian. *Home:* Bracebridge, Ontario, Canada. *Agent:* c/o P.O. Box 2468, Bracebridge, Ontario, Canada P0B 1C0. *Office:* Playwrights Union of Canada, 8 York St, 6th Fl., Toronto, Ontario, Canada M5J 1R2.

CAREER: Writer, 1977—. Playwright-in-Residence, Theatre on the Move, Frog Print Theatre, 1982-83. *Member:* Playwrights Union of Canada; Amnesty International; Canadian Society of Children's Authors, Illustrators and Performers; Ontario Puppetry Association; Performing Artists for Nuclear Disarmament. *Awards, honors:* Chalmers Foundation Award honorable mention, children's play category, 1982, and Dora Mavor Moore Award for Best Children's Play 1983, both for "The Food Show"; Ontario Arts Council grant, annually 1982-88, for playwriting and the "Artists in the Schools" program.

WRITINGS—All plays unless otherwise indicated: *The Bling Said Hello/You'll Never Be the Same: Two Plays for Young People,* Playwrights Co-op, 1979; *Kids Plays* (anthology), Playwrights Press, 1980; (with Jim Biros and Paul Shilton) "The Food Show," first produced by Theatre on the Move, Toronto, 1981; *Sense and Feeling* (anthology), Copp Clark, 1982; (with P. Shilton) "Sky's the Limit," first produced by Theatre on the Move, Toronto, 1982; "Dreamagic," first produced by Theatre on the Move, Toronto, 1983; *I'll Tell You at Recess* (first produced by Theatre on the Move, Toronto, 1978), Playwrights Union of Canada, 1986.

WORK IN PROGRESS: A collection of short stories about people as gemstones; *Significant Moments,* a novel about memory and childhood; a collection of poetry; "In Search of a Voice," an opera about a young soprano's passage into manhood, utilizing large puppets; *The Wheat Book,* a book on the essential place of wheat in the culture of Canada and the world.

SIDELIGHTS: "I am profoundly moved by all art forms, especially music. I am particularly fond of writing lyrics for songs, as music's universality reaches so many. In this regard, it has been my great fortune to work with an extraordinary composer, Paul Shilton. Over the years we have learned to read each other's minds, to challenge one another, and to work and work until we are happy with our song.

"I grew up speaking French and English and attended the bilingual St. Edmond School in Windsor, Ontario. My grandparents were instrumental in the founding of this school, collecting names on a petition door-to-door. My grandmother always said 'When the language dies, the culture dies,' and I believe this to be true. Growing up French in an English community often exposed me to extremes of prejudice that were shocking. Although there were many times as I was growing up that I resented having to speak French at home, I'm now very glad that my mother and grandmother were so strict. I was lucky enough to grow up with my grandmother living with us and thus had two mothers and the influence of a whole other generation of experience. I learned that to grow old is not to rot, but to come into full flower, albeit a different kind of flower from one's youth. My grandmother died at 92 of a stroke. I hope to live as long and as joyfully as she did.

"Because of my experience at Ontario Writers' Retreats, sponsored by the Writers' Development Trust, I was able to make contact with other writers whose work and attitudes had a profound effect on me. Diane Keating encouraged my work in poetry and served as a glowing example of the spirit and dedication of the true poet. Many friendships were made and maintained through these retreats, helping to heal the loneliness that being a writer can bring.

"My brother Paul, a gemologist, introduced me to *The Interior World of Gemstones* a beautiful, authorative book on the subject. I have been keenly interested in this area ever since and plan a collection of short stories about people as gemstones—full of occlusions which enhance their individuality and beauty.

"I have been in and out of psychiatric hospitals since the age of fourteen. This has had a profound impact on my life and my work. It is in these hospitals that I have met the greatest number of sensitive, intelligent people, young and old, all gathered together in one place and joined in a common suffering. The ignorance surrouding psychiatric hospitals and patients is shocking. There is not enough that could be written on the subject. A huge gulf needs desperately to be bridged, or at least traversed.

"My teaching experience brought me back into contact with the unique world of children and this led me into the extremely rewarding field of children's writing. As I became a full time writer, the Ontario Arts Council programme 'Artists in the Schools,' helped me to become more intensely involved with children and their art. Playwrights Union of Canada Touring Programme also enabled me to reach many children and teachers and for them to reach me, as an artist. These programmes are essential to our educational system and to our culture.

"Children shared many of their dreams with me and these became the foundation of my play 'Dreamagic.' Instrumental to this work was the inspired mime and puppeteer, Nikki Tilroe, artistic director of Frog Print Theatre. I cannot give enough thanks to the Ontario Arts Council's Playwrights-in-Residence Programme which brought the two of us together and also introduced me to the fine puppet maker and artist, Karen Valleau, who designed the puppets for *Dreamagic.*

"My family, notably my husband, Bob Simms, has given me support and encouragement in the pursuit of writing as a life-work. This has helped me through many a dark night, blank page and impending deadline. Now, my daughter, Nicole, and son, Adam, inspire me afresh every day. They are the greatest joy in my life. I thank God for the miracle of their being and for the many miracles. . . . A close group of friends help me often to keep the wolves at bay.

"Plans for the future include a lot of travel, painting, sculpting and, of course, given the courage and stamina, writing."

HOBBIES AND OTHER INTERESTS: Knitting, long walks, painting, reading, crossword puzzles, Scrabble.

HARRIS, Geraldine (Rachel) 1951-

PERSONAL: Born October 17, 1951; adopted daughter of Leslie George (a company director) and Mary Edith (Wood) Harris; married Richard Gilmore Eric Pinch (a number theorist), January 7, 1978. *Education:* Cambridge University, B.A., 1977; doctoral study at Oxford University, 1977-84. *Politics:* Social Democrat. *Religion:* Anglican. *Home:* Wolstenholme, 5 Oxford Rd., Cambridge CB4 3PH, England.

CAREER: Free-lance lecturer, writer and television consultant, 1984—. *Member:* Society of Authors, Folklore Society, Egypt Exploration Society, Jomsborg (meadkeeper, 1975-77).

WRITINGS: White Cranes Castle, Macmillan, 1979; *Gods and Pharaohs from Egyptian Mythology,* Eurobooks, 1982; *Seven*

GERALDINE HARRIS

Citadels, Greenwillow, Volume I: *Prince of the Godborn,* 1982, Volume II: *The Children of the Wind,* 1982, Volume III: *The Dead Kingdom,* 1983, Volume IV: *The Seventh Gate,* 1983; *Votive Offerings to Hathor,* Griffith Institute, 1988; *Dancing Day,* Macmillan, 1989. Contributor to journals, including *Folklore* and *Orientalia.*

WORK IN PROGRESS: The Eye of the Sun, a juvenile novel set in ancient Egypt; script for "Ra," an animated film about Egyptian mythology.

SIDELIGHTS: "I divide my time between very dry academic work and creative writing and find that this balance suits me very well. My main interest as a writer is exploring religious questions through the medium of fantasy."

HAVILAND, Virginia 1911-1988

*OBITUARY NOTICE—*See sketch in *SATA* Volume 6: Born May 21, 1911, in Rochester, N.Y.; died of a stroke, January 6, 1988, in Washington, D.C. Librarian and author of children's books. Haviland devoted much of her life to promoting and improving the quality of juvenile literature. Her career began at the Boston Public Library, where she subsequently worked as reader's adviser for children until joining the Library of Congress in 1963. As director of the Children's Book Section there, Haviland reorganized the division into its present form, now called the Children's Literature Center. In addition to her library duties, she served as president of the Children's Services Division of the American Library Association. Haviland began writing about children's books at the request of colleagues and friends. Among her works are *Children's Literature: A Guide to Reference Sources, Children's Books of International Interest,* and *The Openhearted Audience: Ten Authors Talk about Writing for Children.* In addition, she edited sixteen titles in Little, Brown's "Favorite Fairy Tales" series, collections of stories from different countries around the world. She also contributed reviews on children's books to various periodicals, including the *Washington Post* and *Horn Book.* For her overall contribution to children's literature, Haviland received the Catholic Library Association's Regina Medal and an award from Grolier Publishing.

FOR MORE INFORMATION SEE: Contemporary Authors, New Revision Series, Volume 12, Gale, 1984. Obituaries: *Washington Post,* January 8, 1988; *New York Times,* January 9, 1988; *Facts on File,* January 15, 1988; *School Library Journal,* February, 1988; *Horn Book,* March, 1988.

HEILBRUN, Lois Hussey 1922(?)-1987

OBITUARY NOTICE: Born about 1922 in Norwich, Conn.; died of lymphoma, October 21, 1987. Ornithologist, educator, editor, and author. Heilbrun joined the education department of the American Museum of Natural History in 1945, working as a projectionist and instructor before retiring as assistant department chairman in 1971. While at the museum she wrote, with Catherine M. Pessino, the children's books *Collecting Cocoons, Collecting Small Fossils,* and *Collecting for the City Naturalist.* As a member of the Linnaean Society, which she served as treasurer, archivist, and president, she helped to restore the tern colony on Great Gull Island in Long Island Sound. Heilbrun also edited *American Birds'* Christmas bird count issue from 1972 to 1983.

FOR MORE INFORMATION SEE: Obituaries: *New York Times,* October 28, 1987.

HUNTER, Mollie   1922-
(Maureen Mollie Hunter McIlwraith)

PERSONAL: Born June 30, 1922, in Longniddry, East Lothian, Scotland; daughter of William George (a motor mechanic) and Helen Eliza Smeaton (a confectioner; maiden name, Waitt) McVeigh; married Thomas "Michael" McIlwraith (a hospital catering manager), December 23, 1940; children: Quentin Wright, Brian George. *Education:* Attended Preston Lodge School, East Lothian, Scotland. *Politics:* Scottish Nationalist. *Religion:* Episcopalian. *Home:* "The Shieling," Milton, near Drumnadrochit, Inverness-shire 1V3 6UA, Scotland. *Agent:* A. M. Heath & Co. Ltd., 79 St. Martin's La., London WC2N 4AA, England; McIntosh & Otis, Inc., 475 Fifth Ave., New York, N.Y. 10017.

CAREER: Writer, 1953—. Has lectured in the United States in 1975 and in 1976 toured New Zealand and Australia lecturing under the joint auspices of the British Council, the International Reading Association and the education authorities for New Zealand and Australia; writer-in-residence, Dalhousie University, Halifax, Nova Scotia, 1980, 1981; organized and taught in writer's workshops for both adults and children; teacher of creative writing, Aberlour Summer School for Gifted Children, 1987—. *Member:* The Society of Authors in Scotland (chairman).

AWARDS, HONORS: The Ferlie was selected one of Child Study Association of America's Children's Books of the Year, 1968, *The Walking Stones,* 1970, *The Thirteenth Member,* 1971, *A Sound of Chariots,* and *The Haunted Mountain,* both 1972, *The Stronghold,* 1974, *A Stranger Came Ashore,* 1975, *Talent Is Not Enough,* 1976, *A Furl of Fairy Wind,* 1977 and

MOLLIE HUNTER

Cat, Herself, 1987; *Book World*'s Children's Spring Book Festival honor book, 1970, for *The Lothian Run;* Children's Book Award from the Child Study Association of America, 1973, for *A Sound of Chariots; The Haunted Mountain* and *A Sound of Chariots* were both chosen one of *New York Times* Outstanding Books of the Year, 1972, and *A Stranger Came Ashore,* 1975; Scottish Arts Council Award, 1973, for *The Haunted Mountain;* Carnegie Medal for a Children's Book of Outstanding Merit from the British Library Association, 1974, for *The Stronghold;* May Hill Arbuthnot Lecturer at the University of Pennsylvania, 1975; *A Stranger Came Ashore* was selected one of *School Library Journal*'s Best Children's Books, 1975, and was a *Boston Globe-Horn Book* Award Honor Book, 1976; *The Wicked One* was selected one of *School Library Journal*'s Best Books for Spring, and was selected a Scottish Arts Council award book, both 1977; *You Never Knew Her as I Did!* was selected one of New York Public Library's Books for the Teen Age, and a Notable Children's Trade Book in the Field of Social Studies by the National Council of Social Studies and the Children's Book Council, both 1982; *Cat, Herself* was chosen one of American Library Association's Best Books for Young Adults, and one of *School Library Journal*'s Best Books for Young Adults, both 1986.

WRITINGS—Juvenile, except as indicated: *Patrick Kentigern Keenan* (illustrated by Charles Keeping), Blackie & Son, 1963, published in America as *The Smartest Man in Ireland,* Funk, 1965; *Hi, Johnny* (illustrated by Drake Brookshaw), Evans, 1963; *The Spanish Letters* (illustrated by Elizabeth Grant), Evans, 1964, Funk, 1967; *The Kelpie's Pearls* (ALA Notable Book; *Horn Book* honor list; illustrated by Charles Keeping), Blackie & Son, 1964, [new editions illustrated by Joseph Cellini, Funk, 1966, illustrated by Stephen Gammell, Harper, 1976]; *A Pistol in Greenyards* (illustrated by E. Grant), Evans, 1965, Funk, 1968; *The Ghosts of Glencoe,* Evans, 1966, Funk, 1969; *Thomas and the Warlock* (illustrated by J. Cellini), Funk, 1967; *The Ferlie* (illustrated by Joseph Cellini), Funk, 1968.

The Bodach (illustrated by Gareth Floyd), Blackie & Son, 1970, published in America as *The Walking Stones: A Story of Suspense* (illustrated by Trina Schart Hyman), Harper, 1970; *The Lothian Run,* Funk, 1970; *The Thirteenth Member: A Story of Suspense,* Harper, 1971; *A Sound of Chariots* (young adult; *Horn Book* honor list; ALA Notable Book), Harper, 1972; *The Haunted Mountain: A Story of Suspense* (ALA Notable Book; illustrated by Laszlo Kubinyi), Harper, 1972; *The Stronghold* (ALA Notable Book), Harper, 1974; *A Stranger Came Ashore: A Story of Suspense* (ALA Notable Book), Harper, 1975; *The Wicked One: A Story of Suspense* (ALA Notable Book), Harper, 1977; *A Furl of Fairy Wind: Four Stories* (includes *A Furl of Fairy Wind,* "The Enchanted Boy," "The Brownie," and *Hi, Johnny;* illustrated by S. Gammell), Harper, 1977; *The Third Eye* (young adult; *Horn Book* honor list), Harper, 1979.

You Never Knew Her as I Did!, Harper, 1981; *The Knight of the Golden Plain* (illustrated by Marc Simont), Harper, 1983; *The Dragonfly Years,* Hamish Hamilton, 1983, published in America as *Hold on to Love,* Harper, 1984; *The Three-Day Enchantment* (illustrated by M. Simont), Harper, 1985; *I'll Go My Own Way,* Hamish Hamilton, 1985, published in America as *Cat, Herself,* Harper, 1986; *The Mermaid Summer,* Harper, 1988.

Other: *Talent Is Not Enough: Mollie Hunter on Writing for Children* (*Horn Book* honor list), Harper, 1976.

One-act plays: *A Love-Song for My Lady* (first produced at Empire Theatre, Inverness, Scotland, 1961), Evans, 1962; *Stay*

By the evening of that day,...Cat had forgotten all about her brush with the police. ■ (Jacket illustration by Stephen Seymour from *Cat, Herself* by Mollie Hunter.)

for an Answer (first produced at Empire Theatre, Inverness, 1962), French, 1962.

Contributor of articles to numerous newspapers and magazines, including *Scotsman* and *Glasgow Herald;* contributor to anthologies.

WORK IN PROGRESS: Continuing research into Scottish history and folklore, with emphasis on Celtic folklore.

SIDELIGHTS: Born **June 30, 1922** in the Lowland village of Longniddry, East Lothian, Scotland. The daughter of an Irish father and a Scottish mother, Hunter was the third of five children, and was named Maureen Mollie Hunter McVeigh. From birth she was raised with the traditions of Scottish tales and their tellers. "I was three years old when my great-grandmother Hunter first talked and sang to me of the lawless forays carried out by the men that Scotland knew long ago as 'the Border reivers.' She was ninety-three, her voice long since cracked and wasted, but there was still a wild, strange music in the very names I heard from her—Kerr, Elliot, Graham, Hunter, Armstrong. . . .

"'And you're an Elliot, as well as a Hunter,' she told me. 'You have the Elliot nose.' Which is perfectly true, if unenviable; this feature being somewhat less than handsome. Yet still I recall the marvellous thrill of discovery it gave, to put my hand up then and there, and for the first time realise my nose as a distinctive promontory that gave some sort of meaning to my face, and so to me as an entity; as a person." [Mollie

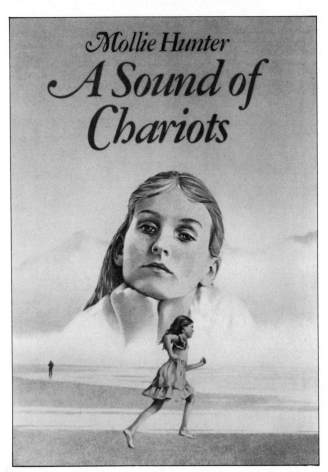

Run, now! Run like the wind, girl! ■ (Jacket illustration by Dave Holmes from *A Sound of Chariots* by Mollie Hunter.)

The seventeenth day of June in the year of 1567; that was when they brought her, captive, to our island. ■ (From *You Never Knew Her as I Did!* by Mollie Hunter.)

Hunter, *Talent Is Not Enough: Mollie Hunter on Writing for Children,* Harper, 1976.[1] Amended by Hunter.]

Scottish village life enriched her imagination, and what began as childish curiosity developed into a lifetime interest in Scotland's history and folklore. "So much the better . . . if the writer is born into an environment which feeds this sense of history—and here, at least, I can speak with the certainty of having experienced this good fortune, for all my childhood impressions are of current time springing naturally from a still-living past.

"The village smithy, where I had watched the forging of that wheel-rim, had fascinated a dozen generations of children before me. In some small fields of the farms around the village there was still seed broadcast by hand; and still, when it came to harvest, the curved rise and fall of shining sickle-blades, the ancient rite of shaping the last sheaf into a corn dolly to perch high on the stacked straw and thereby protect it from unnameable pagan fears of harm.

"The shadow of history fell over me every day. . . . Its shape filled my vision with castle, keep, and cottage, with barn, mill, and dovecote—or 'dookit' as we called this last, in the native

Snowdrops belonged to an old memory, a painful one she had locked away three years before that time. ■ (Jacket illustration by Robert Blake from *The Third Eye* by Mollie Hunter.)

Doric speech which itself has the whole of Scotland's past in its sound and structure.''[1]

Though it has changed, Hunter still has vivid memories of her village. "It is commuter country now, that part of Lowland Scotland which holds the village of my childhood. Tarmac roads lie like a tangle of black spaghetti where once the gold of barley harvest was heavy. The rich red earth ploughed by great teams of shining Clydesdales is sick with spreading bungalow-rash; but in those days our village was only a small place—little more than a farm with cottages grouped around it and a single street of cottages running past the farm.

"Whitewashed and roofed with the mellow red of ogee pantiles, these cottages crouched small in gardens spilling over with wallflowers and hollyhocks, stocks, peonies, and dahlias rioting out of the fertile Lowland earth. The bee-hum that lingered over the flowers' profusion had been disturbed by nothing more than the voice of the martyred George Wishart preaching the Reformation. The village street had seen no more exciting occasion than a contentious little man called John Knox arrogantly preceding the gentle presence of Wishart with the unwanted symbol of a sword borne aloft. The Dene—the lane running from the village to the cold waters of the Firth of Forth—had witnessed no darker sight than a coven of sixteenth-century witches, who had 'convened at the Dene fute, and daunced thir.'

"The village was remarkable only in having remained unremarkable through all the centuries of turbulent history which had washed over that corner of southeast Scotland. Yet history was there in it, the people's history written small in small recurrent events and persisting customs, which only the wondering eye of a child would find worth more than a glance.

"The 'flittings'—the removals when farm laborers exchanged a job in one parish for a job in another—why were they so frequent? Knowing nothing of the complicated agrarian pattern that had produced these landless peasants, I watched them loading carts with their possessions at term time, piling straw on top, then loading their children onto the straw. The dangling boots of the children were tackety-soled and—bought for growth—grotesquely big for their thin legs. The dusty gold of the straw could not conceal how scuffed the furnishings were; and as the carts trundled away, I recognized uneasily that there went people even poorer than my poverty-stricken family.

"At the farm, too, when I gathered with the other children to scramble for the 'poor-oot'—the coins that were always thrown after a wedding—I wondered at the cruelty of the bride's reception. Why did they not throw confetti or rice over her as she ran up the path to the house? Why did they pelt her with stones until she screamed and cried and swore at them, her face all red and ugly above the white dress? The bride reached the door. The hostile stone-throwers became cheerful guests. The bride's anger changed to smiling complacency. She was taken in triumph into the house, and I was acutely aware of a ritual of some kind having been enacted.

There is a mountain by the name of Ben MacDui, and this mountain is haunted. ■ (Jacket illustration by Laszlo Kubinyi from *The Haunted Mountain* by Mollie Hunter.)

"The history of the village was there, too, in the speech of its people—the Doric, which I also spoke then as fluently as the standard English required from me at school. Experience and reading began to come closer together. The reflections grew clearer. I had not known before that Doric was anything except a peasant tongue—a dialect spoken only in such rural areas as my birthplace. Yet here I was discovering from books that until the beginning of the eighteenth century, Doric had been a language in its own right, the language of the country's law and church as well as that of everyday speech in the Lowlands; the language of kings, courtiers, and gentlefolk as well as that of the common people; the language of the greatest among the *makars*—the poets of Scotland.'' [Mollie Hunter, "If You Can Read," *Horn Book,* June, 1978.[2]]

Her family was literate, and instilled in her a love of books and the Scottish style of storytelling. "I had the run of my grandfather's library . . . a collection devoted to works of an 'improving' nature, but the only improvement this achieved for me was that I learned to read very fast. I had to, in order to be able to pick out the action scenes from the long, moralising passages I thought of as 'the dull bits.' My Puritan upbringing balanced the account with feelings of guilty unease over deceiving poor grandfather. Yet despite the guilt, I still resented the dull bits as attempts to lecture me about life, when what I wanted to do was to find out about it for myself. And this latter, it seems to me, is the driving urge of the older child whose basic need to identify has to take account of the expanding realisations of his adolescent years."[1]

1931-1932. Hunter's home was cheerful and full of love, giving her a secure and happy life, until age nine when her adored father died of an illness arising from wounds sustained in World War I. Like her autobiographical heroine, Bridie McShane, in *A Sound of Chariots,* she had then to endure great grief and loneliness. But like Bridie, she was comforted by her love of books and of writing, and was determined to become a writer.

"Long ago, when I had to endure the kindly, adult condescension that asks, 'And what will you be when you grow up?' I used to answer, 'A kennel maid.'

"*They* smiled, reading into this only a childish desire to achieve a life-long romp with the more playful versions of man's faithful friend. *I* smiled, letting them have their delusion, the while I gritted my milk-teeth on a private vision of myself as a commanding figure with wrists of steel tautly controlling a pack of huge and baying hounds, a fearless trainer, an expert tracker, a—

"'Nonsense!' said a teacher who asked me this same question one day and was given my usual answer. 'You'll be a writer.' And passed so firmly on to the child next in line of question that there was no arguing with her decision. The idea that I would be a writer was planted in my head; and for this, at least, I must thank that strong-minded lady—although how she had reached so positive a conclusion can only be a guess with me now. I was talkative, of course—I have to admit that; and even at that tender age I was what I have always continued to be—a storyteller with a great love for words of sweet sound and rich colouring. Yet what neither she nor anyone else could have forecast at that time was that these drives would eventually find their true scope in writing for children; and for this, as for every other form of the art, there is a statement by Ralph Waldo Emerson which makes a shot in the dark out of any prediction for a future in writing.

"'Talent alone cannot make a writer. There must be a man behind the book.'"

Amending this to the "more acceptable" phrasing of "a person behind the book," Hunter calls on a ghost as witness to the initial proof of the statement . . . "the fearsome rheumaticky ghost of the man who was Granpa Cormack."[1]

"He was an acquaintance of my village childhood in the Lowlands of Scotland, this old man, and the sphere of his power was the local market garden. He was very tall and thin, with a hobbling walk aided by a long, heavy stick. His face was small and russet-coloured, heavily wrinkled by age, bad temper, and the pain of his rheumatics. Like ourselves, he used the broad Doric, which was the everyday speech of the Lowlands then; and to him, we village children were always 'they blawstit bairns'—those damn kids.

"Granpa Cormack purely hated children; yet it was to this old curmudgeon we had to apply in the summer holidays for a chance to earn much-needed cash from what we called 'a job at the berries,' and so Granpa was both our terror and our joy. Terror struck when he came hobbling down the rows of raspberry bushes, roaring, and laying about him with that heavy stick. Joy came in the weighing-house when our berry-picking for the day was checked, wages were paid, and we all scuffled about gleefully trying to confuse Granpa's calculations with practical jokes—such as hiding stones in the baskets to increase their weight, and then stealthily abstracting the same.

He stepped into the water. The icy chill of it gripped his knees like an iron band. ■ (From *The Kelpie's Pearls* by Mollie Hunter. Illustrated by Stephen Gammell.)

"It was still from Granpa Cormack, all the same, that I learned to recognise at least one aspect of the truth implicit in my theme, for berry-pickers under his rule were never allowed to do anything in half-hearted fashion. The basket for holding the fruit had to be slung around the neck so that both hands were free to work. Otherwise, like some ancient Demon King shooting through a stage trapdoor, Granpa would burst from the bushes roaring,

"'Yase baith eer haunds!'

"The English of this is 'use both your hands,' and it indicates the basic and very obvious sense in which talent is not enough. Even the greatest talent, lacking the craft to develop it, is no more than an itch in the mind; and the higher the potential, of course, the greater the effort needed to bring it to peak achievement.

"To sustain the effort, however, means cultivating the capacity to endure loneliness—not that loneliness itself is peculiar to the creative mind. Far from that, the mere fact of being human implies an essential loneliness in each of us—microcosmic as we all are; for universe may communicate with universe, but by their very nature they cannot mingle.

"To say, then, that the writer's lot is a lonely one is not to complain of this, but simply to make the point that to be creative is to be different from those who are not; and so, to that extent also, to be cut off from those others. Yet, ironically, it is out of this even deeper loneliness that the writer hopes to be able to communicate to an extent denied the non-creative ones; and the irony is accentuated by his awareness that he will never really be able to tell how far he has succeeded in this.

"A writer, indeed, could be likened to a person locked for life in a cell—someone to whom the mere fact of imprisonment has taught things he wants desperately to convey. He compiles a code, spends the rest of his life using this to tap out messages on the wall of his cell, and all the time he taps he is asking himself,

"'*Is there anyone out there listening? Can they hear me? Do they understand?*'"[1]

1936. Like Bridie McShane, Hunter had to leave school at a tender age for work in Edinburgh. But the pattern of her schooling had at least given her a solid grounding in grammar—and she was still determined to be a writer.

"I left school thinking that my only equipment for this aim was a fluency in reading and a great love of words; but although I did not then recognize it as such, I also had a writer's ear for the fall of language, and to guide my first efforts, I had that solid grounding in grammar. Again, however, I did not recognize the fortune of such a grounding, nor could I then guess at its essential nature. My only clear feeling was that I might be able secretly to plunder the stores of knowledge otherwise denied me but which seemed so vital to achieving my ambition; and so, at the first moment possible, I trailed my ragbag of questions into the most august library I could find. There I took out my biggest question—the one clearly labeled 'GOD'—and sat down and began to read.

"Very soon, then, I discovered that God has many faces, and from the thickets of comparative religion I began to disentangle the stems making up the pattern of Celtic folklore. I also began to see that a people's folklore is only one face of a coin of which the other face is that people's written history. I be-

came aware of reflections in both sides of this particular coin—reflections of many things about my own village that had puzzled me before that time and which still intrigued me.

"Here I was, in fact, taking the first steps to explore the two great interests of my life—the history and folklore which were later to provide the source material for the greater part of my writing—and beginning to prove, in this process, the truth of the dictum I was later to state in very different circumstances: 'If you can read, you can educate yourself.'"[2]

It was in research and reading that Hunter found a lifetime joy that she was able to share with others through her writing. "And this, of course, is the whole reward of reading: to have one's imagination carried soaring on the wings of another's imagination; to be made more aware of the possibilities of one's mind through the workings of another mind; to be thrilled, amazed, amused, awed, enchanted—in worlds unknown until discovered through the medium of language and to find in those worlds one's own petty horizons growing ever wider, ever higher." [Mollie Hunter, "If You Can Read," *Horn Book,* August, 1978.[3]]

1940. Married Thomas McIlwraith (popularly known as "Michael"). Hunter's World War II circumstances were not conducive to furthering a career as a writer. The two sons of the marriage were post-war babies, Quentin in 1951, and Brian in 1953.

1952. Settled in the Highlands of Scotland near Inverness at first, and then in a village close to Drumnadrochit and Loch

For the next three days after that there was peace of a sort for Colin and his family. ■ (Jacket illustration by Stephen Gammell from *The Wicked One* by Mollie Hunter.)

Ness, in a cottage named "The Shieling." It was from then on that Hunter began to make her mark as a writer, in journalism, plays, and various other forms, with her career as a children's writer finally taking precedence.

"... I like children, I like their interest and enthusiasm. Their comparative lack of inhibition sorts well with my own ebullience, and in their company I am easy. Furthermore, I was born with the gift of the gab and the instinct to perform, and there is no better spotlight than the attention of children.

"All of which adds up the fact that I have always enjoyed telling stories to children—my own included. Occasionally also, I enjoyed taking time off from other forms of writing to set down some of these stories. Nevertheless, it was still only at the insistence of my two young sons that I wrote my first children's book, they being much charmed with two short stories I had written for them in a style which was then new to me." [Mollie Hunter, "The Last Lord of Redhouse Castle," *The Thorny Paradise: Writers on Writing for Children*, edited by Edward Blishen, Kestrel, 1975.⁴]

"... The book they coaxed from me was expanded from stories I had previously made up for them; but for me it was also a sustained attempt at a form of language that could ring true only if it hit a particular note—a traditional note, evolved from many, many past centuries of the music in the storyteller's voice. I took the children with me on the way to rediscovery of that music, reading the book to them by installments in the course of its writing. And even although I realised it was only the beam of my own imagination reflecting back at me from their pleasure in this tale, I still had the feeling of being on a road where *someone* had placed lights ahead for me.

"There was one other thing happened in the course of all this to convince me that this lit road was the one I would travel thenceforth, and always. At a certain point in the story, my eight-year-old son wept—more than that, he wept in a way I had never seen happen before with him, or with any other child. He sat bolt upright, never ceasing to listen to my reading, his gaze never shifting from me. There was no blinking, no sniffling, not a tremor of his features. The tears simply rose up, filled his eyes, then spilled over, and bounced like drops of broken crystal down his cheeks. The child seemed unaware he *was* weeping, in fact; and to me, it was a very moving thing, for spontaneous tears like this come from some suddenly-touched and very deep level of emotion.

"I read further on, and the tears no longer came. But duration of an emotion is not gauge of its intensity. Moreover, the range of a child's emotion has the same extent as that of an adult, and all the child lacks, by comparison, is the vocabulary to match his range—yet still there are ways of supplying this defect. So variable are the uses of language, so infinitely flexible their application, that the storyteller may turn the simplest of words into poetry powerful enough to express the deepest, most complex of emotions; and this note of strong and simple poetry was the very one I had been attempting to strike in my choice of language for that particular book.

"Those soundless tears, then, did more than move me. I felt them as an honour, for the story situation that drew them was poignant beyond the child's own power to express; but he had understood my form of words for it, and they had spoken for him. And so at last, it seemed to me than, I had discovered my particular code—one that would indulge my keen delight in all the effects of sound and rhythm and meaning in language, as much as it satisfied my instinctive urge to turn everything, everything, *everything,* into a story!

"A synthesis of two loves had brought me to this point—my writing and my children. Yet it does not follow that the writer who loves children can or should be a lion-tamer. Love can be blind, inept, a bore. Understanding is Argus-eyed, and shrewd in realising the child's need for story-characters through whom he can identify with the rest of humankind, and so discover who *he* is, how he 'belongs.'"¹

October, 1956. Events in Europe, meanwhile had been a maturing influence on her life and on her work. "... The rising of the Hungarian people against Soviet Communist rule. The last pathetic broadcast to the rest of Europe, asking for the help that never came. The pictured glimpse of a girl's face—round, serious, innocent, as she marched along under a banner that asked for nothing more than peace and freedom. Another glimpse of the same child—she could not have been more than fifteen—lying dead from machine-gun fire. The heart-breaking message sent with the children rushed out of Budapest and over the Austrian border—*We are staying to fight. Please look after our children.*

"We never missed a news broadcast at that time, my husband and I. The tension in our household took on an unbearable edge. Then, at the end of a bulletin one day, the Red Cross made an appeal for people to help in the dangerous work of getting these children over the Austro-Hungarian border, and suddenly I felt a great, cracking release at the very deepest level of my emotions.

"Children are important to me. I look at the eyes of an eight-year-old and see a wonder shining there which, in every generation, is innocence renewed; and I am moved to tenderness. I look at the eyes of an adolescent and see there the conflicting eagerness and uncertainty of the between years; and I find myself touched by a strong compassion.

"My own two children were the most important things in the world to me at that time. My love for my husband was deep. My fear of death for myself was an obsession which had haunted me every day from the moment when the death of my father—loved to the point of idolatry—had shattered my nine-year-old life. Yet in that sudden moment of emotional release, nothing of all this mattered any more. My loves were unaltered, I was still desperately afraid of dying, but I knew I had to do *something* to save even one at least of those child victims—anything at all, supposing it was only protecting the child from death with my own body. Otherwise, I realised, I would either have to live with the memory of a betrayal; or, like Judas, go hang myself, for I could never bear to look myself in the face again.

"I told my husband I was going straight out to answer the Red Cross appeal. I can see yet his look of sadness; but he was—and is—a man of conscience, and he made no attempt to stop me. And so off I went to volunteer—and found my noble gesture ending in bathos, for I had none of the special skills the Red Cross work needed, and another dead body would have been only an embarrassment to them.

"My offer of help was not accepted; yet still my moment of self-confrontation retained its value, for out of it I had learned that there are worse things in life than dying, and that some things are worth dying for.

"I found myself looking at my life with new eyes, the eyes of self-knowledge. I began the painful process of coming to terms with what I saw, of developing some philosophy out of it; and because I am a writer, the maturing of such talent as I had ran parallel to this process. In time, some aspect or other of this slowly-forming philosophy became integral to everything I wrote; and so in time also, I arrived at my final clear criteria for deciding what place to assign the terms 'suitable' and 'unsuitable' in children's reading."[1]

1963. Her first book, written at the insistence of her children, was published, and attracted considerable notice in Great Britain. *Patrick Kentigern Keenan* was later changed to *The Smartest Man in Ireland* by an editor who used the book to launch Hunter on the American public. It was also the first of those works of fantasy that was eventually to mark her work as a unique exponent at the folk-lore style of story-telling. It was not an easy task, she found, to reproduce what she calls "The authentic voice of folk-lore!"

"*I will take the world for my pillow.* Thus the hero of the Celtic tale speaks, traditionally, as he sets out on a journey which is also a quest through life. Thus the narrative of folk-lore flows in a style as spare and smooth as polished bone; and thus the high poetic insight of its verbal imagery. And so I hesitated. Yet the challenge of such an exercise in language excited me. There were all sorts of folk-lore beliefs I wanted to work into such a book, and the turns of speech so characteristic of the Celt were mine by right of birth and upbringing. Besides which, the spotlight was on me . . . !

"I had given my Patrick the gift of laughter, a wife patiently enduring of his folly, and a young son dearly loved. Now I set him growing in stature as he pursued a running conflict in which he lost every battle, yet always learned a little wisdom in the process. And gained a small loser's prize too, for Patrick's opponents were fairies who always left some trace of their magic behind them—but no gossamer-winged sprites of the modern picture-book, these fairies!

"These were the lordly and beautiful ones of the hollow hills; the skilful magicians of the Otherworld, the soul-less ones who were the ancient terror of men. . . . I sensed the grue running up my children's backs as I read, the fascination of being within touching distance of that terror—yet always with the comfort of knowing there was Patrick's saving grace of laughter between it and them, always aware of the safe ground of human warmth to which they could retreat.

"Until the moment finally came when it seemed there was no more room for laughter, or courage, or cunning; for this was the moment when Patrick's small son became a hostage in the conflict with the fairies, and Patrick was stripped of every weapon save his great love for the boy.

"Yet still the hostage did not become the victim, for this— the love of one human for another—is the very thing the soul-less ones can never experience or understand, and over which they have therefore no power. And so Patrick won home with his son, not permanently sobered by his experience, but almost a wise man at last. So at last, also, the children had their 'proper book' about him, and in basing its outcome on the triumph of human love over the dark powers of the soul-less ones, I had laid the cornerstone of my whole life's philosophy.

"Before I realized this latter was the case, however, I had a lot more writing to do, alternating further fantasies with historical novels for children; for now I had discovered the great seed-bed of fertility all those years of research had laid down in my mind. Ideas were sprouting fast. The storytelling current was running strong, carrying with it an uneasy feeling lingering from my own childhood days."[4]

That uneasy feeling was the genesis of Hunter's first historical novel, *Hi Johnny*, also published in 1963; and so began a

pattern of writing different types of books to draw upon her dual loves of history and folklore. She wrote fantasy for younger readers, historical novels for the early teens, and more "realistic" novels for young adults—her declared aim in all this being to entertain her readers at the same time as she interwove Scottish culture from past and present with poetic images which could express universal truths.

1964. Second historical novel, *The Spanish Letters,* was published. "I was back in my favourite sixteenth century, in Edinburgh, my favourite of cities. I knew the time as well as I know my own; the plan of the city as intimately as the layout of my own garden. I could feel the cobbles of the High Street slippery under my feet, smell the ordure piled in the closes and vennels opening off it, see the lights of Holyrood Palace, and hear the State secrets whispered there reaching me as clearly as did the gossip of the change-house at its gates. Above all, I knew the character of my sixteenth-century Edinburgh, and this was the character of the boy who emerged from the story I told impromptu that day—Jamie Morton, hero of *The Spanish Letters;* a fifteen-year-old as tough, proud, dirty, and honest as the city which had bred him.

"Jamie, the sixteenth-century street-boy, was also my challenge to the cosy tradition of middle-class heroes in historical novels for children; and with satisfaction, when I came to write this book, I knew I was not addressing it to the privileged minority of readers for whom the tradition had been invented. I was writing it for all those in the shared state of being called childhood; and charging headlong with Jamie, I was going to demolish the barriers which prevented that sharing.

"There were problems in all this, of course; the first being the one peculiar to Scottish writers in this field—how to set the scene in a country whose history is unknown to non-Scottish children. Secondly, I had to deal with an extension of the difficulty facing all writers attempting to convey the flavour of period dialogue without falling into the 'prithee' and 'sirrah' bog; for any dialogue in a Lowland Scots setting had also to give at least the impression of being conducted in the dialect proper to it. In narrative also, the Scot naturally uses dialect words which are infinitely richer in meaning than their nearest equivalent in standard English, and since I was determined to retain this native piquancy of expression, I had to find ways of making it self-explanatory in context."[4]

1965. For her next historical novel, Hunter chose an obscure event and dared to use a new technique. "Its scene was the Scottish Highlands. The time was the nineteenth century when thousands of poor crofting folk were 'cleared'—a euphemism for being driven with guns and dogs and whips from their native glens—to make way for sheep-farming. The incident which had gripped my imagination was that of a boy in the glen called Greenyards, unexpectedly pulling a pistol on a Sheriff Officer serving writs of eviction there; and through this action, appearing briefly in history as the central figure in a short, doomed resistance to that particular clearance.

"This boy haunted me. Looking at Ardgay Hill, from whence he and the other children of the glen had kept watch for the arrival of the Sheriff's forces, I found the thought of those other children also haunting me. I read letters, diaries, newspapers of the period. I talked to old people with intimate experience of crofting life, and got from them old tales and childhood memories. In Gaelic-speaking company I sat apart, letting the music of the old tongue fill my ears. Summer day after summer day I left my own comfortable home in the Highlands to wander among the poor little ruins of stone houses which mark the sites of the clearances, and the pain of the parting which had happened there was keen again.

"I knew much already of the Highlander's passionate, almost mystic attachment to his native land. Now I was reliving the despair of spirit which had filled them in the knowledge they were being driven from it, never to return. I was touching the edge of a sorrow so great that some of these people had literally died of it. But how to convey all this in a story for children? How to convey also the sense of kinship among these people, their respect for learning, their innate courtesy? Most of all, how to convey the courage of that pathetic little resistance?

"I needed a new writing technique for this. I had my journeyman skill as a novelist. In the three fantasies I had written by this time, I had continued to refine the art of projecting verbal imagery. Now I needed to synthesize these separate skills into a first-person narrative spoken swiftly, bitterly, angrily, yet still with all the beauty of phrasing which comes naturally to the Highland tongue. And because children were an integral part of my story, it was the voice of a boy that was called for—the boy who had pulled the pistol on the Sheriff Officer in Greenyards.

"I was unaware at the time of thinking this out, of course, that I was one with other iconoclasts then busily breaking all the rules previously observed in writing for children. I live in isolation from other writers, and always have done. To my publishers' cry that nobody, but *nobody* had heard of the Highland Clearances, I turned a deaf ear. I brushed aside their objections to the bloody—but true—incident in which a posse of constables batoned a group of unresisting women and children almost to death.

"Nor did it even occur to me that I was ripping away convention in allowing the voice of poetry to come through a boy's narrative; or by drawing this boy's character in depth so that, by showing all the linking strands of his emotions, I could also show the emotions of his people.

"I had figured out a method of presenting the brutality of the attack on the women in a manner which would cause the young reader to rise in indignation rather than recoil in horror. I was eager to meet the challenge of language in my chosen medium. I had my title—*A Pistol in Greenyards*. And clearest of all in my mind was a picture of the children who had kept watch on Ardgay Hill.

"I felt a rage of pity for the innocent courage of these children. For they were real—they had lived through what I had to tell. And surely one child could cry out to another over any gap of years? Surely, surely, it was possible for other children to hear the courage in the cry? With a sense of total involvement in the lives of my characters, I wrote the first sentence of their story, setting its beginning on the emigrant ship carrying them away, in defeat, from the beloved glen: '*I saw him coming along the deck of the ship towards me, and even though I owed him my life, I hated the very look of him.*'

"The book which grew from this was dedicated to the children who had kept watch on Ardgay Hill, and to their descendants; and by an odd chance, not long after it was published, I happened to meet one of these descendants—a grandson of one of the watchers. Many and many a time, this man told me, he had heard his grandfather telling of how it was in the clearance of Greenyards. And, he added, when he read my book: 'It could have been my grandfather himself talking.''[4] "I have *never* been paid a greater compliment on any of my writing."

This book marked her as a revolutionary in children's literature, a role she welcomed. "All this may not answer to what children's writers, in fact, are; but that does not invalidate any

theory of what their talent should be. The touchstone of truth is in the children themselves; and I look back with gratitude to having my own two children to inform me so. I had another good fortune at that time, however, and that was in having reached a point in my life where I was ready to rebel sharply against all the conventions which then ruled the world of children's writing.

"It was wrong and stupid, in my opinion, that this should be dominated by a middle-class syndrome which was no more than a hangover from the days of Victorian nurseries; downright ridiculous that juvenile hero-characters should always be children of this class engineered into excitement through such highly-coincidental unlikelihoods as parents called suddenly to visit sick Aunt Jessie, jewel thieves in the neighbourhood, and the only policeman available being either stupid, deaf, or venal. This was pre-masticated pap, regurgitated for a mythical 'child-reader' by adults who were themselves examples of retarded mental development.

"In my view also, all those publishers with fixations on stories of English boarding-school life came into this same retarded category. Such stories, I guessed, were more than just alien to my native Scots tradition. They must certainly also be incomprehensible to all children not of the elite minority processed through such unnatural institutions. As a parent, I was angered by the humiliations of poor children perpetually confronted in their reading by the cruel implication that they were the exceptions to the rule of people never having to worry about the rent, or getting enough to eat, or being cold and ragged. As for the historical novels written for children, I considered it was high time someone put paid to all those cardboard figures flouncing about in period dress, and delicately flourishing anachronistic handkerchiefs.

"If a seventeenth-century commoner blew his nose with his fingers, let him do that! And why not write about commoners anyway, instead of allowing an endless parade of aristocrats to dominate the scene? Commoners are the very stuff of history. The feel, the taste, the smell of history is what comes through their lives—'the rascal multitude,' the *canaille*—those who beg and starve and steal, or labour skilfully if they have been lucky enough to have the chance of learning a trade; and through the centuries, die in the cannon's mouth. Let them speak, for a change!

"So I argued—hotly. But of course I was only one of a considerable number of authors who were then briskly engaged in freeing the whole scene of children's writing from its artificial conventions; and now this freedom has been so well accomplished that one finds it hard to believe these conventions ever existed.''[1]

1966. Hunter followed *A Pistol in Greenyards* with *The Ghost of Glencoe,* based on yet another incident in Scottish history—the fearsome Massacre of Glencoe. "A sixteen-year-old ordered to kill stealthily and in cold blood the people who have been his friends is no different in 1692 from a youngster of similar age in our own and other centuries. The horns of his dilemma are still the same—to obey the law, or to follow his conscience. So it was Robert Stewart's agony of conscience which became the theme of the book about Glencoe. And so it became a children's book, for Stewart's agony was the universal and timeless one which lies in wait for all young people compelled to take their first look at the distorted face of the adult world.

"'History is people.' I have said this often enough to adults as well as to children, and this is the sum of all my research;

this is the basis of everything I have learned about the historical novel. History is ordinary people shaped and shaken by the winds of their time, as we in our time are shaped and shaken by the wind of current events. And so, to write about the people of any time, one must know them so well that it would be possible to go back and live undetected among them.

"Rather than writing from the outside looking in, then, one will write from the inside looking out. Then also, as when a raised window permits interior and exterior to merge in the air and sunlight flowing into a room, the past will merge with the present. The feelings of past and present will be shared. There will be engagement between reader and characters, irrespective of superficial differences in dress, speech, and habit; and in identifying with these characters, the reader will find his own identity.''[4]

1972. *A Sound of Chariots* was published, after being hidden in a drawer for eight years. This autobiographical novel won the Child Study Association of America award a year later. In it, Hunter came to terms with the painful loss of her father. "I lived with his ghost for 30 years. That book was my therapy." [Mary Hoffman, "Scottish Story Weaver," *Times Educational Supplement*, January 13, 1984.[5]]

Her family was unaware she was writing this book. "... I wrote it one hot summer when the rest of my world was going about its business not realizing I was exploring into the great pain of my childhood which had been the beginning of my knowledge that I would be a writer. I finished it, put it in a drawer, and lived in peace at last, with my ghosts.''[4]

This was in 1963, and it was not until eight years later that Hunter discovered the truth of the Scottish saying, *"There's a providence that looks after bairns, fools, and drunk men."*

"Years later, this book was accidentally brought to an editor's notice, and considered by her to be a children's book. Yet I had never thought of it as such, for writing it had involved me in total recall of that childhood pain. Processing this into a book had strained my personal and professional capacities almost to breaking point; and vaguely I felt that after all this agony I might have written something which would one day be considered notable.

"So it was, in this editor's opinion—a notable children's book.

"I re-read the manuscript for the first time in all those years, and saw also for the first time how I had unconsciously demonstrated there ... that I was first, last, and foremost a children's writer. For it was not an adult's remembered view of experience which came off the page, but a child's urgent view of living that experience.

"With relief then, I realized how well the providence had looked after me, for although it was clearly a children's book, it was clearly also one which could never have been published as such unless there had been a revolution in children's writing during the years it lay hidden.''[4]

Discussing here also the self-preoccupation for which writers are notorious, Hunter notes, "There must be inward-lookingness, of course, but only in order to project outwards what one finds in one's inmost feelings; only for purposes of identifying in that projection with one's fellow human beings. And with that God—whatever face he wears—with whom we must all finally seek to identify, or be ever held in thrall to the soulless ones.''[4]

These same "soulless ones" are typified in her work by the supernaturals emanating from the "Otherworld" of Celtic folklore, specifically so in fantasies such as *The Haunted Mountain* of which books she writes: "I will continuing to pursue the philosophy which had led me to climax the first fantasy with the triumph of human love over the dark power of the soulless ones; and it was language used like a sharp tool which enabled me to penetrate to this depth, for here the suspense came from that duality of feeling which traditionally characterizes men's attitude to the Otherword itself.

"It was a world of perfection which held for them all the attraction of a golden age; a world without sickness, pain, or death, yet still a world without love in it, and thus hollow at the heart. For this was the world of the beautiful soul-less ones; and any man who entered it would be hopelessly in their thrall and become prisoner—as they were—of their desolate Eden.

"And so, always between themselves and the temptation to enter this world, men interposed the barrier of this fearful knowledge. Always, for those who had been abducted to it, they clung to the redeeming promise in the power of human love. For this, men have always dimly known, is the essential of their lives. This is the thread in folk-lore that binds Greece to Connemara. That a man should retain the power to look up and see the face of his God—whatever face that god may wear. That a man should be able to stretch out a hand in the illimitable darkness of eternity, and always from somewhere in that darkness, feel the warmth and comforting touch of another human hand.

(Jacket illustration by **Michael Nakai** from *A Stranger Came Ashore* by Mollie Hunter.)

"A one-to-one contact between man and God, and between man and man; this is all that ultimately matters."[4]

1974. For _The Stronghold,_ Hunter researched the Orkney Islands, where hundreds of huge, circular towers of stone called "brochs" were built in the first century. To try to sense something of the supernatural forces so much dreaded by the people of her story, she stood alone one dark night in one of "their" holy places. "I felt as if my body was being drained of life and I became quite hollow. I turned and ran back to the car. Never have I been so glad of my little modern box of glass and steel."[5]

April-May, 1975. Chosen the May Hill Arbuthnot Lecturer, Hunter went on a lecture tour of the United States. On April 25, she spoke on "Talent is Not Enough" at the University of Pennsylvania. On April 29, in Baltimore, her topic was "One World," and on May 1 she gave the lecture "Shoulder the Sky" at the New York Public Library.

Hunter continues to write in her second-story study at "The Shieling" which overlooks a beautiful glen. She enjoys walking the countryside with her dogs, travelling, music, theatre, and children. Her own words sum up her attitude to her life's work: ". . . The essence of creativeness is the ability to produce a work which is more than the sum of its parts. The artist's own life is only one of the many lives which form these parts, and the basis of his achievement is in realising and accepting his involvement with those others. Its significance is in having transmuted this acceptance into a form which has beauty and meaning for them also.

"Any other claim for the artist is sheer humbug, for not to accept involvement is to admit to a talent too feeble to direct the true springs of creativity. Where children are concerned, it is pernicious humbug, for children have no experience against which they may assess the artifice of such a claim. They have not yet learned what it is to ask for bread, and be given a stone. . . .

"The eye of self-knowledge informs me that such values as I have are not mine by right. Nor have I done anything to earn my basic abilities as a writer. All these are part of something life has given me; therefore something I owe. And what I owe I must give back, along with the natural increase due to experience. This, it seems to me, is merely what honesty demands; and true honesty is itself the only true morality. I find my way of giving through children, because I am a children's writer. . . .

"The child that was myself was born with a little talent, and I have worked hard, hard, hard, to shape it. Yet even this could not have made me a writer, for there is no book can tell anything worth saying unless life itself has first said it to the person who conceived that book. A philosophy _has_ to be hammered out, a mind shaped, a spirit tempered. This is true for all of the craft. It is the basic process which must happen before literature can be created. It is also the final situation in which the artist is fully fledged; and because of the responsibilities involved, these truths apply most sharply to the writer who aspires to create literature for children.

"Especially for this writer, talent is not enough—no, by God it is not! Hear this, critics, editors, publishers, parents, teachers, librarians—all you who will shortly pick up a children's book to read it, or even glance idly through it. There _must_ be a person behind that book."[1]

A number of Hunter's books have been serialized on BBC-Radio programs, including _The Kelpie's Pearls, The Lothian_ Run, "The Enchanted Whistle" (based on _The Ferlie). A Stranger Came Ashore_ has been read in serial form on Swedish radio, _A Furl of Fairy Wind_ was published in cassette form, and _The Walking Stones_ and _The Wicked One_ have been featured in Yorkshire TV's "Book Tower" program.

HOBBIES AND OTHER INTERESTS: Theatre, music, physical exercise, traveling to new places. "Like dogs (useful ones only) and places without people. Company preferred—children."

FOR MORE INFORMATION SEE: Eleanor Cameron, _The Green and Burning Tree,_ Atlantic-Little, Brown, 1969; _Horn Book,_ June, 1970, February, 1971, December, 1975, June, 1978, August, 1978; Martha E. Ward and Dorothy A. Marquardt, _Authors of Books for Young People,_ 2nd edition, Scarecrow, 1971; Doris de Montreville and Donna Hill, editors, _Third Book of Junior Authors,_ H. W. Wilson, 1972; _Author's Choice 2,_ Crowell, 1974; Mollie Hunter, "Talent Is Not Enough," _Top of the News,_ June, 1975; Edward Blishen, editor, _The Thorny Paradise: Writers on Writing for Children,_ Kestrel, 1975; Mollie Hunter, _Talent Is Not Enough: Mollie Hunter on Writing for Children,_ Harper, 1976; Peter Hollindale, "World Enough and Time: The Work of Mollie Hunter," _Children's Literature in Education,_ autumn, 1977; D. L. Kirkpatrick, _Twentieth Century Children's Writers,_ St. Martin's, 1978, 2nd edition, 1983; Janet Hickman, "Profile: The Person behind the Book—Mollie Hunter," _Language Arts,_ March, 1979; Mary Hoffman, "Scottish Story Weaver," _Times Educational Supplement,_ January 13, 1984.

HURD, Clement (G.)   1908-1988

OBITUARY NOTICE—See sketch in _SATA_ Volume 2: Born January 12, 1908, in New York, N.Y.; died of Alzheimer's and Parkinson's diseases, February 5, 1988, in San Francisco, Calif. Artist, illustrator, and author. Hurd was best known as an illustrator of children's books, particularly _Goodnight Moon_ and _The Runaway Bunny,_ two classics for the very young written by Margaret Wise Brown. He wrote _Town, Country, The Race, The Merry Chase,_ and _Run, Run, Run._ Among the other children's books Hurd illustrated were more than forty written by his wife, Edith Thacher Hurd, including an "I Can Read" series for Harper & Row. Before pursuing a career in illustrating, Hurd studied painting in Paris and worked as a free-lance designer in New York City.

FOR MORE INFORMATION SEE: Contemporary Authors, New Revision Series, Volume 9, Gale, 1983. Obituaries: _Washington Post,_ February 8, 1988; _Los Angeles Times,_ February 10, 1988; _New York Times,_ February 10, 1988; _Newsweek,_ February 22, 1988; _Time,_ February 22, 1988; _Publishers Weekly,_ February 26, 1988.

ISADORA, Rachel   1953(?)-

PERSONAL: Born about 1953, in New York, N.Y.; married Robert Maiorano (a ballet dancer and author), September 7, 1977 (divorced, May, 1982). _Education:_ Attended American School of Ballet. _Residence:_ New York, N.Y.

CAREER: Ballet dancer with the Boston Ballet Company, Boston, Mass.; free-lance author and illustrator of children's

And Jonathan and Ben have lollipops. ■ (From *The Potter's Kitchen* by Rachel Isadora. Illustrated by the author.)

books. *Awards, honors: Max* was chosen one of Child Study Association's Children's Books of the Year, 1976, *I Hear,* and *I See,* 1985, and *Flossie and the Fox,* and *Cutlass in the Snow,* 1986; *Max* was selected a Children's Choice by the International Reading Association and the Children's Book Council, 1976, included in the Children's Book Showcase of the Children's Book Council, 1977; *Boston Globe-Horn Book Honor Book* for Illustration, and one of *School Library Journal*'s Best Books for Spring, both 1979, Caldecott Honor Book from the American Library Association, 1980, all for *Ben's Trumpet; A Little Interlude* was included in the American Institute of Graphic Arts Book Show, 1981; *The White Stallion* was selected one of *School Library Journal*'s Best Books, 1982; *City Seen from A to Z* was selected one of New York Public Library's Children's Books, 1983; *I Touch* was selected

an Outstanding Science Trade Book by the National Council for Social Studies and the Children's Book Council, 1985.

WRITINGS—All for children; all self-illustrated; all published by Greenwillow, except as indicated: *Max* (ALA Notable Book; Reading Rainbow selection), Macmillan, 1976; *The Potters' Kitchen,* 1977; *Willaby* (Junior Literary Guild selection), Macmillan, 1977; (with Robert Maiorano) *Backstage,* 1978, large print edition, 1978; *Ben's Trumpet* (*Horn Book* honor list), 1979, large print edition, 1979; *My Ballet Class,* 1980, large print edition, 1980; *No, Agatha!,* 1980, large print edition, 1980; *Jesse & Abe,* 1981; (reteller) *The Nutcracker,* Macmillan, 1981; *City Seen from A to Z,* 1983, large print edition, 1983; *Opening Night,* 1984, large print edition, 1984; *I Hear,* 1985, large print edition, 1985; *I See,* 1985, large print edition, 1985; *I Touch*, 1985; *The Pirates of Bedford Street*, 1988.

Illustrator: Robert Maiorano, *Francisco*, Macmillan, 1987; Elizabeth Shub, *Seeing Is Believing*, Greenwillow, 1979; R. Maiorano, *A Little Interlude*, Coward, 1980; E. Shub, *The White Stallion* (ALA Notable Book), Greenwillow, 1982; E. Shub, *Cutlass in the Snow*, Greenwillow, 1986; Patricia C. McKissack, *Flossie and the Fox* (*Horn Book* honor list), Dial, 1986; Hans Christian Andersen, *The Little Match Girl*, Putnam, 1987.

ADAPTATIONS: "Ben's Trumpet" (filmstrip with cassette; videocassette; ALA Notable Filmstrip), Random House.

SIDELIGHTS: Isadora was raised in an artistic environment in New York City where she was encouraged to pursue dancing. She started dancing as a toddler, becoming a professional ballerina by the age of eleven, although she was rather introverted and shy. "I'm not a natural performer. Even when I was little in ballet class, I would see them doing what I wanted to do, but I didn't copy it right then and there. After class I'd go into a studio by myself, and I'd knock my brains out until I got it.

"... Ballet was very real to me: my world. To escape it, I drew—so *that* became my fantasy world. I could express my thoughts in it, I could even express my anger. I couldn't do that as a dancer." ["PW Interviews: Rachel Isadora and Robert Maiorano," *Publishers Weekly*, February 27, 1981.[1]]

After seven high-pressure years of preparing for the stage, when asked to sign on professionally with Balanchine's company, seventeen-year-old Isadora fell apart. "I went into my room and didn't come out for three months."[1]

RACHEL ISADORA

Her first book, *Max*, was the result of encouragement from Elizabeth Shub, then an editor with Macmillan. Isadora developed her artistic talents on her own without professional lessons. "I had always drawn for my own entertainment, but I'd never had any instruction, and I wasn't sure how to proceed. So I just took a whole collection of sketches—odds and ends on bits of paper—to the first editor who would see me. She suggested I do a book about what I knew best."

Max, published in 1976, told the story of a boy who discovered how useful ballet could be in developing his baseball skills. It was praised by critics for having a nonsexist attitude. "Max is really me. He loves to dance, but he's also committed to the outside world. He wants both." Reported *School Library Journal*, "The message is clear—dance is for everyone—and the medium is warm and winning."

Max, an ALA Notable Book selection and a Children's Choice of the International Reading Association, was followed by two other books in 1977, *The Potters' Kitchen* and *Willaby*. That same year she married Robert Maiorano, a ballet dancer and author, and together they created *Backstage* (1978). Before their marriage ended in divorce in 1982, Isadora had illustrated two other books by Maiorano, *Francisco* (1978) and *A Little Interlude* (1980).

Isadora has also illustrated books by Elizabeth Shub and Patricia C. McKissack. She finds this difficult because she usually works from pictures to words. "It's backwards to me. The words are already there, and I'm not free to revise them so I can draw what I want."

Her own books have won critical praise, although she writes for herself, rather than for critical adulation. "I've asked my editors not to send me reviews anymore. When I'm working on a book, when I'm doing something and it's clicking, I'm creating this world I can live in. It's not just a drawing or a painting, it's a whole life."[1]

When beginning a new project, "I 'see' each illustration separately. I write a description of what I envision on each page; then I go over it with my editor and make revisions. Next I do the actual drawing, and finally the text."

Most of her main characters are also "doing something on their own, by themselves ... because *they* want to. And all of a sudden, it's not what peers think, not what the world around them thinks, but the joy of doing it *by themselves*."[1]

"Work like this is a dancer's fantasy. Because ballet is so demanding, dancers' stage careers are short. They can only dream of going on and on forever. With art, I can go on and on, and for me it's the only work that compares in intensity and joy."

FOR MORE INFORMATION SEE: New York Times Book Review, March 1, 1981; *Publishers Weekly*, February 27, 1981.

JOHNSON, Eleanor (Murdock)   1892-1987

OBITUARY NOTICE: Born December 10, 1892, in Washington County, Md.; died of cancer (one source says pneumonia), October 8 (one source says October 9), 1987, in Gaithersburg, Md. Administrator, educator, editor, and author. Johnson was best known as the founder of *Weekly Reader*, a four-to-eight-page classroom newspaper for elementary students. According to the *New York Times*, she came upon the idea "to present selected, well-written news of interest and value to children with accuracy and fairness, colorful but uncolored,'' while working as a public school administrator in Pennsylvania during the late 1920s. The first issue was dated September 21, 1928, and circulation reached one hundred thousand in its first year. In the late 1960s the paper expanded to seven editions, one for each grade from pre-school to sixth, and its circulation reached thirteen million. Forty percent of American elementary schoolchildren read *Weekly Reader,* and the periodical's publisher estimates that two-thirds of American adults read the paper during their school years.

In 1935 Johnson left school administration to work full time as editor-in-chief of *Weekly Reader,* a post she held until her semi-retirement in 1961. She remained a consultant until 1978. In addition to her role at *Weekly Reader,* Johnson wrote more than fifty elementary-school workbooks on reading, math, and geography, including *Junior Language Skills* and *Spelling for Word Mastery.* She was also co-author of several children's book series, including "Child Story Readers" and "Treasury of Literature," contributor to education periodicals, member of the editorial board of *Education* magazine, and a visiting professor at Columbia University, the University of Pittsburgh, and the University of Chicago.

FOR MORE INFORMATION SEE—Obituaries: *Los Angeles Times,* October 10, 1987; *New York Times,* October 10, 1987; *Washington Post,* October 10, 1987; *Chicago Tribune,* October 11, 1987; *Newsweek,* October 19, 1987; *Time,* October 19, 1987.

JOHNSTON, Dorothy Grunbock 1915-1979

PERSONAL: Born July 30, 1915, in Seattle, Wash.; died in 1979; daughter of John Frederick and Mabel (Noyes) Grunbock; married Monroe Bailey Johnston (a printer), November 24, 1944; children: Judy, Susan, Wayne, Dick, Gregory. *Education:* Attended University of Washington, Seattle, two years, and Moody Bible Institute; Prairie Bible Institute, Three Hills, Alberta, Canada, graduate, 1938. *Religion:* Baptist.

CAREER: As Aunt Dorothy, read children's books and stories daily on Radio Station KGDN, Seattle, Wash., for five years; contract writer of Sunday school materials for Union Gospel Press, Cleveland, Ohio, beginning, 1965.

WRITINGS: A Bible Verse for You to Learn, Moody, 1943; *Every Good Gift,* Moody, 1943; *Yakalo,* Moody, 1944; *Ching Lin,* Moody, 1945; *Tognia,* Moody, 1947; *God Feeds Them,* Moody, 1950; *Four Teens,* Scripture Press, 1956; *All About Babies: A Book to Teach Young Boys and Girls About Life,* Zondervan, 1962; *Bob and Betty Wonder,* Scripture Press, 1964; *Hey, Mom!* (collection of "Kitchen Kathedral" columns), Scripture Press, 1965; *Pounding Hooves,* illustrated by Pers Crowell, David Cook, 1976; *Stop, Look, Listen,* Standard Publishing, 1977. Also author of *Church Time for Children.*

"Ginger" series; published by Scripture Press: *Ginger at Dogfish Bay,* 1949; *. . . in Alaska,* 1951; *. . . and the Turkey Raids,* 1952; *. . .and the Glacier Express,* 1953; *. . . in the Jungles,* 1954; *. . . and the Witch Doctor,* 1955.

"Pete and Penny" series; published by Scripture Press: *Pete and Penny Play and Pray,* 1954; *. . . Know and Grow,* 1957; *. . . Live and Learn,* 1963; *. . . Think and Thank,* 1972.

"Wagon Train" series; published by Scripture Press: *Cathy and Carl of the Covered Wagon,* 1954; *. . . Captured,* 1954; *. . . Join the Gold Rush,* 1955; *. . . Shipwrecked,* 1956; *. . . and the Sea Horse Mystery,* 1957; *. . . Ride the Pony Express,* 1958.

Also author of Sunday school papers and lesson materials. Author of monthly column, "Kitchen Kathedral," for *Christian Parent,* for two years, and of "Hey, Mom!," for *Power,* 1963-66.

SIDELIGHTS: Johnston found much of her material at the family horse ranch where the family spent weekends.

FOR MORE INFORMATION SEE: Seattle Post-Intelligencer, April 18, 1965.

JONES, Betty Millsaps 1940-

PERSONAL: Born June 23, 1940, in Chattanooga, Tenn.; daughter of Willard Newton (a teacher) and Lucille (a teacher; maiden name, Springfield) Millsaps; married William B. Jones (a college teacher), August 17, 1963; children: Bruce, Brad. *Education:* Vanderbilt University, B.A., 1962, M.A.T., 1963, M.A., 1965. *Religion:* Methodist. *Home:* 120 Convention Dr., Virginia Beach, Va. 23462. *Office:* Norfolk Collegiate School, 7336 Granby St., Norfolk, Va. 23505.

CAREER: English teacher at public schools in Nashville, Tenn., 1963-64; teacher of English and mathematics at private school in Charlottesville, Va., 1964-69; teacher of English and history at private school in Gainesville, Fla., 1970-75; Norfolk Collegiate School, Norfolk, Va., counselor and teacher, 1975—. *Member:* Authors Guild, Romance Writers of America, Society of Children's Book Writers, Delta Kappa Gamma.

WRITINGS—Juvenile: Nancy Lieberman: Basketball's Magic Lady, Harvey House, 1980; *Wonder Women of Sports,* Random House, 1981; (adapter) *King Solomon's Mines,* Random House, 1982. Contributor of articles and reviews to *Highlights, Jack and Jill, Women's Sports, Scholastic Scope, Young Athlete,* and *Home Life.*

WORK IN PROGRESS: A book on women's basketball; a historical novel; research for a juvenile biography of Henry Knox.

SIDELIGHTS: "At present I combine my writing with teaching, counseling, and motherhood. The keys to becoming a writer are belief in one's abilities, dedication, persistence, and a willingness to do market research.

"My first published work was a story in *Jack and Jill.* Approximately one thousand words long, it was written as a class assignment in a noncredit writing course taught by a local writer. This instructor had much impact upon my writing career because she stressed that 'writers' must not only 'write': they must *submit* what they write to publishers.

"Two of my books and many of my magazine articles have dealt with sports. Although I did not play sports when I was in school, I have always been a sports fan. My father, who played professional baseball in the 1930s, was a tremendous influence upon me, and his intense interest in athletics was passed on to me. My first book, *Nancy Lieberman: Basketball's Magic Lady,* was contracted after I had written several articles about her. As the 1976 Olympian and as the 1979 and 1980 Wade Trophy winner, she led her Old Dominion University teammates (the Lady Monarchs) to two national championships. Since my husband is a professor at Old Dominion, I was able to follow her career closely.

Billie Jean had won many championships. She was twenty-five years younger than Bobby Riggs. ■ (Photograph from *Wonder Women of Sports* by Betty Millsaps Jones.)

"*King Solomon's Mines* is an adaptation of the nineteenth-century novel by H. Rider Haggard. Set in 'Africa, the book is an adventure story of a search for a fabulous treasure. The searchers must overcome the cruelties of nature as well as those of man before achieving their goal.

"A serious illness has limited my writing in recent months. However, I am now able to resume my writing and hope to complete a biography of Henry Knox within the next twelve months. I am also working on a historical novel but am finding the writing very, very 'slow going.' I greatly admire the historical novels of Roberta Gellis. Her erudition and craftsmanship are a powerful combination for which I have great respect."

KAREN, Ruth 1922-1987

OBITUARY NOTICE—See sketch in *SATA* Volume 9: Born February 18, 1922, in Germany; died of cancer, July 11, 1987, in New York, N.Y. Business executive, journalist, editor, and author. Karen's diverse career included service as a war correspondent for both the British Army and the U.S. Army from 1947 to 1953, as well as fifteen years' employment with *Reporter* magazine, the *Toronto Star*, and World Wide Press. Beginning in 1966 she worked her way from editor to vice-president and director of Business International Corporation, a publishing, research, and consulting firm serving multinational corporations. Karen wrote several books based on her varied interests and experiences, including a trilogy for young people about the great pre-Columbian civilizations: *Song of the Quail: The Wondrous World of the Maya, Kingdom of the Sun: The Inca, Empire Builders of the Americas,* and *Feathered Serpent: The Rise and Fall of the Aztecs.* Her books for adults mainly concern international business, and include the novel *Questionable Practices, Terrorism: The Corporate Implications,* and *Toward the Year 2000: A View from the Private Sector.*

FOR MORE INFORMATION SEE: Contemporary Authors, New Revision Series, Volume 11, Gale, 1984; *Who's Who of American Women,* 15th edition, Marquis, 1986; *The Writers Directory: 1986-1988,* St. James Press, 1986.

KOUHI, Elizabeth 1917-

PERSONAL: Born November 24, 1917, in Lappe, Ontario, Canada; daughter of Antti (a farmer) and Aliina (a homemaker and farmer; maiden name, Keisteri) Kaija; married George A. Kouhi, July 1, 1951; children: Christine Hallemeier, Aline Klemencic, Philip, Emily Lavender. *Education:* McGill University, B.A., 1949; Ontario College of Education, teaching certificate, 1964. *Politics:* New Democratic Party. *Religion:* Lutheran. *Home:* 224 N. Norah St., Thunder Bay, Ontario, Canada P7C 4H2.

CAREER: Writer, 1946—; Raith Public School, Raith, Ontario, Canada, teacher, 1950-53; Northwood High School, Thunder Bay, Ontario, teacher, 1963-66; Sir Winston Churchill High School, Thunder Bay, teacher, 1966-82. Public Awareness chairman for the Lakehead Association for the Mentally Retarded, 1983—. *Military service:* Royal Canadian Air Force, 1942-45. *Member:* Writers' Union of Canada, League of Canadian Poets, Canadian Society of Children's Authors, Illustrators, and Performers. *Awards, honors:* Ontario Arts Council Award, 1977, for *Jamie of Thunder Bay,* and 1983, for *Round Trip Home.*

WRITINGS—Juvenile, except as noted: *Jamie of Thunder Bay* (novel), Borealis, 1977; *North Country Spring: A Book of Verse for Children* (illustrated by Robert Rickels), Penumbra, 1980; *The Story of Philip* (illustrated by Helga Miller), Queenston, 1981; *Round Trip Home* (adult poetry), Penumbra, 1983; *Sarah Jane of Silver Islet* (novel; illustrated by Jeanette Lightwood), Queenston, 1984.

WORK IN PROGRESS: Book of poetry; a completed children's historical novel entitled *No Words in English,* set in northwestern Ontario in a Finnish pioneer settlement; another children's novel.

SIDELIGHTS: ''I was born in a northwestern Ontario pioneering community, settled by people from Finland. I learned English when I started in the one room schoolhouse that my father had helped build. When I was young my chief recreation was reading and roaming around the homestead. I had favourite places that I visited regularly. I connected some of those places with places in the books I read. For instance, I named one large rock 'spyglass' from *Treasure Island.*

''After grade eight (senior fourth in those days) I had one year of high school (in Port Arthur, the closest town and now part of Thunder Bay), but then came the Depression and my parents could no longer afford to send me to school in town. I worked at home on the farm for four years, but always with the feeling that I must do something else. My grade eight teacher was still at the school—I'd visit her and we would read and study.

''Finally, I left home to work in town and at the same time go to school. I got a job as a domestic where I kept the small apartment clean, looked after a ten year old girl and did the washing and ironing by hand—all in the evenings. I was paid five dollars a month. I took the commercial course at the local technical school where I learned typing and some office work skills. (I hated it and I wasn't very good at it.) I worked at

Elizabeth Kouhi on a Lapland Fell.

various jobs, and then in 1942 joined the Royal Canadian Air Force as a clerk. I was posted to Toronto, where, for the first time, I was able to go to concerts, plays, art galleries and museums. After three and a half years, at the end of the war I was able to continue school. The Canadian government established rehabilitation schools across the country where one could finish high school.

''I finished the required high school subjects in ten months and entered McGill University in January, 1947, graduating with a B.A. in 1949. At McGill I met people who were also interested in writing. For years I had written verse and some prose, but now I finally had people around me who were knowledgeable and critical. However, after McGill I had to make a living and began to teach in a little one room schoolhouse. I married and had four children. Later, I took summer courses in education and taught in high schools for nineteen years, retiring in 1982.

''I started *Jamie of Thunder Bay* when the children were small, working mostly early in the morning and during summers. It took all of fifteen years to get published.

''Now I try to spend from four to six hours daily on writing, first on poetry and then on prose. I have just finished the first draft of a children's novel set in the pioneering days of my childhood community.

''My husband and I enjoy our summer cabin and we enjoy travelling—Britain, Italy, Lapland, etc. We delight in visiting our five grandchildren. I am a very amateurish bird watcher. I enjoy music, art and theatre. I am active in my church and with the local association for the mentally retarded.

''Students in schools often ask me if I enjoy writing. I answer, 'Not always. Often I have to force myself to sit by my typewriter or desk (I always do my first draft in long hand), but if I don't, I begin to feel very dissatisfied and upset.' I sometimes think that the desire to write is some kind of incurable disease, but there are times when I feel exhilarated as I am writing.''

LARSEN, Rebecca 1944-

PERSONAL: Born August 19, 1944, in Milwaukee, Wis.; daughter of Harry J. (in public relations) and Haddy E. (a housewife; maiden name, Schmitt) Welch; married Alan R.

I joined the crowd at the pool's edge to watch the last of the relay races that day. ■ (From *Slow as a Panda* by Rebecca Larsen.)

REBECCA LARSEN

Larsen (a certified public accountant), August 13, 1966; children: Timothy, Sara, Elizabeth. *Education:* Northwestern University, B.S., 1966; University of California, Berkeley, M.S.J., 1972. *Religion:* Baptist. *Home:* 5 Pebble Beach, Novato, Calif. 94947. *Office:* Marin Independent Journal, 150 Alameda del Prado, Novato, Calif. 94947.

CAREER: Milwaukee Journal, Milwaukee, Wis., journalist, 1966-68; *Marin Independent Journal,* Novato, Calif., journalist, 1973—. Worked for the National Safety Council, 1968-73. *Member:* Society of Children's Book Writers.

WRITINGS: Balancing Act (juvenile novel), Avon, 1985; *Slow as a Panada* (juvenile novel), Dillon, 1986; *Oppenheimer and the Atomic Bomb* (biography), F. Watts, 1988.

Contributor to magazines, including *California Living, San Francisco, Christian Century, Lady's Circle,* and *Family Weekly.*

WORK IN PROGRESS: Two children's novels.

SIDELIGHTS: "My children and their interest in sports got me started writing my first two novels. But it was more than that. Every time I start writing a book, it gives me the same wonderful feeling I used to get as a child when I opened a new book for the first time. I'm filled with anticipation and excitement, and I wonder what's going to happen next."

LAWRENCE, Ann (Margaret) 1942-1987

OBITUARY NOTICE—See sketch in *SATA* Volume 41: Born December 18, 1942, in Tring, Hertfordshire, England; died May, 1987. Author and educator. After graduating from the University of Southampton in 1964, Lawrence pursued her

interest in wildlife by working for the British Trust for Ornithology. She began teaching in 1966, and then turned to writing for children in 1971. Her latest full-length novel for adolescents, *The Hawk of May,* was runner-up for the Guardian Award in 1981. Some of her works have a historical background, such as *The Half-Brothers, There and Back Again,* and *Merlin the Wizard.* She also wrote many books about country animals for younger children, including three about the adventures of a hedgehog named Oggy: *The Travels of Oggy, Oggy at Home,* and *Oggy and the Holiday.* Her final book is a collection of ghostly love stories entitled *Summer's End.*

FOR MORE INFORMATION SEE: Contemporary Authors, Volume 104, Gale, 1982; *Twentieth-Century Children's Writers,* 2nd edition, St. Martin's, 1983. Obituaries: *Junior Bookshelf,* October, 1987.

LEASOR, (Thomas) James 1923-

PERSONAL: Born December 20, 1923, in Erith, Kent, England; son of Richard (a teacher) and Christine (a teacher; maiden name, Hall) Leasor; married Joan Margaret Bevan (a barrister-at-law), December 1, 1951; children: Jeremy, Andrew, Stuart. *Education:* Attended City of London School; Oriel College, Oxford, B.A., 1948, M.A., 1952. *Politics:* Conservative. *Religion:* Episcopalian. *Home and office:* Swallowcliffe Manor, Salisbury, Wiltshire, England; and Casa do Zimbro, Praia da Luz, Algarve, Portugal.

CAREER: The Isis (students' weekly magazine), Oxford University, Oxford, England, editor, 1948; *London Daily Express,* London, England, reporter, foreign correspondent, feature writer, columnist, and personal assistant to publisher, 1948-55; writer, 1966—; George Newnes & C. Arthur Pearson, London, editorial adviser to women's magazines, 1955-69; director, Elm Tree Books Ltd., 1970-74; Lloyds of London, London, England, underwriter, 1973—. Member, Order of St. John. *Member:* P.E.N., Garrick Club, Oxford Union Society. *Awards, honors: The Red Fort* and *The Millionth Chance* chosen by the *New York Times* among the best hundred books, 1957-59; *Boarding Party* was selected one of New York Public Library's Books for the Teen Age, 1981.

JAMES LEASOR

WRITINGS—Fiction; published by Heinemann, except as indicated: *Not Such a Bad Day*, Blackfriars, 1946; *The Strong Delusion*, Harrap, 1951; *N.T.R.: Nothing to Report*, Laurie, 1955; *Passport to Oblivion*, 1964, Lippincott, 1965; *Spylight*, Lippincott, 1966 (published in England as *Passport to Peril*, 1966); *Passport in Suspense*, 1967; *Passport for a Pilgrim*, 1968, Doubleday, 1969; *The Yang Meridian*, Putnam, 1968; *They Don't Make Them Like That Any More*, 1969, Doubleday, 1970; *A Week of Love*, 1969; *Never Had a Spanner on Her*, 1970; *Love All*, 1971; *Follow the Drum*, 1972, Morrow, 1973; *Host of Extras*, 1973; *Mandarin-Gold*, 1973, Morrow, 1974; *The Chinese Window*, 1975; *The Jade Gate*, 1976; *Love and the Land Beyond*, 1979; *Open Secret*, Collins, 1985; *Ship of Gold*, Collins, 1986; *Tank of Serpents*, Collins, 1987.

Non-fiction: *The Monday Story*, Oxford University Press, 1951; *Author by Profession*, Cleaver-Hume, 1952; *Wheels of Fortune: A Brief Account of the Life and Times of William Morris, Viscount Nuffield*, Bodley Head, 1954; *The Serjeant Major*, Harrap, 1955; *The Red Fort: An Account of the Siege of Delhi in 1857*, Laurie, 1956, Reynal, 1957; (with Kendal Burt) *The One That Got Away*, M. Joseph, 1956, Random House, 1957; *The Millionth Chance*, Reynal, 1957; *The Clock with Four Hands: Based on the Experiences of General Sir Leslie Hollis*, Reynal, 1959 (published in England as *War at the Top: Based on the Experiences of General Sir Leslie Hollis*, M. Joseph, 1959); (with Peter Eton) *Wall of Silence*, Bobbs-Merrill, 1960 (published in England as *Conspiracy of Silence*, Angus & Robertson, 1960); *The Plague and the Fire*, McGraw, 1961; *The Uninvited Envoy*, McGraw, 1962; *Singapore: The Battle That Changed the World*, Doubleday, 1968; *Green Beach*, Morrow, 1975; *Boarding Party*, Heinemann, 1978, Houghton, 1979; *The Unknown Warrior*, Houghton, 1980; *Who Killed Sir Harry Oakes?*, Houghton, 1984; *The Marine from Mandalay*, Heinemann, 1988. Also author of scripts for television series, "The Michaels in Africa." Contributor to magazines and newspapers.

WORK IN PROGRESS: "I am writing a new adventure novel, to be published by Grafton, featuring a character I created in the 1960s, Dr. Jason Love. It is set largely in Pakistan, where I spent some time researching it."

SIDELIGHTS: "Doctor Johnson once declared that no one but a blockhead writes unless for money. So far as I was concerned, this was true, but the money was so slight that this rather mercenary admission needs explanation.

"When I was about seven years old in the 1930s, I discovered several magazines for boys, with such evocative titles as *The Hotspur, The Wizard, The Rover*. In those days, these cost tuppence—two pennies—each, and my pocket money was only one penny a week. I found that the local newsagent would sell last week's issues for one penny, but I was a quick reader, and could finish a whole issue of the magazine in an evening. How, then, to earn enough money to buy more copies? Every morning I travelled to school by bus, a distance of two miles, which cost one penny return. I, therefore, decided to walk to school, save these pennies and buy more magazines. My journey took me through a rough area, where I was sometimes set upon by gangs of boys, simply because wearing a school cap I aroused their antagonism.

"As a measure of defence, I persuaded other boys from the school to walk with me. When they expressed reluctance, I explained I would tell them a story as we walked. This I did for several weeks, but found that such constant talking, taking the different parts of characters I invented, was very tiring. Accordingly, I decided to write down my stories in pages of

an exercise book, and lent them out at a halfpenny a time. I think that this must be the first recorded instance of the Public Lending Right in operation! I soon found that I was making more money than I could spend on magazines and also that I enjoyed the escape into a fantasy world of my own imagination. So I became a professional writer."

HOBBIES AND OTHER INTERESTS: Vintage sports cars, walking dogs, swimming, collecting eighteenth-century sporting prints and antique carriage lamps.

FOR MORE INFORMATION SEE: New York Times, April 21, 1957; *New York Herald Tribune Book Review*, May 5, 1957; *New York Times Book Review*, February 11, 1968, March 29, 1970, August 17, 1975, February 18, 1979; *Book World*, July 7, 1968; *Times Literary Supplement*, May 1, 1969; *Spectator*, June 7, 1969; *Best Sellers*, June, 1975.

LeBLANC, L(ee) 1913-

PERSONAL: Born October 5, 1913, in Powers, Mich.; son of Vincent Ferrier (in business) and Alice (a homemaker; maiden name, Charboneau) LeBlanc; married Lucille Hayworth (in business), June 21, 1962; children: Patricia. *Education:* Attended Frank Wiggins Trade School, La France Art Institute, Art Students League, Choinard School of Art, and Jepsen Art School; studied under Will Foster and Nicolai Fechin. *Home and office:* 3819 W. Brule Lake Rd., Iron River, Mich. 49935. *Agent:* Petersen Publishing Co., 6725 Sunset Blvd., Los Angeles, Calif. 90028.

CAREER: Western Lithography, Los Angeles, Calif., commercial artist, 1938; Walt Disney Studios, Burbank, Calif., artist, 1938; Merry Melodies-Looney Tunes, Los Angeles, Calif., cartoonist, 1939-42; Twentieth Century-Fox Studios, Los Angeles, assistant department head, 1942-56; Metro-Goldwyn-Mayer, Culver City, Calif., department administrator of special photographic effects, 1956-62; free-lance illustrator and artist, 1962—. West Iron County School Board, 1963-65. *Military service:* U.S. Maritime, 1944. *Member:* Audubon American Ornithologist Union, Society of Animal Artists, Ducks Unlimited, Cornell Laboratory of Ornithology, National Wildlife Federation.

AWARDS, HONORS: Federal Duck Stamp Design Contest, second place, 1972-73, first place, 1973-74; Golden Mallard Award from the Arkansas Wildlife Federation, 1975; Artist of the Year from Tennessee Ducks Unlimited, 1976; Michigan

L. Le BLANC

State Duck Stamp Contest, second place, 1977; Michigan Migratory Bird Hunting Stamp Competition, finalist, 1978, 1979; Michigan Ducks Unlimited Waterfowl Artist Award, 1978; Michigan Trout Stamp Competition, finalist, 1979; Conservation Service Award from the Atlanta chapter of Ducks Unlimited, 1979; Crawdad Award from the Baton Rouge Sportsmens League, 1979; Artist of the Year from National Ducks Unlimited, 1980; selected artist for the Southeast Wildlife Exposition in Charleston, South Carolina, 1982; finalist, "Art for the Parks" National Contest, 1987.

WRITINGS—Self-illustrated: *Little Frog Learns to Sing*, Oddo, 1967.

Illustrator; all published by Oddo: C. F. Emery, *Horny*, 1967; I. Green, *Where Is Duckling Three?*, 1967; E. A. Olsen, *Adrift on a Raft*, 1970; E. A. Olsen, *Killer in the Trap*, 1970; E. A. Olsen, *Lobster King*, 1970; E. A. Olsen, *Mystery at Salvage Rock*, 1970; E. A. Olsen, *Rockets and Crackers*, 1970. Contributor of illustrations to *Ducks Unlimited* and *Out of Doors*.

ADAPTATIONS—Cassettes; all produced by Oddo: "Little Frog Learns to Sing," 1967; "Adrift on a Raft," 1970; "Killer in the Trap," 1970.

SIDELIGHTS: LeBlanc was chosen by the states of Arkansas and South Carolina to design their "First of State" Migratory Waterfowl Hunting Stamp for 1981. He also designed the 1981 "Deer Unlimited" stamp and print, the 1982 print and stamp for the "Wild Turkey Federation," and the 1982 print and stamp for the "Striped Bass Association."

HOBBIES AND OTHER INTERESTS: Photography and sports.

LOREEN LEEDY

LEEDY, Loreen (Janelle) 1959-

PERSONAL: Born June 15, 1959, in Wilmington, Del.; daughter of James Allwyn (an auditor) and Grace Anne (a homemaker; maiden name, Williams) Leedy. *Education:* Attended Indiana University—Bloomington, 1978-79; University of Delaware, B.A. (cum laude), 1981. *Religion:* Catholic. *Home and office:* 503 Park North Ct., Winter Park, Fla. 32789.

CAREER: Craftsperson, specializing in jewelry, 1982-84; writer and illustrator, 1984—. Conducts writing workshops. *Member:* Ardensingers (community theater company; board of directors, 1985-86). *Awards, honors:* Parents' Choice Honor Book for Illustration from the Parents' Choice Foundation, 1987, for *Big, Small, Short, Tall*.

WRITINGS—Self-illustrated children's books: *A Number of Dragons*, Holiday House, 1985; *The Dragon ABC Hunt*, Holiday House, 1986; *The Dragon Halloween Party*, Holiday House, 1986; *Big, Small, Short, Tall*, Holiday House, 1987; *The Bunny Play*, Holiday House, 1988; *A Dragon Christmas*, Holiday House, 1988.

SIDELIGHTS: "Books have been a part of my life since I was very young. I would beg my parents to read aloud to me, and soon learned to read by myself. I liked to look at beautiful pictures, and used pencils and crayons to make my own drawings of cats and horses and funny houses. In school, I wrote poems and stories and reports, sometimes adding an illustration.

"All my life, I have gone to the library to read about animals, gardens, crafts, music, and many other things. I like to read about how other people live—their customs, their food, their clothes, their ideas. I like to read about how animals live—what they eat, how they hide, how they have babies, how they survive. I like to read about how machines work—how they get invented, how the different parts fit together, what makes them run. And I like to read stories that take me to another place, another time, to see the world through someone else's eyes. All of these things are waiting inside books, waiting for me to read about them.

"And now I make my own books. Writing and illustrating picture books for children allows me to share my abilities and interests in an inspiring way. In *The Dragon Halloween Party*, for example, the dragons decide to throw a party. Woven into the story are specific directions for making costumes, decorations, and Halloween treats. When the guests arrive, Ma tells a ghost story, they play Pin-the-Hat-on-the-Witch, and have a wonderful time. Readers can use the book as a springboard for their own Halloween festivities. In *The Bunny Play*, a group of bunnies go through all the steps of putting on a play. They hold tryouts, paint scenery, hang posters, have rehearsals, have dress rehearsals, and finally, perform the play in front of an audience. Readers can gain a clear idea of the fun and work involved in a theatrical production. My hope for all of my books is that they will playfully enlighten and entertain children.

"Many things are interesting to me, and may someday show up in one of my books. I like dolls, trolls, cats, camping, traveling, canoeing, junk yards, dilapidated buildings, mermaids, the beach, science fiction, philosophy, physics, and religion, to name a few. I hope to keep writing and illustrating picture books as long as people want to read them."

FOR MORE INFORMATION SEE: Delaware Today, October, 1986.

LEESON, Muriel   1920-

PERSONAL: Born January 7, 1920, in Wolverhampton, Staffordshire, England; daughter of William Hartill (a draper) and Florence (a milliner and homemaker; maiden name, Bentley) Bayliss; married Robert A. Leeson (a retired high school teacher), August 28, 1943; children: Robert, Mark, John. *Education:* Attended University of Winnipeg, 1966-68. *Politics:* Conservative. *Religion:* Protestant. *Home:* 189 John Forsyth Rd., Winnipeg, Manitoba R2N 1R3, Canada.

CAREER: Homemaker and writer. Has worked in millinery in small stores in Winnipeg, Canada, 1938-43; Hudson's Bay Company, Book Department, clerk, 1943-44, librarian, 1944-45. *Member:* Manitoba Christian Writers Association (president, 1984-85), Penhandlers (secretary/treasurer, 1984-85).

WRITINGS—Juvenile, except as indicated: *Oranges and U.F.O.'s* (illustrated by Affie Mohammed), Scholastic-TAB, 1975, published under title *The Promise-Keeper*, Moody, 1984; *I Escaped the Holocaust* (adult), Horizon House, 1978; *Path of the Promise-Keeper* (sequel to *The Promise Keeper*), Moody, 1984; *The Bedford Adventure*, Herald Press, 1987; *Journey to Freedom*, Herald Press, in press.

Contributor to "Impressions" anthology, Holt, 1986. Contributor of adult inspirational articles and juvenile fiction, mostly to Christian magazines, including *Woman's Touch, Guideposts, Jack and Jill, Aglow,* and *Lookout.*

ADAPTATIONS: "The Promise Keeper" and "Path of the Promise-Keeper" have been broadcast on WMHK-Radio, Columbia, S.C.

WORK IN PROGRESS: Never Say "Columbus", a fantasy with historical rather than other planet tie-in.

He looked up, expecting to see a Dark One in the trees. ■ (Cover illustration from *Path of the Promise-Keeper* by Muriel Leeson.)

MURIEL LEESON

SIDELIGHTS: "My motivation for writing, as an adult, came through a dream. After our first son started school and before the second began kindergarten, I realized that I needed something in life 'just for me,' in preparation for the time when my mother role would be over, in the everyday sense. I experimented in various creative areas such as painting, clay modeling, etc. Nothing worked. Finally I did what, as a professing Christian, I should have done in the first place. I asked God to show me what *He* wanted me to do. That same night I had a disturbing dream in which I woke up before the dream problem was solved. I began to try and write this incident as a story, in longhand, in an old exercise book. (My husband asked if I was copying recipes.) About then I remembered how much I used to enjoy writing in school. In grade nine I'd won a prize for the best short story in our room contest, and in grade ten, a teacher whose sister was a well-known Canadian author, suggested I submit a story to a magazine. My dad, aware of my slim chance of success, advised against this and I listened to him, not my teacher. (I was the kind of child who, at an early age, drove teachers crazy by saying, 'My daddy says this . . .' at every opportunity.) After that, youthful activities, World War II, romance, marriage and motherhood took over and writing was forgotten.

"In my early thirties, after the dream episode, I taught myself to type on a rented machine and eventually began to send out manuscripts. The day I made my first sale my husband brought home a cake to celebrate the occasion. He'd already bought me a typewriter.

"Writing juveniles began much later when our third son was old enough to read and said, 'That's the best story I ever heard,' after I read him something I'd written for children. I began to wonder if that was where my talent lay. I moved into juvenile fiction and eventually wrote my first book, *Oranges and U.F.O.'s*, which was published in 1975.

"Ideas for stories come from incidents in my life and the lives of those around me. *Oranges and U.F.O's* grew out of what happened when this third son built a model U.F.O. and fooled the neighborhood with a trick picture, now on the back of the Scholastic-TAB edition of the book.

"I've learned to say, 'God if You don't need this, don't let it be published,' when I send something out. That way I feel assured I'll never hurt a child by what I write. (I should add that the first time I prayed this way was before my book was accepted and for me as a writer, it was like putting Isaac on the altar.) I suppose some would say that's a simplistic solution to a problem. Nevertheless, I feel children are influenced by what they read in a way that adults are not and that puts a heavy responsibility on me not to stumble them.

"I'm glad I enjoy writing because I'm hopeless at sports and always have been. Writing is my way of resting from life's duties. My other way is reading. As a child, my idea of a good Christmas or birthday present was a book. Both my parents were great readers. My husband shares this pleasure. Even when planning holidays, we seem attracted to places of historical and/or literary significance, rather than 'fun in the sun' tours.

"Because books have always held a place of importance in my life, it would be nice to feel my work could be of value to children—a way of putting something back into the pot, perhaps."

FOR MORE INFORMATION SEE: Ed Hughes, "Local Author Successful in Book Market," *Winnipeg Free Press*, August 30, 1980; "Writing for Children Not Easy," *Prairie Messenger*, April 11, 1982; Sonja Mullan, *Connections Two: Writers and the Land*, Manitoba School Library Audio Visual Association, 1983.

LEVINE, Abby 1943-

PERSONAL: Born September 27, 1943, in New York, N.Y.; daughter of Charles A. (a businessman) and Edna (a librarian; maiden name, Deshel) Bernstein; married Jonathan Levine (a human relations executive), June 13, 1965; children: Sarah, Susannah. *Education:* Cornell University, B.A., 1964, M.Ed., 1966. *Home:* 9509 Ridgeway Ave., Evanston, Ill. 60203. *Office:* Albert Whitman & Co., 5747 West Howard, Niles, Ill. 60648.

CAREER: Free-lance editor, 1970-80, 1981-83; University of Pittsburgh Press, Pittsburgh, Pa., editor, 1980-81; Albert Whitman & Co., Niles, Ill., editor, 1983—. *Member:* Children's Reading Round Table.

WRITINGS—Juvenile: (With daughter, Sarah Levine) *Sometimes I Wish I Were Mindy* (*My Weekly Reader* selection; illustrated by Blanche Sims), A. Whitman, 1986; *What Did Mommy Do Before You?* (illustrated by Dyanne DiSalvo-Ryan), A. Whitman, 1988; *You Push, I Ride* (illustrated by Margot Apple), A. Whitman, 1988.

WORK IN PROGRESS: A fourth children's book.

SIDELIGHTS: "Like so many children who read a lot, I also wrote. But it was not until I had been a children's book editor for several years, immersed in other people's writing, that I began to think of writing children's books myself.

"My three picture books so far have all been triggered by things I heard children say. I try extra hard now to always listen to kids!"

LOBEL, Arnold (Stark) 1933-1987

OBITUARY NOTICE—See sketch in *SATA* Volume 6: Born May 22, 1933, in Los Angeles, Calif.; died of cardiac arrest, December 4, 1987, in New York, N.Y. Children's book illustrator and author. Best known for his four studies about a frog and toad who share many adventures, Lobel illustrated nearly one hundred children's books throughout his career, many of which he also wrote. Among the latter are *Mouse Tales, Treeful of Pigs, Uncle Elephant, Ming-Lo Moves the Mountain*, and the "Frog and Toad" series. Lobel accumulated numerous awards and honors for his works, including a Newbery Honor Book award in 1973 for *Frog and Toad Together* and the 1981 Caldecott Medal for *Fables*. His Caldecott Honor books include *Frog and Toad Are Friends, Hildilid's Night*, and *On Market Street*. He also received Christopher Awards for *On the Day Peter Stuyvesant Sailed Into Town* and *Frog and Toad All Year*.

FOR MORE INFORMATION SEE: Illustrators of Children's Books: 1967-1976, Horn Book, 1978; *Authors in the News*, Volume 1, Gale, 1981; *Contemporary Authors, New Revision Series*, Volume 2, Gale, 1981; *Children's Literature Review*, Volume 5, Gale, 1983; *Twentieth-Century Children's Writers*, 2nd edition, St. Martin's, 1983. Obituaries: *New York Times*, December 6, 1987; *Facts on File*, December 11, 1987; *Publishers Weekly*, December 25, 1987; *School Library Journal*, January, 1988; *AB Bookman's Weekly*, February 8, 1988.

MacDONALD, Suse 1940-

PERSONAL: Given name rhymes with "news"; born March 3, 1940, in Evanston, Ill.; daughter of Stewart Y. (a professor) and Constance R. (a writer) McMullen; married Stuart G. MacDonald (a designer and builder), July 14, 1962; children: Alison Heath, Ripley Graeme. *Education:* Attended Chatham College, 1958-60; University of Iowa, B.A., 1962; also attended Radcliffe College, Art Institute, and New England School of Art and Design. *Home and studio:* P.O. Box 25, South Londonderry, Vt. 05155. *Agent:* Phyllis Wender, 3 East 48th St., New York, N.Y. 10017.

CAREER: Caru Studios, New York City, textbook illustrator, 1964-69; MacDonald & Swan Construction, South Londonderry, Vt., architectural designer, 1969-76; author and illustrator, 1976—. *Member:* Society of Children's Book Writers, Authors Guild. *Awards, honors: Alphabatics* was one of *Booklist*'s Editor's Choices, one of *School Library Journal*'s Best Books of the Year, one of Child Study Association of America's Children's Books of the Year, and one of American Booksellers Association's Pick of the Lists, all 1986, and selected a Caldecott Honor Book by the American Library Association, and received the Golden Kite Award from the Society of Children's Book Writers, both 1987.

WRITINGS—Juvenile: Alphabatics (Junior Literary Guild selection; self-illustrated), Bradbury, 1986; (with Bill Oakes) *Numblers* (self-illustrated with B. Oakes), Dial, 1988.

(From *Alphabatics* by Suse MacDonald. Illustrated by the author.)

WORK IN PROGRESS: Another discovery book which uses numbers in new and inventive ways, with Bill Oakes.

SIDELIGHTS: Suse MacDonald was raised in Glencoe, Illinois, a suburb of Chicago. Her father, a professor at Northwestern University, took his family to an old farm in Weston, Vermont for the summers, where MacDonald enjoyed swimming and collecting specimens in the pond, horseback riding, and investigating the mysteries of an old barn in which she kept a playhouse, several forts and numerous catwalks and perches. She worked at the local summer theater handling the box office, pounding nails and painting sets.

She attended Chatham College in Pittsburgh for two years, completing her B.A. at the State University of Iowa. She settled in New York after her marriage, hoping to get a job using her artistic talents, but several years passed before she landed a position at Caru Studios, where she illustrated textbooks.

After five years, she and her husband returned to the family farm in Vermont, and took over a construction company for ten years while raising two children. When her second child entered first grade, MacDonald decided to return to school to study illustration. She drove back and forth between Vermont and Boston for four years, attending classes at Radcliffe, the

Art Institute, the New England School of Art and Design, and other schools in the city where she took courses in illustration, silkscreening, paper making, sketching, drawing, design, topography, and writing. "It's hard to pinpoint the time when I decided that children's book illustration was the field in which I wanted to concentrate my energies. My interests always seemed to lean in that direction."

Eventually she enrolled in Marion Parry's class in children's book writing and illustration at Radcliffe. It was then that MacDonald really became involved in children's books. She wrote and illustrated several stories, and learned how to make the pencil and color dummies which are a necessary part of the publication process for all picture books.

After completing her studies, MacDonald bought an old house in South Londonderry, Vermont, in partnership with two other artists. They spent six months renovating the building and setting up five artist's studios, one for each of them and two which they rent. She then put together a portfolio and began to look for work, in both advertising and the children's book field. Her first assignments were paper sculpture for advertising. These jobs kept her going financially as she began to make the rounds of the publishers.

SUSE MacDONALD

The idea for *Alphabatics* emerged from the wealth of information which she gathered while taking a topography course in art school. She worked exclusively with letter forms, shrinking and expanding them and manipulating their shapes in various ways. She was intrigued by the process and felt there were possibilities for a book, but it was several years before she sold the idea to Bradbury Press.

"*Alphabatics* relates the shape of each letter in the alphabet to an object whose name starts with that letter. By changing the letter's shape, MacDonald makes it evolve into something which is familiar but exciting to a child. This removes the alphabet from the adult world of letters on pages and brings it into the child's world of action and visual image. This book, which is my first, has been very exciting. I love the picture book format and feel it offers challenging opportunities for creative illustration."

MANUSHKIN, Fran(ces) 1942-

PERSONAL: Surname is pronounced Ma-*nush*-kin; born November 2, 1942, in Chicago, Ill.; daughter of Meyer (a furniture salesman) and Beatrice (a housewife; maiden name, Kessler) Manushkin. *Education:* Attended University of Illinois and Roosevelt University; Chicago Teachers College, North Campus (now Northeastern Illinois University), B.A., 1964. *Home and office:* 121 East 88th St., New York, N.Y. 10128. *Agent:* Amy Berkower, Writers House, 21 West 26th St., New York, N.Y. 10010.

CAREER: Elementary teacher in Chicago, Ill., 1964-65; Lincoln Center for Performing Arts, New York City, tour guide, 1966; Holt, Rinehart & Winston, Inc., New York City, secretary to college psychology editor, 1967-68; Harper & Row Publishers, Inc., New York City, secretary, 1968-72, associ-

ate editor of Harper Junior Books, 1973-78; Random House, Inc., New York City, editor of Clubhouse K-2 (student paperback book club), 1978-80. *Member:* P.E.N., Author's League of America, National Audubon Society. *Awards, honors:* Dutch Silver Pencil Award from the Committee for the General Promotion of the Dutch Book (Netherlands), 1974, for *Baby*.

WRITINGS—Juvenile: *Baby* (picturebook; illustrated by Ronald Himler), Harper, 1972; *Bubblebath!* (picturebook; illustrated by R. Himler), Harper, 1974; *Shirleybird* (illustrated by Carl Stuart), Harper, 1975; *Swinging and Swinging* (picturebook; illustrated by Thomas DiGrazia), Harper, 1976.

The Perfect Christmas Picture (illustrated by Karen A. Weinhaus), Harper, 1980, large print edition, 1980, new edition, 1987; *Annie Finds Sandy* (illustrated by George Wildman), Random House, 1981; *Annie Goes to the Jungle* (illustrated by G. Wildman), Random House, 1981; *Annie and the Desert Treasure* (illustrated by G. Wildman), Random House, 1982; *Annie and the Party Thieves* (illustrated by G. Wildman), Random House, 1982; *Moon Dragon* (illustrated by Geoffrey Hayes), Macmillan, 1982; *The Tickle Tree* (illustrated by Yuri Salzman), Houghton, 1982; *The Roller Coaster Ghost* (illustrated by Dave Ross), Scholastic, 1983; *Hocus and Pocus at the Circus* (illustrated by G. Hayes), Harper, 1983, large print edition, 1983; *The Adventures of Cap'n O. G. Readmore: To the Tune of "The Cat Came Back"* (illustrated by Manny Campana), Scholastic, 1984; *Baby, Come Out!* (illustrated by R. Himler), Harper, 1984; *Buster Loves Buttons!* (illustrated by Dirk Zimmer), Harper, 1985; *Jumping Jacky* (illustrated by Carolyn Bracken), Golden Books, 1986; *Little Rabbit's Baby Brother* (illustrated by Diane De Groat), Crown, 1986; *Ketchup, Catch Up!* (illustrated by Julie Durrell), Golden Books, 1987.

WORK IN PROGRESS: Baby Rabbit Takes a Tumble, a sequel to *Little Rabbit's Baby Brother; Latkes and Applesauce: A Hanukah Story; Beach Day,* a "Little Golden Book"; and a novel for seven- to nine-year-old readers.

SIDELIGHTS: "It never occurred to me that one day I would be an author. I was always an avid reader and fantasizer, but gave no real indication of a literary predilection. My family is from Chicago and I was a city kid through and through.

FRAN MANUSHKIN

Their hugs were very icy! ■ (From *Little Rabbit's Baby Brother*, created by Lucy Bate. Story by Fran Manushkin. Illustrated by Diane de Groat.)

One of my favorite places to play was the loading docks of Sears, Roebuck on weekends when the warehouse was closed. The docks were raised platforms, and had ladders leading up to them. I used to climb up and tap dance and sing to my heart's content. Generally no one else was around. Alas, they missed a great show!

"My family had a currency exchange where people would cash checks, pay their utility bills, have their taxes prepared, and so on. I worked there during my teens and was often left alone with thousands of dollars—an awesome responsibility now that I think of it. I belonged to Junior Achievement, where kids create and run their own businesses with supervision from adults in the business world. I eventually became president of their bank, which serviced all of their other enterprises. We were even paid a salary by check—very official.

"Junior Achievement provided virtually all of my social life— dances and outings with a large cross-section of people from all over Chicago. There were no cliques. I had friends from all kinds of neighborhoods, people I would not otherwise have met.

"I pretty much avoided the 'goings-on' in my high school. I couldn't find a niche with the cheerleader and scientist/professor types. There was no middle ground. An average student, I learned only two useful things in high school: the parts of speech and the art of typing.

"As much as I enjoyed Junior Achievement it instilled in me no concrete ambitions. The pressures on a girl growing up in the fifties was to find someone wonderful and get married. The only thing I was certain I wanted to do was to live in New

York. It seemed to me that anything worth happening was happening in New York. I went to college and got a teaching degree thinking that this would enable me to get a job easily, and save enough money to go to New York.

"I was a substitute teacher for about four months. By April I was in New York with a job at the Illinois pavillion of the 1964 World's Fair. I told my parents I was just going for the summer, but I had no intention of returning.

"After the World's Fair job ended I found a job in the adult college textbook department at Holt, Rinehart and Winston. Shortly thereafter I met Ezra Jack Keats, an artist whose friendship changed my life. He knew of an opening at Harper & Row in the children's book department. I worked there from 1966 until 1976, the most important years of my career. I came in as an assistant and eventually became an associate editor. The sixties and early seventies constituted a 'golden age' in American children's books and some of the finest books were being done at Harper's. Ursula Nordstrom, who headed the department, had a genius not only for recognizing and attracting highly unusual talent, but for instilling that gift in those who worked for her. We all actively encouraged writers and artists who were breaking taboos. Lillian Hoban, Tomi Ungerer, Leonard Kessler, Syd Hoff, Myra Levoy, and Bruce Degen were some of the writers and artists I edited.

"There was something else extraordinary about Harper's—they encouraged their editors to be writers. Virtually all the editors wrote books. Until I worked at Harper's I had no literary aspirations, but the atmosphere was so stimulating it was hard not to become a writer. Charlotte Zolotow kept encouraging me to try my hand, but I resisted until another editor, someone about my age, wrote a book that was accepted by them. 'If she can do it, I can,' I thought. But that was not what made me a writer. When Ursula Nordstrom saw my first manuscript, she said, 'Dear, you can be more original.' I believe that if she had accepted that first effort, I never would have gone on to do anything unusual. I would have been satisfied with writing stories that were basically realistic, and never discovered the true impetus for my work—whimsy, fantasy. I think that Ursula's gentle, encouraging rejection of my first book ignited the first spark of ambition in me.

"While working at Harper's I also began writing poetry. Looking at the world and letting images grab me is the best way for me to write. I have also found that this type of writing easily lends itself, in fact often leads, to picture books. I never would have been able to write *Baby* unless I had been writing poetry.

"My stories tend to grow from a single image. *Baby*, for example, blossomed from an image I had in my head of a mother communicating with her newborn baby. That image metamorphosed into a mother communicating with the child she is carrying in her womb. When the child said, 'I don't want to be born,' it just happened, I did not plan it. I didn't have a plot in mind. In fact I never start with a plot, and never know in advance how a book is going to end. If I knew, the work would be so boring. One of the pleasures of writing is that it is a form of entertainment for the writer. Only after the entertainment is over, do I learn what the unconscious underpinnings of the story are. Whether you know it or not, every book you write is about yourself. *Hocus and Pocus at the Circus*, for example, is about my sister and myself—but I'm not telling who the nice sister is! *The Perfect Christmas Picture* is about my family—the way I wish my family had been. I suppose the 'message' in that book has to do with acceptance in a rather odd, madcap family. But I never start out with a

theme, or consciously write to a theme. This, too, is something I discover afterwards, and often it is other people who will tell me, 'Well, the theme here clearly is. . . .' I am not one for heavy, ponderous, problem-laden situations. My imagination is whimsical, light, which is not to say that my situations have no emotional depth or charge. It's just that I approach the 'heavy stuff' very, very indirectly.

"It's hard to generalize about how long it takes me to write a book. Some of my best books were written very quickly, almost in one sitting. *Baby* was one, as was *Swinging, Swinging*, about a little girl on a swing. *Hocus and Pocus* and *The Perfect Christmas Picture* took longer. In early drafts of both books, I had episodes my editors felt were too 'outrageous,' 'implausible,' or just literally impossible. Plot has never been my strong suit; my imagination is too wild, I guess, to readily adapt itself to constricting stories.

"Generally publishers keep the author and illustrator apart, with the editor and art director serving as go-betweens. Because I had worked extensively with illustrators while working at Harper & Row, I insisted that I be allowed to see the artist's dummies for my books. Any comments or suggestions I have I pass on to the editor, who presumably passes at least some

"I don't want to be born," said Baby. ∎ (From *Baby Come Out!* by Fran Manushkin. Illustrated by Ronald Himler.)

of them on to the artist. Looking at the art work gives me ideas for improving the story. Generally after seeing the illustrations, I do a considerable amount of cutting on the text. While it sometimes hurts to excise a line, I'm not a prima donna about my language. There is nothing worse than a boring, word-heavy picture book. I often implant cues for the illustrator about the characters: what they're doing, what they're wearing, what they look like, and so on. After the artist incorporates this information into his drawings I cut the descriptions from the text. There's no sense in the language and pictures imparting the same information. Picture books are very scary because the writer is at the mercy of the artist's talent. Even if you write a wonderful book, it can be destroyed by the wrong illustrator. Matching artists and writers is a very delicate business. In my opinion picture book writers are comparatively unsung. It's the artist who usually garners most of the attention. I don't think enough people realize that the picture book is a literary genre unto itself, and a very difficult one. The writing is rhythmic and telegraphic, not unlike poetry. In fact, I would say that the language of a good picture book is much more like poetry than prose.

"I usually type the first draft of a book and then handwrite revisions and corrections. I retype this and then, if necessary, make more handwritten changes. When I'm really working, the thoughts come flying and I can keep up more easily on the typewriter. I also like the 'clackety-clack' of the machine. Very writerly. Although I have had my computer for well over a year I still compose more naturally by hand or on the typewriter. The computer is best for plugging in changes and moving text around.

"In addition to read-aloud picture books, I have also done a number of 'I-Can-Read' titles. I'm happy to say that more and more schools are turning away from those boring primers they seem to have used for the last three hundred years where sentence structure was consistently the same: subject, verb, object. The 'I-Can-Reads' allow for creativity—stories within stories, games, and even invented words. Beginning-to-read books should show children that words are delicious and, once kids realize that, they will love to read.

"When I am not working, I love birdwatching. Early morning, particularly in April and May, are the best times when everything is so fresh. This is a recent passion, only five or six years old. I'm late in appreciating nature, having spent my whole life in cities. Now I walk and hike in the woods as much as I possibly can. There are so many wonderful sounds, many quite subtle, unlike most city sounds which grab you and won't let go.

"I try to write in my diary as often as possible. My journal entries take a poetic rather than prose form. No doubt this stems from the fact that images are always the impetus for my writing. Poetry and poets have always been extremely important to me. I guess if I had to choose, I would say that Rilke is my all-time favorite. His poems are like air to me. The prose writers I most favor—Chekhov, Proust, Colette, and Virginia Woolf—are very poetic to my way of thinking, because they are first and foremost image makers. They are not rhetorical."

Manushkin keeps a file cabinet "full of ideas and fragments, some of which go back ten years. Living up to ideas is not as easy as having them, however. And sometimes what seems to be a fantastic idea is just that—an idea but not a good premise for a book. Ideas come to me in the strangest circumstances. Recently I was shopping in Dean & Deluca, one of the most wonderful gourmet shops in the world. On display was an exquisite angel food cake. Suddenly I found myself lost in a fantasy of a little girl making a cake so light and magical that it rises, carrying her into the sky.

"For several years now, I have been part of a group of writers and illustrators who meet once a month to eat out, talk shop, and socialize. Paul Zelinsky, Myra Levoy, Mary Szilagyi, Miriam Schlein, Amy Schwartz, Bruce Degan, Linda Heller, Marvin Glass, Mirra Ginsburg, among others, are part of the group. We go to a restaurant in a different neighborhood each time we meet. It's great fun and keeps our spirits high.

"It can be discouraging to be a writer. But I am convinced that good publishers are always on the lookout for new talent. It makes their day to receive an unsolicited manuscript that turns out to be a gem. In my years as a writer and editor I have learned a few things I would like to pass on: don't give up on a book even if lots of editors reject it, keep sending it around (stories you hear about authors having been turned down forty times before being accepted are true), and don't be nervous if you've started writing something but don't know where it is going—be willing to discover the book as it evolves. I used to think that books existed in a pure state in authors' heads, perfect unto themselves. That simply isn't true. Books develop according to their own time. You cannot dictate that a book be born; neither can you dictate to a book. Listen, really listen, and your book will speak."

—Based on an interview by Marguerite Feitlowitz

HOBBIES AND OTHER INTERESTS: Swimming, bird watching, cat watching, reading, book collecting, movie and theatergoing.

MAREK, Margot L. 1934(?)-1987

OBITUARY NOTICE: Born about 1934; died of a brain tumor, September 29, 1987, in New York, N.Y. Specialist in learning disabilities, educator, and author. Marek, who taught learning-disabled students in her home, wrote *Different, Not Dumb,* a nonfiction book about individuals with impaired learning abilities. She also completed a novel for young readers, *Matt's Crusade,* which is scheduled for posthumous publication.

FOR MORE INFORMATION SEE—Obituaries: *New York Times,* October 1, 1987.

MAUGHAM, W(illiam) Somerset 1874-1965

PERSONAL: Surname pronounced Mawm; born January 25, 1874, in Paris, France; died December 15, 1965, in Nice, France; son of Robert Ormond (solicitor to the British Embassy) and Edith Mary (Snell) Maugham; married Syrie Barnardo Wellcome, May 26, 1917 (divorced, 1927); children: Liza, now Lady Glendevon. *Education:* Studied under a British tutor on the French Riviera; attended lectures at University of Heidelberg, 1890-92; briefly studied accountancy in Kent, England; St. Thomas Hospital, L.R.C.P., M.R.C.S., 1897. *Religion:* Rationalist. *Home:* Villa Mauresque, St. Jean-Cap Ferrat, A.M., France.

CAREER: Writer, 1896-1965. *Military service:* Served with a Red Cross ambulance unit and as a medical officer, later with the British Intelligence Corps in Switzerland, during World War I; served with the British Ministry of Information in Paris during World War II. *Member:* Garrick Club. *Awards, honors:*

Chevalier of the Legion of Honor, 1929; Commander, Legion of Honour, 1939; D.Litt., Oxford University, 1952; Companion of Honour, 1954; D.Litt., University of Toulouse; Royal Society of Literature, Fellow and Companion of Literature, 1961; Honorary Fellow, Library of Congress, Washington, D.C.; Honorary Senator, University of Heidelberg, 1961.

WRITINGS—Novels: *Liza of Lambeth,* Unwin, 1897, Doran, 1921, reprinted, Arno Press, 1977; *The Making of a Saint,* L. C. Page, 1898, new edition published as *The Making of a Saint: A Romance of Mediaeval Italy,* Arno Press, 1977; *The Hero,* Hutchinson, 1901, reprinted, Arno Press, 1977; *Mrs. Craddock,* Heinemann, 1902, Doran, 1920, new edition, Arno Press, 1977; *The Merry-Go-Round,* Heinemann, 1904; *The Bishop's Apron: A Study in the Origins of a Great Family,* Chapman & Hall, 1906, reprinted, Arno Press, 1977; *The Explorer* (novelization of play with same title), Heinemann, 1908, Baker and Taylor, 1909, reprinted, Arno Press, 1977; *The Magician,* Heinemann, 1908, Duffield, 1909, reprinted, Arno Press, 1977; *Of Human Bondage,* Doran, 1915; *The Moon and Sixpence,* Doran, 1919, reprinted, Arno Press, 1977.

The Painted Veil, Doran, 1925, new edition, Arno Press, 1977; *Ashenden; or, The British Agent,* Doubleday, Doran, 1928, new edition, Arno Press, 1977; *Cakes and Ale; or, The Skeleton in the Cupboard,* Doubleday, Doran, 1930; *The Book-Bag,* G. Orioli, 1932; *The Narrow Corner,* Doubleday, Doran, 1932, reprinted, Arno Press, 1977; *Theatre,* Doubleday, Doran, 1937, reprinted, Arno Press, 1977; *Christmas Holiday,* Doubleday, Doran, 1937, new edition, Arno Press, 1977; *Up at the Villa,* Doubleday, Doran, 1941, reprinted, Arno Press, 1977; *The Hour before the Dawn,* Doubleday, Doran, 1942, reprinted, Arno Press, 1977; *The Razor's Edge,* Doubleday, Doran, 1944; *Then and Now,* Doubleday, 1946, reprinted, Arno Press, 1977, also published as *Fools and Their Folly,* Avon, 1949; *Catalina: A Romance,* Heinemann, 1948, Doubleday, 1949, reprinted, Arno Press, 1977; *The Selected Novels,* 3 volumes, Heinemann, 1953; *The Explorer [and] The Land of the Blessed Virgin,* Heron, 1968; *Cakes and Ale; The Painted Veil; Liza of Lambeth; The Razor's Edge; Theatre; The Moon and Sixpence,* Heinemann, 1979.

Short Stories: *Orientations,* Unwin, 1899; *The Trembling of a Leaf: Little Stories of the South Sea Islands,* Doran, 1921, new edition, Arno Press, 1977, published as *Rain and Other Stories,* Grosset, 1932; *The Casuarina Tree: Six Stories,* Doran, 1926, reprinted, Arno Press, 1977; *Six Stories Written in the First Person Singular,* Doubleday, Doran, 1931, reprinted, Arno Press, 1977; *Ah King: Six Stories,* Doubleday, Doran, 1933, reprinted, Arno Press, 1977; *East and West: The Collected Short Stories of W. Somerset Maugham,* Doubleday, Doran, 1934 (published in England as *Altogether: Being the Collected Stories of W. Somerset Maugham,* Heinemann, 1934); *The Judgment Seat,* Centaur, 1934; *Cosmopolitans,* Doubleday, Doran, 1936, new edition, Arno Press, 1977; *The Favorite Short Stories of W. Somerset Maugham,* Doubleday, Doran, 1937.

The Mixture as Before, Doubleday, Doran, 1940, new edition, Arno Press, 1977; *The Unconquered,* House of Books, 1944; *Creatures of Circumstance,* Doubleday, 1947, reprinted, Arno Press, 1977; *Stories of Love and Intrigue* (from *The Mixture as Before*), Avon, 1947; *East of Suez: Great Stories of the Tropics,* Avon, 1948; *Here and There: Short Stories,* Heinemann, 1948; *Quartet: Stories by W. Somerset Maugham, Screen-Plays by R. C. Sheriff,* Heinemann, 1948, Doubleday, 1949; *The Complete Short Stories of W. Somerset Maugham,* Heinemann, 1951, Doubleday, 1952; *The World Over: Stories of Manifold Places and People,* Doubleday, 1952; *Encore: Orig-*

If I have given the reader an impression that Elliott Templeton was a despicable character I have done him an injustice. ■ (Cover illustration "Martin Coleman" by Glyn Philpot from *The Razor's Edge* by W. Somerset Maugham.)

inal Stories by W. Somerset Maugham, Screen-Plays by T.E.B. Clarke, Arthur Macrae and Eric Ambler, Doubleday, 1952; *South Sea Stories of W. Somerset Maugham,* Pocket Books, 1956; *The Best Short Stories,* selected by J. Beecroft, Modern Library, 1957.

Favorite Stories, Avon, 1960; *The Kite, and Other Stories,* Heinemann, 1963; *A Maugham Twelve: Stories,* selected by Angus Wilson, Heinemann, 1966, bound with *Cakes and Ale,* Doubleday, 1967; *Maugham's Malaysian Stories,* selected and with an introduction by Anthony Burgess, Heinemann Educational, 1969; *Seventeen Lost Stories,* compiled by Craig Showalter, Doubleday, 1969, reprinted, Arno Press, 1977; *A Baker's Dozen: Thirteen Short Stories,* Heinemann, 1969; *A Second Baker's Dozen: Thirteen Short Stories,* Heinemann, 1970; *Four Short Stories,* Hallmark Editions, 1971; *Hairless Mexican [and] The Traitor,* Heinemann Educational, 1974; *Footprints in the Jungle and Two Other Stories,* edited by Rod Sinclair, Heinemann Educational, 1975; *The Collected Short Stories of W. Somerset Maugham,* Volumes I-IV, Pan Books, 1976; *Sixty-five Short Stories,* Octopus, 1976; *Four Modern*

Story-Tellers, edited by M. T. Fain, Heinemann Educational, 1977; *W. Somerset Maugham: Selected Stories*, Franklin Library, 1979; *Tales from the East and the West* (illustrated by Mitchell Hooks), Franklin Library, 1979; *Thirty Great Short Stories*, Chancellor, 1983; *Short Stories*, selected and with an introduction by Sue Bradbury, Folio, 1985. A short story, "The Vessel of Wrath," was published by Dell as *The Beachcomber*.

Plays: *Marriages Are Made in Heaven* (first produced as "Schiffbrüchig" in Berlin at Schall and Rauch, January 3, 1902), Baillie, 1903; *A Man of Honour* (tragedy; first produced in London at Imperial Theatre, February 22, 1903), Chapman & Hall, 1903, Dramatic Publishing, 1912; *Jack Straw* (farce; first produced in London at Vaudeville Theatre, March 26, 1908), Heinemann, 1911, Dramatic Publishing, 1912; *Lady Frederick* (comedy; first produced in London at Royal Court Theatre, October 26, 1907), Heinemann, 1911, Dramatic Publishing, 1912; *Penelope* (comedy; first produced in London at Comedy Theatre, January 9, 1909), Dramatic Publishing, 1912; *The Explorer: A Melodrama* (first produced in London at Lyric Theatre, June 13, 1908), Dramatic Publishing, 1912; *Mrs. Dot* (farce; first produced in London at Comedy Theatre, April 27, 1908), Dramatic Publishing, 1912; *The Land of Promise* (comedy; first produced in New York at Lyceum Theatre, December 25, 1913), Bickers, 1913; *Smith* (comedy; first produced in London at Comedy Theatre, September 30, 1909), Dramatic Publishing, 1913; *Landed Gentry* (comedy; first produced as "Grace" in London at Duke of York's Theatre, October 15, 1910), Dramatic Publishing, 1913; *The Tenth Man: A Tragic Comedy* (first produced in London at Globe Theatre, February 24, 1910), Dramatic Publishing, 1913.

The Unknown (first produced in London at Aldwych Theatre, August 9, 1920), Heinemann, 1920, Doran, 1929; *The Circle* (comedy; first produced in London at Haymarket Theatre, March 3, 1921), Doran, 1921; *Caesar's Wife* (comedy; first produced in London at Royalty Theatre, March 27, 1919), Heinemann, 1922, Doran, 1923; *East of Suez* (first produced in London at His Majesty's Theatre, September 2, 1922), Doran, 1922, reprinted, Arno Press, 1977; *Our Betters* (comedy; first produced in New York at Hudson Theatre, March 12, 1917), Heinemann, 1923, Doran, 1924; *Home and Beauty: A Farce in Three Acts* (first produced in London at Playhouse, August 30, 1919; also produced as "Too Many Husbands" in New York at Booth Theatre, October 8, 1919), Heinemann, 1923; *The Unattainable* (farce; first produced as "Caroline" in London at New Theatre, February 8, 1916), Heinemann, 1923, S. French, 1926; *Loaves and Fishes* (comedy; first produced in London at Duke of York's Theatre, February 24, 1911), Heinemann, 1924; *The Letter* (based on *The Casuarina Tree;* first produced in London at Playhouse, February 24, 1927), Doran, 1927, reprinted, Arno Press, 1977; *The Constant Wife* (comedy; first produced in New York at Maxine Elliott's Theatre, November 29, 1926), Doran, 1927; *The Sacred Flame* (first produced in New York at Henry Miller's Theatre, November 19, 1928), Doubleday, Doran, 1928, reprinted, Arno Press, 1977.

The Breadwinner (comedy; first produced in London at Vaudeville Theatre, September 30, 1930), Heinemann, 1930, Doubleday, Doran, 1931; *Dramatic Works*, Volumes I-IV, Heinemann, 1931-1934, published as *The Collected Plays*, Volumes I-III, 1952; *Plays by W. Somerset Maugham*, Heinemann, 1931; *For Services Rendered* (first produced in London at Globe Theatre, November 1, 1932), Heinemann, 1932, Doubleday, Doran, 1933, reprinted, Arno Press, 1977; *Sheppey* (first produced in London at Wyndham's Theatre, September 14, 1933), Heinemann, 1933, Baker, 1949, reprinted, Arno Press, 1977;

Six Comedies (contains *The Unattainable, Home and Beauty, The Circle, Our Betters, The Constant Wife*, and *The Breadwinner*), Doubleday, Doran, 1937, reprinted, Arno Press, 1977; (with Guy Reginald Bolton) *Theatre* (comedy), S. French, 1942; (with R. C. Sheriff and Noel Langley) *Trio: Stories and Screen Adaptations*, Doubleday, 1950; *The Noble Spaniard: A Comedy in Three Acts* (adapted from Ernest Grenat-Dancourt's *Les Gaités du veuvage;* first produced in London at Royalty Theatre, March 20, 1909), Evans, 1953; *Three Dramas of W. Somerset Maugham*, Washington Square, 1968; *Three Comedies of W. Somerset Maugham*, Washington Square, 1969; *Plays by W. Somerset Maugham*, Volumes I-III, Heron, 1969; *The Selected Plays of W. Somerset Maugham*, Pan Books, 1976; *For Services Rendered; The Letter; Home and Beauty*, Pan Books, 1980.

W. Somerset Maugham, 1949.

Unpublished plays: "Mademoiselle Zampa," first produced in London at Avenue Theatre, February 18, 1904; "A Trip to Brighton" (adaptation of a play by Abel Tarride), produced in London, 1911; "The Perfect Gentleman" (adapted from Molière's *Le Bourgeois Gentilhomme*), first produced in London at His Majesty's Theatre, May 27, 1913; "Mrs. Beamish" (unproduced), 1917; "The Keys to Heaven" (unproduced), 1917; "Love in a Cottage," first produced in London at Globe Theatre, January 26, 1918; "The Camel's Back," first produced in New York at Vanderbilt Theatre, November 13, 1923; "The Road Uphill" (unproduced), 1924; "The Force of Nature" (unproduced), 1928; "The Mask and the Face" (adaptation of a play by Luigi Chiavelli), first produced in New York at Fifty-Second Street Theatre, May 8, 1933.

Editor: (With Laurence Housman) *The Venture Annual of Art and Literature*, Baillie, 1903; (with L. Housman) *The Venture Annual of Art and Literature, 1905*, Simpkin Marshall, 1904; Charles Henry Hawtrey, *The Truth at Last*, Little, Brown, 1924; *The Traveller's Library*, Doubleday, Doran, 1933, reissued as *Fifty Modern English Writers*, Doubleday, Doran, 1933, also published as *The Traveller's Library compiled with Notes*, Norwood Editions, 1986; (with Joseph Frederick Green) *Wisdom of Life: An Anthology of Noble Thoughts*, Watts, 1938; (and author of introduction) George Douglas, *The House with the Green Shutters*, Oxford University Press, 1938; *Tellers of Tales: One Hundred Short Stories from the United States, England, France, Russia, and Germany*, Doubleday, Doran, 1939, published as *The Greatest Stories of All Times*, Garden City Publishing, 1943.

Great Modern Reading, Doubleday, 1943; *The Greatest Stories of All Times*, Garden City Publishing, 1943; Charles Dickens, *David Copperfield*, Winston, 1948; Henry Fielding, *Tom Jones*, Winston, 1948; Feodor Dostoevski, *The Brothers Karamazov*, Winston, 1949; Gustave Flaubert, *Madame Bovary*, Winston, 1949; Herman Melville, *Moby Dick*, Winston, 1949; Honore de Balzac, *Old Man Goriot*, Winston, 1949; Jane Austen, *Pride and Prejudice*, Winston, 1949; Stendahl, *The Red and the Black*, Winston, 1949; Leo Tolstoi, *War and Peace*, Winston, 1949; Emily Brontë, *Wuthering Heights*, Winston, 1949; *A Choice of Kipling's Prose*, Macmillan, 1952, published as *Maugham's Choice of Kipling's Best*, Doubleday, 1953.

Other: *The Land of the Blessed Virgin: Sketches and Impressions of Andalusia*, Heinemann, 1905, published in America under same title and also as *Andalusia, Sketches and Impressions*, Knopf, 1920, new edition published as *Andalusia, "The Land of the Blessed Virgin,"* Arno Press, 1977; *On a Chinese Screen*, Doran, 1922, facsimile edition, Oxford University Press, 1985; *The Gentleman in the Parlour: A Record of a Journey from Rangoon to Haiphong*, Doubleday, Doran, 1930, reprinted, Arno Press, 1977; *The Non-Dramatic Works*, 28 volumes, Heinemann, 1934-69; *Don Fernando; or, Variations on Some Spanish Themes*, Doubleday, Doran, 1935, new edition, Arno Press, 1977; *My South Sea Island*, privately printed, 1936; *The Summing Up*, Doubleday, Doran, 1938, reprinted, Arno Press, 1977; *Princess September and the Nightingale* (from *The Gentleman in the Parlour*), Oxford University Press, 1939, also published as *Princess September* (illustrated by Jacqueline Ayer), Harcourt, 1969.

Books and You, Doubleday, Doran, 1940, reprinted, Arno Press, 1977; *France at War*, Doubleday, Doran, 1940, reprinted, Arno Press, 1977; *Strictly Personal*, Doubleday, Doran, 1941, new edition, Arno Press, 1977; *The W. Somerset Maugham Sampler*, edited by Jerome Weidman, Garden City Publishing, 1943, published as *The Somerset Maugham Pocket Book*, Pocket

She shook her head, unable to speak, and the tears rolled down her cheeks. ∎ (Cover illustration "The Cafe" by Graham Bell from *Of Human Bondage* by W. Somerset Maugham.)

Books, 1944; *W. Somerset Maugham's Introduction to Modern English and American Literature*, New Home Library, 1943; *Of Human Bondage, with a Digression on the Art of Fiction: An Address*, U.S. Government Printing Office, 1946, reprinted, Folcroft, 1977.

Great Novelists and Their Novels: Essays on the Ten Greatest Novels of the World and the Men and Women Who Wrote Them, Winston, 1940, revised edition published as *Ten Novels and Their Authors*, Heinemann, 1954, published in America as *The Art of Fiction*, Doubleday, 1955, reprinted, Arno Press, 1977; *A Writer's Notebook*, Doubleday, 1949, new edition, Arno Press, 1977; *A Maugham Reader*, edited by Glenway Wescott, Doubleday, 1950; *The Writer's Point of View*, Cambridge University Press, 1951, Folcroft, 1969, reprinted, Norwood Editions, 1977; *The Vagrant Mood: Six Essays*, Heinemann, 1952, Doubleday, 1953, reprinted, Arno Press, 1977; *The Partial View* (contains *The Summing Up* and *A Writer's Notebook*), Heinemann, 1954; *Mr. Maugham Himself*, se-

Maugham in 1929.

lected by John Beecroft, Doubleday, 1954; *The Travel Books,* Heinemann, 1955; *The Magician, a Novel, together with a Fragment of Autobiography,* Heinemann, 1956, Doubleday, 1957; *Points of View,* Heinemann, 1958, published in America as *Points of View: Five Essays,* Doubleday, 1959, new edition, Arno Press, 1977.

Purely for My Pleasure, Doubleday, 1962; *Selected Prefaces and Introductions of W. Somerset Maugham,* Doubleday, 1963, reprinted, Arno Press, 1977; *Wit and Wisdom,* edited by Cecil Hewetson, Duckworth, 1966; *Essays on Literature,* New American Library, 1967; *The Vagrant Mood [and] Ten Novels and Their Authors,* Heron Books, 1969; *The Letters of William Somerset Maugham to Lady Juliet Duff,* selected and with an introduction by Loren R. Rothschild, Rasselas Press, 1982; *A Traveller in Romance: Uncollected Writings 1901-1964,* edited by John Whitehead, C. N. Potter, 1984.

ADAPTATIONS—Motion pictures: "Smith," Jury (London), 1917; "The Land of Promise," Famous Players Film, 1917; "The Divorcee" (based on play *Lady Frederick*), Metro Pictures, 1919; "Jack Straw," Paramount, 1920; "The Circle," Metro-Goldwyn-Mayer, 1925; "The Canadian" (based on play *The Land of Promise*), starring Thomas Meighan and Mona Palma, Paramount, 1926; "Sadie Thompson," starring Gloria Swanson and Lionel Barrymore, United Artists, 1928, remade as "Rain," starring Joan Crawford and Walter Huston, United Artists, 1932, remade as "Miss Sadie Thompson," starring Rita Hayworth and José Ferrer, Columbia, 1954; "Charming Sinners" (based on play *The Constant Wife*), Paramount, 1929; "The Sacred Flame," Warner, 1929; "The Letter," starring Jeanne Eagels, Paramount, 1929, remade, starring Bette Davis and Herbert Marshall, Warner Bros., 1940.

"Strictly Unconventional" (based on play *The Circle*), Metro-Goldwyn-Mayer, 1930; "Our Betters," R.K.O. Radio Pictures, 1933; "The Narrow Corner," Warner, 1933; "Of Human Bondage," starring Leslie Howard and Bette Davis, RKO, 1934, remade, starring Paul Ilenreid and Eleanor Parker, Warner Bros., 1946, remade, starring Laurence Harvey and Kim Novak, Metro-Goldwyn-Mayer, 1964; "The Painted Veil," starring Greta Garbo and Herbert Marshall, Metro-Goldwyn-Mayer, 1934; "The Right to Live" (based on novel *The Sacred Flame*), Warner, 1935; "The Secret Agent" (based on novel *Ashenden*), Gaumont British, 1936; "Isle of Fury" (based on novel *Narrow Corner*), Warner, 1936; "The Tenth Man," Wardour Films, 1937; "The Beachcomber" (based on "The Vessel of Wrath"), starring Charles Laughton and Elsa Lanchester, Paramount, 1938.

"Too Many Husbands," starring Jean Arthur and Fred MacMurray, Columbia, 1940, remade as "Three for the Show," starring Gower Champion and Betty Grable, Columbia, 1955; "The Moon and Sixpence," starring George Sanders and Her-

(From the movie "The Razor's Edge," starring Gene Tierney and Tyrone Power. Twentieth Century-Fox, 1946.)

bert Marshall, United Artists, 1943; "The Hour before Dawn," Paramount, 1944; "Christmas Holiday," Universal Pictures, 1944; "The Razor's Edge," starring Tyrone Power and Gene Tierney, Twentieth Century-Fox, 1947, remade, starring Bill Murray, Columbia, 1984; "Quartet" (film version of "The Facts of Life," "The Alien Corn," "The Kite," and "The Colonel's Lady"), starring Basil Radford and Cecil Parker, J. Arthur Rank, 1949.

"Trio," starring Jean Simmons and Michael Rennie, Paramount, 1951; "Encore" (film version of "The Ant and the Grasshopper," "Winter Cruise," and "Gigolo and Gigolette"), starring Roland Culver and Glynis Johns, J. Arthur Rank, 1952; "The Seventh Sin" (based on novel *The Painted Veil*), Metro-Goldwyn-Mayer, 1957; "Adorable Julia," Films-Etoile, 1964; "Overnight Sensation," (16mm or videocassette; based on short story "The Colonel's Lady"), Pyramid Films, 1984.

Plays: "Rain" (dramatization of "Miss Thompson"; starring Jeanne Eagels; produced in New York at Maxine Elliott Theater, 1922), Boni & Liveright, 1923, S. French, 1948; "The Moon and Sixpence," first produced in London at New Theatre, September 24, 1925; "The Letter," starring Katherine Cornell, first produced at Morosco Theater, September 26, 1927; "Sadie Thompson" (musical adaptation), produced in

New York, 1944; "Before the Party" (dramatization of a short story), S. French, 1950; "Larger Than Life" (based on the novel *Theatre*), S. French, 1951; "Jane" (dramatization of a short story; produced in New York, 1952), Random House, 1952.

Television: "The Letter," starring Madeleine Carroll, "Lucky Strike Theatre," NBC-TV, January 30, 1950; "Teller of Tales" (also known as "The Somerset Maugham Theater"), narrated by Somerset Maugham, 40 one-half hour episodes, CBS-TV, October 18, 1950-March 28, 1952, seven one-hour episodes, NBC-TV, April 2, 1951-December 10, 1951; "The Letter," starring Siobhan McKenna, "Producer's Showcase," NBC-TV, October 15, 1956; "The Moon and Sixpence," starring Laurence Olivier, NBC-TV Special, October 30, 1959; "Cakes and Ale," "Masterpiece Theatre," PBS-TV, April, 1976.

Opera: "The Moon and Sixpence," first produced in London at Sadler's Wells Theatre, May 24, 1957.

Cassettes, except as noted: "Of Human Bondage" (recording), Metacom, 1948; "The Three Fat Women of Antibes" (recorded with "Gigolo and Gigolette"), Columbia, 1955, (cassette) Caedmon, 1983(?); "Short Stories" (recording), Listening Library, 197(?); "The Razor's Edge," Books on Tape, 1977; "Theatre," Books on Tape, 1979; "Cakes and

(From the 1934 MGM movie "The Painted Veil," starring Greta Garbo and George Brent.)

(From the movie "The Letter," starring Herbert Marshall and Bette Davis. Copyright 1940 by Warner Brothers First National Pictures, Inc.)

Ale'' (recorded with "Up at the Villa"), Books on Tape, 1980; "The Narrow Corner," Books on Tape, 1980; "Liza of Lambeth," Books on Tape, 1980; "The Lotus Eater," Caedmon, 1981; "The Moon and Sixpence," G. K. Hall; "The Summing Up," Books on Tape, 1984; "The Explorer," Books on Tape, 1985; "The Hero," Books on Tape, 1985; "The Moon and Sixpence," Caedmon, 1986; "Mrs. Craddock," Books on Tape, 1986; "The Making of a Saint," Books on Tape, 1986; "Cakes and Ale; or, The Skeleton in the Cupboard," G. K. Hall, 1987; "The Merry-Go-Round," Books on Tape, 1987.

SIDELIGHTS: **January 25, 1874.** Maugham, who preferred to be called "Willie," was born in the British Embassy in Paris, France. Although the family did not live in the embassy, his mother gave birth there to insure her fourth son's British citizenship and to avoid his conscription into the French army. ". . . My father, I do not know why unless he was drawn by some such restlessness for the unknown as has consumed his son, went to Paris and became solicitor to the British Embassy.

"He was forty when he married my mother, who was more than twenty years younger. She was a very beautiful woman and he was a very ugly man. I have been told that they were known in the Paris of that day as Beauty and the Beast.

"My mother was very small, with large brown eyes and hair of a rich reddish gold, exquisite features and a lovely skin. She was very much admired. One of her great friends was

Lady Anglesey, an American woman who died at an advanced age . . . and she told me that she had once said to my mother: 'You're so beautiful and there are so many people in love with you, why are you faithful to that ugly little man you've married?' And my mother answered: 'He never hurts my feelings.'

"She suffered from tuberculosis of the lungs and I remember the string of donkeys that stopped at the door to provide her with asses' milk, which at that time was thought to be good for that malady.

"Once when she was lying in bed, I suppose after a hemorrhage, and knew she could not live much longer, the thought came to her that her sons when they grew up would not know what she was like when she died, so she called her maid, had herself dressed in an evening gown of white satin and went to the photographer's. She had six sons and died in childbirth. The doctors of the period had a theory that to have a child was beneficial to women suffering from consumption. She was thirty-eight." [W. Somerset Maugham, *The Summing Up*, Doubleday, Doran, 1938.¹]

The tragedy of his mother's death in 1882 had a profound effect on eight-year-old Maugham, who never fully recovered from it. He developed a life-long stammer. At ninety-one, he wrote: "Perhaps the most vivid memory left to me is the one which has tortured me for more than 80 years—that of the death of my mother. . . . Even today the pain of her passing is as keen as when it happened in our home in Paris." [W.

(From the movie "Too Many Husbands," starring Jean Arthur and Fred MacMurray. Copyright 1940 by Columbia Pictures Corporation.)

Somerset Maugham, *A Traveller in Romance: Uncollected Writings 1901-1964*, edited by John Whitehead, Clarkson N. Potter, 1984.[2]]

"After my mother's death, her maid became my nurse. I had till then had French nurses and I had been sent to a French school for children. My knowledge of English must have been slight. I have been told that on one occasion seeing a horse out of the window of a railway carriage, I cried: *'Regardez, Maman, voila un 'orse.'*

"I had been taken away from the French school and went for my lessons every day to the apartment of the English clergyman at the church attached to the Embassy. His method of teaching me English was to make me read aloud the police-court news in *The Standard* and I can still remember the horror with which I read the ghastly details of a murder in the train between Paris and Calais. I must then have been nine. I was for long uncertain about the pronunciation of English words and I have never forgotten the roar of laughter that abashed me when in my preparatory school I read out the phrase 'unstable as water' as though unstable rhymed with Dunstable.

"I have never had more than two English lessons in my life, for though I wrote essays at school, I do not remember that I ever received any instruction on how to put sentences together."[1]

Maugham lived with his father and brothers in an apartment near the embassy. His father, however, had grander plans for the family, and spent freely to accomplish his dream. "I think my father had a romantic mind. He took it into his head to build a house to live in during the summer. He bought a piece of land on the top of a hill at Suresnes. The view was splendid over the plain, and in the distance was Paris. There was a road down to the river and by the river lay a little village. It was to be like a villa on the Bosphorus and on the top floor it was surrounded by loggias. I used to go down with him every Sunday by the Seine on a *bateau-mouche* to see how it was getting on. When the roof was on, my father began to furnish it by buying a pair of antique fire irons. He ordered a great quantity of glass on which he had engraved a sign against the Evil Eye which he had found in Morocco. . . . It was a white house and the shutters were painted red. The garden was laid out. The rooms were furnished and then my father died."[1]

Maugham was sent to live with his uncle, Henry MacDonald Maugham, and his German wife, Sophia, in rural Whitstable, England, far from metropolitan Paris. His beloved nurse was sent back immediately. His uncle was a stern vicar, and since the couple was childless and Maugham spoke little English, he felt miserably out of place in his new home.

His suffering increased when he was sent to the King's School in Canterbury, Kent. "I had many disabilities. I was small; I

Maugham dining at the Villa Mauresque with his secretary, Alan Searle.

had endurance but little physical strength; I stammered; I was shy; I had poor health. I had no facility for games, which play so great a part in the normal life of Englishmen; and I had, whether for any of these reasons or from nature I do not know, an instinctive shrinking from my fellow men that has made it difficult for me to enter into any familiarity with them. I have loved individuals; I have never cared for men in the mass. I have none of that engaging come-hitherness that makes people take to one another on first acquaintance. Though in the course of years I have learnt to assume an air of heartiness when forced into contact with a stranger, I have never liked anyone at first sight.

". . . I find social intercourse fatiguing. Most persons, I think, are both exhilarated and rested by conversation; to me it has always been an effort. . . . It is a relief to me when I can get away and read a book."[1]

"I left school early. I had been unhappy at the preparatory school to which I was sent. . . . It was an annex of the King's School, an ancient foundation, and to this when I was thirteen I duly went. After I had got out of the lower forms, the masters of which were frightening bullies, I was contented enough, and I was miserable when an illness forced me to spend a term in the South of France. . . . (When it was found that my lungs were affected [by tuberculosis] my uncle and aunt were concerned. I was placed at a tutor's at Hyeres.) When I went back to Canterbury I did not like it so well. My friends had made new friends. I was lonely. I had been moved into a higher form in which, with three months lost, I could not find my place. My form-master nagged me. I persuaded my uncle that it would be very good for my lungs if instead of staying at school I spent the following winter on the Riviera and that it would be of value to me after that to go to Germany and learn German. I could continue to work there on the subjects which were necessary for me to get into Cambridge. He was a weak man and my arguments were specious. He did not much like me, for which I cannot blame him, since I do not think I was a likeable boy, and as it was my own money that was being spent on my education, he was willing enough to let me do as I chose. My aunt greatly favoured my plan. She was herself German. . . . It was she who arranged that I should go to a family in Heidelberg whom she had heard of through her relations in Munich."[1]

In Heidelberg, Maugham found a new beginning. His studies at the university introduced him to the works of Schopenhauer and Spinoza, and he found in their philosophical pessimism an echo of his own experience. His bitter awareness of how chance and circumstance shape a life led to an atheistic perspective.

"Most people live haphazard lives subject to the varying winds of fortune. Many are forced by the situation in which they were born and the necessity of earning a living to keep to a straight and narrow road in which there is no possibility of turning to the right or to the left. Upon these the pattern is imposed. Life itself has forced it on them. There is no reason why such a pattern should not be as complete as that which anyone has tried self-consciously to make. But the artist is in a privileged position.

"The artist can within certain limits make what he likes of his life. In other callings, in medicine for instance or the law, you are free to choose whether you will adopt them or not, but having chosen, you are free no longer. You are bound by the rules of your profession; a standard of conduct is imposed upon you. The pattern is predetermined. It is only the artist, and maybe the criminal, who can make his own.

". . . The passing moment is all we can be sure of; it is only common sense to extract its utmost value from it; the future will one day be the present and will seem as unimportant as the present does now. But common sense avails me little. I do not find the present unsatisfactory; I merely take it for granted. It is interwoven in the pattern and what interests me is what remains to come."[1]

Heidelberg further exposed Maugham to the music of Wagner, the drama of Ibsen, and the scientific method. "I was glad to learn that the mind of man (himself the product of natural causes) was a function of the brain subject like the rest of his body to the laws of cause and effect and that these laws were the same as those that governed the movements of star and atom. I exulted at the thought that the universe was no more than a vast machine in which every event was determined by a preceding event so that nothing could be other than it was. These conceptions not only appealed to my dramatic instinct; they filled me besides with a very delectable sense of liberation.

"With the ferocity of youth I welcomed the hypothesis of the Survival of the Fittest. It gave me much satisfaction to learn that the earth was a speck of mud whirling round a second-rate star which was gradually cooling; and that evolution, which had produced man, would by forcing him to adapt himself to his environment deprive him of all the qualities he had acquired but those that were necessary to enable him to combat the increasing cold till at last the planet, an icy cinder, would no longer support even a vestige of life. I believed that we were wretched puppets at the mercy of a ruthless fate; and that, bound by the inexorable laws of nature, we were doomed to take part in the ceaseless struggle for existence with nothing to look forward to but inevitable defeat. I learnt that men were moved by a savage egoism, that love was only the dirty trick nature played on us to achieve the continuation of the species, and I decided that, whatever aims men set themselves, they were deluded, for it was impossible for them to aim at anything but their own selfish pleasures. . . .

"I was violently pessimistic. All the same, having abundant vitality, I was getting on the whole a lot of fun out of life."[1]

At the university, Maugham experienced the first freedom of his youth. It was during this interlude that he had his first homosexual encounter with an older dilettante and dandy, John Ellingham Brooks. Later he was to renounce Brooks' ideas, but the pattern was set for a lifelong attraction to men.

". . . When I came back from Germany, aged eighteen, I had very decided views of my own about my future. I had been happier than ever before. I had for the first time tasted freedom and I could not bear the thought of going to Cambridge and being subjected once more to restraint. I felt myself a man and I had a great eagerness to enter at once upon life. I felt that there was not a moment to waste. My uncle had always hoped that I would go into the church, though he should have known that, stammering as I did, no profession could have been more unsuitable; and when I told him that I wouldn't, he accepted with his usual indifference my refusal to go to Cambridge. I still remember the rather absurd arguments that were held about the calling I should adopt. A suggestion was made that I should become a civil servant and my uncle wrote to an old Oxford friend of his who held an important position in the Home Office for his advice. It was that, owing to the system of examinations and the class of persons it had introduced into the government service, it was now no place for a gentleman. That settled that. It was finally decided that I should become a doctor.

(From the movie "Rain," starring Walter Huston and Joan Crawford. Released by United Artists, 1932.)

(From the movie "Sadie Thompson," starring Gloria Swanson and Lionel Barrymore. Released by United Artists, 1928.)

(From the movie "Miss Sadie Thompson," starring Rita Hayworth. Released by Columbia Pictures Corporation, 1954.)

"I did not want to be a doctor. I did not want to be anything but a writer, but I was much too shy to say so, and in any case at that time it was unheard of that a boy of eighteen, belonging to a respectable family, should adopt literature as a profession. The notion was so preposterous that I never even dreamt of imparting it to anybody. I had always supposed that I should enter the law, but my three brothers, much older than I, were practising it and there did not seem room for me too.

"The medical profession did not interest me, but it gave me the chance of living in London and so gaining the experience of life that I hankered after. I entered St Thomas's Hospital . . . [and] I found the first two years of the curriculum very dull and gave my work no more attention than was necessary to scrape through the examinations. I was an unsatisfactory student. But I had the freedom I yearned for. I liked having lodgings of my own, where I could be by myself; I took pride in making them pretty and comfortable. All my spare time, and much that I should have devoted to my medical studies, I spent reading and writing. I read enormously; I filled notebooks with ideas for stories and plays, scraps of dialogue and reflections, very ingenuous ones, on what my reading and the various experiences that I was undergoing suggested to me. I entered little into the life of the hospital and made few friends

there, for I was occupied with other things; but when, after two years, I became a clerk in the outpatients' departments I began to grow interested. In due course I started to work in the wards and then my interest so much increased that when I caught septic tonsillitis through doing a postmortem on a corpse that was in an unreasonable state of decomposition and had to take to my bed, I could not wait to get well to resume my duties. I had to attend a certain number of confinements to get a certificate and this meant going into the slums of Lambeth, often into foul courts that the police hesitated to enter, but in which my black bag amply protected me: I found the work absorbing. For a short period I was on accident duty day and night to give first aid to urgent cases. It left me tired out but wonderfully exhilarated.

"For here I was in contact with what I most wanted, life in the raw. In those three years I must have witnessed pretty well every emotion of which man is capable. It appealed to my dramatic instinct. It excited the novelist in me. Even now . . . I can remember certain people so exactly that I could draw a picture of them. Phrases that I heard then still linger on my ears. I saw how men died. I saw how they bore pain. I saw what hope looked like, fear and relief; I saw the dark lines that despair drew on a face; I saw courage and steadfastness.

Maugham with Syrie Wellcome shortly after their marriage.

(From the "Masterpiece Theatre" presentation of "Cakes and Ale," starring Judy Cornwell. Produced by the BBC, it was broadcast on PBS-TV, April, 1976.)

I saw faith shine in the eyes of those who trusted in what I could only think was an illusion and I saw the gallantry that made a man greet the prognosis of death with an ironic joke because he was too proud to let those about him see the terror of his soul.

"All this was a valuable experience to me. I do not know a better training for a writer than to spend some years in the medical profession. . . ."[1]

Maugham's first novel was published the same year he received his certificate. The immediate success of *Liza of Lambeth,* about the slum life he had observed in his training, encouraged him to abandon the medical profession.

Travelled to Spain, Italy and Capri. "Presently I was qualified. I had already published a novel and it had had an unexpected success. I thought my fortune was made, and, abandoning medicine to become a writer, I went to Spain. I was then twenty-three. I was much more ignorant than are, it seems to me, young men of that age at the present day. I settled down in Seville. I grew a moustache, smoked Filipino cigars, learnt the guitar, bought a broad-brimmed hat with a flat crown,

in which I swaggered down the Sierpes, and hankered for a flowing cape, lined with green and red velvet. But on account of the expense I did not buy it. I rode about the countryside on a horse lent me by a friend. Life was too pleasant to allow me to give an undivided attention to literature. My plan was to spend a year there till I had learnt Spanish, then go to Rome which I knew only as a tripper and perfect my superficial knowledge of Italian, follow that up with a journey to Greece where I intended to learn the vernacular as an approach to ancient Greek, and finally go to Cairo and learn Arabic. It was an ambitious programme, but I am glad now that I did not carry it out. I duly went to Rome (where I wrote my first play) but then I went back to Spain; for something had occurred that I had not anticipated. I fell in love with Seville and the life one led there and incidentally with a young thing with green eyes and a gay smile (but I got over that) and I could not resist its lure. I returned year after year. I wandered through the white and silent streets and strolled along the Guadalquivir, I dawdled about the Cathedral, I went to bullfights and made light love to pretty little creatures whose demands on me were no more than my exiguous means could satisfy. It was heavenly to live in Seville in the flower of one's youth. I postponed my education to a more convenient moment. . . ."[1]

Maugham at the entrance to Villa Mauresque.

(From the movie "The Moon and Sixpence," starring George Sanders and Herbert Marshall. Copyright 1942 by United Artists Corporation.)

During this time, Maugham wrote a manuscript entitled *The Artistic Temperament of Stephen Carey*, a precursor to *Of Human Bondage*. He also wrote travel essays, plays, magazine stories and continued to travel.

1903. First play, *A Man of Honour* was produced by The Stage Society, a group promoting unknown plays.

1905. Went to Paris for a year and met many of the famous artists and writers of the Montparnasse cafe society. One of them became his life-long friend, Gerald Kelly, who later painted many portraits of Maugham.

Plays brought Maugham colossal success. He had four on the London stage at once, an unheard-of event. However popular, his plays met with critics' disapproval, an incongruity which continued throughout his career. At the height of his success, he decided to retire from the stage and write a novel in order to study himself. ". . . I was but just firmly established as a popular playwright when I began to be obsessed by the teeming memories of my past life. The loss of my mother and then the break-up of my home, the wretchedness of my first years at school for which my French childhood had so ill-prepared me and which my stammering made so difficult, the delight of those easy, monotonous and exciting days in Heidelberg, when I first entered upon the intellectual life, the irksomeness of my few years at the hospital and the thrill of London; it all came back to me so pressingly, in my sleep, on my walks, when I was rehearsing plays, when I was at a party, it became such a burden to me that I made up my mind that I could only

regain my peace by writing it all down in the form of a novel. I knew it would be a long one and I wanted to be undisturbed, so I refused the contracts managers were anxious to give me and temporarily retired from the stage.

"I called my book *Beauty from Ashes*, which is a quotation from Isaiah, but finding that this title had been recently used, I chose instead the title of one of the books in Spinoza's *Ethics* and called it *Of Human Bondage*. It is not an autobiography, but an autobiographical novel; fact and fiction are inextricably mingled; the emotions are my own, but not all the incidents are related as they happened and some of them are transferred to my hero not from my own life, but from that of persons with whom I was intimate. The book did for me what I wanted, and when it was issued to the world (a world in the throes of a terrible war and too much concerned with its own sufferings to bother with the adventures of a creature of fiction) I found myself free forever from those pains and unhappy recollections. I put into it everything I then knew and having at last finished it prepared to make a fresh start."[1]

Maugham's intimacies with both men and women were beginning to cause him a great deal of frustration. "I was tired. I was tired not only of the people and thoughts that had so long occupied me; I was tired of the people I lived with and the life I was leading. I felt that I had got all that I was capable of getting out of the world in which I had been moving; my success as a playwright and the luxurious existence it had brought me; the social round, the grand dinners at the houses of the great, the brilliant balls and the week-end parties at country houses; the company of clever and brilliant people, writers, painters, actors; the love affairs I had had and the easy companionship of my friends; the comfortableness and security of life. It was stifling me and I hankered after a different mode of existence and new experiences. But I did not know where to turn for them. I thought of travelling. I was tired of the man I was, and it seemed to me that by a long journey to some far-distant country I might renew myself.

"I was forty. If I meant to marry and have children it was high time I did so and for some time I had amused my imagination with pictures of myself in the married state. There was no one I particularly wanted to marry. It was the condition that attracted me. It seemed a necessary motif in the pattern of life that I had designed, and to my ingenuous fancy (for though no longer young and thinking myself so worldly wise, I was still in many ways incredibly naive) it offered peace; . . . peace that would enable me to write all I wanted to write without the loss of precious time or disturbance of mind; peace and a settled and dignified way of life. I sought freedom and I thought I could find it in marriage."[1]

He then met Syrie Barnardo Wellcome, a socialite separated from her millionaire husband. They began an affair which bore Maugham a daughter, Liza, on September 1, 1915 before they were legally married. The events caused a big stir in the London tabloids.

Maugham volunteered for the Ambulance Corps in Belgium and France during World War I where he met American Gerald Haxton, the love of his life. Haxton, an extroverted alcoholic and gambler was charmingly brash and quite in contrast to the reserved, self-conscious Maugham.

1915. Recruited by the British Intelligence Department as a secret agent in Switzerland, Maugham used his writing as a

Jeanne Eagels in the stage production of "Rain,"
Maxine Elliott Theatre, 1922.

cover. ". . . I joined the Intelligence Department where it looked as though I could be more useful than in somewhat inadequately driving an ambulance. The work appealed both to my sense of romance and my sense of the ridiculous. The methods I was instructed to use in order to foil persons who were following me; the secret interviews with agents in unlikely places; the conveying of messages in a mysterious fashion; the reports smuggled over a frontier; it was all doubtless very necessary but so reminiscent of what was then known as the shilling shocker that for me it took most of its reality away from the war and I could not but look upon it as little more than material that might one day be of use to me. But it was so hackneyed that I doubted whether I should ever be able to profit by it. After a year in Switzerland my work there came to an end."[1]

Of Human Bondage was published, but was unpopular with war-time readers looking for more cheerful subjects.

Maugham travelled to Tahiti and the Pacific Islands with Gerald Haxton to research the life of Gauguin. Here he formed impressions he used in his famous short story, "Rain," and the novel *Moon and Sixpence*. "I went, looking for beauty and romance and glad to put a great ocean between me and the trouble that harassed me. I found beauty and romance, but I found also something I had never expected. I found a new self. Ever since I left St Thomas's Hospital I had lived with people who attached value to culture. I had come to think that there was nothing in the world more important than art. I looked for a meaning in the universe and the only one I could find was the beauty that men here and there produced. On the surface my life was varied and exciting; but beneath it was narrow. Now I entered a new world, and all the instinct in me of a novelist went out with exhilaration to absorb the novelty. It was not only the beauty of the islands that took me, . . . nor was it their ramshackle, slightly adventurous, easy life; what excited me was to meet one person after another who was new to me. I was like a naturalist who comes into a country where the fauna are of an unimaginable variety. Some I recognized; they were old types that I had read of and they gave me just the same feeling of delighted surprise that I had once in the Malayan Archipelago when I saw sitting on the branch of a tree a bird that I had never seen before but in a zoo. For the first moment I thought it must have escaped from a cage. Others were strange to me and they thrilled me as Wallace was thrilled when he came upon a new species. I found them easy to get on with. They were of all sorts; indeed, the variety would have been bewildering but that my powers of observation were by now well trained and I found it possible without conscious effort to pigeon-hole each one in my awareness. Few of them had culture. They had learnt life in a different school from mine and had come to different conclusions. They led it on a different plane; I could not, with my sense of humour, go on thinking mine a higher one. It was different. Their lives too formed themselves to the discerning eye into a pattern that had order and finally coherence."[1]

May 26, 1917. Married Syrie in New Jersey, and they continued to live together in escalating disharmony for ten years. Haxton was clearly Maugham's love, and both men grew to hate Wellcome.

When he returned to England, he was once again approached by the Intelligence Department to act as a secret agent—this time in Russia. Although he failed in his mission to prevent a Bolshevik takeover, he gathered important background material, and met many spies, terrorists, and double agents.

1917-1918. Contracted tuberculosis and spent a year in a Scottish sanitarium, where he gathered impressions of invalids and recluses, adding to his collection of human characters.

(From the movie "The Razor's Edge," starring Bill Murray. Released by Columbia Pictures Corporation, 1984.)

1919-1928. Travelled with Haxton to China, Malaysia, Borneo, the Pacific Islands and Burma. They had many adventures, including attacks by bandits, near drownings and jungle fever. "I filled notebooks with descriptions of places and persons and the stories they suggested. I became aware of the specific benefit I was capable of getting from travel; before, it had been only an instinctive feeling. This was freedom of the spirit on the one hand, and on the other, the collection of all manner of persons who might serve my purposes. After that I travelled to many countries. I journeyed over a dozen seas, in liners, in tramps, in schooners; I went by train, by car, by chair, on foot or on horseback. I kept my eyes open for character, oddness and personality. I learnt very quickly when a place promised me something and when I waited till I had got it. Otherwise I passed on. I accepted every experience that came my way. When I could I travelled as comfortably as my ample means allowed, for it seemed to me merely silly to rough it for the sake of roughing it; but I do not think I ever hesitated to do anything because it was uncomfortable or dangerous.

"I have never been much of a sightseer. So much enthusiasm has been expended over the great sights of the world that I can summon up very little when I am confronted with them. I have preferred common things, a wooden house on piles nestling among fruit trees, the bend of a little bay lined with coconuts, or a group of bamboos by the wayside. My interest has been in men and the lives they led. I am shy of making acquaintance with strangers, but I was fortunate enough to have on my journeys a companion who had an inestimable social gift. He had an amiability of disposition that enabled him in a very short time to make friends with people in ships, clubs, bar-rooms and hotels, so that through him I was able to get into easy contact with an immense number of persons whom otherwise I should have known only from a distance."[1]

Maugham never stopped travelling, and years later, he repeated many of his journeys with a new companion, his secretary, Alan Searle.

1928. By now his marriage to Syrie was a sham, and they were divorced. Maugham bought a home on the French Riviera at St. Jean Cap Ferrat, shared it with Haxton, and named it the Villa Mauresque. He kept a strict discipline of writing every morning. Afternoons and evenings were spent entertaining such notables as the Duke and Duchess of Windsor, Winston Churchill and the Aga Kahn. Maugham knew many painters, many of whom did his portrait, and he amassed a huge and valuable collection of art. He continued to have many theatrical successes and was a very popular novelist, but critical acclaim eluded him.

Travelled to India with Haxton, armed with introductions to Rajas and Princes known to the Aga Kahn. They met mystics, yogis, scholars and poets, and gathered background for *The Razor's Edge.*

1939. The British Ministry of Information asked Maugham to move to the United States and write propaganda urging the United States to join England in the war effort. Haxton joined him and they moved from New York to California, where Maugham met movie producers and religious seekers who were studying Eastern mysticism. Later these contacts resulted in an American television series and movie dramatizations of his work.

Toward the end of the war, Haxton moved to Washington, D.C. and Maugham went to live on the estate of Nelson and Ellen Doubleday, at Parker's Ferry near Yemassee, South Carolina. Haxton died in 1944 at the age of fifty-two. Maugham, aged seventy, was devastated, and returned to the Villa Mauresque. He resumed his regimen of writing and entertaining with Alan Searle as his secretary and companion. By the age of eighty-eight, Maugham was suffering from senile dementia. During moments of lucidity, he and Searle burned much of Maugham's autobiographical writings.

December 15, 1965. Died, just before his ninety-second birthday. Maugham was buried, by his request, on the grounds of The King's School, Canterbury, England. "Somewhat early, but at what age I cannot remember, I made up my mind that, having but one life, I should like to get the most I could out of it. I wanted to make a pattern of my life, in which writing would be an essential element, but which would include all the other activities proper to man, and which death would in the end round off in complete fulfilment."[2]

FOR MORE INFORMATION SEE: Somerset Maugham, *Traveller's Library,* Garden City Publishing, 1937; S. Maugham, *Teller of Tales,* Doubleday, Doran, 1939; John Brophy, *Somerset Maugham,* Longmans, Green, 1952, revised edition, 1958; Harvey Breit, editor, *The Writer Observed,* World, 1956; Sven A. Jensen, *William Somerset Maugham: Some Aspects of the Man and His Work,* Folcroft, 1957; *Newsweek,* January 27, 1958, March 17, 1980; *New York Times Magazine,* January 25, 1959; Frank Swinnerton, *The Saturday Review Gallery,* Simon & Schuster, 1959; Karl Graham Pfeiffer, *W. Somerset Maugham: A Candid Portrait,* Norton, 1959.

Richard Albert Cordell, *Somerset Maugham: A Biography and Critical Study,* Indiana University Press, 1961; *Saturday Review,* October 14, 1961, November 5, 1966, March 15, 1980; *Time,* April 20, 1962; L. Brander, *Somerset Maugham,* Barnes & Noble, 1963; *New York Herald Tribune,* December 17, 1965; *New York Times,* December 17, 1965; W. Menard, *The Two Worlds of Somerset Maugham,* Sherbourne, 1965; Garson Kanin, *Remembering Mr. Maugham,* Atheneum, 1966; *Playboy,* January, 1966; Robin Maugham, *Somerset and All the Maughams,* New American Library, 1966; Will Durant and Ariel Durant, *Interpretations of Life,* Simon & Schuster, 1970; Jonas, editor, *The World of Somerset Maugham,* Greenwood, 1972; *Contemporary Literary Criticism,* Gale, Volume I, 1973, Volume II, 1974, Volume XV, 1980; Anthony Curtis, *Somerset Maugham,* Macmillan, 1977; Richard Aldington, *W. Someset Maugham: An Appreciation,* Folcroft, 1977; Robert Maugham, *Conversations with Willie: Recollections of W. Somerset Maugham,* Simon & Schuster, 1978; W. Menard, "Maugham in Hollywood," *American Film,* April, 1979; Ted Morgan, *Maugham: A Biography,* Simon & Schuster, 1980; *New Republic,* March 8, 1980; Bason, editor, *Bibliography of the Writings of W. Somerset Maugham,* Haskell House, 1982;

Ian Scott-Kilvert, editor, *British Writers,* Volume VI, Scribner, 1983; *McGraw-Hill Encyclopedia of World Drama,* 2nd edition, McGraw, 1984; Forrest D. Burt, *W. Somerset Maugham,* Twayne, 1985; John M. Reilly, editor, *Twentieth-Century Crime and Mystery Writers,* St. Martin's Press, 1985; *Dictionary of Literary Biography,* Volume 36, Gale, 1985; Archie Loss, *W. Somerset Maugham,* Ungar, 1988.

Obituaries: *New York Times,* December 16, 1965; *Publishers Weekly,* December 27, 1965; *Reporter,* December 30, 1965; *Antiquarian Bookman,* January 3-10, 1966; *Current Biography,* January, 1966; *Books Abroad,* spring, 1966; *Britannica Book of the Year,* 1966; *Current Biography Yearbook 1966,* H. W. Wilson, 1967.

Collections: Maugham's archives are maintained by the Yale University Library.

NELSON, Cordner (Bruce) 1918-

PERSONAL: Born August 6, 1918, in San Diego, Calif.; son of Albert (a produce dealer) and Uradel (a homemaker; maiden name, Bruce) Nelson; married Mary Kenyon (a homemaker), February 4, 1941; children: Elizabeth, Rebecca (Mrs. Robert Covington), Nancy. *Education:* University of the Pacific, A.B., 1940; Oklahoma University, graduate study, 1946-47. *Politics:* "Registered as nonpartisan." *Religion:* Unitarian. *Address:* P.O. Box 6476, Carmel, Calif. 93921.

CAREER: Writer, 1946—; Risso & Nelson (farming and produce firm), Stockton, Calif., manager, 1947-65; *Track & Field News,* Los Altos, Calif., editor, 1948-70. *Military service:* U.S. Army, 1941-45; became major; received China-Burma-India theater combat star; U.S. Army Reserve, 1945-68; now colonel (retired). *Member:* Authors League of America. *Awards, honors:* United States Track and Field Hall of Fame, 1975.

CORDNER NELSON

WRITINGS: The Jim Ryun Story (young adult biography), Tafnews, 1967; *The Miler* (young adult novel), S. G. Phillips, 1969; *Track and Field: The Great Ones,* Pelham Books, 1970, new edition published as *Track's Greatest Champions,* Tafnews, 1986; (with Roberto Quercetani) *Runners and Races: 1500m-Mile,* Tafnews, 1973, new edition published as *The Milers: A History of the Mile-1500m,* 1985; *Runners' World Advanced Running Book,* Anderson World, 1983; *Excelling in Sports: Training to Be a Winner* (young adult), Rosen, 1985; *Track and Field,* World Book Encyclopedia, 1988.

WORK IN PROGRESS: The Thunderbolt Peril, a suspense novel.

SIDELIGHTS: "I don't know about everybody else, but it is easy for me to connect the main activities of my life with my early interests.

"Before I was a teen-ager I had two main passions, reading and sports. Outside of school I did little else. I lived half a block from a library in a small town in southern California, and people called me a bookworm. I read books by the dozens, usually completing one author's works before I became enthusiastic about the next. Unfortunately, nobody directed my reading and so I remember a lot of mysteries and stories about Indians and cowboys but no classics. When I was fourteen, *The Count of Monte Cristo* seemed to be the best book I'd ever read. My love of reading led me to try to write, and when I was twelve I wrote a 'novel,' filling a tablet with penciled words about boys in sports and adventures.

"Much as I loved reading, I spent as much or more time at sports. I read about sports, in books and newspapers, and I played. I played the year 'round, mostly softball and touch football with a mixture of other sports. When I was thirteen I became a 'track nut' and competed for nine years. My competitive career slowed to a halt because I discovered I was in the wrong sport for me. I had more talent in accuracy sports like golf, tennis and basketball, but I licked track. About the same time I fell in love with Mary, graduated from college, and went into the army for five years of World War II.

"For more than ten years I had wanted to be a track coach, but when the war ended I had two children and I was advised to do something to earn some money. Instead, I took a writing course at Oklahoma University, living on our savings and the G.I. Bill. I sold some pulp stories, mostly sports and mysteries, but not enough to earn a living. So I went to work for my father on his ranch and in his produce business.

"In 1948, my brother Bert and I founded *Track and Field News,* more or less as a hobby. This combined my love of writing and track, but it took a lot of time and so my freelance writing had to stop for a while. I never stopped wanting to be a writer, though, and I wrote several books which have never been published. In 1966, I wrote *The Jim Ryun Story,* which became something of a sports best-seller.

"This success gave me the confidence to revise one of my unpublished manuscripts, and I sold *The Miler.* Then a British publisher asked me to write a book about the top dozen track athletes of all time, which they added to their series called "The Great Ones." Doubleday gave me a contract to write a book on training for distance running, and as soon as I finished, I took a month to write a book on training for all sports. I was paid for both books, but their plans for the series fell through and they held my books for, believe it or not, twelve years! When they released them to me, the books sold to other publishers immediately. The *Advanced Running Book* has also been published in French.

'Meanwhile, in 1973, our European editor, Roberto Quercetani, furnished the statistics and I wrote the text for a history of the mile run. In the next few years I strayed from my interest in track and wrote several unsold book manuscripts and some short material. In 1984 I was asked to update the twelve-year-old book on the history of the mile *(The Milers)* and also the biographical book about great track men *(Track's Greatest Champions).* The latter has been published in Japanese.

"So you can see what I mean about early interests shaping a whole life. I wanted to write, but my only real writing success has been on the subject of track, my other early interest. My conclusion: Be careful what you want; it may mean more then you think."

HOBBIES AND OTHER INTERESTS: Reading, tennis, conversation, computers.

FOR MORE INFORMATION SEE: Kirkus Reviews, September 15, 1969; *Library Journal,* December 15, 1969.

OWENS, Gail   1939-

PERSONAL: Born March 13, 1939, in Detroit, Mich.; daughter of Gershon A. (a salesman) and Janet Macbeth (a homemaker; maiden name, Cotton) Owens; children: Owen L. Geisz, Devon C. Mossa (daughter). *Home:* West Burlington, N.Y. 13482.

CAREER: Illustrator of books for young people. Has also worked as a fashion illustrator, and as a designer and art director in advertising. *Awards, honors: A Bedtime Story* and *The Santa Claus Mystery* were both chosen one of Child Study Association of America's Children's Books of the Year, 1975, *The Eels' Strange Journey* and *I'll Tell on You,* 1976, *The Hot and Cold Summer* and *The Adventures of Ali Baba Bernstein,* 1985, and *Cassie Bowen Takes Witch Lessons* and *Tac's Island,* 1986; *The Cybil War* was chosen one of *School Library Journal's* Notable Children's books, 1981, and one of International Reading Association/Children's Book Council's Children's Choices, 1982; *That Julia Redfern* was chosen one of *School Library Journal's* Best Books, 1982.

ILLUSTRATOR—All juvenile; all fiction, except as noted: Rubie Saunders, *Smart Shopping and Consumerism,* (nonfiction), F. Watts, 1973; Matt Christopher, *Stranded,* Little, Brown, 1974; Barbara Corcoran, *The Winds of Time,* Atheneum, 1974; Mabel E. Allan, *Romansgrove,* Atheneum, 1975; Joan Goldman Levine, *A Bedtime Story,* Dutton, 1975; J. G. Levine, *The Santa Claus Mystery,* Dutton, 1975; Phyllis Reynolds Naylor, *Witch's Sister* (part of a trilogy with *Witch Water* and *The Witch Herself*), Atheneum, 1975; Anne Alexander, *Connie,* Atheneum, 1976; Mary Anderson, *F*T*C Superstar,* Atheneum, 1976; Judi Friedman, *The Eels' Strange Journey* (nonfiction), Crowell, 1976; Joan Lexau, *I'll Tell on You,* Dutton, 1976; Jenifer Wayne, *Sprout,* new edition (Owens was not associated with earlier edition), McGraw, 1976; J. Wayne, *Sprout's Window Cleaner,* new edition (Owens was not associated with earlier edition), McGraw, 1976.

Eleanor Cameron, *Julia and the Hand of God (Horn Book* honor list; Junior Literary Guild selection), Dutton, 1977; Louise Moeri, *A Horse for X.Y.Z.* (Junior Literary Guild selection), Dutton, 1977; P. R. Naylor, *Witch Water* (part of a trilogy with *Witch's Sister* and *The Witch Herself*), Atheneum, 1977; J. Wayne, *Sprout and the Dogsitter,* new edition (Owens was not associated with earlier edition), McGraw, 1977; J. Wayne,

Sprout and the Helicopter, McGraw, 1977; J. Wayne, *Sprout and the Magician,* McGraw, 1977; Natalie Savage Carlson, *Jaky or Dodo?,* Scribner, 1978; Ellen Conford, *Hail, Hail, Camp Timberwood* (Junior Literary Guild selection), Little, Brown, 1978; Eleanor B. Heady, *Trees Are Forever: How They Grow from Seeds to Forests* (nonfiction), Parents Magazine Press, 1978; Eve Merriam, *Unhurry Harry,* Four Winds, 1978; P. R. Naylor, *The Witch Herself* (part of a trilogy with *Witch's Sister* and *Witch Water*), Atheneum, 1978; Carolyn Polese, *Something about a Mermaid,* Dutton, 1978; Anne Rose, adapter, *Spider in the Sky,* Harper, 1978; Sydney Taylor, *Ella of All-of-a-Kind Family,* Dutton, 1978.

Caroline B. Cooney, *Safe as the Grave* (Junior Literary Guild selection), Coward, 1979; J. M. Lexau, *I Hate Red Rover,* Dutton, 1979; Joanne Ryder, *Fog in the Meadow,* Harper, 1979; Jay Williams, *The Magic Grandfather,* Four Winds, 1979; Patricia Goehner Baehr, *The Way to Windra,* Warne, 1980; Aileen Fisher, *Out in the Dark and Daylight* (poetry), Harper, 1980; (contributor) A. A. Milne, *Pooh's Bedtime Book* (poetry and fiction; original illustrations by Ernest H. Shepard), Dutton, 1980; (contributor) A. A. Milne, *Winnie the Pooh's Calendar Book: 1981* (original illustrations by E. H. Shepard), Dutton, 1980; S. Taylor, *Danny Loves a Holiday,* edited by Ann Durell, Dutton, 1980; Betsy Byars, *The Cybil War,* Viking, 1981; C. B. Cooney, *The Paper Caper* (Junior

"What are voodoo shoes?" she asked. "Do you think I'm a witch?" (From *Ash Brooks: Super Ranger* by Wanda Vanhoy Smith. Illustrated by Gail Owens.)

Literary Guild selection), Coward, 1981; LouAnn Gaeddert, *Just Like Sisters,* Dutton, 1981; Elaine Knox-Wagner, *The Oldest Kid,* edited by Kathleen Tucker, A. Whitman, 1981; Donald J. Sobol, *Angie's First Case,* Four Winds, 1981.

E. Cameron, *That Julia Redfern* (ALA Notable Book), Dutton, 1982; Victoria Boutis, *Katy Did It,* Greenwillow, 1982; Pat Rhoads Mauser, *A Bundle of Sticks,* Atheneum, 1982; Peggy Parish, *Mr. Adams's Mistake,* Macmillan, 1982; Faith McNulty, *Hurricane,* Harper, 1983; (contributor) *Winnie-the-Pooh's Calendar Book, 1984* (original illustrations by E. H. Shepard), Dutton, 1983; E. Cameron, *Julia's Magic* (sequel to *That Julia Redfern*), Dutton, 1984; Johanna Hurwitz, *The Hot and Cold Summer,* Morrow, 1984; Ada B. Litchfield, *Making Room for Uncle Joe,* A. Whitman, 1984; Penny Pollock, *Stall Buddies,* Putnam, 1984; Wanda V. Smith, *Ash Brooks: Super Ranger,* Scribner, 1984; D. J. Sobol, *Encyclopedia Brown and the Case of the Mysterious Handprints,* Morrow, 1985; Jean Van Leeuwen, *Benjy the Football Hero,* Dial, 1985; Anna Grossnickle Hines, *Cassie Bowen Takes Witch Lessons,* Dutton, 1985; J. Hurwitz, *The Adventures of Ali Baba Bernstein,* Morrow, 1985; Ruth Yaffe Radin, *Tac's Island,* Macmillan, 1986; Clement C. Moore, *The Night before Christmas Coloring Book,* Simon & Schuster, 1986; Bonnie Pryor, *Vinegar Pancakes and Vanishing Cream,* Morrow, 1987; R. Y. Radin, *Tac's Turn,* Macmillan, 1987; Susan Saunders, *The Daring Rescue of Marlon the Swimming Pig,* Random House, 1987; Janice Cohn, *I Had a Friend Named Peter; Talking to Children about the Death of a Friend,* Morrow, 1987; Donald Sobol, *Encyclopedia Brown and the Case of the Treasure Hunt,* Morrow, 1988. Also illustrator of *Addie Across the Prairie,* A. Whitman.

WORK IN PROGRESS: Books for Morrow and Holiday House.

SIDELIGHTS: **March 13, 1939.** Born in Detroit, Michigan. "My mother was a homemaker and my father a carpet and floorcovering salesman. Detroit is a flat, grey, industrial city, although the rest of Michigan is remarkably beautiful. People didn't move here for the weather—they came to work hard in the factories. Until recently, I was unaware of how growing up in this city had influenced my artwork. You see, I have always been very interested in the edges of things—in that moment when 'all' becomes 'nothing.' Detroit, with all its brick buildings and barren urban landscape, is about that tension. Now I can see how growing up here has everything to do with my becoming interested in drawing faces, and in portraying interaction between people, a compensation, I think, for the fact that there was no landscape to look at. The street scenes were never rich or beautiful as they are in Rome or Florence—walk down any street in those incredible cities and you can easily see what inspired the Italian painters! We had no special light to capture, no magical streets, but we had *people.* My intrigue in relationships and people remains essential subjects for my illustration.

"I began drawing at an early age, and seriously from about the age of eleven, signing up for life drawing as a young girl with a letter of permission from my mother.

"I recall my mother's collection of the 'Book of the Month Club' novels, which she acquired in the 1930s. I read them all, and was particularly taken with the work of Louis Bromfield. Louisa May Alcott's *Little Women* was a favorite I still re-read once a year. Alcott, often referred to as a light author, has had more influence on our society than we give her credit. Think of all the women who have read her books, and then raised their own kids on them! Yet when authors list their literary influences, Alcott is never mentioned. She was a rather

We'll just have ourselves a little tea and math party. ■ (From *Cassie Bowen Takes Witch Lessons* by Anna Grossnickle Hines. Illustrated by Gail Owens.)

somber, dark person, and people were disappointed that she was not as lively as Jo, her central character. She once retaliated to the charge, saying, 'Just because it's fun to read my books, does not mean it is fun to write them.' I often say the same to children about illustration, 'Just because it's fun to look at, does not mean it is fun to draw.' I find that I am always starting over, and I am often surprised how something like drawing which began as such a pleasure, can turn into such torture. It seems the more I engage myself, the more difficult the work becomes.

"I was never lucky enough to have a professor fall in love with my work, telling me, 'Dear, someday you will really be something.' Quite the contrary! But I possessed a very rebellious 'I'll show you!' attitude.

"I graduated high school at seventeen and started to work as a freelance artist for department stores at sixteen. I had taken several courses in fashion illustration and was attracted to it, mostly because it was the only kind of illustration which involved drawing the human figure. The stores would give me clothes, and I'd find a model and make fashion illustrations.

"I never thought I would become an artist, however. After all, an artist was a very interesting person, not at all boring and routine as I was. I had been raised to take care of people, something no artist is supposed to have time or energy to do.

That kind of tunnel vision is perhaps unattractive, even unhealthy, but, I admit, sometimes necessary for the complete commitment to their work. It took a long time for me to come to terms with all that, but finally I have struck a balance.

"I received my best art instruction before I was eighteen. Once I came to New York, I was very disappointed. I often chose schools because I admired the work of their alumni, but by the time I reached the schools, the quality of the teaching had usually disintegrated when the good teachers moved on to greener pastures. I spent two wasted years in a very bad school. I have, therefore, taken a vow not to teach. I know what an incompetent teacher can do to someone. A student remembers everything—every work, and every lift of the eyebrow can be so influential. Teaching is a terrible responsibility and I'm just not confident enough to take it on."

Owens made Brooklyn, New York her home for thirteen years, rearing her son and daughter, and working in various advertising agencies in Manhattan. "Drawing seemed to be the only thing I was capable of doing—I didn't know how to type or take dictation. I might have given up working in the field of art altogether had it not been for the hard, economic fact of having to support my two children. As a young artist, it is so easy to get discouraged, but I didn't have that luxury. Even when I thought my work was terrible, which it very often was, I had to turn it in. I couldn't stall or take more time or make

She fastened the green-striped lace bikini panties with clothespins and another pair of tights for her legs. It made a pretty good person. ■ (From *The Paper Caper* by Caroline B. Cooney. Illustrated by Gail Owens.)

excuses—I needed the paycheck. So I give my kids the credit! Without them, I may have given up long ago. I held many jobs over the years—graphic designer, art director, layout person. As much as I liked my jobs, I began to worry about my children having to walk to and from school alone, so I learned to drive and moved us all upstate. It was a good move.

"I never decided to become an illustrator; it just happened. If I hadn't left New York City, I might never have committed myself to book illustration. New York was so stimulating, I found it difficult to concentrate on certain kinds of work there. It wasn't until I moved away, into a quiet, less hectic atmosphere, that I was able to conserve enough energy to turn inward. I like book illustration because it is much more of an individual effort than advertising.

"My experience in advertising helped me learn composition, however. Doing layouts to sell refrigerators or cosmetics and making storyboards for television commercials is excellent practice for a would-be book illustrator. You learn to move things along and to pace visual elements. Still, for many years I only *worked* as an artist, but never identified myself as such. The fact that I was an illustrator didn't really hit me until I was in my mid-thirties.

"I started doing children's books when my kids began to attend high school. I had been commuting to New York City from upstate, about a two-hour drive each way. I'd leave home at seven in the morning and return home at eight at night. I

The net broke the surface without a splash. ∎ (From *Tac's Island* by Ruth Yaffe Radin. Illustrated by Gail Owens.)

decided to break into publishing in order to spend more time at home with my kids. At first, I was assigned to illustrate magazine articles. Then I got a book, and then another, but I couldn't afford to quit my nine-to-five job as yet. For two years I worked all day at the agency, came home, cooked dinner, helped with homework, put us all to bed at nine, set the alarm for three in the morning and worked on illustration till six. By seven I'd hit the road again for the two-hour drive into Manhattan. I finally decided to quit and stay home. Many mothers think that the early years are the most important time to be around, but I felt the teenage years were better when bigger kids get into bigger trouble. It was good—I became a regular mother, I nagged the kids, and worked on my book illustration. It was a terrible financial disaster at first because books don't pay well, and I had been making a decent salary in advertising. I was finally able to support us on my freelance jobs, however."

Owens is "firmly rooted in modern day," and her illustrations reflect this. "I love Formica, Saran Wrap and Handi-Wipes. I like contemporary stories, and while I admire looking at things from the past, I don't have enough obsessional interest in it to sustain me. I am very happy to be living now, and, if anything, would like to have been born twenty years later. It would have been much easier in regard to my schooling and to my struggle to perceive myself as an artist. I grew up during a time when expectations in terms of women and achievement were mercilessly shallow. In order to be popular and successful, a girl was expected to be blonde, blue-eyed, with some-

The stopper slid right out of her hand. ∎ (From *Julie's Magic* by Eleanor Cameron. Illustrated by Gail Owens.)

She caught him up and buried her face in his cool, clean, night-smelling fur. ■ (From *That Julia Redfern* by Eleanor Cameron . Illustrated by Gail Owens.)

thing which people called a 'good personality.' Well, I wasn't blonde, or blue-eyed, but I did put a lot of energy into my personality, and was a minor success at that. Still, it was such a waste of energy. Kids aren't under the same social pressures today, although they deal with the drug scene, among other problems. But a major improvement is that young women have a greater sense of identity and higher expectations which surpass a 'good personality,' having to marry and beginning a family.

"The kind of stories I work on do not take place in imaginary landscapes; they aren't about elves or fairies or giants. They are modern, up-to-date stories, which don't require great doses of inspiration to begin working. I read the manuscript carefully, and begin to sketch through all the drawings, going back over them again and again until they fall into place. When I'm working on a book, I think of all the illustrations as one big illustration. It is like planning a menu. When you first start to cook, you want every course to be spectacular, and it used to be that I tried to be 'spectacular' in every single illustration I did. Now I've come to view the illustration as a giant puzzle. I work on the parts as I work on the whole, and I make a game of it. I very often repeat the general composition in every illustration, or I'll retain the center of interest in successive illustrations. Sometimes I use a particular picture construction at the beginning of a book and try to return to the same scene at the end. And sometimes I shake the illustration up—make it a little out of kilter. Anything I can do to reveal character through composition, pacing, I will do.

"Many people seem to think that I spend a long time on the faces, but in actuality, I spend very little time, and usually do them last. If I set the basic structure of a picture in such a way as to create a mood, the faces seem to slip right into place. A strange thing happens when I begin to work. At first I think of boys as being boys, the grandfather as being the grandfather, grass as grass, sky as sky, but as I work on the composition, these elements become quite abstract. I can almost work on them upside down, and often get carried away to the point that objects no longer look like what they *should* look like. I may be so focused on having the curve of a hair ribbon reflect the curve of a wallpaper pattern that the ribbon begins to look like something totally different. When all is said and done, the picture either works or it doesn't. If it's good, then it feels alive with the kind of harmony which I strive for."

Owens uses reference material to achieve her highly detailed illustration. "I use the library and my own collection of books. The Sears, Roebuck catalogues are a terrific help, as are my books on interiors. When it comes to fashion, however, I don't have to fuss much with research. I began as a fashion illustrator, and took courses in the history of costumes and clothing, so as a minor expert, I can draw most any period of American and European fashion from 1750 without reference."

For *Making Room for Uncle Joe,* a story about a family coping with Down's Syndrome, Owens research brought her to the local Association for Health of Retarded Children. "I also worked from some literature the author sent concerning the texture of the skin, hair, as well as facial construction common to people with Down's Syndrome. The character, Joe, however, is a composite and bears no resemblance to an actual person.

"I use actual children as models. I realized early on if I continued to work without models, all the kids in my books would wind up looking like my own! There were certain facial characteristics that kept repeating themselves. My drawings improved because I was able to observe so many different body types, gestures and facial expressions in action.

"You can't get three hamburgers in one bun," he called cheerfully. ■ (From *The Cybil War* by Betsy Byars. Illustrated by Gail Owens.)

"For most of the young models, working with me is their first real job. Sometimes it's easy work, sometimes it's quite difficult, I have discovered that middle children in a family tend to work out best. They seem to be physically very sophisticated, and move particularly well. Eldest children tend to be a little self-conscious, and the youngest are definitely hams. Middle kids also have a tough time in the family, and I suspect the work they do with me helps to raise their status a bit. Working with them is in some ways the best part of my work. I learn a lot from them—we talk about sneakers, and they tell me their latest jokes.

"I also work from Polaroid photographs. I can't actually see much detail in the snapshots themselves, but they serve as reminders of certain movements during the action. By sketching and getting to know the kids, I'm able to imagine what a certain gesture should look like. Think of all the possible positions someone could get into while playing a game of soccer, for example. It is particularly difficult to portray a figure from a variety of positions and still retain consistency of characterization. The drawing of position 'a' and the position 'b' can be anatomically correct in terms of the figure, but if the drawing is off, the same character will appear to be two totally different people. These differences are so subtle, and correcting them can be a matter of shifting the position of the figure a sixteenth of an inch. That's when Polaroids come in very handy.

All I have to do is snip off those few extra hairs and it'll be fine. ■ (From *Ella of All of a Kind Family* by Sydney Taylor. Illustrated by Gail Owens.)

(From *Julia and the Hand of God* by Eleanor Cameron. Illustrated by Gail Owens.)

"It has taken me a long time to develop consistency in my work. Unlike some artists who start out with a rather high level of quality in their work, my illustration has progressed slowly over a period of time. It is perhaps difficult to locate the central elements of my style, because my work is constantly changing.

"Artists today rarely deal with relationships between people. Instead we are given canvases in which the two central and alienated figures turn away from each other. Critics describe this as 'sensitivity,' but I think it is facile. The hardest thing to portray visually is two, or ten, or fifteen people *communicating* with their bodies, their gestures, and their glances.

"It's no accident that Da Vinci's 'The Last Supper' is such a famous painting and technical masterpiece. Dinner scenes—which I have frequently had to illustrate—are a killer. Meal time is a very intense time for most families, and an illustrator must portray all of the attendant tensions within the very confined space of a table. One must deal with each of the items on the table, and with their varying proportion. A glass of milk is perhaps tiny and insignificant to an adult viewer, but to the child, it appears huge. If I choose to put a turkey on a table, I must deal with the fact that in our minds, turkeys seem enormous. I constantly struggle to balance the actual proportion and size of everyday objects with our perception of them. This is what illustration is about—creating illusions in order to create a reality.

"That is the most difficult thing about illustration: you never draw anything real, and yet, you must build the illusion of reality. Artists like Degas were, of course, always working with this principle. They would sketch and sketch and finally make a painting. Then art got away from that way of working, and we now have either life studies, drawn from a more or less inanimate model, or abstract art which has no relationship to natural people, whatsoever. But illustration still works through illusion, and illusion is very difficult to create. My work is naturalistic, and so most people assume that I work directly from photographs or from life. This is not so, I work from life, but I never directly mimic life."

Illustration, Owens feels, is not really art. "Subject matter is crucially important to an artist, but the illustrator is rarely given the opportunity to choose his or her subject. Another important difference is that the illustrator's work is never seen in its original quality. Illustration is meant to be reproduced, and as a result, is worked, not for the eyes of a human audience, but for the eyes of a camera, which has fast become the mediator between what we artists produce and the final book. There is a big difference between original artwork and final reproduction. Sometimes our work can be prepared in a rather routine fashion and really glow in print. Other times, stunning original artwork is transformed into something very pedestrian. One can identify when Norman Rockwell began to work for the camera. In his early work, which reproduced more subtly because it didn't have any sharp definition of form, Rockwell tended to build forms through paint (a very painterly quality). In his later work, he retained the dark outline for the sake of clarity.

"Illlustrating books doesn't require that you become a public figure with a strong, charismatic personality. As a matter of fact, you can be rather anonymous. That precious anonymity has enabled me to try different things in order to develop. With each new project, I learn new technique."

Along with anonymity, Owens never deals directly with the authors whose books she illustrates. "I never hear from authors, except when they write to tell me they like my illustrations. That is very rewarding. I guess they are happy when an artist takes the time to be faithful to the details of their text. But we don't work alone in children's books. We deal with editors and art directors. For the most part I have tremendous respect for them, but I sense that publishing is undergoing a change. Things have become less personal. For example, I frequently have difficulty obtaining the information I need to begin a book, and now wind up dealing with several, usually conflicting, sources. I would really prefer one contact at a publishing house, but that is virtually impossible these days.

"I work for the age group I like best—eight to twelve-year-old middle readers. These kids are a terrific audience, and I'm only sorry that publishers won't give them more of the illustration they really seem to want. I love working in black and white, but have yet to meet a child who responds enthusiastically to it. Middle readers also love complete figures. I noticed this first with my own children. Each time I drew a picture of my daughter's head and put it on the wall, she would come along and add legs and arms. Later, when I began to talk to school children, I discovered they want characters to be on the page from head to toe. They like to see a complete figure, and they want everything in color—drawn as big as possible. Left to my own devices, I prefer cropped figures—I think every artist does—because they are exciting and fun to do and make dramatic compositions. But keeping in mind what kids like, I will often show complete figures in all the illustrations of characters. This is very difficult—one figure is okay, but three, four . . . ten, and your problems multiply. You have to animate the characters, get them swinging within the very limited space of a five- by eight-inch rectangle. Recently I've been trying to talk publishers into using double-page spreads in my books, and have had some success. The double-page illustrations always get the best response from art directors, editors, authors, and, most important, from the kids."

For black and white, Owens works with pencil, pen and ink, and wash; for full color, she uses "whatever will get me there—watercolor, pastel, colored pencil—I don't have a preference. I don't have a strong art training background, so I tend to set my sights on the end result, and am willing to try anything that'll get me there. My technique is not as refined as illustrators who are experts in watercolor or oil. I envision the final product and try to achieve it. I hate cluttered details, I like to shake a drawing hard when I've finished and let all the loose ends fall away, leaving only what I really need."

——*Based on an interview by Rachel Koenig*

FOR MORE INFORMATION SEE: Lee Kingman and others, compilers, *Illustrators of Children's Books: 1967-1976,* Horn Book, 1978.

PATTERSON, Geoffrey 1943-

PERSONAL: Born October 6, 1943, in Wimbledon, London, England; son of Walter (a carnival hat designer) and Yvonne (Still) Patterson; married Rosumund Mary Inglis, 1970; children: Ruth, Oliver. *Education:* Attended private boys' school. *Home and office:* Beech Farm, Wingfield, Eye, Suffolk IP21 5RE, England.

CAREER: John Siddeley (interior designer), London, England, designer, 1961-64; BBC-TV London, set designer, 1964-77; writer, 1977—. Teacher of visual and three-dimensional arts. *Member:* Society of Industrial Artists.

The pig trotted up to the farm gate and looked through it. There was an old wooden shed in the yard and it looked warm and inviting. The pig had seen the little girl take a bag of feed into the shed. She decided to have a look herself.

(From *A Pig's Tale* by Geoffrey Patterson. Illustrated by the author.)

WRITINGS—Self-illustrated children's books; all published by Deutsch: *The Oak*, 1978; *Chestnut Farm 1860*, 1980; *The Story of Hay*, 1983; *A Pig's Tale*, 1984; *Dairy Farming*, 1984; *All about Bread*, 1985; *The Working Horse*, 1985; *The Goose That Laid the Golden Egg: Re-Told from Aesop*, 1986; *The Story of Wool*, 1986. *Awards, honors: All about Bread* was selected one of Child Study Association of America's Children's Books

of the Year, and was exhibited at Bologna International Children's Book Fair, both 1985; Smarties Prize (England), 1986, for *The Goose That Laid the Golden Egg*.

SIDELIGHTS: "All my life I have managed to earn my living with one skill—drawing. My first job was working for John Siddeley, an interior designer based in Knightsbridge, London. I got this job because I could draw. At the interview I presented my future employer with some visuals of interiors I copied from *House and Garden,* an interior design magazine. This got me the job and at this time I learned how to do technical drawing.

"I was always reasonable at drawing. My father was a carnival hat designer and my two brothers are artists, one a Royal Academy painter, the other a puppet maker with his own company. My mother paints and draws well also.

"My art education was not academic but picked up on the way. The interior design work opened my eyes. I was getting paid £6 a week and the clients were spending thousands of pounds on their Italian black marble baths, but I didn't care, I was learning. My technical drawing skill and free-hand visualizing of interiors got me a job at the BBC in the design department as a set designer.

"The BBC was a breath of fresh air, with a fair turn around of work. One play would last a month. To be working at the BBC with people from all kinds of backgrounds was refreshing. Directors and producers say to designers, 'Well, what's it going to look like.' You can't tell them you have to draw it then and there on the spot.

"At the BBC I met Graham Oakley a set designer like me; he originally was a designer at Covent Garden, London. He was writing and illustrating his first 'Church Mouse' story for Macmillan which now sells around the world. He is very successful and has won every award going for his beautiful books.

"I wrote and illustrated a book for children and asked him to look at it. Considering how dreadful it was, he was very kind and gave me an introduction at Macmillan. They said, 'Very nice but not for us! Try over at Deutsch.' At Deutsch I met Pamela Royds (chief children's book editor) who took a chance on me and took my first book, *The Oak.* Since then I have written seven other books.

"I try to write in such a way that new words describing the story will not put children off. I never write what I illustrate and vice versa; drawings and text should compliment each other—Graham Oakley taught me this. Pam Royds often reshapes what I have written and is invaluable.

"My drawing is changing all the time, you never learn how to do it, that's the joy of it.

"Anyone can draw if you work hard enough and practice.

"I live in the country where things have changed very little in many ways over the last fifty years. So I write about and illustrate English country life as it used to be and is now. The books are always for children, six to twelve years old.

"I am concerned about the changing landscape of the English countryside and with the disappearance of the hedgerows and trees in the name of progress and modern farming; quite often it is just greed. So in the children's books I illustrate and write, I try to make the next generation aware of what they will lose and are losing. The books also show that the old ways of farming, although incredibly hard and not as romantic as you may imagine, gave the community a feeling of strength and closeness to the land.

"Everything about country life fascinates me. In my spare time I run my small holding and restore my sixteenth-century farmhouse to its former glory."

PAULSEN, Gary   1939-

PERSONAL: Born May 17, 1939, in Minneapolis, Minn.; son of Oscar (an army officer) and Eunice Paulsen; married second wife, Ruth Ellen Wright (an artist), May 4, 1971; children: James Wright. *Education:* Attended Bemidji College, 1957-58, and University of Colorado, 1976. *Politics:* "As Solzhenitsyn has said, 'If we limit ourselves to political structures we are not artists.'" *Religion:* "I believe in spiritual progress." *Residence:* Leonard, Minn. *Agent:* Ray Peekner Literary Agency, 2625 North 36th St., Milwaukee, Wis. 53210.

CAREER: Writer. Has also worked variously as a teacher, field engineer, editor, soldier, actor, director, farmer, rancher, truck driver, trapper, professional archer, migrant farm worker, singer, and sailor. *Military service:* U.S. Army, 1959-62; became sergeant. *Awards, honors:* Central Missouri Award for Children's Literature, 1976; *The Green Recruit* was chosen one of New York Public Library's Books for the Teen Age, 1980, 1981 and 1982, and *Sailing: From Jibs to Jibing,* 1982; *Dancing Carl* was selected one of American Library Association's Best Young Adult Books, 1983, *Tracker,* 1984; Society of Midland Authors Award, 1985, for *Tracker;* Newbury Honor Book, 1986, for *Dogsong,* and 1988, for *Hatchet; Dogsong* was chosen one of Child Study Association of America's Children's Books of the Year, 1986.

Even now with the tracks gone, there is a line of gravel and skunkweed where there used to be ties and steel. ■ (Jacket illustration by Andrew Rhodes from *Popcorn Days and Buttermilk Nights* by Gary Paulsen.)

GARY PAULSEN

WRITINGS—Juvenile books: *Mr. Tucket*, Funk & Wagnalls, 1968; (with Dan Theis) *Martin Luther King: The Man Who Climbed the Mountain*, Raintree, 1976; *The Small Ones* (illustrated by K. Goff and with photographs by Wilford Miller), Raintree, 1976; *The Grass-Eaters: Real Animals* (illustrated by K. Goff and with photographs by W. Miller), Raintree, 1976; *Dribbling, Shooting, and Scoring Sometimes*, Raintree, 1976; *Hitting, Pitching, and Running Maybe*, Raintree, 1976; *Tackling, Running, and Kicking—Now and Again*, Raintree, 1977; *Riding, Roping, and Bulldogging—Almost*, Raintree, 1977; *Careers in an Airport* (illustrated with photographs by Roger Nye), Raintree, 1977; *The CB Radio Caper* (illustrated by John Asquith), Raintree, 1977; *The Curse of the Cobra* (illustrated by J. Asquith), Raintree, 1977; *The Golden Stick*, Raintree, 1977.

Running, Jumping, and Throwing—If You Can (illustrated by Heinz Kluetmeier), Raintree, 1978; *Forehanding and Backhanding—If You're Lucky* (illustrated with photographs by H. Kluetmeier), Raintree, 1978; *Downhill, Hotdogging and Cross-Country—If the Snow Isn't Sticky* (illustrated with photographs by Willis Wood and H. Kluetmeier), Raintree, 1979; *Facing Off, Checking and Goaltending—Perhaps* (illustrated with photographs by Melchior DiGiacomo and H. Kluetmeier), Raintree, 1979; *Going Very Fast in a Circle—If You Don't Run Out of Gas* (illustrated with photographs by H. Kluetmeier and Bob D'Olivo), Raintree, 1979; *Launching, Floating High and Landing—If Your Pilot Light Doesn't Go Out* (illustrated with photographs by H. Kluetmeier), Raintree, 1979; *Pummeling, Falling and Getting Up—Sometimes* (illustrated with photographs by H. Kluetmeier and Joe DiMaggio), Raintree, 1979; *Track, Enduro and Motocross—Unless You Fall Over* (illustrated with photographs by H. Kluetmeier and others), Raintree, 1979; (with Art Browne, Jr.) *TV and Movie Animals*,

Messner, 1980; *Sailing: From Jibs to Jibing* (illustrated by wife, Ruth W. Paulsen), Messner, 1981.

Novels: *The Implosion Effect*, Major Books, 1976; *The Death Specialists*, Major Books, 1976; *Winterkill*, T. Nelson, 1977; *The Foxman*, T. Nelson, 1977; *Tiltawhirl John*, T. Nelson, 1977; *C. B. Jockey*, Major Books, 1977; *The Night the White Deer Died*, T. Nelson, 1978; *Hope and a Hatchet*, T. Nelson, 1978; (with Ray Peekner) *The Green Recruit*, Independence Press, 1978; *The Spitball Gang*, Elsevier/Nelson, 1980; *Campkill*, Pinnacle Books, 1981; *The Sweeper*, Harlequin, 1981; *Clutterkill*, Harlequin, 1982; *Popcorn Days and Buttermilk Nights*, Lodestar Books, 1983; *Dancing Carl*, Bradbury, 1983; *Tracker*, Bradbury, 1984; *Dogsong*, Bradbury, 1985; *Sentries*, Bradbury, 1986; *Murphy*, Walker, 1987; *The Crossing*, F. Watts, 1987; *Hatchet*, Bradbury, 1987.

Nonfiction: *The Special War*, Sirkay, 1966; *Some Birds Don't Fly*, Rand McNally, 1969; *The Building a New, Buying an Old, Remodeling a Used Comprehensive Home and Shelter Book*, Prentice-Hall, 1976; *Farm: A History and Celebration of the American Farmer*, Prentice-Hall, 1977; (with John Morris) *Hiking and Backpacking* (illustrated by Ruth Wright), Simon & Schuster, 1978; (with J. Morris) *Canoeing, Kayaking, and Rafting* (illustrated by John Peterson and Jack Storholm), Simon & Schuster, 1979; *Beat the System: A Survival Guide*, Pinnacle Books, 1983.

Plays: "Communications" (one-act), first produced in New Mexico at a local group theatre, 1974; "Together-Apart" (one-act), first produced in Denver at Changing Scene Theatre, 1976.

Also author of *Meteor*, and more than 200 short stories and articles.

WORK IN PROGRESS: Madonna, a collection of stories; collaborating on a book with a Soviet writer.

SIDELIGHTS: Born **May 17, 1939** in Minneapolis, Minnesota. "I'm only a second-generation American. My father's family came to this country from Denmark; my mother's people emigrated from Norway and Sweden. My father was a career military man who served as an officer on General Patton's staff during World War II. He spent most of my childhood years fighting the Germans, and my mother spent the war years working in a munitions plant in Chicago—'Rosie the Riveter' type stuff. I was reared by my grandmother and several aunts. I first saw my father when I was seven in the Philippines where my parents and I lived from 1946 until 1949.

"After we returned to the States, we moved around constantly. I lived in every state. The longest time I spent in one school was for about five months. I was an 'Army brat,' and it was a miserable life. School was a nightmare because I was unbelievably shy, and terrible at sports. I had no friends, and teachers ridiculed me. I wound up skipping most of the ninth grade and had to make it up during the tenth grade so I could graduate on time. As it was, I squeezed through with 'C's and 'D's. And there were family problems. My father drank a lot, and there would be terrible arguments. Again, I was sent to live with relatives. In order to buy clothes and have some spending money, I worked at a young age. For a while I sold *The Grand Forks Herald* in hospitals and bars; during junior high school I set up pins every night in a bowling alley. Had

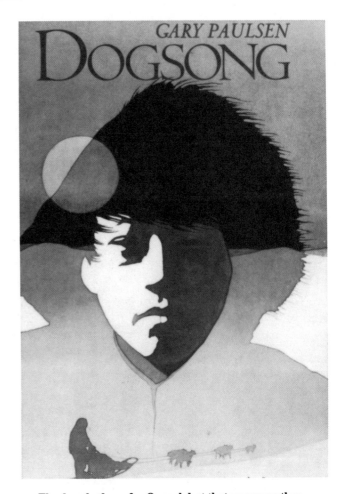

The dogs had run for Oogruk but that was more than two years earlier. They had not run since for anybody.
■ (Jacket illustration by Neil Waldman from *Dogsong* by Gary Paulsen.)

teen suicide been a topic in the news as it is today, had it in any way suggested a way out, I know I would have seriously considered the possibility.

"But I did have 'safety nets'—all of them women. My grandmother and aunts were terribly important to me. And there was someone else. One day as I was walking past the public library in twenty below temperatures, I could see the reading room bathed in a beautiful golden light. I went in to get warm and to my absolute astonishment the librarian walked up to me and asked if I wanted a library card. She didn't care if I looked right, wore the right clothes, dated the right girls, was popular at sports—none of those prejudices existed in the public library. When she handed me the card, she handed me the world. I can't even describe how liberating it was. She recommended westerns and science fiction but every now and then would slip in a classic. I roared through everything she gave me and in the summer read a book a day. It was as though I had been dying of thirst and the librarian had handed me a five-gallon bucket of water. I drank and drank."

1957-1958. Attended Bemidji College. "As I'd grown up hunting and trapping, I was able to pay my way through the first year by laying trap lines for the State of Minnesota."

1959-62. Served in the U.S. Army; attained rank of Sergeant. "I worked with missiles. When I got out of the service, I took

(Jacket illustration by Jon Weiman from *Tracker* by Gary Paulsen.)

Maybe Carl wasn't dancing, but just being and they didn't know how to do that. ■ (Jacket illustration by Jon Weiman from *Dancing Carl* by Gary Paulsen.)

extension courses and accrued enough credits to become a field engineer.''

1962-1966. Worked as a field engineer in the aerospace departments of Bendix and Lockheed. ''I worked on the Gemini shots, the Mariner probes and on designing the guidance section for the Shrike, an anti-radar missile. I was good at my work, but didn't like it.''

''I was sitting in a satellite tracking station in California in front of a massive console and related computers . . . I'd finished reading a magazine article on flight-testing a new airplane during an inactive period, and thought, *Gad,* what a way to make a living—writing about something you like and getting paid for it! I remembered writing some of my past reports, some fictionalized versions I'd included. And I thought: What the hell, I *am* an engineering writer.

''But, conversely, I also realized I didn't know a thing about writing—*professionally.* After several hours of hard thinking, a way to earn came to me. All I had to do was go to work editing a magazine.'' [Franz Serdahely, ''Prolific Paulsen,'' *Writer's Digest,* January, 1980.[1]]

''So I wrote a totally fictitious resume which landed me an associate editorship on a men's magazine in Hollywood, California. It took them about two day to find out that I knew nothing about publishing. I didn't know what a lay-out sheet was, let alone how to do one. My secretary—who was all of

(Jacket illustration by Richard Cuffari from *The Foxman* by Gary Paulsen.)

nineteen years old—edited my first three issues. They could see I was serious about wanting to learn, and they were willing to teach me. We published some excellent writers—Steinbeck, Bradbury, Ellison—which was great training and exposure for me.''

''I was there for about a year, and it was the best of all possible ways to learn about writing. It probably did more to improve my craft and ability than any other single event in my life.''[1]

While living in California, Paulsen did a considerable amount of work as a film extra. ''Once I played a drunken Indian in a movie called *Flap* starring Anthony Quinn. I was on screen for about thirty-five seconds.'' Paulsen also took up sculpting, and won 'Best in Show' at an exhibit in Santa Barbara. ''I worked mostly at wood carving, which I love. But by then I knew I wanted to be writing, and backed off from sculpture. I didn't feel I could do justice to both.''

His first book, *The Special War,* was based on interviews he did with servicemen returning from Viet Nam. ''The other war story I covered was the Watts riot. And let me tell you, the racial 'disturbances' as they were sometimes referred to then, were out-and-out battles.''

After twelve years as a writer, Paulsen had become one of the most prolific authors in the country, having published nearly 40 books, over 200 magazine articles and short stories, and two plays. He wrote nonfiction on hunting, trapping, farming, animals, medicine and outdoor life, as well as juvenile and adult fiction. On a bet with a friend, he once wrote eleven articles and short stories inside four days and sold all of them. To burn off tension, he was given to long walks around his Minnesota farm during which he would ''blow the hell out of a hillside''[1] with a rifle.

Paulsen's life was changed radically and abruptly after the 1977 publication of his novel *Winterkill;* he was sued for libel. ''My attorney, Margaret Troyer, a full-blooded Chippewa, is now a reservation Magistrate. Our case went all the way up to the Minnesota Supreme Court, where we finally won. It was a good fight, and I'd do it all over again, but it brought me to the edge of bankruptcy. And I didn't get the support I'd expected from my publisher. In fact, the whole situation was so nasty and ugly that I stopped writing. I wanted nothing more to do with publishing and burned my bridges, so to speak.

''So there I was, living deep in the country in northern Minnesota with no way to earn a living. Having no choice in the matter, I went back to trapping for the state. It was predator control work, aimed at coyotes and beavers. The traps we used were snares, which kill the animals right away. It's not pleasant, but it's humane, if death can be humane. I was working a 60-mile line mostly on foot, sometimes on skis, going out in the early morning and heading home at night. Very slow work.

''One day a guy name Bob McWilliams came to my house saying he had four dogs—sprint team used to doing 12-mile races—he couldn't keep. As we were so broke we didn't even have a car, the prospect of *any* sort of transportation was very inviting. And besides, the dogs were free. This team was real slow, but they did make my work much easier. One day about midnight we were crossing Clear Water Lake, which is about three miles long. There was a full moon shining so brightly on the snow you could read by it. There was no one around, and all I could hear was the rhythm of the dogs' breathing as they pulled the sled. We came to the top of a hill, the steam from the dogs' breath all but hid their bodies—the entire world, seemed to glisten. It almost stopped my heart; I'd never seen anything so beautiful. I stayed out with the dogs for seven days. I didn't go home—my wife was frantic,—I didn't check line, I just ran the dogs, sixty to seventy miles an hour. We covered a lot of northern Minnesota. For food, we had a few beaver carcasses. You know, you don't train these northern breeds to pull sleds. It's part of their genetic make-up. When a puppy gets to be seven months old, you put a harness on him and he'll pull a sled. I was initiated into this incredibly ancient and very beautiful bond, and it was as if everything that had happened to me before ceased to exist. When I came off that seven-day run, I pulled all my traps, having resolved never again to kill.

"Shortly afterward, McWilliams told me about the Iditarod, a 1200-mile dogsled race that goes from Iditarod, an old mining town in the middle of Alaska, to Nome. On the spur of the moment, I announced, 'Sure, I'll run.' I had no idea what I was in for. And I certainly never figured I could raise the money it takes to get a team together and so on. It was getting down to the wire when Richard Jackson, the publisher of Bradbury Press, called wanting to know what I was writing. Now I had never met or worked with Jackson. 'I'm not writing! I'm running dogs!' I told him. I was hard up for the upcoming Iditarod. 'I'll send you the money,' he said, 'and when you get around to writing something, let me be the first to see it.'

"So I ran the Iditarod—a mind-boggling experience. You don't sleep for seventeen days. You begin to hallucinate. You are not allowed any outside assistance. If you make a mistake, you are left to die. Even the CBS helicopters covering the event can't intervene. You have no physical contact with your dogs—it's all voice commands given from where you stand on the back of the sled. If your lead dog doesn't like and respect you, the odds are good that you will die. If the dogs sense that you are losing your nerve, they may simply stop, make craters in the snow, roll up in a ball and sleep for days. That's called 'cratering' and once they start, there's absolutely nothing you can do to stop it. The dogs may also go berserk and trash the sled. And there you are, all alone in the middle of Alaska. The dogs are deeply intuitive and incredibly smart, far more intelligent than most people.

"When you first start the race, you feel great, exhilarated by the unbelievable beauty of your surroundings. After about eight miles of navigating the Arctic Circle, you start to feel scared. After twelve miles, you realize that you are nothing and the dogs are everything. To survive, you must be in deep harmony with your team. The Iditarod may sound like a macho thrill, but it's the opposite. You go where death goes, and death doesn't give a damn about macho. Besides, the last two races were won by women.

"Here's something that was brought home to me: macho is a lie. It's testicular garbage. Core toughness and compassion are the opposite of macho. The absence of fear comes with knowledge, not strength or bravura. More people should be telling this to young people, instead of 'climb the highest mountain and kill something.'"

Paulsen's experiences with the dogs and the resulting transformations motivated him to continue with his writing. *Dancing Carl* was published in 1983 by Richard Jackson's Bradbury Press and had its first incarnation as a dance. "I began it when I was trapping beaver. It was a narrative ballet for two dancers with original music by John Collins and choreography by Nancy Keller. A seven-minute version of this piece was aired on Minnesota Public Television."

(Jacket illustration by Jon Weiman from *Sentries* by Gary Paulsen.)

Tracker, brought out a year later, deals with the metaphysics of tracking an animal. John, the thirteen-year-old protagonist, faces his first season of hunting alone, while his grandfather lay dying of cancer. Said Paulsen, "they're a farm family in northern Minnesota; they have always hunted their meat. 'We take meat with a gun,' John's grandfather tells him. 'It doesn't make you a man. It doesn't make you anything to kill.' What I'm exploring is the almost mystical relationship that develops between the hunter and the hunted. It's a relationship with its own integrity, not to be violated. There is, in the book, the concept of 'giving death' to the deer. I've seen this. At a certain point, the animal senses death coming and accepts it. This acceptance of death is something I was trying to write about in *Tracker.*"

Dogsong also deals with an adolescent boy struggling to become deeply humane. Russell, a fourteen-year-old Eskimo, has sought guidance from Oogruk, a tribal wise man, who counsels him to take his dog team across Alaska and back. En route, Russell finds a pregnant girl about his age, dying of exposure. Helping her to give birth, he does his best to save her life. "I wrote *Dogsong* in camp while I was training my team for the Iditarod. It'd be twenty below, and there I'd sit by the fire writing longhand in my notebook. You know, I miss *Dogsong*. I wish I could keep writing it. It's like a friend who's gone away." The book was named a Newbery Honor Book in 1986, and in 1988, *Hatchet* was also named. "It's like things have come full circle. I felt like nothing the first time I walked into a library, and now library associations are giving me awards. It means a lot to me."

Paulsen is currently working on *Madonna,* a collection of stories intended as a tribute to women who, by virtue of what he calls "core toughness" have deeply impressed him. "It started with Gloria, a friend of mine, who's two sons (out of a total of five kids) were born with spina bifida, and a husband with a drinking problem. Not only has she kept her family together for twenty-five years, but she's recently gone to college for a nursing degree and has consistently been at the top of her class. That got me started looking at the ladies in my family. They amaze me. Women are inevitably emotionally tougher than men. I want to understand their kind of toughness, and so feel that I must write about it."

"I don't think there's any attempt on the part of men (writers) to understand what women are or the influence they have on our lives. Incidentally, my grandmother taught me how to crochet. When I was in battle or doing some of the other hard things in life, I found I had a tempering, a soft influence that I could use. It saved me many hours of agony. The male thing is to have an objective and go out and get it done. You can't stop. . . . And when you try one of these things and fail, you have this feminine influence to fall back on. You can lean back and say, all right, maybe the male side is crushed because I didn't make it, but I can also have compassion. I can try to understand my failure and I can try to learn from it." [Maryann N. Weidt, "Gary Paulsen: A Sentry for Peace," *Voice of Youth Advocates,* August/October, 1986.[2]]

"I have about seven stories so far for *Madonna.* I've been doing performances of them with John Collins who has composed music. Some of the pieces are read, others sung. I don't know if they'll eventually find their form in a book, or if they are meant to be sung, painted, or danced.

"I write because it's all I can do," admits Paulsen. "Every time I've tried to do something else I cannot, and have to come back to writing, though often I hate it—hate it and love it. It's much like being a slave, I suppose, and in slavery there is a kind of freedom that I find in writing: a perverse thing. I'm not 'motivated,' as you put it. Nor am I particularly driven. I write because it's all there is."

Paulsen writes for a youth market because for his part he feels that it's "artistically fruitless to write for adults. Adults created the mess which we are struggling to outlive. Adults have their minds set. Art reaches out for newness, and adults aren't new. And Adults aren't truthful. The concept behind . . . *Sentries,* is that young people know the score. *Sentries* is mostly a lot of questions, and I'm betting that young people have the answers."

His work habits have changed considerably over the years. He now does most of his writing on computer. "I even have a portable Radio Shack model I can take camping with me. When I was training dogs, we would run six hours on, four off. During my 'down time' in camp, I'd write. But these days, I'm camping less and less, and hardly running dogs at all. I'm building an office on my property with more advanced computers, modem links and the like. I find I do a lot more revision now that I work on computer. Diskettes are perfect for raw research. It's a new form and perfect for experimentation."

Paulsen gives public readings, performances, and storytelling in small towns near his Minnesota farm. "It's real nice. Generally, it takes place in a town hall. People bring coffee, bake cakes and pies. There's a coal stove. Everyone sits around listening and swapping tales.

"I'm also building a garden. The first thing I do every day is go into my garden and meditate. I try to become serene and write from whatever reservoir of serenity I find within myself."

Paulsen also devotes a good deal of his time to nuclear disarmament causes. "I believe that governments are standing in the way of solving this thing. It's up to private citizens. We cannot let our children grow up terrified of being blown apart by a thermonuclear device. Last spring, my fifteen-year-old son and I sat down and wrote a letter to the Soviet Writers Union. A simple letter to let them know we have no desire to blow them up, that we do not consider them the 'Evil Empire' (as does our President). Everyone should write letters—it makes a difference." In response to the letter Paulsen was invited to discuss his work with a delegation of Russian writers who met in Minneapolis. Furthermore, one of the Soviet writers and Paulsen plan to collaborate on a book in an effort to spread good will between our two nations.

—Based on an interview by Marguerite Feitlowitz

FOR MORE INFORMATION SEE: Franz Serdahely, "Prolific Paulsen," *Writer's Digest,* January, 1980; Maryann N. Weidt, "Gary Paulsen: A Sentry for Peace," *Voice of Youth Advocates,* August/October, 1986.

PEAVY, Linda 1943-

PERSONAL: Born November 5, 1943, in Hattiesburg, Miss.; daughter of Wyatt Gaines (a forest products dealer) and Claribel (a teacher; maiden name, Hickman) Sellers; married Howard Sidney Peavy (a professor of environmental engineering), December 21, 1962; children: Erica, Don. Education: Mississippi College, B.A., 1964; University of North Carolina, M.A., 1970. Home: 521 South Sixth, Bozeman, Mont. 59715. Office: P.S., A Partnership, 1104 South Fifth, Bozeman, Mont. 59715.

LINDA PEAVY

CAREER: Central High School, Jackson, Miss., teacher of English and journalism, 1964-66; Glen Oaks Senior High School, Baton Rouge, La., teacher of English, 1966-69; Oklahoma Baptist University, Shawnee, instructor in English, 1970-74; free-lance writer, 1974—; P.S., A Partnership, Bozeman, Mont., partner and writer, 1980—. Poet/writer with Montana Arts Council, 1982—. Gives readings (sometimes on radio programs) and workshops. *Member:* Society of Children's Book Writers, Montana Institute of the Arts, Author's Guild, National Women's Studies Association. *Awards, honors:* With Ursula Smith, Paladin Award for Best Article in *Montana, the Magazine of Western History,* 1985; *Dreams into Deeds* was selected a Notable Children's Trade Book in the Field of Social Studies by the National Council for Social Studies and the Children's Book Council, 1986, and one of Child Study Association's Children's Books of the Year, 1987; fiction writing residency, Ucross Foundation, Ucross, Wyo., 1987; grants from the American Association of University Women and the Montana Committee for "Molders and Shapers: Montana Women's Community Builders," 1987; with U. Smith, residency in nonfiction at Centrum, Port Townsend, Wash., 1988.

WRITINGS—For young people: *Allison's Grandfather* (picture book; illustrated by Ronald Himler), Scribner, 1981; (with Ursula Smith) *Food, Nutrition, and You,* Scribner, 1982; (with U. Smith) *Women Who Changed Things: Nine Lives That Made a Difference,* Scribner, 1983; (with U. Smith) *Dreams into Deeds: Nine Women Who Dared,* Scribner, 1985.

Other: (With Jere Day) *The Complete Book of Rockcrafting,* Drake, 1976; *Have a Healthy Baby: A Guide to Prenatal Nu-* *trition and Nutrition for Nursing Mothers,* Drake, 1977; *Canyon Cookery: A Gathering of Recipes and Recollections from Montana's Scenic Bridger Canyon,* Artcraft, 1978; (with Andrea Pagenkopf) *Grow Healthy Kids! A Parents' Guide to Sound Nutrition,* Grosset, 1980; *A Feathered Shadow* (poetry), Pierian Press (Canada), 1984; "Family: A Portrait for Today" (musical; arrangements by Michael McGill), first produced by Missoula Children's Theatre, 1984; (with U. Smith) "Pamelia" (three-act opera; music by Eric Funk), choral version produced at Carnegie Hall, New York, N.Y., spring, 1989.

Work represented in anthologies, including *With Joy: Poems for Children,* edited by T. E. Wade, Jr., Gazelle, 1976; *The Poetry of Horses,* edited by William Cole, Scribner, 1979; *Rapunzel, Rapunzel,* edited by Katharyn Machan Aal, McBooks Press, 1980; *Cracks in the Ark,* edited by Richard Morgan and Phyllis Fischer, Writers for Animal Rights, 1982. Contributor of poems, articles and stories to periodicals, including *Papers of the Bibliographical Society of America, Shakespeare Quarterly, Oklahoma Teacher, South Dakota Review, Mothering, New Oxford Review, Frontiers, Cobblestone, Texas Review, Cottonwood Review, South Dakota Review, Pierian Spring, Southern Exposure, Antigonish Review,* and *Old Hickory Review.*

WORK IN PROGRESS: The Widows of Little Falls, with U. Smith; *When Papa Comes Home,* a juvenile historical novel, with U. Smith; *You, Me, and Poetry,* a text on writing poetry; *A Tangle of Kudzu,* stories for adults; *Women in Waiting: The Home Frontier in the Westward Movement,* with U. Smith.

Erica remembered Allison's grandfather on the ranch. He hadn't been dying then. ■ (From *Allison's Grandfather* by Linda Peavy. Illustrated by Ronald Himler.)

SIDELIGHTS: "Poetry and fiction allow me to express the feelings that are mine during one small moment in time. The poem or story that results from this expression of feeling about a single event, person, or place represents my own personal perspective on this one aspect of life. It is simply that—a single person's view on a single aspect of life. Only when it is shared with others does the intensely personal expression take on another dimension.

"Different kinds of sharing bring different rewards. Since readers seldom correspond with authors, I have only the re-actions of editors, critics, and friends by which to judge whether my published work has spoken to others. Conversely, read-ings, workshops, and presentations in schools and communi-ties all allow for a more direct sharing. It is in that sharing that I realize my poems have value for those fellow travelers who seem to need to have their private perceptions expressed by a writer. It is as if such an expression somehow validates the worth of the inward journey for us all.

"For two of my nonfiction books, *The Complete Book of Rockcrafting* and *Grow Healthy Kids!,* I was the writer and another woman was the expert, and I thoroughly enjoyed both projects. But I've found my greatest satisfaction in working with another writer whose love of research, writing, and ed-iting are equal to my own. Though my writing partner and I have worked together (as well as separately) on many nonfic-tion projects, working on women's biographies has become our obsession. We're fierce admirers of those women whose accomplishments show that they never regarded overwhelming odds against success as insurmountable obstacles.

"Many beginning writers seem to see writing for children as an 'easy' way to break into print, I consider writing for chil-dren and young adults as one of the greatest challenges a se-rious writer can accept."

HOBBIES AND OTHER INTERESTS: Hiking, birdwatching, backpacking, cross-country skiing.

LOUISE DICKINSON RICH

RICH, Louise Dickinson   1903-

PERSONAL: Born June 14, 1903, in Huntington, Mass.; daughter of James Henry (a newspaper editor) and Florence Myrtie (Stewart) Dickinson; married Ralph Eugene Rich (a businessman), August 27, 1934 (died, 1945); children: Rufus, Dinah. *Education:* Massachusetts State Teachers' College, B.Sc., 1924.

CAREER: Has worked as a high school English teacher in New Hampshire, New Jersey and Bridgewater, Mass.; writer. *Awards, honors:* New York Herald Tribune's Children's Spring Book Festival Award, 1949, for *Start of the Trail: The Story of a Young Maine Guide; Star Island Boy* was chosen one of Child Study Association of America's Children's Books of the Year, 1968, and *King Philip's War, 1675-76,* 1972.

WRITINGS: We Took to the Woods, Lippincott, 1942; *Happy the Land,* Lippincott, 1946; *Start of the Trail: The Story of a Young Maine Guide* (young adult), Lippincott, 1949; *My Neck of the Woods,* Lippincott, 1950; *Trail to the North* (young adult), Lippincott, 1952; *Only Parent,* Lippincott, 1953; *In-nocence under the Elms,* Lippincott, 1955; *The Coast of Maine: An Informal History,* Crowell, 1956; *Mindy,* Lippincott, 1959.

The First Book of New World Explorers, F. Watts, 1960; *The First Book of the Early Settlers,* F. Watts, 1960; *The First Book of the Vikings,* F. Watts, 1962; *The Natural World of Louise Dickinson Rich,* Dodd, 1962; *The Forest Years* (con-tains *We Took to the Woods* and *My Neck of the Woods*), Lippincott, 1963; *The First Book of China Clippers,* F. Watts, 1963; *State O'Maine,* Harper, 1964; *The First Book of the Fur Trade,* F. Watts, 1965; *The First Book of Lumbering,* F. Watts, 1967; *The Kennebec River,* Holt, 1967; *Star Island Boy* (il-lustrated by Elinor Jaeger), F. Watts, 1968; *Three of a Kind* (Junior Literary Guild selection; illustrated by William M. Hutchinson), F. Watts, 1970; *The Peninsula,* Chatham Press, 1971; *King Philip's War, 1675-76: The New England Indians Fight the Colonists,* F. Watts, 1972; *Summer at High Kingdom* (Junior Literary Guild selection), F. Watts, 1975.

Contributor to periodicals, including *Reader's Digest, Out-door Life,* and *Woman's Day.*

SIDELIGHTS: Born on **June 14, 1903** in Huntington, Massa-chusetts; raised in the small town of Bridgewater. "That's the way Bridgewater is now, and that's the way it was when I was a child: just another New England town.

"When I was a child, though, it didn't seem like that. It didn't seem *like* anything. It was where my sister Alice and I lived with our mother and father, and that was all there was to it. There wasn't any other place, any other trees and streets and houses and people and dogs and horses and cats, anywhere in our experience.

"Bridgewater wasn't subject to any opinion or judgment. It wasn't a pretty town or an ugly town or a wonderful or deadly town. It just *was* to be seen, heard, smelled, touched and tasted, but never questioned. We knew what water was, nat-urally, and what a bridge was. And yet we didn't wonder why a village nowhere near a body of water and certainly not con-spicuously overstocked with bridges should be called Bridgewater.

"Our family occupied a rather equivocal position in Bridge-water, which, like all New England towns of the day, had a fairly rigid social structure. There were the Old Families, whose ancestors were original settlers, or nearly enough as didn't

(Cover illustration from *Summer at High Kingdom* by Louise Dickinson Rich.)

matter, and who lived in the houses that had been handed down to them through several generations. . . .

"At the other extreme were the Foreigners, the immigrants who in those days before the Immigration Act of 1921, with its establishment of quotas, poured into this country. . . . Most of them were Italians, Portuguese, Armenians and Poles—known as Polanders, and the term Polander included Lithuanians, Latvians, and Estonians—with a few Greeks, Russians and Spaniards thrown in. The Irish didn't count as Foreigners, probably because they spoke English, or perhaps because they so quickly made themselves so thoroughly at home. The real Foreigners often couldn't speak any English at all when they arrived, and they lived down across the railroad tracks, keeping themselves pretty much to themselves. . . .

"In between these two extremes were several classifications. There was the Normal Click. At least that's the way it was pronounced and the way I thought it was spelled, although it must have been the local version of *clique*. This consisted of the teachers at the Normal School and their families. They rated high on the social scale, combining as they did respectability with the intellectual. So did the ministers of the six Protestant churches. . . .

"We Dickinsons didn't fall into any of these categories. We came from Huntington, two hundred miles away at the other end of the state, a long way in the days when the automobile was only a fad of the wealthy and doomed to short favor. It's true, we rated as Old Settlers back there. One ancestor founded South Hadley and another not only founded but was scalped by the Indians at Northfield; a collateral relation, Emily, was the talk of Amherst and the literary world with her eccentric behavior and her poetry; another of the Dickinson girls married Cyrus Field, who astonished his in-laws by becoming responsible for the laying of the Atlantic cable; my own grandfather was a Congregational minister known and loved throughout the Berkshires; and the city of Springfield was full of Dickinson Streets and Dickinson Squares. But all this cut no ice in Bridgewater, where we were just fly-by-nights, or dark horses, or whatever else anybody wanted to call us, except Foreigners. . . ." [Louise Dickinson Rich, *Innocence under the Elms*, Lippincott, 1955.[1]]

Her father was sole owner-editor-publisher-printer of a local newspaper. ". . . The *Independent* was strictly a one-man enterprise, involving no social, business, or fraternal bonds. . . . It wasn't friendship that had put my father on the track of the *Independent*. He'd been working on the Westfield *Valley Echo* and fostering the newspaperman's dream of owning his own little weekly. So when he saw one advertised for sale, he bought it from a man named Pliny Jewell, a total stranger.

"Why did he do it? Because he wanted to be left alone to go his own pace. Because he wanted not only to think his own thoughts, but to express them without censorship; not only to hold his own opinions, but to declare them openly. Because he wanted nobody to tell him what to do or say or think except his own conscience and intelligence. Because he'd rather have less and be more. Because, in brief, he was a Dickinson.

Gulls are more teachable than I would have thought possible for birdbrains. ■ (From *The Peninsula* by Louise Dickinson Rich. Illustrated by Grattan Condon.)

"Our father was not a particularly imposing figure. He was a rather small man, with a low voice, a mild manner, and a habit of listening, more than he talked. He had blue eyes and fine, blond, curly hair, a fact that struck [my sister] Alice and me, stuck with our mother's brown eyes and straight hair, as being supremely unfair. But there wasn't much we could do about it except fuss.

"It's possible that our father's quiet ways were the result of having to live with three talkative females. If driven to it by lack of other audience, we sometimes talked to the cats or to ourselves, and our father must sometimes have found it hard to get a word in edgewise. I don't think it bothered him much.

He just let the clatter go in one ear and out the other, while he pursued his own thoughts. He didn't miss much by not listening to us. We never had anything very important to say anyhow; and the same thing was true of our father that I have observed in other quiet and thoughtful people. They seem to have some sort of subconscious monitor that warns them when they'd better come back to earth and take an interest in proceedings. Our father always heard anything worth hearing.

"As to what else he and the *Independent* gave Alice and me, it's hard to say. I know that doctors' sons frequently turn out to be good mechanics, and ditch-diggers' daughters often make wonderful fashion designers or concert pianists. So maybe it's

Rich with son, Rufus, and Kyak.

Rich with husband, Ralph, and son, Rufus.

only by coincidence that today Alice is an editor of children's books, and I call myself a writer.

"The climax of the week for the Dickinson family was, of course, Thursday, Publication Day. Everything built up to press time—late afternoon, early evening, or late night, depending on a lot of things. The day started at seven in the morning and ended when the mail sacks of papers were safely bestowed in the vestibule of the Post Office, which could be in the small hours of Friday morning. In any case, the Post Office was always closed and the lucky, lucky employees, who had a definite quitting time, gone about their private affairs. So the vestibule was left unlocked for us, so that the papers could be left for distribution into boxes and delivery sacks by the first clerk to arrive next day.

"The *Independent* had to be in circulation Friday morning. Not only was our father's professional pride at stake, but there was also the matter of the Advertisers who were running ads for weekend sales, which would be so much wasted ink if we failed in our contract.

"The whole family moved to the Office on Publication Day. When we were very young, there wasn't very much Alice and I could do to expedite progress except be quiet and keep out from under foot. We found a number of ways to amuse ourselves in what might have seemed to the uninitiated eye an unpromising and sterile field, the tiny, cramped Office corner

to which we were confined in the interests of not bothering those at work. We sat at the desk, and drew pictures and wrote stories. We typed our manuscripts on the old Oliver, although between its eccentricities and our lack of skill, they were seldom recognizable as English composition. We made jewelry for ourselves by linking paper clips into chains. We took everything out of the desk drawers, dusted them, and returned the contents neatly. We could do this every Thursday, since in a week's time the drawers would again be hoorah's nests.

"Someone had left a whole file of old bound copies of a children's magazine called *The Chatterbox* piled up in a corner—I don't know why, since they had no bearing whatsoever on the functioning of the *Independent*—and we spent hours and hours reading them. They were full of quaint moral tales about little girls who even to our inexperience seemed innocent to the point of feeble-mindedness. But they were something to read. In fair weather, before it grew dark, we made frequent sallies down into the Square, just to see what was going on.

"I'm sure my father was operating on a shoestring.... That is undoubtedly why during all my childhood we always lived in rented houses, in a town where almost everybody owned his own home.... Be that as it may, Alice and I have no Olde Family Homestead to look back on with nostalgia. We have a series of them.

"Nobody told my mother that moving all over town was going to give us a sense of insecurity; and I guess it wouldn't have

Wash day at Forest Lodge.

made any difference if they had, except to provide her with one more thing to worry about. When we had to move, we had to move. By the time we were old enough to pay attention to what went on, moving was an old story to us. In fact, we grew to like moving. . . .

"In a day when it was neither fashionable nor common for wives and mothers in good standing to work outside the home, our mother worked. Nobody else's mother did, and we tried to convince ourselves that what our mother did was not really working, but just helping our father. For some reason, that made it seem a little less peculiar, and us a little less unlike other children. Our mother worked, all right, no matter how we chose to regard it. She worked hard, selling advertising space, setting type, correcting proof, and collecting local news items, all day Wednesday and Thursday and a large part of Tuesday. Nobody had to tell us, because it was in the very air we breathed, that nothing could interfere with getting out the paper. The sun rose in the morning, water ran down hill, and the *Independent* was printed late on Thursday, for sale Friday morning.

"There were other constants in our lives besides the brooding shadow of publication day, which made all this flittering about

from one house that had seen better days to another of the same ilk less unsettling than it might have been. We never had to change schools for one thing, or Sunday Schools. You could move from one side of the town to the opposite side and still be within easy walking distance of Central Square and the church and school. We didn't have to break into a new gang, either. No matter where we moved, we already knew the children who lived in that neighborhood, from school association. At first, of course, we didn't know them as well as the ones we'd left behind, but very soon the emphasis shifted, so that boon companions of yesteryear became this year's recess-time-only cronies. We didn't have secrets with them any more, but we still liked them. Our secrets we reserved for those with whom we spent our Saturdays, those who now lived closest; all except for the top secrets. Those were between Alice and me, serving as fixed points in each others' shifting frames of reference. We took the same beat-up old furniture along with us wherever we went, too, and the same pets, and the same family institutions. We learned early that short of death, possibly, there is no escape. Wherever you may run, certain things go along with you."[1]

Rich's constant childhood companion was Alice, her sister who was two years younger. "When I was very young indeed,

I thought that everybody had a sister like mine, a second self, who thought and felt and acted in complete accord and sympathy with one. Later, naturally, when school attendance exposed me to the facts of life, I found that such was not the case. . . . Some girls had sisters whom they didn't even like very much; and some poor girls didn't have any sisters. All this I knew, because I saw it with my own eyes; but I couldn't imagine it being my lot, and I still can't.

"There is—or there can be—a very special relationship between near and dear and only sisters that is like no other relationship on earth. I know. I don't say that it is better than the bond between brother and sister, or mother and child, or husband and wife. There just isn't any comparison possible. . . .

"With your sister, if she is of about your own age, you share everything. You're of the same sex, with its emotional and physiological idiosyncrasies; you have the same parents and uncles and aunts and cousins, the same home background, the same training and cumulative daily experience, the same heredity. You eat the same food, wash with the same brand of soap, read the same books, breathe the same air. You suffer the same apprehensions (The Black Stick), uphold the same standards ('*We* don't cry'), cherish the same dreams (Wally Reid under the stairs), and giggle at the same jokes which nobody else finds funny, since they have been developed bit by microscopic bit over years that no one else has shared in such intimate and complete detail. You have private catchwords by which you can convey volumes to your sister, but which to anybody else sound like incomprehensible doubletalk. How can you help being close to a person like that?

"It wasn't in our minds only that Alice and I were as inseparable as the two halves of an apple. Everybody always spoke of us, and probably thought of us, as linked—the Dickinson sisters, or Louisenalice Dickinson. This started when we were very young indeed, in the first and third grades, before Alice gained a year on me scholastically."[1]

Together the Dickinson girls explored their new neighborhoods. When not outdoors, they explored books. "Our ruling passion was books. I can remember well the day I discovered that I could read. Up to that time, our parents had read to us. It didn't make any difference what they read. If our father was reading to himself, he just went on from wherever he was, aloud. We probably didn't understand a tenth of what was read to us, but some of it stuck, and we liked to be read to anyhow. We'd sit as still as mice while the reader's voice went on and on, giving us glimpses of a fabulous world outside our experience. What we didn't understand we asked about, and if the explanation didn't clear matters up, we pretended that it did, so that the reading would go on.

"Besides the books that we withdrew from the library, we read everything else, appropriate or inappropriate, that we could lay hands on. The only thing I was never able to get through was the *Pickwick Papers;* and I haven't succeeded to this day. I found it dull then, and I find it dull now. . . . For some reason it was a matter of honor to read a book through, if once you started it; and our long-range program was eventually to read every book in the world. . . .

"We had a lot of games that we played together, and a great many of them were based on our reading. One of the best was Robinson Crusoe, but we couldn't play this very often, since we'd laid down some binding rules in connection with it. There was no reason why we had to abide by these rules or, if it comes to that, no particular sense to the rules in the first place. But the young have deep-seated craving for order, and the

observance of rules provides it, especially if they are rules of your own making.

"We became completely enamored of and absorbed in the outdoors, and I think perhaps that's one of the reasons we grew up so slowly. When other girls of our age were going to dance school, we were brushing out and blazing a trail through the underbrush to the hut we'd built on the edge of the creek. We refused flatly to have any part of dancing school, a silly waste of time and money. When other girls were spending cold winter afternoons stewing in the house and talking about clothes and boys, we were down at the pond skating, or out in the woods tracking rabbits; or on a hot summer day, instead of sitting in hammocks and preserving our complexions, we were in the sun-drenched fields or shadowy woods, looking, listening, tasting, smelling. It was a phase we should have succumbed to and recovered from at a much earlier age, probably, but we didn't. . . ."[1]

Rich's intense love for the outdoors made it difficult for her to sit in school during the year. "The only time during my childhood when I did not feel the grim shadow of school hanging over me was for about three weeks each summer during July. It took me that long to shake off the effect of the school year just completed; and then August loomed. By any calendar I had ever seen, the end of August meant the first of September, and September meant hated, inevitable school. I loathed school so much that just thinking about it gave me a stomachache; and sometimes during February I would wonder with a sick despair whether I could ever live out the time until June. I always had, but I'd feel that this year was the straw that was going to break this camel's back.

"This wasn't any attitude that I *took*. On the contrary, it took me. In some subjects—reading and composition especially— I did as well as anybody did, and better than most. I was poor in arithmetic, but history and geography offered no special problems. In general, I got pretty good report cards, although not as good as Alice did. Having that fact periodically pointed out at home didn't further endear school to me, in all probability; but it wasn't bad enough to account for my bone-deep and abiding hatred.

"I guess it was primarily a matter of the Dickinson temperament. Dickinsons are not and never have been group-minded. They prefer to operate on their own. They function better alone than with others. They resent—and this is a bad fault—being told anything; and while you can sometimes influence them if you know the right spell to say—for all true Dickinsons have a fatal weakness for words—you can neither drive nor lead them.

"They won't go where the flock goes, even if wandering off to the other end of the range by themselves means that they are going to be hungry and cold. They're not going to be lonesome, that's one sure thing. You can't ever punish a Dickinson by shutting her up in a paddock alone. She enjoys her own company too much. The only time Dickinsons are lonely is when they are in crowds, trying to adjust their slightly offbeat thinking to the accepted trend. They are eccentric in the purely mechanical sense of being a little bit off center.

"Emily Dickinson is an extreme example of Dickinson behavior, but there are plenty of others to illustrate my point. John Dickinson signed the Declaration of Independence, I feel sure, partly because he was seduced by the fine sound of the name of the document, but more because it was at the time the less popular political course to take.

"The old stock has become considerably watered down and weakened of later days; but enough of the former stubborn, nonconformist flavor remains so that I couldn't bear to be shut up with a lot of other kids, being bossed around. I wanted out.

"That's the only way I can account for my first, instinctive, and deathless revolt against going to school. My initial experience was pleasant enough so that I should, had it not been for this heritage, have loved school very much. Bridgewater had one of the few school systems anywhere around in those days to boast a kindergarten. This was because of a set-up peculiar to those towns in which Normal Schools were located. The grade school was partly supported by the state and operated in connection with the State Normal School as a training ground for would-be teachers, and also as a sort of laboratory in which to try out, or to demonstrate to visitors, new ideas in the field of education. . . .

"That's the way things were when I was a child. It's easy to say that things were different and better in one's youth; in fact, so easy that too many people do say it. They were different, yes; but whether they were better or not, I can't say, because I don't know.

"Perhaps it is not the world that is different. Perhaps it is we who have changed. To the eyes of a child, perhaps the world is still a place of wonder and beauty and high adventure. The material and shoddy and meretricious things that have taken the place of our golden dreams and great hopes and instinctive faith may not exist at all except as we have brought them into existence, each one for himself. Perhaps when we started to consider and to weigh, we forgot how to feel; when we started to question, we lost a sure knowledge; when we began to seek, we gave up what we possessed. The elements of which the magic of youth was composed still exist in the universe around us; and if the compound is less rich, less glowing than it used to be, perhaps we have no one but ourselves to blame."[1]

Although she disliked the confines of public school, Rich continued her public education at Massachusetts State Teachers College in Bridgewater. Beginning in 1924, she taught high school English in New Hampshire, New Jersey and Massachusetts and later worked in an institution for the retarded.

On a 1934 canoe trip in northern Maine with her sister, Rich met her future husband, Ralph, a Chicago businessman and Harvard graduate. "We saw a man splitting wood in the yard of the only house we had seen in days, and we stopped to talk to him. He had just arrived there that morning, and he was about to build his first fire and cook his first meal. He invited us to stay and eat with him, because he felt like celebrating. He'd bought the place for a summer camp during the boom years, but he hadn't been able to come East from Chicago, where he lived, since 1929. Now, however, he'd sold some patent rights and not only was he going to spend the summer there, but if things turned out right, the rest of his life. We were all touched and amused, I remember, by his enthusiasm.

"The Winter House," the original Forest Lodge. ■ (From *We Took to the Woods* by Louise Dickinson Rich.)

Jake threw vests into the crowd below. ■ (From *The First Book of Lumbering* by Louise Dickinson Rich. Illustrated by Victor Mays.)

"Now that I know Ralph better, I know that there was nothing strange about his inviting us all to spend the rest of the week with him. . . . But at the time I thought, and I guess all the others thought, that he was crazy. We stayed, though.

"We stayed, and we had a lovely time. We fished and sunbathed and swam, and in between times I found out why a man so obviously dry behind the ears should want to bury himself in the woods for the rest of his life. Ever since he was twelve years old, he had been spending his summers at Coburn's, and his winters wishing it were summer so he could go back to Coburn's. Middle Dam was the place in all the world where he was happiest, and he'd always told himself that someday he's live there permanently. It took a long time and a lot of doing, but finally he'd managed. You see, Ralph, unlike me, has a single-track mind.

"My mind, however, did fall into a single track before that week was over. I became obsessed with the idea that if I didn't see more—a lot more—of this Ralph Rich, I'd quietly go into a decline and die. It's a common phenomenon, I believe, both in fact and in fiction. It doesn't need any explanation, if indeed it can be explained. It's seldom fatal, I understand, so probably I'd have recovered if I'd had to. I didn't have to.

"Almost immediately upon my return to Massachusetts, while I was trying to think up a reasonably plausible excuse for happening back to the Rangeley region at the time of year when people just don't go there, I began getting letters, telegrams, and finally telephone calls, almost daily from Ralph. Then he began spending his time and money on the long and painful trek from Maine to Boston. It was, in short, a Courtship, and ended in the usual manner with our deciding that this was a lot of expensive nonsense, so why didn't we get married?. . . The timing was perfect, and that's how I happen to live in the woods." [Louise Dickinson Rich, *We Took to the Woods in the Forest Years*, Lippincott, 1963.[2]]

During their years in the Maine wilderness, they lived in their camp, Forrest Lodge, on the banks of the Rapid River, and Rich began to write for publication. ". . . I wrote a little number about Maine guides, at my sister's suggestion, for *Scribner's* Life in the United States Contest. I finished it in May, and the contest didn't close until September, so I thought I'd try it out on a couple of dogs first. I'd get it back in plenty of time to qualify.

"Now this is not mock modesty. I was absolutely stupified when the *Saturday Evening Post* bought it. Ralph was, too. But we rallied sufficiently to write another entry for the *Scribner's* contest, since our first had been scratched, as it were, and it won a prize. This double success so went to our heads that we decided that from then on we would be writers.

"We weren't, of course, because being a writer involves a lot more than just thinking it would be nice to be one. We sold our first attempt at fiction—which was probably bad for us as it gave us false confidence—and then we settled down to discover that writing is not all beer and skittles.

"But I think that now, at last, we are nearly writers. We don't wait for inspiration any more, having found that inspiration is mostly the application of the seat of the pants to the seat of a chair. We stall around, trying to put off writing, which I understand is the occupational disease of writers. We earn most of our living by the written word. And we are utterly impatient with people who say, 'I've often thought I could write myself.'"[2] Rich's first book, *We Took to the Woods*, described her Thoreau-like life style. It became a Book-of-the-Month Club selection and was well received by the critics—Clifton Fadiman, writing in the *New Yorker*, called it "uncommonly good reading." A critic from the New York *Herald Tribune* said: "There are moments in her book when she comes close to writing literature."

Working on the principle that you must write about that material which you know best, Rich's next books were also written about her exploits in Northwest Maine, where she lived with her husband, stepdaughter, son and daughter. "When I set out to write . . . I knew exactly what I wanted to do. It had occurred to me that while I had written before of my life and the country here, I had been too selfishly preoccupied with my own problems and the background against which they have

been—more or less—successfully solved to have paid proper attention to one of the chief factors in making that life good, or even possible for me: my friends and neighbors. I wanted—and it sounds quite simple—to tell about them in such a way that others could know and appreciate what kind of people they are and why I admire them so much. . . .

"It is unfortunately true that the writer seldom does what he wants to do; he only does the best he can. Within his heart and mind are feelings and ideas which he wishes to convey; which, indeed, he *must* at least attempt to convey, since he acts under a real compulsion which he cannot deny and remain whole. These ideas may not be important to anyone else, but they are important enough to the writer so that he is willing to spend a great deal of time and energy—and yes, mental anguish, exaggerated as that may sound—on their proper expression, in order that they may be shared with others. Usually he is only partly successful, and that is what makes writing, much of the time, a painful and frustrating occupation: the fact that the product of the labor, in cold print, falls so far short of the living, glowing concept.

"When I read over what I have written, I ordinarily feel just as I do when I try to sing, only worse, because I don't pretend to be a singer and I do try to think that I'm a writer. I can run through whole arias in my head, hearing the full, rich, pear-shaped tons as clearly as anything; and then when I open my mouth all that comes out is a thin, reedy, pitiful squawk. It's damn discouraging. The compensation of writing, I ought to add, comes once in a blue moon, when you recognize with a certainty that nothing can shake that you have somehow managed, for once, to say exactly what you wanted to say, have portrayed a character exactly as he is, have painted a scene in its true colors. Those are the moments which deter a writer from pitching his typewriter into the river and starting to take in washing, as being an easier and surer way of earning a living."[2]

In 1945 her husband died and it became impossible for Rich to cope alone with the hazards of wilderness life and raising her children. In subsequent years she moved to several different small towns in Maine, earning her living writing books and articles for magazines.

She also wrote books for teenagers along with autobiographical books and historical books for children. In 1970 *Three of a Kind* was chosen a Junior Literary Guild selection. It was based on an actual situation. "A few years ago the town of Frenchboro, which is on a small island off the Maine coast, was threatened with the closure of its school because there were too few children to bring the enrollment up to the standards necessary for State aid. Someone suggested the placing of homeless children with island families. Very doubtfully and with many reservations, the Child Welfare Department finally agreed to this. The experiment was wildly successful, and is continued to this day.

"The characters in the book are entirely imaginary; the background is not. The only real person in the book is the cat, Ree-ject, whom I copied from my own homely, self-sufficient cat. But the people, although not real, are exactly like my neighbors and friends along this stretch of the down-East coast. They talk the same and act the same, earn their living from the sea, and entertain themselves in the same ways, whether on the island or the Main. So, in a way, the book is true."

Rich was exploring back roads in Maine and came upon an abandoned house which led to her book *Summer at High Kingdom*. "The windows were broken, the doors sagged, and the clapboards were warped and curling, but even in ruin it was a beautiful house, overlooking a fertile valley far below. Somehow it haunted me. I'd wake up on stormy nights, snug in my own home, and think about it standing there with the wine howling through the empty rooms and the snow gathering on the roof. It was a symbol of loneliness and desertion; and I'd wish someone lived there and loved it. But who?

"During this time the hippies started to come in small groups to the little village where I lived. They were not welcome. They seemed to represent everything distasteful to the prudent, conventional State of Mainers. In time, however, they came to be accepted as the harmless, gentle people they for the most part were.

"It occurred to me that these would be ideal occupants for my old house. They would love its high isolation, its airy view, its spacious rooms and utter peace as much as I did. So I started to write *Summer at High Kingdom*. When it was done I went back for the first time to the house on the ridge. The road was now completely washed out and I had to cover the last mile on foot. Only the chimneys remained standing, rising nobly from a heap of rotting timbers. But strangely, it did not seem as forlorn as I remembered it; and I was glad that I had peopled it, even with imaginary tenants. I could think of it now as having been, if only in my mind, full of life and laughter."

Rich lives in Maine in an old house by the sea. "The house sags with age and old lilac bushes lean on it. I love it—even the doors that won't quite close and the windows that won't stay open. There's a fireplace in every room and the sound of surf all around. I never go much of anywhere. I like it too much here to waste time in other places."

HOBBIES AND OTHER INTERESTS: Fly-tying, fly-fishing, canoeing, knitting, walking, and spending long evenings with books.

FOR MORE INFORMATION SEE: Saturday Review of Literature, November, 21, 1942; *New York Times Book Review,* November 22, 1942; *New York Herald Tribune Books,* November 22, 1942; Douglas Gilbert, "Woman Wrote Best Seller on Maine by Happenstance," *New York World-Telegram,* March 18, 1943; Emma Bugbee, "Louise Rich, Maine Forest Writer, Gets Extra Canned Goods Supply," *New York Herald Tribune,* March 22, 1943; *Good Housekeeping,* October, 1943; *Woman's Home Companion,* October, 1943, March, 1944, May, 1944, October, 1944; *Current Biography,* H. W. Wilson, 1943; *New York Herald Tribune Book Review,* October 8, 1950; Stanley J. Kunitz and Vineta Colby, *Twentieth Century Authors,* first supplement, H. W. Wilson, 1955; *Woman's Day,* August, 1957; *Reader's Digest,* October, 1957, April, 1960; Martha E. Ward and Dorothy A. Marquardt, *Authors of Books for Young People,* Scarecrow, 1971.

RIVERA, Geraldo (Miguel)   1943-

PERSONAL: First name pronounced Hare-*al*-doe; born July 4, 1943, in New York, N.Y.; son of Cruz Allen (a cab driver and restaurant worker) and Lillian (a waitress; maiden name, Friedman) Rivera; married second wife, Edith Bucket Vonnegut (an artist and fashion designer), December 14, 1971 (marriage ended); married Sherryl Raymond (a film producer), December 31, 1976 (marriage ended); married C. C. Dyer (a producer), July, 1987; children: Gabriel Miguel. *Education:* Attended State University of New York Maritime College, and New York City Community College of Applied Arts and Sci-

GERALDO RIVERA

ences; University of Arizona, B.S., 1965; Brooklyn Law School, J.D., 1969; graduate study at University of Pennsylvania, 1969, and Columbia School of Journalism, 1970. *Religion:* Jewish. *Home and office:* 157 Columbus Ave., New York, N.Y. 10023.

CAREER: Harlem Assertion of Rights, and Community Action for Legal Services (anti-poverty neighborhood law firms), New York City, clerk, 1968-70; admitted to the Bar of New York State, 1970; American Broadcasting Co. (ABC-TV), member of *Eyewitness News* team, 1970-75, host of "Good Night America" program, contributor to "Good Morning America" program 1974-78, special correspondent on "20/20" program, 1978-85, special correspondent for "Entertainment Tonight"; host of "Geraldo," 1987—. Documentaries and specials aired on ABC-TV, included "Willowbrook: The Last Disgrace," "The Littlest Junkie: A Children's Story," "Migrants: Dirt Cheap," "Tell Me Where I Can Go," "Marching Home Again," "Barriers: The View from a Wheelchair," "Working Class Heroes." *Military service:* Served in the U.S. Merchant Marine for two years. *Member:* One-to-One (former chairman). *Awards, honors:* Award from the Associated Press Broadcasters Association of New York, 1971, for "Drug Crisis in East Harlem"; named Broadcaster of the Year by the New York State Associated Press, 1971, 1972, and 1974; George Foster Peabody Broadcasting Award, 1972, for "Willowbrook: The Last Disgrace"; Robert F. Kennedy Journalism Award, 1973 and 1975; two Alfred I. du Pont-Columbia University citations; seven Emmy awards from the National Academy of Television Arts and Sciences.

WRITINGS—All for young people: (With Edith Rivera) *Miguel Robles—So Far* (illustrated by E. Rivera), Harcourt, 1973; *Puerto Rico: Island of Contrasts* (illustrated by William Negron), Parents Magazine Press, 1973; *A Special Kind of Courage: Profiles of Young Americans* (illustrated by E. Rivera), Simon & Schuster, 1976.

30 MILLION WITNESS SPECTACULAR EVENT.*

GERALDO RIVERA'S SPECIAL
"MURDER: LIVE FROM DEATH ROW."

The Geraldo Rivera Specials ratings success story continues with his latest live special, delivering a 20.1* rating nationally! It also rated #1 in these major markets.

Rating/Share

#1 NEW YORK-14.9/24
#1 LOS ANGELES-22.9/34
#1 CHICAGO-18.5/31
#1 SAN FRANCISCO-18.7/31
#1 DETROIT-18.5/29
#1 DALLAS-16.1/29
#1 SEATTLE-14.1/22
#1 MIAMI-14.1/21
#1 DENVER-13.8/46
#1 HARTFORD-15.1/24

A spectacular accomplishment! Because first, there was "The Mystery of Al Capone's Vaults," the highest-rated syndicated special of all-time. Now, following that success, three out of the five Geraldo Rivera Specials also share the distinctive honor of being among the 20 top-rated syndicated specials of all-time.

It's also been a spectacular effort on the part of Geraldo Rivera, his staff, the sponsors and the 160 stations who aired this show. From all of us at Tribune Entertainment and TeleTrib, thank you.

TRIBUNE ENTERTAINMENT Company

© 1988. A subsidiary of Tribune Broadcasting Company.

Represented nationally by **TELETRIB**
Source: *GAA
         NSI/Metered Markets
         NTI/NSS (9/73-4/88)

This Daily Variety ad attests to Rivera's enormous viewer popularity.

Other: *Willowbrook: A Report on How It Is and Why It Doesn't Have to Be That Way* (based on his television special), Random House, 1972.

ADAPTATIONS: "What Is Puerto Rico? and Miguel Robles—So Far" (cassette), Caedmon.

SIDELIGHTS: Born in New York City in 1943, Rivera was raised in the Williamsburgh section of Brooklyn. His father had been the valedictorian of his class in Puerto Rico, but when he emigrated to the United States in 1940 he found work wherever he could: dishwasher, cab driver, counter man. "My dad's Puerto Rican, my mom's Jewish. They met in a cafeteria where he washed dishes and she tended counter. Her folks were so appalled at the idea of a Puerto Rican son-in-law, they died soon after the marriage, literally of shame. . . . [A] strong memory is of my Bar Mitzvah. All my Puerto Rican cousins came, they kept taking off the yarmulkes and putting them over their hearts. . . ." [Tom Burke, "Geraldo Saves," *Esquire,* April, 1974.[1]]

To protect their son from racial prejudice, Rivera's parents often used the surname "Riviera" on school forms.

Although he was a poor student in grade school and in high school, Rivera attended the Bronx Maritime College, served in the Merchant Marine, and received his undergraduate degree from the University of Arizona. His years in Arizona were unhappy. "Here I was, this little hood from New York with a Brooklyn Spanish-American accent. I wanted to be like them, to belong. So I said my name was Jerry Rivers and I did everything I could to please them. But they never accepted me. Me, with my black mohair suit and pointy shoes. . . . When I think of how hard I tried. . . ." [Deborah Haber, "The Angry Newsman from Avenue C," *New York Sunday News,* September 10, 1972.[2]]

Rivera returned to New York City with his undergraduate degree in 1965, enrolled at Brooklyn Law School, and supported himself by working in a department store and clerking for the Harlem Association of Rights. He graduated fifth in a class of 350 students. "[I] got treated for the first time as a Puerto Rican person, got recognized ethnically, it was terrific. Lived in this hovel on Avenue C, thirty-three dollars a month, got involved in block associations, as soon as I got my diploma I started representing neighbors in court. I'd say, 'Your Honor, I know Jose Garcia's turf because I live there, can you blame him for stealing a typewriter? At least he's kicked hard drugs.' And it *worked!*"[1]

While defending the Young Lords, a Puerto Rican street gang, Rivera met a CBS newswoman who told him that ABC-TV was looking for a Puerto Rican television news reporter. Rivera was heard by ABC, sent to Columbia's Graduate School of Journalism, and, in September, 1970, debuted on "Eyewitness News." He quickly graduated from such routine assignments as celebrity parties and circus parades to more relevant news assignments. One of his first special assignments examined drug addiction. So moved was he by one of the accounts of the drug addicts that Rivera wept openly on camera. "I don't think of my role as a conduit of information but of feeling, a certain moral point of view. I won't let a war story pass. There aren't two sides. I'll decide if there is another side. I trust myself implicitly. I'm the Everyman." [Julia Baumgold, "Geraldo the Proud," *New York Magazine,* August 7, 1972.[3]]

Believing that a reporter does not have to be primarily objective, but can analyze the news, give a perspective, and ad-

vocate an appropriate change, Rivera won five Emmys and seventy-four other awards after only four years as a television reporter. He was named Broadcaster of the Year by the New York State Associated Press in 1971, 1972, and 1974. During the 1970s, Rivera was also the author of several books for children, including a 1973 semi-autobiographical book about a young boy growing up "straight" on New York's Lower East Side, *Miguel Robles—So Far.* "I love being a newsman. Given enormous power and responsibility by the network, I have tried to use my position to make the world a slightly better place. Questions of style aside, this is where I differ substantively from conventional news-industry wisdom. Sometimes the reporter has to become involved in helping society change the thing he is complaining about." [Geraldo Rivera, "What Ever Happened to Geraldo Rivera? Who?" *Esquire,* April, 1986.[4]]

During his affiliation with ABC-TV, Rivera was a host of "Good Night America," a semi-weekly ABC-TV program, a contributor to the "Good Morning America" program, and a regular correspondent on "20/20." "'20/20's on-air team of correspondents is fairly close, especially compared to the '60 Minutes' all-stars, who, it is said, barely speak to one another. Walters may be Queen of the May, but she is a sexy and benevolent despot, hardworking and often charming. Hugh Downs is '20/20's philosophical anchor, our public conscience. Brighter and sharper than often given credit for by some younger associates, he is an incredibly accomplished, good man and my friend. Correspondent Bob Brown is our soft-spoken poet, an excellent writer and Middle American everyman. John Stossel, Tom Jarriel, and Sylvia Chase are consistently rated by their peers as being among the best in the business."[4]

In 1985, Rivera agreed to resign from his position on "20/20" following a dispute with the network over its decision to cancel a special report on the Marilyn Monroe-John F. Kennedy and Robert F. Kennedy association that had been investigated by fellow colleague, Sylvia Chase. "Publicly, ABC announced I was leaving 'after fifteen years of hard and honorable work to pursue other goals,' adding they didn't want to stand in my way. I told interviewers, 'It was time for a change.'

"The way I feel about the resignation now? I died of massive, mostly self-inflicted wounds. I'm not even terminally mad at Arledge [ABC news president]. Openly confronted on his Monroe decision, challenged in public, he had no option but to respond firmly. If I'd still had my old access to him, I would just have called and advised against him making an editorial decision bound to mar his otherwise remarkable career. Embarrassed by the entire episode, he has to deal with its stubbornly persistent aftermath. Sylvia [Chase] resigned a month after I did.

"Just an hour or so before my intent to resign was to be announced to the press, I called a meeting of my producers, some of the men and women who worked with me to structure and report the 195 stories I had done for '20/20.' Covering emotion with bravado, I told them why I was resigning, asked them not to believe the libelous rumors they would be hearing, and promised we would all be working together again someday, this wild and passionate team unlike any other in TV news.

"There was Charlie Thompson, my ace and senior man, producer of my first '20/20' segment; I had watched his children grow and his hair get white. My kid brother Craig, a junior producer, was there, listening, knowing he was so closely identified with me that if I left the network, he would soon have to; Danny Goldfarb, my friend since law school; Eric Tate, nineteen-year ABC veteran, a deceptively quiet man with the hidden heart of a Masai; Timmy Cothren, underwater adventurer with lifeguard good looks; Bobby Read, the earnest nephew I had helped into the business; and Jackie Farmer, the fiery, beautiful lady from Philly who reported stories with intelligence and élan.

"After the announcement of the resignation, '20/20' staffers privately described the program as being 'in mourning,' which I appreciated, although some public statements might have been more helpful. Of all the letters of shock and condolence I received from fans, friends, and colleagues, two are most memorable.

"One came from Peter Lance, once one of my producers and now an ambitious on-air reporter, still Irish enough occasionally to wax poetic. 'His rash fierce blaze of riot [could] not last,' Peter wrote, quoting Shakespeare on the early demise of a swaggering soldier of fortune (presumably the role I play in life).

"The other came from Jerry Tully, '20/20's talented young writer. He wrote . . . that it was all for the best because he and his wife couldn't bear the thought 'of Geraldo Rivera growing old on network news.'

"Which, of course, is true unless you are still alive and need to work for a living. Would I do it all over again? Well, in truth, I wish I'd never heard of Marilyn Monroe. Having been brought into the controversy, however, especially in my state of mind, my inflexible hero complex would have mandated the Divine Wind approach. We are on earth to slay dragons or die trying."[4]

Following his departure from "20/20" Rivera starred in the television special "Capone," in which he opened the Chicago vaults of mobster Al Capone, finding nothing but a few dusty bottles. After that he did "American Vice: The Doping of a Nation," which was the fifth-highest rated syndicated show in television history. In 1987 he became host of his own talk show, "Geraldo," for which he is grateful because "I was frustrated being on TV only occasionally. I couldn't follow up, react to happenings, influence the national dialogue. I exist on earth to affect reality, not just report on it." [Alan Richman, "He's Tough, Smart and Honest—Just Ask Him—But Geraldo Rivera Wants Something More: Respect," *People*, December 7, 1987.[5]]

HOBBIES AND OTHER INTERESTS: Reading, ping-pong.

FOR MORE INFORMATION SEE: John J. O'Connor, "He's at Home in the City Jungle," *New York Times Biographical Edition*, November, 1971; "TV Review: A Crusader on Camera," *Life*, June 9, 1972; *Newsweek*, July 17, 1972, November 6, 1972; Julie Baumgold, "Geraldo the Proud," *New York*, August 7, 1972; Deborah Haber, "The Angry Newsman from Avanue C," *Daily News* (N.Y.), September 10, 1972; *Harper's Bazaar*, November, 1972, August, 1974; Carol Burton, "Geraldo Rivera: 'I Try to Be Honest,'" *Newsday* (N.Y.), March 31, 1974; Arthur Unger, "Geraldo Rivera's Rise: 'Classic Case' Expounded," *Christian Science Monitor*, April 3, 1974; "Rock Reporter Rivera," *Time*, May 13, 1974; Jack Booth, "Rivera—Crusader with Camera," *Philadelphia Bulletin*, June 6, 1974; *New York Times*, June 6, 1974; Lauren D'Alessandro, "TV Host Criticizes His Own Success," *Hartford Courant* (Conn.), June 30, 1974; Frank E. Bair, editor, *Biography News*, August, 1974; *Mademoiselle*, August, 1974; *Esquire*, April, 1975, April, 1986; *Nation*, July 19, 1975; *Publishers Weekly*,

February 9, 1976; *Best Sellers*, June, 1976; *Current Biography 1975*, H.W. Wilson, 1976; Martha E. Ward and Dorothy A. Marquardt, *Authors of Books for Young People*, supplement to the 2nd edition, Scarecrow, 1979; Alan Richman, "He's Tough, Smart and Honest—Just Ask Him—But Geraldo Rivera Wants Something More: Respect," *People*, December 7, 1987.

ROBINSON, Dorothy W. 1929-

PERSONAL: Born October 1, 1929, in Waycross, Ga.; daughter of Theodore and Mildred (Summers) Washington; married Paul L. Robinson, August 26, 1951 (divorced, 1975); children: Paul, Jr., Tracy Lynn. *Education:* Fisk University, B.A., 1950; Atlanta University, M.L.S., 1951. *Home* 8040 South Wabash Ave., Chicago, Ill. 60619.

CAREER: Chicago Public Library, Chicago, Ill., children's librarian, 1951-59; Northeastern Illinois University Center for Inner City Studies, Chicago, librarian, 1969-71; Chicago public schools, school librarian, 1963-68, 1971—. *Member:* American Library Association, Children's Reading Roundtable, Friends of Woodson Library. *Awards, honors:* Coretta Scott King Award from the American Library Association, 1975, for *The Legend of Africania*.

WRITINGS—Juvenile: *The Legend of Africania* (illustrated by Herbert Temple), Johnson Publishing, 1974; *Martin Luther King and the Civil Rights Movement*, Jehara, 1986. Contributor of articles to *American Libraries*, *Wilson Library Bulletin*, and *School Library Journal*.

SIDELIGHTS: "I am primarily interested in helping young people realize that they have a special and unique talent of their very own and that they must find it and work to develop it fully. My writing revolves around this message.

"My work as a children's librarian led me into a fascination with folk and fairy tales. When I found that they held the interest and attention of children of all ages, I began to study the tales for their form and meaning. I found that they could be interpreted in many different ways, but that most of them carry very clear instructions for helping people realize their potential.

"This prompted me to write *The Legend of Africania*, using the form and the symbols of the traditional fairy tale. It is the story of the individual's quest for freedom and self-fulfillment.

"For me, writing is a means of telling young people that they each have a very important gift to bring to the world. If I could sing, I would sing that message. If I could dance, I would dance it. Getting that message across has become my reason for being."

ROGERS, Paul 1950-

PERSONAL: Born June 16, 1950, in London, England; son of Franklin (a company director) and Alice (a housewife; maiden name, Nuttman) Rogers; married Emma Jane Rothwell-Evans (a writer), October 15, 1977; children: Toby, Thea, Joshua. *Education:* University of Sussex, B.A. (with honors), 1973; also attended University of Freiburg. *Home:* Somerset, England.

CAREER: Northease Manor School, Lewes, Sussex, England, teacher, 1974-78; Tideway School, Newhaven, Sussex, teacher,

1978-81; Sydenham Community School, Bridgwater, Somerset, England, teacher of French, German, Spanish, and Latin and head of language department, 1981—.

WRITINGS—Juvenile: Forget-Me-Not (illustrated by Celia Berridge), Viking, 1984; *Sheepchase* (illustrated by C. Berridge), Viking, 1986; *From Me to You* (illustrated by Jane Johnson), Orchard Books, 1987; *Rain and Shine* (illustrated by Chris Burke), Orchard Books, 1987; *Tumbledown* (illustrated by Robin Bell Corfield), Walker, 1987; (with wife, Emma Rogers) *The Get Better Book,* Orchard Books, 1988; *Lily's Picnic* (illustrated by John Prater), Bodley Head, 1988; *The Somebody Stories* (illustrated by R. B. Cornfield), Bodley Head, 1988.

Other: *Alles Klar* (textbook; title means "Everything Made Clear"), Harrap, 1981; *Understanding Grammar*, Harrap, 1982; *La Grammaire en clair* (title means "Grammar Made Clear"), Harrap, 1983; *Zick Zack* (German textbook), Arnold Wheaton, Volume I, 1987, Volume II, 1988, Volume III, 1989.

WORK IN PROGRESS: Children's books; others in progress, including a collection of poems.

SIDELIGHTS: "As a child I was not very interested in books. I preferred to be drawing pictures or climbing up a tree. I did fill an exercise book with two rambling stories. I also remember subjecting several friends to rehearsals of an 'Aladin' play I had written, whose immortal first line was 'My feet are killing me.' Theatre, in fact, excited me much more than books, and I was lucky to be taken quite often to musical in the West End of London by my father, who was company secretary of Chappells. He was happy to encourage my interest in the theatre by taking me backstage during the interval, but was very disappointed when my choice of musical instrument turned out to be nothing more tuneful than the drums.

"These two interests, however, stayed with me throughout my teens and into university. I produced plays, made films and played in bands. In their own way, I think these contributed to my interest in the visual side of story-telling and to my fascination with the rhythm of words. It was during my time as a student that I first truly discovered the joy of books, and began to feel that writing was what I would really like to do.

"When I went to live in Andalucia at the age of twenty-three, my main language was a suitcase full of books. They are still there—I hope. During my time in Spain, I wrote lots of very bad poetry, inspired by the poet I admired most, the German, Rilke. On my return to England I lived at a pottery in Sussex, teaching French, German and Spanish part time at a nearby school. It was here that I met Emma—who later became my wife. I shall never forget the first time I benefitted from her literary criticism. Her reaction, when I read her a poem I had been working on, was to say: 'You mean you've spent all afternoon doing *that?!*' I went off to cut the spinach for supper with uncustomary cruelty. Since that time her criticisms have never failed to help, and now we have also written several children's books together.

"It was the birth of son Toby that first gave me the idea of writing something for children. We were then living in Lewes, Sussex. First Emma, then I, had published several school books. But reading to Toby made us aware of the shortage of well-written, well-structured books for young children. By chance I met Celia Berridge, whose illustrations for *Postman Pat* have since made her well-known in Britain. I asked her if she would be interested in doing some drawings for a text I had written called *Forget-Me-Not.* A sales representative at a book fair cautioned me about the number of unsolicited manuscripts submitted, but gave me the address of Penguin Books. We decided to try anyway. The book came out in 1984.

"That year we moved to Somerset. Living in an old house in a beautiful place certainly encouraged me to write. It is also a wonderful playground for our (now three) children, who have indirectly inspired many of the things I have written. I like to work on several things at once and greatly enjoy working with a variety of illustrators. But I am still looking forward to the day when I have more time for reading. Perhaps some things never change."

HOBBIES AND OTHER INTERESTS: Playing folk and classical guitar, ancient Hebrew.

FOR MORE INFORMATION SEE: Sarah Carpenter, "Collaborative Creations," *Times Literary Supplement*, June 6, 1986.

PAUL ROGERS

ROOP, Constance Betzer 1951- (Connie Roop)

PERSONAL: Born June 18, 1951, in Elkhorn, Wis.; daughter of Robert Sterling (a funeral director) and Marjorie (a homemaker; maiden name, Gray) Betzer; married Peter G. Roop (an educator and author), August 4, 1973; children: Sterling Gray, Heidi Anne. *Education:* Lawrence University, B.A., 1973; attended University of Wisconsin—Madison, and Colorado School of Mines, 1974; Boston College, M.S.T., 1980. *Politics:* Independent. *Religion:* Christian. *Home and office:* 2601 North Union St., Appleton, Wis. 54911.

Connie and Peter Roop.

CAREER: Appleton Area School District, Appleton, Wis., science teacher, 1973—. Fulbright exchange teacher at Lady Hawkins School, Kingston, England, 1976-77. Consultant, D.C. Heath Company, 1986-87; workshop coordinator, Duquesne University, 1986—. Member of Appleton Energy Task Force. *Member:* American Association of University Women (chairperson of international relations, 1984-87; issue chairman, 1987-88), National Education Association, Society of Children's Book Writers, Wisconsin Society of Science Teachers, Wisconsin Society of Earth Science Teachers (treasurer, 1987—), Wisconsin Regional Writers, American Field Service, Friends of the Appleton Library (board of directors for community nursery school, 1986-87). *Awards, honors:* Children's Choice Award from the International Reading Association and the Children's Book Council, 1984, for *Out to Lunch!* and *Space Out!; Keep the Lights Burning, Abbie* was selected one of Child Study Association of America's Children's Books of the Year, 1985, and *Buttons for General Washington,* 1986; Irma Simonton Black Award Honor Book, and Children's Book of the Year Award, both from Bank Street College of Education, and Outstanding Trade Book in the Language Arts from the National Council of Teachers of English, all 1986, all for *Keep the Lights Burning, Abbie;* Outstanding Trade Book in the Field of Social Studies from the National Council for Social Studies and the Children's Book Council, 1986, for *Buttons for General Washington.*

WRITINGS—Children's books; under name Connie Roop; with husband, Peter Roop: *Keep the Lights Burning, Abbie* ("Reading Rainbow" selection; illustrated by Peter E. Hanson), Carolrhoda, 1985; *Buttons for General Washington* (illustrated by

P. E. Hanson), Carolrhoda, 1986; *Snips the Tinker,* Milliken, 1988; *Seasons of the Cranes,* Walker, 1989.

"Make Me Laugh" series; juvenile; under name Connie Roop; with P. Roop; all illustrated by Joan Hanson; all published by Lerner: *Space Out! Jokes about Outer Space,* 1984; *Go Hog Wild! Jokes from down on the Farm,* 1984; *Out to Lunch! Jokes about Food,* 1984; *Stick Out Your Tongue! Jokes about Doctors and Patients,* 1986; *Going Buggy! Jokes about Insects* ("Reading Rainbow" selection), 1986; *Let's Celebrate! Jokes about Holidays,* 1986.

"Great Mysteries" series; juvenile; under name Connie Roop; with P. Roop: *Dinosaurs: Opposing Viewpoints,* Greenhaven, 1988; *Poltergeists: Opposing Viewpoints,* Greenhaven, 1988; *The Solar System: Opposing Viewpoints,* Greenhaven, 1988.

Contributor to Harcourt Brace Jovanovich's reading texts. Also contributor of stories, articles and reviews to periodicals, including *Learning, Appraisal, Cricket, Cobblestone,* and *Curriculum Review.*

WORK IN PROGRESS: Ah-Yoka and the Talking Leaves, with P. Roop; joke and riddle books.

SIDELIGHTS: "I grew up in an active and supportive family where reading was a highly valued activity. I loved school and was an avid reader. I won an essay contest as a thirteen-year-old, but never considered this achievement as a credential for becoming an author! I actively participated in everything from bassoon and forensics to scouting where I gained a love for the outdoors. During the summer of my junior year in high school, I lived with an Italian family as an American Field Service student. This experience confirmed my desire to learn and to discover the uniqueness of different cultures.

"In college I intended to become a physician. However, a field camp experience in geology made me decide to study our earth. The vastness of geologic time still humbles me.

"Combining my interest and concern for people with my curiosity about nature, I became a junior high science teacher. Married to an equally adventurous and curious person, Peter and I both took advantage of travel and study opportunities. One of our most exciting experiences was teaching in England for a year as part of the Fulbright Exchange Program.

"My interest in children's books developed while pursuing a Master's degree in science teaching. I began to read many of the books assigned to my husband in his Master's of children's literature program as a welcome change from science journals. Based on this reading, I developed a fiction booklist to supplement the science curriculum in my junior high school science classes. These scientifically accurate and exciting books provided my entry into the world of writing for children and young adults.

"After being initiated into the world of children's books, I wrote several articles for educational journals and I also began

That night the wind blew hard. ■ (From *Keep the Lights Burning, Abbie* by Peter and Connie Roop. Illustrated by Peter E. Hanson.)

to review science books for *Appraisal* magazine as a science specialist.

"Peter and I then collaborated on a variety of projects. The first was a series of six joke and riddle books. They are an extension of our family tradition of word play.

"While researching a travel article off the coast of Maine, Peter and I learned of the lighthouse heroine, Abbie Burgess. This courageous young woman singlehandedly kept two lighthouses lit during a month of stormy weather in 1856. The resulting book, *Keep the Lights Burning, Abbie,* was featured on the Public Broadcasting System's 'Reading Rainbow' in 1987. We are very proud of this book. *Buttons for General Washington* is another historical story we wrote for young readers. We have many more ideas about historic and heroic young people and we hope to write additional historical fiction books.

"With our backgrounds in science, it is natural that we write non-fiction science books. Two of these, *Dinosaurs* and *Solar System,* are topics incorporated into my earth science curriculum. I was especially pleased to write for this series as it explores the mysteries yet unsolved by science. Scientific debate, key to the scientific process, is a critical element of these books. I believe young people need to realize that there are many unanswered questions in science and that they can be part of solving these questions. We are presently working on two more science books, one on earthquakes and another on whooping cranes.

"I look forward to writing projects on a variety of topics as my involvement with science, literature, history, and reading continues. Through travel, camping and reading, our family discovers new outlets for our creativity.

"Peter and I are committed to children. I hope to always be able to look at the world with the eyes of a young person—full of fresh wonder, awe, and surprise. I am hopeful that through our books we can help young people discover the joy of learning. This is a precious gift that Peter and I possess and treasure and hope to share with others."

HOBBIES AND OTHER INTERESTS: Reading, traveling, camping, sewing, skiing and activities with her husband and children.

ROOP, Peter (G.)   1951-

PERSONAL: Born March 8, 1951, in Winchester, Mass.; son of Daniel Morehead (an engineer) and Dorothy (a homemaker; maiden name, Danenhower) Roop; married Constance Betzer (an educator and author), August 4, 1973; children: Sterling Gray, Heidi Anne. *Education:* Lawrence University, B.A., 1973; Simmons College, M.A., 1980; also attended University of Wisconsin—Madison. *Politics:* Independent. *Home and office:* 2601 North Union St., Appleton, Wis. 54911.

CAREER: Appleton Area School District, Appleton, Wis., teacher, 1973—; writer, 1977—. Fulbright exchange teacher at Kingston County Primary School, Kingston, England, 1976-77; University of Wisconsin—Fox Valley, Menasha, Wis., instructor, 1983-84; University of Wisconsin, School of the Arts, Rhinelander, Wis., instructor, 1986-87. Workshop coordinator, Duquesne University, 1986—; consultant, D.C. Heath Company, 1986-87; teacher consultant for *Learning* magazine, 1988—. Member of board of directors of Friends of the Ap-

"Now march," he ordered. ∎ (From *Buttons for General Washington* by Peter and Connie Roop. Illustrated by Peter E. Hanson.)

pleton Public Library, 1974-84, and board of trustees of Appleton Public Library, 1983-89. *Member:* Children's Literature Association, Society of Children's Book Writers, National Council of Teachers of English, National Education Association, Wisconsin Regional Writers (president, 1983-86), Council for Wisconsin Writers, Chicago Reading Roundtable, Children's Literature Assembly (board of directors, 1987—).

AWARDS, HONORS: Jade Ring Award from the Wisconsin Regional Writers Association, 1979, for play "Who Buries the Funeral Director?" and 1982, for *The Cry of the Conch;* Reading Teacher of the Year from the Mideast Wisconsin Reading Council, 1983; Children's Choice Award from the International Reading Association and the Children's Book Council, 1985, for *Out to Lunch!* and *Space Out!; Keep the Lights Burning, Abbie* was selected one of Child Study Association of America's Children's Books of the Year, 1985, and *Buttons for General Washington,* 1986; Teacher of the Year, and Outstanding Elementary Educator for Wisconsin both from the Wisconsin Department of Public Instruction, both 1986; Outstanding Elementary Educator in Appleton from the Mielke Foundation, 1986; Children's Book of the Year Award, and Irma Simonton Black Award Honor Book, both from Bank Street College of Education, and Outstanding Trade Book in the Language Arts from the National Council of Teachers of English, all 1986, all for *Keep the Lights Burning, Abbie;* Outstanding Trade Book in the Field of Social Studies from the National Council for Social Studies and the Children's Book Council, 1986, for *Buttons for General Washington;* "In Honor of Excellence Award" from the Burger King Corp., 1987, for excellence in education.

WRITINGS—Juvenile: The Cry of the Conch (illustrated by Patric), Press Pacifica, 1984; *Little Blaze and the Buffalo Jump* (illustrated by Jesse Wells), Montana Council for Indian Education, 1984; *Sik-Ki-Mi* (illustrated by Shawn Running Crane), Montana Council for Indian Education, 1984; *Natosi: Strong Medicine* (illustrated by S. Running Crane), Montana Council for Indian Education, 1984.

Juvenile; with wife, Connie Roop: *Keep the Lights Burning, Abbie* ("Reading Rainbow" selection; illustrated by Peter E. Hanson), Carolrhoda, 1985; *Buttons for General Washington* (illustrated by P. E. Hanson), Carolrhoda, 1986; *Snips the Tinker,* Milliken, 1988; *Seasons of the Cranes,* Walker, 1989.

"Make Me Laugh" series; juvenile; all with C. Roop; all illustrated by Joan Hanson: *Space Out! Jokes about Outer Space,* Lerner, 1984; *Go Hog Wild! Jokes from down on the Farm,* Lerner, 1984; *Out to Lunch! Jokes about Food,* Lerner, 1984; *Stick Out Your Tongue! Jokes about Doctors and Patients,* Lerner, 1986; *Let's Celebrate! Jokes about Holidays,* Lerner, 1986; *Going Buggy! Jokes about Insects* ("Reading Rainbow" selection), Lerner, 1986.

"Great Mysteries" series; juvenile; all with C. Roop: *Dinosaurs: Opposing Viewpoints,* Greenhaven, 1988; *Poltergeists: Opposing Viewpoints,* Greenhaven, 1988; *The Solar System: Opposing Viewpoints,* Greenhaven, 1988.

Author of "Who Buries the Funeral Director?" (juvenile one-act play). Contributor to Harcourt Brace Jovanovich's reading texts. Also contributor of articles and reviews to newspapers and magazines, including *Cobblestone, Jack and Jill, Cricket, History Today, Discovery, Wisconsin English Journal, Curriculum Review, Learning, Appraisal, Milwaukee Journal, Post Crescent, School Library Journal, Science Books and Films,* and *Language Arts.*

PETER ROOP

WORK IN PROGRESS: Ah-Yoka and the Talking Leaves, with C. Roop; *Quake!* to be published by Random House; four joke and riddle books.

SIDELIGHTS: "My work in the elementary classroom is one of the prime motivations for my writing for children. Although I had written many short stories while in college, I had never considered writing for publication.

"When I began my career in education, teaching grades one through four, I was reading numerous children's books. I said to myself, 'I can write these stories.' Little then did I realize the scope of children's literature and the skills it would take to write quality stories for children. The 'easy' appearance of many children's books hides the hours of hard work involved in creating a worthwhile book for young readers.

"For several years after college I had talked about it, but I did no real writing. Then, while teaching in England as a Fulbright exchange teacher, I decided to stop talking and start writing. That year I wrote four children's stories and articles, two of which were eventually published in magazines. My route to writing children's books was focused first on writing for the many children's magazines. By taking this approach I hoped to gain the necessary background in the profession, to hone my writing skills, and to establish a name in preparation for writing books.

"In 1980, to enhance my knowledge of children's books for my work as an educator, as well as for my writing, I completed my master's degree in children's literature at the Center for the Study of Children's Literature at Simmons College in Boston. The work at Simmons was pivotal in my understanding of children's literature and in writing for children. I studied with noted authors Nancy Bond and Scott O'Dell. The books of Scott O'Dell, especially *Island of the Blue Dolphins,* have been the mainstay of my perspective on writing for children. O'Dell's style, sensitivity, and adept mixing of history and fiction are models for my own writing efforts.

"An intense interesting history has led me to write historical stories, articles, and books. As a writer on assignment for

Cobblestone, a history magazine, I researched and wrote about topics ranging from the origins of Native Americans to the creation of video games. Fascinated with the lives of pre-European contact peoples, I have written three books for the Blackfeet Nation. A fourth book, *The Cry of the Conch,* is about ancient Hawaii.

"After I had been writing by myself for about six years, my wife, Connie, and I began collaborating. Inspired by a walk along the coast of Maine, we wrote a joke and riddle book about the seashore. This idea developed into a six-book series. Playing with words has long been a family tradition, one which we turned into award-winning books for children.

"Our abiding interest in Maine led us to write *Keep the Lights Burning, Abbie,* a historical story about Abbie Burgess, a brave young woman who singlehandedly kept two lighthouses going during a month-long siege of bad weather in 1856. This book, featured on Public Broadcasting System's 'Reading Rainbow' in 1987, will hopefully create more opportunities for our future.

"We are interested in writing the stories of children who, like Abbie, are 'footnotes in history.' By researching and writing these heroic stories, we hope to provide children with an exciting glimpse into the past.

"Our combined backgrounds in science have involved us in writing nonfiction books as well. Our most recent work, a three-book series, explores such great mysteries as the extinction of the dinosaurs, the existence of poltergeists, and the marvels of the solar system.

"My interest in travel has provided the backdrop for many of my books. As a writer I believe that getting the right sense of setting is critical to the impact of a story. Experiencing the sacredness of a *pu'unhonua* in Hawaii was essential to *The Cry of the Conch.* Feeling the chilling blasts of a nor'easter was vital in creating the atmosphere of *Keep the Lights Burning, Abbie.* Walking the cobbled streets of Philadelphia established the feeling of place in *Buttons for George Washington.*

"Writing the best books possible for young readers is my goal. By providing the best for children, I can open more vistas and distant horizons to their wondering eyes and minds. What better role for a writer?"

HOBBIES AND OTHER INTERESTS: Reading, traveling, speaking to educators, librarians and writers, playing with his children.

ROSS, Judy 1942-

PERSONAL: Born October 3, 1942, in Toronto, Ontario, Canada; daughter of Charles H. (a stockbroker) and Robina (a housewife; maiden name, Robb) Thompson; married Robert Ross (a publisher), December 19, 1964; children: Noelle, Aimee. *Religion:* Protestant. *Education:* University of Toronto, B.A., 1963. *Home:* 333 St. Clair Ave. East, Toronto, Ontario, Canada M4T 1P3.

CAREER: J. Walter Thompson (advertising agency), Montreal and Toronto, Canada, copywriter, 1963-67; Screen Gems, Toronto, researcher for the television show, "The Pierre Berton Show," 1967-68; Canadian Broadcasting Corporation, Toronto, story editor for a daily television series, 1968-74; freelance writer, 1974—. *Member:* Periodical Writers Association of Canada, Toronto Lawn Tennis Club, Muskoka Lakes Association. *Awards, honors:* Canada Council Grant, 1980.

JUDY ROSS

WRITINGS—Juvenile; published by D. C. Heath Canada, except as noted: *Brum, the Siberian Tiger,* 1978; *Lobo, the Timber Wolf,* 1978; *Snowflake, the Polar Bear,* 1978; *Tequila, the African Elephant,* 1978; *Dassen, the Penguin,* 1979; *Falstaff, the Hippopotamus,* 1979; *Khan, the Camel,* 1979; *Mias, the Orangutan,* 1979; *Amanda the Gorilla,* 1980; *Castor the Beaver,* 1980; *Tonto the South African Fur Seal,* 1980; *Turk the Moose,* 1980; *Canada Goose,* Grolier, 1985; *Loons,* Grolier, 1985; *Wolves,* Grolier, 1985; *Moose,* Grolier, 1985.

Adult: (With David Allen and Nina Czegledy-Nagy) *Down to Earth: Canadian Potters at Work,* Thomas Nelson, 1980.

Also author of "The History of the Muskoka Lakes Association" published in the *Muskoka Lakes Association Yearbook,* 1984. Contributor of articles on travel, lifestyle and design to magazines, including *Homemaker's, Canadian Living, En Route, Town and Country, Western Living, Travel a La Carte, Destinations,* and *Globehopper.* Homes editor of *Ontario Living.*

WORK IN PROGRESS: A book with color photographs and contemporary and historical text about the lake district of Muskoka, Ontario, with photographer John De Visser.

SIDELIGHTS: "I am enjoying an eclectic variety of writing assignments—and focusing more on travel as a specialty."

I know well that only the rarest kind of best in anything can be good enough for the young.
—Walter de la Mare

JOEL L. SCHWARTZ

SCHWARTZ, Joel L. 1940-

PERSONAL: Born April 23, 1940, in Philadelphia, Pa.; son of Reuben B. (a physician) and Elinor (Shickman) Schwartz; married Charlotte Rodoff (a teacher of the deaf), June 23, 1963; children: Ronald, Toby, Deborah. *Education:* Franklin and Marshall College, B.A., 1962; Hahnemann University, M.D., 1965, postdoctoral study, 1968-69, 1971-72. *Home:* 1333 Dillon Rd., Fort Washington, Pa. 19034. *Agent:* Ray Lincoln, 4 Surrey Rd., Melrose Park, Pa. 19126. *Office:* 830 Twining Rd., Dresher, Pa. 19025.

CAREER: Board certified in child, adolescent, and adult psychoanalysis. Albert Einstein Medical Center, Philadelphia, Pa., intern, 1965-66; Institute of Living, Hartford, Conn., resident in adult psychiatry, 1966-68; private practice of psychiatry, 1972—. Director of CHILD/Adolescent fellowship at Hahnemann University, 1980—. *Military service:* U. S. Air Force, Medical Corps, 1969-71; became major. *Member:* American Psychiatric Association, American Psychoanalytic Association, American Academy of Child Psychiatry, Pennsylvania Psychiatric Society, Philadelphia Association for Psychoanalysis, Phi Beta Kappa.

WRITINGS: Upchuck Summer (juvenile; illustrated by Bruce Degan), Delacorte, 1982; *Best Friends Don't Come in Three's* (juvenile; sequel to *Upchuck Summer;* illustrated by B. Degan), Dell, 1985; *Shrink* (juvenile), Dell, 1986.

WORK IN PROGRESS: The Cinekyd, to be published by Dell.

SIDELIGHTS: "My books are about boys from a boy's point of view."

A house full of books, and a garden of flowers.
—Andrew Lang

SEARCY, Margaret Z(ehmer) 1926-

PERSONAL: Born October 26, 1926, in Raleigh, N.C.; daughter of John Adrain (in engineering sales) and Agnes Tyler (Johnson) Zehmer; married Joseph Alexander Searcy (a real estate broker), June 23, 1948; children: Margaret Tyler, Joseph Alexander III, Elizabeth Baskerville. *Education:* Duke University, B.A., 1946; University of Alabama, M.A., 1959; further graduate study at University of the Americas. *Religion:* Presbyterian. *Home:* 1 Oaklana, Tuscaloosa, Ala. 35401. *Office:* Department of Anthropology, University of Alabama, Box #6135, University, Ala. 35486.

CAREER: University of Alabama, instructor in anthropology, 1964—; author of books for children. Visiting lecturer at University of South Dakota. Public lecturer and consultant. *Member:* American Anthropological Association, Guild of Professional Writers for Children (chairwoman), Alabama Academy of Science (past vice-president), Alabama Archaeological Society (past president), Alpha Kappa Delta. *Awards, honors:* University of Alabama faculty grant, 1969; grants from Alabama Consortium for Higher Education, 1973, for study in Mexico and Guatemala; Charlton W. Tebeau Literary Award from the Florida Historical Society, 1975, for *Ikwa of the Temple Mounds;* Author's Award from the Alabama Library Association, 1980, for *Tiny Bat and the Ball Game.*

WRITINGS—All for children: *Ikwa of the Temple Mounds,* University of Alabama Press, 1974; *Tiny Bat and the Ball Game* (illustrated by Lu Celia Wise), Portals Press, 1978; *Alli Gator Gets a Bump on His Nose* (illustrated by L. Wise), Portals Press, 1978; *The Race of Flitty Hummingbird and Flappy Crane: An Indian Legend,* Portals Press, 1978; *The Charm of the Bear Claw Necklace: A Story of Stone-Age Southeastern Indians,* University of Alabama Press, 1981; *Wolf Dog of the Woodland Indians,* University of Alabama Press, 1982. Contributor to professional journals.

ADAPTATIONS: "Ikwa of the Temple Mounds," Alabama Public Television, 1978; "The Race of Flitty Hummingbird and Flappy Crane: An Indian Legend," Alabama Public Television, 1978.

SIDELIGHTS: Searcy writes that her Portals Press books, part of the "Fact and Fantasy" series, are "based upon Southeastern Indian myths. The series is designed to acquaint the reader with southeastern flora and fauna while helping to eliminate problems for the child who is 'different.' All of my books are designed to present some positive aspects of a culture."

SHEA, George 1940-

PERSONAL: Born June 12, 1940, in New York, N.Y.; son of George Vincent, Sr. and Mary Agnes (Foley) Shea; married Anique Taylor, May 28, 1980 (divorced July 9, 1981); children: Madeleine Todd. *Education:* Attended College of the Holy Cross, 1957-58; Fordham University, B.A., 1963; graduate study at New York University, 1966-67. *Home:* 96 St. Mark's Pl., New York, N.Y. 10009. *Agent:* Amy Berkower, Writer's House, Inc., 21 West 26th St., New York, N.Y. 10010.

CAREER: Substitute nursery school teacher in New York City, 1968-70; Raw Guts and American Know-How, New York City, improvisational comedy actor, 1969-71; Paul Bunyan Playhouse, Bemidji, Minn., actor, 1973; National Public Radio, Minneapolis, Minn., radio comedy actor, 1973-76; writer,

1976—. Improvisational comedy actor at Dudley Riggs Brave New Workshop, 1973-74. *Member:* Dramatists Guild.

WRITINGS—Juvenile: *Alligators* (illustrated by Scott W. Earle), EMC, 1977; *Bats* (illustrated by S. W. Earle), EMC, 1977; *Spiders* (illustrated by S. W. Earle), 1977; *Wolves* (illustrated by S. W. Earle), EMC, 1977; *I Died Here*, Childrens Press, 1979; *Nightmare Nina*, Bowmar/Noble, 1979; *Big Bad Ernie*, Bowmar/Noble, 1979; *Cheap Skates*, Scholastic Book Services, 1980; *Jody*, Scholastic Book Services, 1980; *Whales* (illustrated by Anne M. Runvon), EMC, 1981; *Big Cats* (illustrated by A. M. Runvon), EMC, 1981; *Bears* (illustrated by A. M. Runvon), EMC, 1981; *Snakes* (illustrated by A. M. Runvon), EMC, 1981; *Dolphins* (illustrated by A. M. Runvon), EMC, 1981; *Silly Quizzes*, Scholastic Book Services, 1981; *Strike Two*, Children's Press, 1981; (with Anique Taylor) *What to Do When You're Bored*, Simon & Schuster, 1982; *Manage Your Own Baseball Team: Make the Playoffs! Blues vs. Sharks*, Wanderer Books, 1983; *Coach Your Own Football Team: Make It to the Superbowl! Panthers vs. Grizzlies*, Wanderer Books, 1983; *ESP McGee to the Rescue*, Avon, 1984. Also author of *How Many Nerds Does It Take to Screw in a Lightbulb?*, *Danger in Eagle Park*, and *The Great Talking Contest*, all Scholastic Book Services.

Stage plays: "Mad Dog" (one-act comedy), first produced at Playwrights Horizons, 1976; "Until the Last Christian Has Been Eaten" (series of one-act plays), first produced at Playwrights Horizons, October, 1977; "Bless Me, Father, for I Have Sinned" (three-act comedy), first produced off-Broadway at Phoenix Theatre, November, 1980.

Television scripts: "Who Killed Susie Smith?" (juvenile documentary; "Afterschool Special"), first broadcast by ABC-TV, Highgate Pictures; "The Animal Snatchers" (juvenile; episode for animated series "Jana of the Jungle"), first broadcast by NBC-TV, Hanna-Barbera; "Flakes" (comedy pilot), released by Videotape Network and Universal Pictures Television; "The ABC's of Love and Sex" (comedy special), released by Home Box Office.

Writer for advertising and promotional films and other audio-visual productions. Writer for radio programs, "Hour Times" and "All Things Considered." Contributor to children's magazines, including *Sprint, Action, Scholastic Search,* and *Scholastic Science Monthly.* Contributing editor of *Attenzione,* 1980-82.

WORK IN PROGRESS: "Goodbye, Broadway, Hello World War Three!," a stage play.

SMITH, Janice Lee   1949-

PERSONAL: Born May 12, 1949, in Fowler, Kan.; daughter of James Elmer (a businessman) and Olivia (a nurse; maiden name, Burgin) Lee; married James Foster Smith (a department head for AT&T), July 14, 1968; children: Bryan Foster, Jaymi Lee. *Education:* Rutgers University, B.A. (magna cum laude), 1977. *Politics:* Republican. *Religion:* Protestant. *Home and office:* 5029 211th St., Noblesville, Ind. 46060. *Agent:* Dorothy Markinko, McIntosh & Otis, Inc., 310 Madison Ave., New York, N.Y. 10017.

CAREER: Writer, 1978—; Lee-Smith Enterprises (land developers), Hamilton County, Ind., 1988—. Member of *Mademoiselle* marketing board, 1977-87. *Member:* Society of Children's Book Writers. *Awards, honors:* Bread Loaf Con-

JANICE LEE SMITH

ference Scholarship, 1981, for children's writing; Outstanding Young Woman of America, 1981; Master Fellowship Grant from the Indiana Arts Commission and the National Endowment for the Arts, 1984, for *The Show and Tell War; The Kid Next Door and Other Headaches* was selected one of International Reading Association's Children's Choices, 1985; Bread Loaf Writers' Conference Fellowship, 1986; Addi Award, 1987, for advertising booklet.

WRITINGS—Juvenile; all illustrated by Dick Gackenbach: *The Monster in the Third Dresser Drawer: And Other Stories about Adam Joshua*, Harper, 1981; *The Kid Next Door and Other Headaches: Stories about Adam Joshua*, Harper, 1984, published in paperback as *The Kid Next Door and Other Headaches: More Stories about Adam Joshua*, Harper, 1986; *The Show-and-Tell War: And Other Stories about Adam Joshua*, Harper, 1988; *Pet Day: Yet More Stories about Adam Joshua*, Harper, 1989.

WORK IN PROGRESS: A fifth book in the Adam Joshua series, *Nelson in Love: Stories about Adam Joshua;* a variety of other writing projects.

SIDELIGHTS: "My husband, Jim, and I were raised in Minneola, a tiny town of 600 that sits across the Chisolm Trail and lies between Dodge City and No Man's Land. Our grandparents traveled there as children in covered wagons. Our great-grandparents homesteaded it. It was a very isolated part of the country in which to spend a childhood, but it was filled with storytellers. I would sit for hours listening to those stories of the early days of Kansas, and then I'd line up dolls, dogs, cats, and my baby brother as a captive audience and practice telling the stories myself. It was an ideal start for a creative writer." [Marie T. Baker, "Area Author, Janice Lee Smith," *Right Here,* January/February, 1985.]

An editor at Harper & Row noticed Smith when an article of hers was published in *Mademoiselle* in 1977, the year she was guest editor. ''They wrote me a letter saying they'd like to be my publishers, and I should send my portfolio . . . I didn't have one.''[1]

The Kid Next Door is based on memories of a childhood friend. ''He cut off my hair when I was four—I made him eat a box of dog biscuits when he was six—and generally, we managed to get into a great deal of trouble. He was, however, such delightful fun, that I grew up to marry him. He is still my best friend, and we take turns reminding one another that someone really should get to the cooking and cleaning because we're supposed to be adults now.''[1]

''My husband and I are enthusiastic photographers, and the entire family is addicted to travel. China, Japan, Greece, Spain, Hawaii, and the Bahamas have been recent adventurous delights! (It still isn't enough!)

''Our other new addiction is Cobweb, our newly built Victorian farm house and its thirty acres of woods and meadows. I tried to get them to leave the kitchen off in favor of more porches, but we ended up with a happy balance. We have a resident herd of deer, a loose brick in the fireplace for secret messages, and a small, but mysterious secret passage. My writing loft looks out over the family's breakfast room and fireplace—and I had them put the largest picture window pos-

In the drawer there were sacks and shoestrings and sweat shirts, but no monsters. ■ (From ''The Monster in the Third Dresser Drawer'' in *The Monster in the Third Dresser Drawer and Other Stories about Adam Joshua* by Janice Lee Smith. Illustrated by Dick Gackenbach.)

sible by my desk. It looks out toward a woods with hundred-year-old beech trees, wildflowers and wildlife (including my two teens and their friends). It's a lovely place for dreaming up books! (And for getting out of cooking!)''

''I'm lucky to live in a family of eccentrics, and I do draw most of my ideas from my children and the children of friends.''[1]

FOR MORE INFORMATION SEE: Helen Janousek, ''She Grew Up to Tell Tales,'' *Indianapolis News,* August 7, 1984; Marie T. Baker, ''Area Author, Janice Lee Smith,'' *Right Here,* January/February, 1985; Chris Kennedy-Daniels, ''Mischievous Child Becomes a Storyteller,'' *Commercial Review* (Portland, Ind.), January 20, 1986; John Flora, ''Story Teller Visits School Children,'' *Indianapolis News,* December 4, 1986; Pat Watson, ''Children's Book Author Says She's 'Stubborn,' '' *Arts Insight,* January, 1987; Elizabeth Jacobson, ''Noblesville Author Prints More Adam Joshua Antics,'' *Noblesville Ledger* (Ind.), February 13, 1988.

SMITH, Joan (Mary) 1933-

PERSONAL: Born January 11, 1933, in Birmingham, England; daughter of Kenneth (a brewer) and Dora (a buyer; maiden name, Hayward) Thompson; married David Smith (a managing director), September 16, 1961; children: Caroline, Rachel and Matthew (twins). *Education:* Queen Elizabeth Hospital School of Physiotherapy, member of the Chartered Society of Physiotherapy, 1953; Open University, B.A., 1987. *Politics:* Social Democrat Party. *Religion:* Church of England. *Home:* 14 Burlington Rd., Leicester LE2 3DD, England. *Office:* Jubb Containers, Chiswick Rd., Freemens Common, Leicester LE2 3DD, England.

CAREER: Physiotherapist in Leicester and Nottingham, England, 1954-63; Jubb Containers, Leicester, England, company secretary, 1971—; free-lance writer, 1971—. *Member:* Society of Authors.

WRITINGS—Juvenile: *Just Like Corduroy* (illustrated by Jane Paton), Hamish Hamilton, 1972; *The Folk Doll of Sion* (illustrated by Prudence Seward), Hamish Hamilton, 1973; *The Dittany Bush* (illustrated by Tessa Jordan), Hamish Hamilton, 1975; *Pilgrim's Way* (illustrated by Janet Duchesne), Hamish Hamilton, 1976; *November and the Truffle Pig* (illustrated by J. Duchesne), Hamish Hamilton, 1977; *The Hole in the Road* (illustrated by J. Duchesne), Hamish Hamilton, 1979; *Saturday and the Last Stitch* (illustrated by Susan Sansome), Hamish Hamilton, 1979; *Augusta* (illustrated by Beryl Sanders), Dobson, 1979.

The Great Cube Race (illustrated by Doreen Caldwell), Hamish Hamilton, 1982; *The Gift of Umtal,* Macrae, 1982; *Grandmother's Donkey* (illustrated by Gunvor Edwards), F. Watts, 1983; *We Three Kings from Pepper Street Prime* (illustrated by Nicole Goodwin), Macrae, 1985; *The Pepper Street Papers* (illustrated by N. Goodwin), MacRae, 1987.

WORK IN PROGRESS: A book about Hippocrates.

SIDELIGHTS: ''Like many only children I tended to be inward looking, creating an imaginary family for myself. From an early age I kept a journal, using exercise books, not a diary, so that I could write at length about interesting days, or nothing, as I chose. These two elements are common in many writers beginnings. However, unlike most, I am not a natural storyteller—I never *told* my own children stories when they

With their hands close together, they talked endlessly, neither listening much to the other. ■
(From *Grandmother's Donkey* by Joan Smith. Illustrated by Gunvor Edwards.)

were young, although I read them plenty. The creative urge is to produce a character, and to recreate atmosphere and emotion, or the feel of a place. From the comments of the critics this does seem to be what I am best at; I have never been praised for a clever plot.

"But children's books do need a workmanlike plot, even more than adult works, and I have to work on this. I find legend useful and often tie a modern problem to a local folk tale, frequently one with a foreign location. I took the tumulus grave of a stone age man in Brittany about whom nothing was known in *The Gift of Umtal* and linked it with the problems of a boy coming to terms with the fact he does not have to feel guilty in acknowledging affection for his stepmother. In another, *November and the Truffle Pig,* I took the problem of a truffle pig in the Dordegne area of France, who would not use his sense of smell to seek out the fungus delicacies in the traditional way, and the legend that a statue of a black virgin

in a nearby church could work miracles, which were heralded by the spontaneous ringing of an old church bell.

"Although trained as a physio, I gave this work up when my children were born. By the time they were at school, my husband had started his own business, which is packaging, a plastic bottle and printing firm, and I was pulled in to keep the accounts. The job has expanded and accountants have to explain new skills required of me each year. Luckily, coming to terms (eventually) with a computer is now saving me from working full time.

"Competing with my writing time is my Open University degree, which I adore working on. One half of me regrets not having gone to university at eighteen; the other half is grateful that as an adult, it is possible to enjoy study more.

"I do think writing for children is harder than writing for adults, in that there is a choice—either the well plotted, turn

JOAN SMITH

the page, action story *or* the in-depth, analytical development of character. Children demand action, teachers and librarians demand literary values. Therefore, a children's writer has to satisfy both, not one or the other.

"*November and the Truffle Pig* has been translated into French, and *Pilgrim's Way*, into Welsh. *The Dittany Bush* has been translated into Russian. This was a great thrill because I located a copy in a children's library in Moscow, and they presented it to me, since I had not before seen a copy of the edition. I walked down Gorky Street in the snow with it tucked under my coat."

HOBBIES AND OTHER INTERESTS: Tennis, golf.

SMITH, Ursula 1934-

PERSONAL: Born January 3, 1934, in Santa Maria, Calif.; daughter of Jules (a physician) and Mary Loretta (a nurse; maiden name, Connolly) Bertero; married James Francis Smith (an insurance agent), July 19, 1958 (divorced, 1988); children: James, Jr., Joseph, Christopher, Ursula, Nora. *Education:* San Francisco College for Women, B.A., 1955; San Francisco State University, graduate studies, 1955-56. *Home and office:* 1104 South Fifth, Bozeman, Mont. 59715.

CAREER: Mission High School, San Francisco, Calif., teacher of English, 1956-58; secretary and office manager for computer and real estate firms, Bozeman, Mont., 1977-80; writer, free-lance editor, 1980—. Gives readings, workshops, and presentations in women's history and biography. *Member:* Society of Children's Book Writers, Montana Institute of the Arts, National Women's Studies Association, Editorial Free-

lancers Association. *Awards, honors:* With Linda Peavy, Paladin Award for Best Article in *Montana, the Magazine of Western History,* 1985; *Dreams into Deeds* was selected a Notable Children's Trade Book in the Field of Social Studies by the National Council for Social Studies and the Children's Book Council, 1986, and one of Child Study Association of America's Children's Books of the Year, 1987; with L. Peavy residency in nonfiction at Centrum, Port Townsend, Wash., 1988.

WRITINGS—For young people; all with Linda Peavy: *Food, Nutrition, and You,* Scribner, 1982; *Women Who Changed Things: Nine Lives That Made a Difference,* Scribner, 1983; *Dreams into Deeds: Nine Women Who Dared,* Scribner, 1985.

Other: (With L. Peavy) "Pamelia" (three-act opera; music by Eric Funk), choral version produced at Carnegie Hall, New York, N.Y. 1989.

Also author of articles with L. Peavy in periodicals, including *Nebraska Education News, Plainswoman, Cobblestone, Montana English Journal, Woman's Journal Advocate,* and *Montana, the Magazine of Western History.*

WORK IN PROGRESS—All with Linda Peavy: *When Papa Comes Home,* historical fiction for young adults; *Women in Waiting: The Home Frontier in the Westward Movement; The Widows of Little Falls.*

SIDELIGHTS: "Some truths are slow in coming. Swept as I was by the drama of the stories I read and heard in the history classes I took as a child and as a college student, it never occurred to me to question the accuracy of those texts. I was well over forty before I came to realize that half the story was missing. None of those books I had so enjoyed had given me the role models I needed in order to reach my fullest potential, for none of those books had told me about the women who shaped our past. I had grown up with the subtle message that everything worth writing about had been accomplished by men; women had done nothing worth remembering. I cannot overemphasize the impact that unstated message has had on countless young women.

URSULA SMITH

"Convinced that future generations must not grow up with the same misconceptions, I have spent the last ten years of my life researching and writing the stories of women whose achievements were remarkable, yet unrecorded and largely unremembered. Writing these stories into history validates the lives of those women and somehow validates my own."

SOUTHEY, Robert 1774-1843
(Don Manuel Alvarez Espriella)

PERSONAL: Born August 12, 1774, in Bristol, England; died March 21, 1843, at home, Greta Hall, in Keswick, England; son of a Bristol linen draper and Margaret Hill Southey; married Edith Fricker, November 14, 1795 (died, November 16, 1837); married Caroline Bowles (an author), 1839; children: (first marriage) Margaret, Edith May, Herbert, Emma, Bertha, Katherine, Isabel, Charles Cuthbert. *Education:* Attended Balliol College, Oxford, 1793-94. *Politics:* Pantisocracy; later, Tory. *Religion:* Church of England. *Home:* Greta Hall, Keswick, England.

CAREER: English Romantic poet and prose-writer. *Awards, honors:* Poet Laureate of England, 1813-43; honorary LL.D., Oxford, 1820.

WRITINGS—For children: (Reteller) *The Three Bears* (illustrated by William Moyers; originally published in *The Doctor,* Volume 4; see below), Limited Editions, 1949 [other editions include those illustrated by Feodor Rojankovsky, adapted by Kathleen N. Daly, Golden Press, 1967; Sarah Chamberlain, Chamberlain Press, 1983].

Adult; poems: (With Samuel Taylor Coleridge) *The Fall of Robespierre: An Historic Drama,* W. H. Lums & J. Merrill,

ROBERT SOUTHEY

1794; (wih Robert Lovell) *Poems: Containing the Retrospect, Odes, Elegies, Sonnets,* R. Crutwell, 1795; *Joan of Arc: An Epic Poem,* J. Cottle, 1796, Manning & Loring, 1798; *Poems,* 2 volumes, T. N. Longman & O. Rees, 1799.

Thalaba the Destroyer, 2 volumes, T. N. Longman & O. Rees, 1801, T. B. Wait, 1812; *Metrical Tales and Other Poems,* Longman, Hurst, 1805, C. Williams, 1811; *Madoc,* 2 volumes, Longman, Hurst, 1805, Munroe & Francis, 1806; *The Curse of Kehama,* Longman, Hurst, 1810, D. Longworth, 1811; *Roderick, the Last of the Goths,* Longman, Hurst, 1814; *Odes to His Royal Highness the Prince of Regent, His Imperial Majesty the Emperor of Russia, and His Majesty the King of Prussia,* Longman, Hurst, 1814; *Carmen Triumphale, for the Commencement of the Year 1814,* [London], 1814; *The Lay of the Laureate: Carmen Nuptiale,* Longman, Hurst, 1816; *The Poet's Pilgrimage to Waterloo,* W. B. Gilley, 1816; *Wat Tyler: A Dramatic Poem in Three Acts,* J. Fairburn, 1817; *A Vision of Judgment,* Longman, Hurst, 1821; *A Tale of Paraguay,* Longman, Hurst, 1825, S. G. Goodrich, 1827; *All for Love; and, The Pilgrim to Compostella,* J. Murray, 1829; *Oliver Newman: A New England Tale (Unfinished); with Other Poetical Remains,* Longman, Brown, 1845; (with wife, Caroline Southey) *Robin Hood: A Fragment,* W. Blackwood & Sons, 1847.

Biographies: *The Life of Nelson,* 2 volumes, Eastburn Kirk, 1813, reissued, AMS Press, 1973 [other editions illustrated by Edward Duncan, Birket Foster, and Richard Westall, D. Bogue, 1854; B. Foster, Roberts Brothers, 1883; A. D. McCormick, Houghton, Mifflin, 1916]; *The Life of Wesley, and the Rise and Progress of Methodism,* 2 volumes, E. Duyckinck, 1820; (with son, Charles Cuthbert Southey) *The Life of Reverend Andrew Bell* (Volume 1 by Southey; Volumes 2 & 3 by C. C. Southey), edited by Caroline Southey, J. Murray, 1844; *The Life of Oliver Cromwell,* [London], 1844, [New York], 1854; *The Life of William Cowper,* Phillips, Sampson, 1858.

Histories: *The History of Brazil,* 3 volumes, Longman, Hurst, 1810-19, new edition, B. Franklin, 1971; *The Expedition of Orsua and the Crimes of Aguirre,* Hickman & Hazzard, 1821; *The History of the Peninsular War,* J. Murray, 1823-32; *The Lives of the British Admirals,* 4 volumes, Longman, Rees, 1833-40, Volume 1 published in America as *The Early Naval History of England,* Carey, Lea, 1835.

Editor: *The Annual Anthology,* 2 volumes, T. N. Longman & O. Rees, 1799-1800; (with Joseph Cottle) *The Works of Thomas Chatterton,* 3 volumes, T. N. Longman & O. Rees, 1803, reissued, AMS Press, 1968; *The Remains of Henry Kirke White,* 3 volumes, Longman, Hurst, 1807-22; *Specimens of the Later English Poets,* 3 volumes, Longman, Hurst, 1807; *The Byrth, Lyf, and Actes of King Arthur,* 2 volumes, Longman, Hurst, 1817; *The Pilgrim's Progress, with a Life of John Bunyan,* J. Murray, 1830; *Select Works of the British Poets, from Chaucer to Jonson,* Longman, Rees, 1831; *Attempts in Verse by John Jones, an Old Servant,* J. Murray, 1831, later edition published as *The Lives and Works of the Uneducated Poets,* H. Milford, 1925; *Horae Lyricae: Poems by Isaac Watts,* J. Hatcherd, 1834; *The Works of William Cowper,* 15 volumes, Baldwin & Cradock, 1836-37; reissued, AMS Press, 1971.

Translator: (From the French) Jacques Necker, *On the French Revolution,* Volume 2, T. Cadell & W. Davies, 1797; (from the Spanish) Vasco de Lobeira, *Amadis of Gaul,* 4 volumes, T. N. Longman & O. Rees, 1803; (from the Portuguese) Francisco de Moraes, *Palmerin of England,* 4 volumes, Longman, Hurst, 1807; (from the Spanish) *Chronicle of the Cid,* Longman, Hurst, 1808, D. Bixby, 1846, reissued, Doubleday, 1961.

Robert Southey, 1804. Portrait by H. Eldridge, courtesy of National Portrait Gallery, London.

Other: *Letters Written During a Short Residence in Spain and Portugal,* J. Cottle, 1797; (under pseudonym Don Manuel Alvarez Espriella) *Letters from England,* 3 volumes, Longman, Hurst, 1807, reissued, Cresset Press, 1951, new edition, edited by Jack Simmons, A. Sutton, 1984; *The Origin, Nature, and Object of the New System of Education,* [London], 1812; *A Letter to William Smith, Esq. M. P.,* J. Murray, 1817; (with S. T. Coleridge) *Omniana; or, Horae Otiosiores,* 2 volumes, Longman, Hurst, 1812, new edition, Southern Illinois University Press, 1969; *The Book of the Church,* 2 volumes, J. Murray, 1824, Wells & Lilly, 1825; *Vindiciae Ecclesiae Anglicanae,* J. Murray, 1826; *Sir Thomas More; or, Colloquies on the Progress and Prospects of Society,* 2 volumes, J. Murray, 1829; *Essays, Moral and Political,* 2 volumes, J. Murray, 1832, facsimile edition, Irish University Press, 1971; *Letter to John Murray, Esq., ''Touching'' Lord Nugent,* J. Murray, 1833.

The Doctor, 7 volumes, Longman, Rees, 1834-47 [excerpt published separately as *The Three Bears* (Southey's retelling of an earlier tale; illustrated by William Moyers), Limited Editions, 1949]; *Southey's Common-Place Book,* 4 volumes, edited by John Wood Warter, Harper, 1849-51; *Journal of a Tour in the Netherlands in the Autumn of 1815,* edited by W. R. Nicoll, Houghton, Mifflin, 1902; *English Seamen: Hawkins, Greenville, Devereux, Raleigh,* Methuen, 1904; *Journal of a Tour in Scotland in 1819,* edited by C. H. Herford, J. Murray, 1929, reissued, J. Thin, 1972; *Journals of a Residence in Portugal, 1800-1801, and a Visit to France, 1838,* edited by Adolfo Cabral, Clarendon Press, 1960, reissued, Greenwood Press, 1978.

Collections and selections: *Poems by Robert Southey,* Manning & Loring, 1799; *The Minor Poems of Robert Southey,* 3 volumes, Longman, Hurst, 1815; *The Poetical Works of Robert Southey,* A. & W. Gagliani, 1829; *The Poetical Works of Robert Southey, Collected by Himself,* 10 volumes, Longman, Hurst, 1837-38, D. Appleton, 1842, reissued, Scholarly Press, 1969; *The Life and Correspondence of Robert Southey,* edited by C. C. Southey, 6 volumes, Harper, 1849, reissued, Scholarly Press, 1969; *The Complete Poetical Works of Robert Southey,* D. Appleton, 1851; *Southey's Poems,* 3 volumes, Clarke, Beeton, 1854; *Selections from the Letters of Robert Southey,* edited by J. W. Warter, 4 volumes, Longman & Co., 1856, reissued, AMS Press, 1977.

The Correspondence of Robert Southey with Caroline Bowles, edited by Edward Dowden, [Dublin], 1881; *Robert Southey: The Story of His Life Written in His Letters,* edited by John Dennis, Lothrop, 1887; *Selections from the Poems,* edited by S. R. Thompson, [London], 1888; *Poems,* edited by E. Dowden, [London], 1895; *Poems of Robert Southey,* edited by Maurice H. Fitzgerald, Oxford University Press, 1909; *Letters of Robert Southey: A Selection,* edited by Maurice H. Fitzgerald, Oxford University Press, 1912, reissued, AMS Press, 1977; *Select Prose of Robert Southey,* edited by Jacob Zeitlin, [New York], 1916; *New Letters of Robert Southey,* edited by Kenneth Curry, 2 volumes, Columbia University Press, 1965; *A Choice of Robert Southey's Verse,* edited by Geoffrey Grigson, Faber, 1970; *Letters from the Lake Poets, Samuel Taylor Coleridge, William Wordsworth, Robert Southey to Daniel Stuart, Editor of the Morning Post and the Courier, 1800-1838,* Folcroft, 1974; *The Letters of Robert Southey to John May, 1797-1838,* edited by Charles Ramos, Jenkins, 1976; *The Contributions of Robert Southey to the Morning Post,* edited by K. Curry, University of Alabama Press, 1984.

Contributor to periodicals, including *Monthly, Critical Review, Annual Review, Athenaeum, Quarterly Review, Foreign Quarterly Review, Foreign Review, Edinburgh Annual Register, Morning Post,* and *Courier.*

ADAPTATIONS: ''Goldilocks and the Three Bears and Other Stories'' (cassette), Caedmon, 1986.

SIDELIGHTS: **August 12, 1774.** Born on Wine Street in Bristol, England. Southey's paternal grandfather was a Somerset farmer; his own father was an unsuccessful cloth merchant, and his mother, Margaret Hill, was educated but poor. ''The first child of this marriage was born August 1, 1773, and christened John Cannon. He lived only to be nine or ten months old. He was singularly beautiful; so much so, that, when I made my appearance . . . , I was sadly disparaged by comparison with him. My mother asking if it was a boy, was answered by her nurse in a tone as little favourable to me as the opinion was flattering. 'Ay, a great ugly boy!' and she added, when she told me this, 'God forgive me!—when I saw what a great red creature it was, covered with rolls of fat, I thought I should never be able to love him.''' [Rev. Charles Cuthbert Southey, editor, *The Life and Correspondence of Robert Southey,* Volume I, Longman, Brown, Green and Longmans, 1849.[1]]

Southey and three brothers survived infancy, but three sisters and two other brothers died.

At the age of two, he was sent to Bath, to live with his mother's half-sister, the domineering and eccentric Miss Elizabeth Tyler. ''Here my time was chiefly passed from the age of two till six. I had many indulgences, but more privations, and those of an injurious kind; want of playmates, want of exercise, never being allowed to do anything in which by possibility I might dirt myself; late hours for a child, which I reckon among the privations (having always had the healthiest propensity for going to bed betimes); late hours of rising, which were less painful perhaps, but in other respects worse.

''My aunt chose that I should sleep with her, and this subjected me to a double evil. She used to have her bed warmed, and during the months while this practice was in season I was always put into Molly's bed first, for fear of an accident from the warming-pan, and removed when my aunt went to bed, so that I was regularly wakened out of a sound sleep. This, however, was not half so bad as being obliged to lie till nine, and not unfrequently till ten in the morning, and not daring to make the slightest movement which could disturb her during the hours that I lay awake, and longing to be set free. These were, indeed, early and severe lessons of patience. My poor little wits were upon the alert at those tedious hours of compulsory idleness, fancying figures and combinations of form in the curtains, wondering at the motes in the slant sunbeam, and watching the light from the crevices of the window-shutters, till it served me at last by its progressive motion to measure the lapse of time. Thoroughly injudicious as my education under Miss Tyler was, no part of it was so irksome as this.'' [John Dennis, editor, *Robert Southey: The Story of His Life Written in His Letters,* Lothrop, 1887.[2]]

Miss Tyler loved the theatre, and Southey was introduced to it early. ''Nothing could be more propitious for me, considering my aptitudes and tendency of mind, than Miss Tyler's predilection, I might almost call it passion, for the theatre. Owing to this, Shakespere was in my hands as soon as I could read; and it was long before I had any other knowledge of the history of England than what I gathered from his plays.

''But I acquired imperceptibly from such reading familiarity with the diction, and ear for the blank verse of our great masters.

"You will wonder that this education should not have made me a dramatic writer. I had seen more plays before I was seven years old than I have ever seen since I was twenty, and heard more conversation about the theatre than any other subject."[2]

Despite his exposure to the sophisticated world of the theatre, Southey was kept in skirts until he was sent to school at age six. "Miss Tyler, whose ascendancy over my mother was always that of an imperious older sister, would not suffer me to be breeched till I was six years old, though I was tall of my age. I had a fantastic costume of nankeen for highdays and holydays, trimmed with green fringe; it was called a vest and tunic, or a *jam*. When at last I changed my dress, it was for coat, waistcoat, and breeches of foresters' green; at that time there was no intermediate form of apparel in use. I was then sent as a day scholar to a school on the top of St. Michael's or Mile Hill, which was then esteemed the best in Bristol, kept by Mr. Foot, a dissenting minister of the community called General Baptists, in contradistinction to the Particular of Calvinistic Baptists. He was an old man, and if the school had ever been a good one, it had wofully deteriorated. I was one of the least boys there, I believe the very least, and certainly both as willing and as apt to learn as any teacher could have desired; yet it was the only school where I was ever treated with severity.

"I was shut up during playtime in a closet at the top of the stairs, where there was just light enough through some bars to see my lesson by. Once he caned me cruelly,—the only time that any master ever laid his hand upon me,—and I am sure he deserved a beating much more than I did. There was a great deal of tyranny in the school, from the worst of which I was exempted, because I went home in the evening; but I stood in great fear of the big boys, and saw much more of the evil side of human nature than I should ever have learnt in the course of domestic education."[2]

Southey suffered at school and at Miss Tyler's. He missed his own family, especially his mother, who was in awe of her half-sister's iron will. In later years his greatest joy was quiet family life, in contrast to the eccentric life at Miss Tyler's. "The principle upon which her whole household economy was directed was that of keeping the house clean, and taking more precautions against dust than would have been needful against the plague in an infected city. She labored under a perpetual *dusto-phobia,* and a comical disease it was; but whether I have been most amused or annoyed by it, it would be difficult to say. I had, however, in its consequences, an early lesson how fearfully the mind may be enslaved by indulging its own peculiarities and whimsies, innocent as they may appear at first.

"The discomfort which Miss Tyler's passion for cleanliness produced to herself, as well as to her little household, was truly curious: to herself, indeed, it was a perpetual torment; to the two servants a perpetual vexation, and so it would have been to me if nature had not blest me with an innate hilarity of spirit which nothing but real affliction can overcome. That the better rooms might be kept clean, she took possession of the kitchen, sending the servants to one which was underground; and in this little, dark, confined place, with a rough stone floor, and a skylight (for it must not be supposed that it was a best kitchen, which was always, as it was intended to be, a comfortable sitting-room; this was more like a scullery), we always took our meals, and generally lived. The best room was never opened but for company; except now and then on a fine day to be aired and dusted, if dust could be detected there. In the other parlor, I was allowed sometimes to read, and she wrote her letters, for she had many correspondents; and we sat there sometimes in summer, when a fire was not needed, for fire produced ashes, and ashes occasioned dust, and dust, visible or invisible, was the plague of her life.

"I have seen her order the teakettle to be emptied and refilled, because someone had passed across the hearth while it was on the fire preparing for her breakfast. She had indulged these humors till she had formed for herself notions of uncleanness almost as irrational and inconvenient as those of the Hindoos. She had a cup once buried for six weeks, to purify it from the lips of one whom she accounted unclean; all who were not her favorites were included in that class. A chair in which an unclean person had sat was put out in the garden to be aired; and I never saw her more annoyed than on one occasion when a man, who called upon business, seated himself in her own chair: how the cushion was ever again to be rendered fit for her use, she knew not! On such occasions, her fine features assumed a character either fierce or tragic; her expressions were vehement even to irreverence, and her gesticulations those of the deepest and wildest distress,—hands and eyes uplifted, as if she was in hopeless misery, or in a paroxysm of mental anguish."[2]

1782. On the death of Southey's grandmother, Miss Tyler moved to her house in Bedminster, where Southey enjoyed more freedom. It was here that he first began writing poetry. "I have so many vivid feelings connected with this house at Bedminster, that if it had not been in a vile neighborhood, I believe my heart would have been set upon purchasing it, and fixing my abode there where the happiest days of my childhood were spent. My grandfather built it (about the year 1740, I suppose), and had made it what was then thought a thoroughly commodious and good house for one in his rank of life.

"My chief amusement was in the garden, where I found endless entertainment in the flowers and in observing insects. I had little propensity to any boyish sports, and less expertness in them. My uncles Edward and William used to reproach me with this sometimes, saying they never saw such a boy."[2]

1786-1788. Southey came back home to live in Bristol with his family, but spent the holidays with Miss Tyler. A new school, Williams', was a change for the better. "The pleasantest of my school years were those which I passed at Williams'. What I learnt there, indeed, was worth little; it was just such a knowledge of Latin as a boy of quick parts and not without diligence will acquire under bad teaching.

"Williams, who read well himself and prided himself upon it, was one day very much offended with my reading, and asked me scornfully who taught me to read. I answered, my aunt. 'Then,' said he, 'give my compliments to your aunt; and tell her that my old horse, that has been dead these twenty years, could have taught you as well.' I delivered the message faithfully, to her great indignation. It was never forgotten or forgiven, and perhaps it accelerated the very proper resolution of removing me. My uncle made known his intention of placing me at Westminster. His connection with Christ Church naturally led him to prefer that to any other school. . . ."[2]

In spring, **1788,** Southey entered Westminster at the expense of his Uncle, the Rev. Herbert Hill. He was expelled for writing an article about flogging as the work of the Devil. He returned to Bristol in spring, 1972, the year his father went bankrupt, then died. "I left Westminster in a perilous state— a heart full of poetry and feeling, a head full of Rousseau and *Werther,* and my religious principles shaken by Gibbon; many circumstances tended to give me a wrong bias, none to lead me right except adversity, the wholesomest of all discipline."[2]

The following year he was sent to Balliol college, Oxford, by his Uncle who hoped he would become a clergyman. Instead, he wrote *Joan of Arc* and made friends with Robert Lovell and Samuel Taylor Coleridge. Together they embraced the theories of pantisocracy (the equal government by all) and aspheterism (the generalization of individual property). They formed a visionary plan to emigrate to America and create a Utopian society on the banks of the Susquahanna. Southey eagerly wrote to his brother: "In March we depart for America; Lovell, his wife, brother, and two of his sisters; all the Frickers; my mother, Miss Peggy, and brothers; Heath, apothecary, etc.; G.Burnett, S. T. Coleridge, Robert Allen, and Robert Southey. Of so many we are certain, and expect more. Whatever knowledge of navigation you can obtain will be useful, as we shall be on the bank of a navigable river, and appoint you admiral of a cock-boat. My aunt knows nothing as yet of my intended plan; it will surprise her, but not very agreeably. Everything is in a very fair train, and all parties eager to embark."[2]

But eagerness was all they had. Lovell had married one of the three Fricker sisters, who were educated but poor. Southey was in love with Edith Fricker. Coleridge, though still in love with someone else, was persuaded to marry the third Fricker sister, and lived to regret it. No one had any income or prospects. America was to remain a dream, whose focus shifted later to a farm in Wales, which never materialized either.

When Miss Tyler learned of Southey's plans to marry Edith and emigrate to America, she threw him out of her house on a rainy night, and never spoke to him again.

Coleridge and Southey gave historical lectures to support themselves and each other. "If Coleridge and I can get £150 a year between us, we purpose marrying, and retiring into the country, as our literary business can be carried on there, and practising agriculture till we can raise money for America—still the grand object in view."[2]

November 14, 1795. Married Edith Fricker at Redcliffe Church. The money for the fees and ring were lent to him by his lifelong friend and publisher, Joseph Cottle. This same ring was worn around Edith's neck for months, as the marriage was not publicized. Neither was it consummated, for Southey left within hours for Spain and Portugal. His uncle, the Rev. Hill, had hoped to avert the marriage by taking Southey with him on a six-month trip, little imagining he would marry Edith before going. Southey wrote to his publisher: "I have learnt from Lovell the news from Bristol, public as well as private, and both of an interesting nature. My marriage is become public. You know my only motive for wishing it otherwise, and must know that its publicity can give me no concern. I have done my duty. Perhaps you may hardly think my motives for marrying sufficiently strong. One, and that to me of great weight, I believe was never mentioned to you. There might have arisen feelings of an unpleasant nature, at the idea of receiving support from one not legally a husband; and (do not show this to Edith) should I perish by shipwreck, or any casualty, I have relations whose prejudices would then yield to the anguish of affection, and who would love and cherish, and yield all possible consolation to my widow. Of such an evil there is but possibility: but against possibility it was my duty to guard."[2]

1796. Southey fell in love with Portugal, but he returned to England and Edith in May. Robert Lovell had died a few weeks before Southey's return, and Mary Fricker Lovell soon found a home with the Southeys. They lived for a time in lodgings in Bristol.

During this time, Southey wrote *Madoc,* a long poem, and *Letters from Spain and Portugal.* He was trying to study law

in the hope of supporting Edith, Mary Lovell, his widowed mother, and his younger brother. "To go on with *Madoc* is *almost* necessary to my happiness; I had rather leave off eating than poetizing; but these things must be;—I will feed upon law and digest it, or it shall choke me."[2]

An old friend from Westminster days, C.W.W. Wynn, offered Southey an annuity, and suggested he go to London to study law. Wynn's generosity would support Southey most of his life. "The law will neither amuse me, nor ameliorate me, nor instruct me; but the moment it gives me a comfortable independence—and I have but few wants—then farewell to London.

"I should be the happiest man in the world, if I possessed enough to live with comfort in the country; but in this world we must sacrifice the best part of our lives to acquire that wealth, which generally arrives when the time of enjoying it is past.

"I ardently wish for children; yet, if God shall bless me with any, I shall be unhappy to see them poisoned by the air of London.

"My spirits always sink when I approach it. Green fields are my delight. I am not only better in health, but even in heart, in the country. A fine day exhilarates my heart; if it rains, I behold the grass assume a richer verdure as it drinks the moisture: everything that I behold is very good, except man; and in London I see nothing but man and his works."[2]

Southey and Edith sought the countryside, and took a house with Southey's mother at Westbury on Trym, which they named Martin Hall. Here the most and the best of Southey's poems were written. ". . . We christened the house properly, I assure you, as the martins have colonized all round it, and doubly lucky must the house be on which they so build and bemire. We hesitated between the appropriate names of Rat Hall, Mouse Mansion, Vermin Villa, Cockroach Castle, Cobweb Cottage, and Spider Lodge; but as we routed out the spiders, stopped the rat holes, and found no cockroaches, we bethought of the animals without, and dubbed it Martin Hall." [*A Choice of Robert Southey's Verse,* selected and with an introduction by Geoffrey Grigson, Faber & Faber, 1970.[3]]

Cats were essential to Southey's household and stories about them abound in his later work, *The Doctor.* During this time he met William Wordsworth, whose friendship was to last a lifetime.

1800. Traveled with Edith to Portugal. In a letter to Coleridge, he described their perilous journey. "Here, then, we are, thank God! alive, and recovering from dreadful sickness. I never suffered so much at sea, and Edith was worse than I was; we scarcely ate or slept at all: but the passage was very fine and short; five days and a half brought us to our port, with light winds the whole of the way. The way was not, however, without alarm. On Monday morning, between five and six, the captain was awakened with tidings that a cutter was bearing down upon us, with English colors, indeed, but apparently a French vessel; we made a signal, which was not answered; we fired a gun, she did the same, and preparations were made for action. We had another Lisbon packet in company, mounting six guns; our own force was ten; the cutter was a match, and more, for both, but we did not expect to be taken. You may imagine Edith's terror, awakened on a sick bed—disturbed I should have said—with these tidings! The captain advised me to surround her with mattresses in the cabin, but she would not believe herself in safety there, and I lodged her in the cockpit, and took my station on the quarterdeck with a musket.

Title page from Southey's *The Doctor*, showing the view from the author's study window. Illustration by J. T. Willmore.

How I felt I can hardly tell; the hurry of the scene, the sight of grape-shot, bar-shot, and other ingenious implements of this sort, made an undistinguishable mixture of feelings. The cutter bore down between us; I saw smoke from her matches, we were so near, and not a man on board had the least idea but that an immediate action was to take place. We hailed her; she answered in broken English, and passed on. 'Tis over! cried somebody. Not yet! said the captain; and we expected she was coming round as about to attack our comrade vessel. She was English, however, manned chiefly from Guernsey, and this explained her Frenchified language. You will easily imagine that my sensations, at the ending of the business, were very definable,—one honest simple joy that I was in a whole skin! I laid the musket in the chest with considerably more pleasure than I took it out. I am glad this took place; it has shown me what it is to prepare for action.''[2]

1801. Returned to England. Published *Thalaba the Destroyer* and began *Curse of Kehama*. Worked continuously on *History of Portugal,* which he was still working on up until his death. Southey abandoned all thoughts of the law and had various dreams for making a living. He and Edith visited the Coleridges at Keswick, where they had gone to live near the Wordsworths, in the beautiful Lakes region of England. ''Thus much for the future; for the present I am about to move to Coleridge, who is at the Lakes;—and I am laboring, somewhat blindly indeed, but all to some purpose, about my ways and means; for the foreign expedition that has restored my health, has at the same time picked my pocket; and if I had not good spirits and cheerful industry, I should be somewhat surly and sad. So I am—I hope most truly and ardently for the last

J. T. Willmore's frontispiece illustration from *The Doctor.*

time—pen-and-inking for supplies, not from pure inclination. I am rather heaping bricks and mortar than building; hesitating between this plan and that plan, and preparing for both.''[2]

Southey returned to Bristol with the news of his mother's death. His first born daughter lived for only a year. Their grief prompted them to stay with the Coleridges, hoping their year-old daughter, Sara, would cheer them. The visit expanded to a lifetime. ''To escape from Bristol was a relief. The place was haunted, and it is my wish never to see it again. Here my spirits suffer from the sight of little Sara, who is about her size. However, God knows that I do not repine, and that in my very soul I feel that his will is best. These things do one good: they loosen, one by one, the roots that rivet us to earth; they fix and confirm our faith till the thought of death becomes so inseparably connected with the hope of meeting those whom we have lost, that death itself is no longer considered as an evil.

''Edith suffers deeply and silently. She is kept awake at night by recollections,—and I am harassed by dreams of the poor child's illness and recovery, but this will wear away. Would that you could see these lakes and mountains! how wonderful they are! how awful in their beauty. All the poet-part of me will be fed and fostered here. I feel already in tune, and shall proceed to my work with such a feeling of power as old Samson had when he laid hold of the pillars of the Temple of Dagon.''[2]

Greta Hall, the Coleridges' home, was a three-story house designed for two families. The owner, Willliam Jackson, and his housekeeper, Mrs. Wilson, lived there, in addition to the Coleridges and the Southeys and Mary Lovell. Mrs. Wilson later worked for the Southeys and helped to raise the children. The Wordsworths lived fifteen miles away. Southey had finally found a home. ''This place is better suited for me than you imagine—it tempts me to take far more exercise than I ever took elsewhere, for we have the loveliest scenes possible close at hand; and I have, therefore, seldom or never felt myself in stronger health. And as for good spirits, be sure I have the outward and visible sign, however it may be for the inward and spiritual grace.

''The mountains, on Thursday evening, before the sun was quite down, or the moon bright, were all of one dead-blue color; their rifts, and rocks, and swells, and scars had all disappeared—the surface was perfectly uniform, nothing but the outline distinct; and this even surface of dead blue, from its unnatural uniformity, made them, though not transparent, appear transvious,—as though they were of some soft or cloudy texture through which you could have passed. I never saw any appearance so perfectly unreal. Sometimes a blazing sunset seems to steep them through and through with red light; or it is a cloudy morning, and the sunshine slants down through a rift in the clouds, and the pillar of light makes the spot whereon it falls so emerald green that it looks like a little field of Paradise. At night you lose the mountains, and the wind so stirs up the lake that it looks like the sea by moonlight.''[2]

Southey may have found a lifetime home, but keeping it would prove to be a lifetime challenge. Forced to write editorials, essays and book reviews for a living, he nevertheless kept up a continuous correspondence, wrote verse, and read thousands of books which he collected into a library of 14,000 volumes. ''I must go to work for money; and that also frets me. This hand-to-mouth work is very disheartening, and interferes cruelly with better things,—more important they cannot be called, for the bread-and-cheese is the business of the first necessity.''[2]

To Coleridge he wrote: ''Oh! I have yet such dreams! Is it quite clear that you and I were not meant for some better star, and dropped, by mistake, into this world of pounds, shillings, and pence?''[2]

1804. Coleridge, addicted to opium, and estranged from his wife, went to Malta, and never returned to Keswick to live. Their friendship suffered a change, but Southey supported the Coleridge family and was much loved by the Coleridge children. All three Fricker sisters now lived at Greta Hall. They were his financial burden, but there is no doubt that he was well-cared for. ''Of my own goings on I know not that there is anything which can be said. Imagine me in this great study of mine from breakfast till dinner, from dinner till tea, and from tea till supper, in my old black coat, my corduroys alternately with the long worsted pantaloons and gaiters in one, and the green shade, and sitting at my desk, and you have my picture and my history. I play with Dapper, the dog, downstairs, who loves me as well as ever Cupid did, and the cat up-stairs plays with me; for puss, finding my room the quietest in the house, has thought proper to share it with me. Our weather has been so wet that I have not got out-of-doors for a walk in a month. Now and then I go down to the river, which runs at the bottom of the orchard, and throw stones till my arms ache, and then saunter back again. James Lawson, the carpenter, has made boards for my papers, and a screen, like those in the frame, with a little shelf to hold my ivory knife, etc., and is now making a little table for Edith, of which I shall probably make the most use. I rouse the house to breakfast every morning, and qualify myself for a boatswain's place by this practice; and thus one day passes like another, and never did the days appear to pass so fast. Summer will make a difference.''[2]

A second daughter, Edith May, was born. The depth of Southey's love for his wife and child was expressed in this letter to his wife: ''I need not tell you, my own dear Edith, not to read my letters aloud till you have first of all seen what is written only for yourself. What I have now to say to you is that having been eight days from home, with as little discomfort, and as little reason for discomfort, as a man can reasonably expect, I have yet felt so little comfortable, so great sense of solitariness, and so many homeward yearnings, that certainly I will not go to Lisbon without you. Without you I am not happy. But for your sake as well as my own, and for little Edith's sake, I will not consent to any separation; the growth of a year's love between her and me, to be given up for any light inconveniences either on your part or mine. An absence of a year would make her effectually forget me. But of these things we will talk at leisure; only, dear, dear Edith, we must not part.''[2]

1805. _Madoc_ published. Went to Scotland to meet Sir Walter Scott.

1806. First son, Herbert, born. ''. . . I have had a son born into the world, and baptized into the Church by the name of Herbert, who is now six months old, and bids fair to be as noisy a fellow as his father,—which is saying something; for be it known that I am quite as noisy as ever I was, and should take as much delight as ever in showering stones through the hole of the staircase against your room door, and hearing with what hearty good earnest 'you fool!' was vociferated in indignation against me in return. Oh . . . what a blessing it is to have a boy's heart! it is as great a blessing in carrying one through this world as to have a child's spirit will be in fitting us for the next.''[2]

1809. _The Quarterly Review_ was established by Sir Walter Scott to encourage the British ministry in its war against Napoleon. Southey became a contributor, and received a modest but regular income from it.

**They listened to the Maid,
And they almost believed....**

■(From _Joan of Arc, Ballads, Lyrics, and Minor Poems_ by Robert Southey. Illustrated by John Gilbert.)

Daughter, Bertha, born. Both his son, Herbert, and daughter, Emma, were ill and Southey suffered from a constant fear of their possible death. ''I had a daughter born on the 27th last month; a few days after the birth her mother was taken ill, and for some time there was cause of serious alarm. This, God be thanked, is over. The night before last we had another alarm of the worst kind, though happily this also is passing away. My little boy went to bed with some slight indications of a trifling cold. His mother went up as usual to look at him before supper; she thought he coughed in a strange manner, called me, and I instantly recognized the sound of the croup. We have a good apothecary within three minutes' walk, and luckily he was at home. He immediately confirmed our fears. The child was taken out of bed and bled in the jugular vein, a blister placed on the throat next morning, and by these vigorous and timely remedies we hope and trust the disease is subdued. But what a twelve hours did we pass, knowing the nature of the disease, and only hoping the efficacy of the remedy. Even now I am far, very far, from being at ease. There is a love which passeth the love of women, and which is more lightly alarmed than the wakefullest jealousy.

"I am not a stoic at home: I feel as you do about the fall of an old tree; but, O Christ! what a pang it is to look upon the young shoot and think it will be cut down. And this is the thought which almost at all times haunts me; it comes upon me in moments when I know not whether the tears that start are of love or of bitterness. There is an evil, too, in seeing all things like a poet; circumstances which would glide over a healthier mind sink into mine; everything comes to me with its whole force,—the full meaning of a look, a gesture, a child's imperfect speech, I can perceive, and cannot help perceiving; and thus as I made to remember what I would give the world to forget.''[2]

A month later Southey's fear came true. "We lost Emma yesterday night. Five days ago she was in finer health than we had ever seen her, and I repeatedly remarked it. For a day or two she had been ailing; on Saturday night breathed shortly and was evidently ill. Edmondson repeatedly saw her, thought her better at ten o'clock, and assured us he saw no danger. In half an hour she literally fell asleep without a struggle. Edith is as well as should be expected, and I, perhaps, better. You know I take tooth-ache and tooth-drawings, and I have almost learnt to bear moral pain, not, indeed, with the same levity, but with as few outward and visible signs. In fact, God be thanked for it, there never was a man who had more entirely set his heart upon things permanent and eternal than I have done; the transitoriness of everything here is always present to my feeling as well as my understanding. Were I to speak as sincerely of my family as Wordsworth's little girl, my story [would be] that I have five children; three of them at home, and two under my mother's care in heaven.''[2]

1812. Met Shelley and took him under his wing. "Here is a man at Keswick, who acts upon me as my own ghost would do. He is just what I was in 1794. His name is Shelley, son to the member for Shoreham; with 6000*l*. a year entailed upon him, and as much more in his father's power to cut off. . . .

"He is come to the fittest physician in the world. At present he has got to the Pantheistic stage of philosophy, and, in the course of a week, I expect he will be a Berkeleyan, for I have put him upon a course of Berkeley. It has surprised him a good deal to meet, for the first time in his life, with a man who perfectly understands him, and does him full justice. I tell him that all the difference between us is, that he is nineteen, and I am thirty-seven; and I dare say it will not be very long before I shall succeed in convincing him that he may be a true philosopher, and do a great deal of good, with 6000*l*. a year; the thought of which troubles him a great deal more at present than ever the want of sixpence (for I have known such a want) did me.''[2]

Daughter, Isabel, born; but Southey suffered presentiments of his son Herbert's death. "No child ever promised better, morally and intellectually. He is very quick of comprehension, retentive, observant, diligent, and as fond of a book and as impatient of idleness as I am. Would that I were as well satisfied with his bodily health; but in spite of activity and bodily hilarity, he is pale and puny: just that kind of child of whom old women would say that he is too clever to live. Old women's notions are not often so well founded as this; and having this apprehension before my eyes, the uncertainty of human happiness never comes home to my heart so deeply as when I look at him. God's will be done! I must sow the seed as carefully as if I were sure that the harvest would ripen.''[2]

1813. Made Poet Laureate at the recommendation of Sir Walter Scott, who turned down the post. The small yearly sum eased Southey's mind. "It comes to me as a Godsend, and I have vested it in a life-policy; by making it up 102*l*. It covers an insurance for 3000*l*. upon my own life. I have never felt any painful anxiety as to providing for my family,—my mind is too buoyant, my animal spirits too good, for this care ever to have affected my happiness.''[2]

1814. Began work on *The Doctor,* a personal and autobiographical collection of anecdotes he would publish anonymously twenty years later. The story of the fictional Dr. Daniel Dove and his family and friends, *The Doctor* recounts many traditional stories and proverbs, as well as Southey's opinions on various topics. "Such a variety of ingredients I think never before entered into any book which had a thread of continuity running through it. I promise you there is as much sense as nonsense there. It is very much like a trifle, where you have whipt cream at the top, sweetmeats below, and a good solid foundation of cake well steeped in ratafia. You will find a liberal expenditure of long hoarded stores, such as the reading of few men could supply; satire and speculation; truths, some of which might beseem the bench or the pulpit, and others that require the sanction of the cap and bells for their introduction. And withal a narrative interspersed with interludes of every kind; yet still continuous upon a plan of its own, varying from grave to gay; and taking as wild and yet as natural a course as one of our mountain streams.'' [Kenneth Curry, *Southey,* Routledge & Kegan Paul, 1975.[4]]

1816. Son, Herbert, died. Southey never fully recovered. "Here is an end of hope and of fear, but not of suffering. His sufferings, however, are over, and, thank God, his passage was perfectly easy. He fell asleep, and is now in a better state of existence, for which his nature was more fitted than for this. . . . For years it has been my daily prayer that I might be spared this affliction.

"Oh! that I may be able to leave this country! The wound will never close while I remain in it. You would wonder to see me, how composed I am. Thank God, I can control myself for the sake of others; but it is a lifelong grief, and do what I can to lighten it, the burden will be as heavy as I can bear.

"Many blessings are left me—abundant blessings, more than I have deserved, more than I had ever reason to expect, or even to hope. I have strong ties to life, and many duties yet to perform. Believe me, I see these things as they ought to be seen. Reason will do something, time more, Religion most of all. The loss is but for this world; but as long as I remain in this world I shall feel it.

"Never, perhaps, was child of ten years old so much to his father. Without ever ceasing to treat him as a child, I had made him my companion, as well as playmate and pupil, and he had learnt to interest himself in my pursuits, and take part in all my enjoyments.

"I thank God for the strength with which we have borne this trial. I pray for continued life that I may fulfill my duties towards those whom I love. Many will feel for me, but none can tell what I have lost: the head and flower of my earthly happiness is cut off. But I am *not* unhappy.

"No circumstance of my former life ever brought with it so great a change as that which I daily and hourly feel, and perhaps shall never cease to feel. Yet I am thankful for having possessed this child so long; for worlds I would not but have been his father. Of all the blessings which it has pleased God to vouchsafe me, this was and *is* the greatest.''[2]

Southey's religious beliefs were strengthened during this trial and he became more and more an outspoken supporter of the Church of England.

1819. Son, Charles Cuthbert, born. He would later compile Southey's letters.

1834. Mrs. Southey was committed to the Retreat, a Quaker asylum in York. The same year, Edith May married and left home. "I have been parted from my wife by something worse than death. Forty years has she been the life of my life; and I have left her this day in a lunatic asylum.

"God who has visited me with this affliction, has given me strength to bear it, and will, I know, support me to the end—whatever that may be.

"To-morrow I return to my poor children. There is this great comfort,—that the disease is not hereditary, her family having within all memory been entirely free from it.

"I have much to be thankful for under this visitation. For the first time in my life I am so far beforehand with the world, that my means are provided for the whole of next year; and that I can meet this additional expenditure, considerable in itself, without any difficulty. As I can do this, it is not worth a thought; but it must have cost me much anxiety had my affairs been in their former state."[2]

1835. Third volume of *The Doctor* published.

Offered baronetcy by Sir Robert Peel, but he refused the title on the grounds that he was landless and could not support it. Instead he was granted an increase in his pension. "The confidence which I used to feel in myself is now failing. I was young, in health and heart, on my last birth-day, when I completed my sixtieth year. Since then I have been shaken at the root. It has pleased God to visit me with the severest of all domestic afflictions, those alone excepted into which guilt enters. My wife, a true helpmate as ever man was blessed with, lost her senses a few months ago. She is now in a lunatic asylum; and broken sleep, and anxious thoughts, from which there is no escape in the night season, have made me feel how more than possible it is that a sudden stroke may deprive me of those faculties, by the exercise of which this poor family has hitherto been supported. Even in the event of my death, their condition would, by our recent calamity, be materially altered for the worse; but if I were rendered helpless, all our available means would procure only a respite from actual distress.

"Under these circumstances, your letter, Sir, would in other times have encouraged me to ask for such an increase of pension as might relieve me from anxiety on this score.' "[2]

1836. Mrs. Southey returned home to die. "There is no change for the better in our domestic circumstances. All hope is extinguished, while anxiety remains unabated, so sudden are the transitions of this awful malady. . . . "[2]

1837. Fourth volume of *The Doctor* published, in which the tale of "The Three Bears" appears as a story Dr. Dove is said to have heard from his uncle. No doubt Southey had heard the story himself and was familiar with various versions of the interloper who tries out the porridge and the beds. In Southey's telling, an old woman, rather than Goldilocks, visits the bears, and each bear's speech is marked by either gothic, large capitals or small italic type. It was not until 1950 that an earlier written version, by Eleanor Mure, was found to exist, thus disproving the theory that Southey was the originator of the story.

November 16, 1837. Wife died. "This event could not have been regarded otherwise than as a deliverance at any time since there ceased to be a hope of mental restoration; and for several weeks it was devoutly to be desired. Yet it has left a sense of bereavement which I had not expected to feel, lost as she had been to me for the last three years, and worse than lost. During more than two-thirds of my life she had been the chief object of my thoughts, and I of hers. No man ever had a truer helpmate! no children a more careful mother. No family was ever more wisely ordered, no housekeeping ever conducted with greater prudence, or greater comfort. Every thing was left to her management, and managed so quietly and so well, that except in times of sickness and sorrow, I had literally no cares."[2]

1839. Southey married the poet Caroline Bowles, with whom he had corresponded since 1818. "I have now only one daughter left, and my son divides the year between college and home. Oxford has done him no harm; indeed, I never apprehended any. Reduced in number as my family has been within the last few years, my spirits would hardly recover their habitual and healthful cheerfulness, if I hadn't prevailed upon Miss Bowles to share my lot for the remainder of our lives. There is just such a disparity of age as is fitting; we have been well acquainted with each other more than twenty years, and a more perfect comformity of disposition could not exist; so that, in resolving upon what must be either the weakest or wisest act of a sexagenarian's life, I am well assured that, according to human foresight, I have judged well and acted wisely, both for myself and my remaining daughter."[2]

March 21, 1843. Died. Buried in Crossthwaite Churchyard, in Keswick. A bust of Southey appears in Poet's Corner in Westminster Abbey. ". . . When I add, what has been the greatest of all advantages, that I have passed more than half my life in retirement, conversing with books rather than men, constantly and unweariedly engaged in literary pursuits, communing with my own heart, and taking that course which, upon mature consideration, seemed best to myself, I have said everything necessary to account for the characteristics of my poetry, whatever they may be." [William Haller, *The Early Life of Robert Southey: 1774-1803*, Octagon Books, 1966.[5]]

FOR MORE INFORMATION SEE: Joseph Cottle, *Reminiscences of Samuel Taylor Coleridge and Robert Southey*, Houlston & Stoneman, 1847, reissued, Lime Tree Bower Press, 1970; Charles Cuthbert Southey, editor, *The Life and Correspondence of Robert Southey*, 6 volumes, Harper, 1849, reissued, Scholarly Press, 1969; Edward Dowden, *Southey*, Harper, 1880, reissued, Folcroft, 1973; John Dennis, editor, *Robert Southey: The Story of His Life Written in His Letters*, Lothrop, 1887; Maurice H. Fitzgerald, editor, *Letters of Robert Southey*, Oxford University Press, 1912, reissued, AMS Press, 1976; William Haller, *The Early Life of Robert Southey, 1774-1803*, Columbia University Press, 1917, reissued, Octagon, 1966; Jack Simmons, *Southey*, Collins, 1945, Yale University Press, 1948, reissued, R. West, 1973; Malcolm Elwin, *The First Romantics*, Longmans, Green, 1947, reissued, Russell, 1967; Elizabeth R. Montgomery, *The Story behind Great Stories* (juvenile), McBride, 1947.

Kenneth Hopkins, *The Poets Laureate*, Library Publications, 1955; Louis Untermeyer, *Lives of the Poets*, Simon & Schuster, 1959; Geoffrey Carnall, *Robert Southey and His Age: The Development of a Conservative Mind*, Clarendon, 1960; G. Carnall, *Robert Southey*, Longman, Green, 1964, St. Martin's, 1980; Joan M. Lexau, "The Story of The Three Bears and the Man Who Didn't Write It," *Horn Book*, February, 1964; May Hill Arbuthnot, *Children and Books*, 3rd edition, Scott, Foresman, 1964; Kenneth Curry, editor, *New Letters of Robert Southey*, Columbia University Press, 1965; Roger Lancelyn Green, *Tellers of Tales*, F. Watts, 1965; Brian Doyle, editor, *The Who's Who of Children's Literature*, Schocken Books, 1968; Goeffrey Grigson, editor, *A Choice of Robert Southey's Verse*, Faber, 1970; Lionel Madden, editor, *Robert Southey: The Critical Heritage*, Routledge & Kegan Paul, 1972; K. Curry, *Southey*, Routledge & Kegan Paul, 1975; Charles Ramos, editor, *The Letters of Robert Southey to John May 1797-1838*, Jenkins, 1976; Ernest Bernhardt-Kabisch, *Robert Southey*, Twayne, 1977; G. Carnall, ''Robert Southey'' in *The Romantic Period Excluding the Novel*, edited by James Vinson, Macmillan, 1980, St. Martin's, 1981; G. Carnall, ''Robert Southey'' in *British Writers*, edited by Ian Scott-Kilvert, Volume 4, Scribner, 1981.

SOUTHGATE, Vera

PERSONAL: Born in Durham, England; married Douglas Booth, December 14, 1961. *Education:* Attended Neville's Cross College, and University of Birmingham, 1949-56. *Home and office:* 3 Mere Ct., Chester Rd., Mere, Cheshire WA16 6LQ, England.

CAREER: Writer and lecturer on the teaching of reading; author of children's books. School teacher until 1949; Remedial Education Service, Worcester, England, director, 1954-60; University of Manchester, Manchester, England, lecturer in curriculum development, 1960-72, senior lecturer in education, 1972-79. Member of Bullock Committee (Committee of Inquiry into Reading and the Use of English), Department of Education and Science, University of London, 1972-74; director of Schools Council research project, Extending Beginning Reading, 1973-77. *Member:* International Reading Association, United Kingdom Reading Association (founding member; president, 1970-71). *Awards, honors:* Research Award from the United Kingdom Reading Association, 1982, for best piece of reading research published in the United Kingdom in 1981.

WRITINGS: (With John Havenhand) *Sounds and Words*, six books, University of London Press, 1960; (with J. Havenhand) *The Fireman* (juvenile; illustrated by John Berry), Ladybird Books, 1962; (with J. Havenhand) *The Policeman* (juvenile; illustrated by J. Berry), Ladybird Books, 1962; (with J. Havenhand) *The Nurse* (juvenile; illustrated by J. Berry), Ladybird Books, 1963; (with J. Havenhand) *Penny the Poodle* (juvenile; illustrated by Patricia McGrogan), E. J. Arnold, 1964; *The Story of Cricket* (juvenile; illustrated by Jack Matthew), Ladybird Books, 1964; *The Story of Football* (juvenile; illustrated by J. Matthew), Ladybird Books, 1964; *The Postman and the Postal Service* (juvenile; illustrated by J. Berry), Ladybird Books, 1965; (with Francis W. Warburton) *i.t.a.: An Independent Evaluation*, J. Murray, 1969.

i.t.a.: What Is the Evidence? A Book for Parents and Teachers, J. Murray, 1970; (with Geoffrey R. Roberts) *Reading: Which Approach?*, University of London Press, 1970, Verry, 1976; *Beginning Reading*, University of London Press, 1972; (editor) *Literacy at All Levels: Proceedings of the Eighth Annual Study Conference of the United Kingdom Reading Association*, Ward, Lock, 1972; (with others) *Extending Beginning Reading*, Heinemann, 1981; *Almond Blossom* (illustrated by Maggie Read), Macmillan Educational, 1983; *Planning for Reading Success*, Book 2: *Reading*, Macmillan Educational, 1985.

Reteller; all for children: *Cinderella* (illustrated by Eric Winter), Ladybird Books, 1964, new edition (illustrated by Brian Price Thomas), Ladybird Books, 1981; *Pancake Tuesday* (illustrated by A. Saul), E. J. Arnold, 1964; *Jack and the Beanstalk* (illustrated by E. Winter), Ladybird Books, 1965, revised edition, Ladybird Books, 1983; *The Elves and the Shoemaker* (illustrated by Robert Lumley), Ladybird Books, 1965; *Sleeping Beauty* (illustrated by E. Winter), Ladybird Books, 1965; *The Three Little Pigs* (illustrated by R. Lumley), Ladybird Books, 1965, revised edition (illustrated by Chris Russell), Ladybird Books, 1986.

Dick Whittington and His Cat (illustrated by E. Winter), Ladybird Books, 1966, revised edition (illustrated by Martin Aitchison), Ladybird Books, 1986; *The Gingerbread Boy* (illustrated by R. Lumley), Ladybird Books, 1966; *The Little Red Hen* (illustrated by R. Lumley), Ladybird Books, 1966, revised edition (illustrated by Stephen Holmes), Ladybird Books, 1986; *Second Book of Nursery Rhymes*, Ladybird Books, 1966; *Puss in Boots* (illustrated by E. Winter), Ladybird Books, 1967; *Beauty and the Beast* (illustrated by E. Winter), Merry Thoughts, 1968; *Rapunzel* (illustrated by E. Winter), Merry Thoughts, 1968, revised edition (illustrated by M. Aitchison), Ladybird Books, 1985; *Rumpelstiltskin* (illustrated by E. Winter), Merry Thoughts, 1968, revised edition (illustrated by M. Aitchison), Ladybird Books, 1985; *The Sly Fox and the Little Red Hen* (illustrated by R. Lumley), Merry Thoughts, 1968, revised edition (illustrated by B. P. Thomas), Ladybird Books, 1985; *The Three Billy Goats Gruff* (illustrated by R. Lumley), Merry Thoughts, 1968, revised edition (illustrated by Chris Russell), Ladybird Books, 1986; *Chicken Licken*, Ladybird Books, 1969, revised edition, 1983.

The Enormous Turnip (illustrated by R. Lumley), Ladybird Books, 1970, revised edition (illustrated by Christine Owen), 1982; *Goldilocks and the Three Bears* (illustrated by E. Winter), Ladybird Books, 1971; *The Magic Porridge Pot* (illustrated by R. Lumley), Ladybird Books, 1971; *The Big Pancake* (illustrated by R. Lumley), Ladybird Books, 1972, revised edition (illustrated by Gillian Hurry), Ladybird Books, 1982; *Little Red Riding Hood* (illustrated by R. Lumley), Ladybird Books, 1972; *The Old Woman and Her Pig* (illustrated by R. Lumley), Ladybird Books, 1973; *The Princess and the Frog* (illustrated by Capaldi), Ladybird Books, 1973, revised edition (illustrated by M. Aitchison), Ladybird Books, 1986; *The Musicians of Bremen* (illustrated by R. Lumley and J. Berry), Ladybird Books, 1974, revised edition (illustrated by Margaret Gold), Ladybird Books, 1982; *The Princess and the Pea* (illustrated by E. Winter), Ladybird Books, 1979; *Snow White and Rose Red*, Ladybird Books, 1979; *Wolf and the Seven Little Kids*, Ladybird Books, 1979.

Beauty and the Beast (illustrated by Robert Ayton), Ladybird Books, 1980; *Snow White and the Seven Dwarfs*, Ladybird Books, 1980; *The Emperor's New Clothes* (illustrated by Nina O'Connell), Macmillan Educational, 1983; *The Gigantic Turnip* (illustrated by David Bryant), Macmillan Educational, 1983; *Lazy Jack* (illustrated by Maureen Williams), Macmillan Educational, 1983.

Contributor: J. E. Merritt, editor, *Reading and the Curriculum*, Ward, Lock, 1971; M. Clark and A. Milne, editors, *Reading and Related Skills*, Ward, Lock, 1973; D. Moyle, editor, *Reading: What of the Future?*, Ward, Lock, 1974; A. Cashdan, editor, *The Content of Reading*, Ward, Lock, 1976; (with H. Arnold and S. Johnson) E. Hunter-Grundin and H. U. Grundin, editors, *Reading: Implementing the Bullock Report*, Ward, Lock, 1978; (with S. Johnson) G. Bray and T. Pugh, editors, *The Reading Connection*, Ward, Lock, 1980; L. O. Ollila, editor, *Beginning Reading Instruction in Different Countries*, International Reading Association, 1981; A. Henry, editor, *Teaching Reading: The Key Issues*, Heinemann.

Author of "Star" series, twenty-five volumes, Macmillan, 1981. Also author of the *Southgate Group Reading Tests*, 1959-62; editorial consultant, *Education Three to Thirteen* (journal), beginning in 1971. Contributor to professional journals, including *British Journal of Educational Psychology, Educational Research, Educational Review,* and *Reading Research Quarterly.*

SPIER, Peter (Edward) 1927-

PERSONAL: Born June 6, 1927, in Amsterdam, Netherlands; came to the United States in 1951; became citizen, 1958; son of Joseph E. A. (a journalist and illustrator) and Albertine (van Raalte) Spier; married Kathryn M. Pallister, July 12, 1958; children: Thomas Pallister, Kathryn Elizabeth. *Education:* Rijksacademie voor beeldende kunsten, student 1945-47; attended Willems Park School, Amsterdams Lyceum. *Religion:* Reformed Church of America. *Home:* Wardencliff Rd., P.O. Box 210, Shoreham, Long Island, N.Y. 11786.

CAREER: Elsevier's Weekblad, Paris, France, junior editor, 1949-51; Elsevier Publishing, Houston, Tex., junior editor, 1951-52; author and illustrator, 1952—. *Military service:* Royal Netherlands Navy, 1947-51; became lieutenant. *Member:* Netherlands Club (New York).

AWARDS, HONORS: Hans Brinker; or, the Silver Skates was included in the American Institute of Graphic Arts Book Show, 1958-60, *London Bridge Is Falling Down!,* 1967-68, and *Tin Lizzie,* 1976-77; Caldecott Honor Book from the American Library Association, 1962, for *The Fox Went Out on a Chilly Night; Boston Globe-Horn Book* Award for Illustration, 1967, for *London Bridge Is Falling Down!,* Honor Book, 1967, for *To Market! To Market!;* Diploma de Triennale di Milano; *Hurrah, We're Outward Bound!* was chosen one of Child Study Association of America's Children's Books of the Year, 1968, *And So My Garden Grows,* 1969, *The Erie Canal,* 1970, *Crash! Bang! Boom!,* 1972, *Tin Lizzie,* 1975, *The Legend of New Amsterdam,* 1979, and *Dreams,* 1987.

Christopher Award, 1971, for *The Erie Canal; Gobble, Growl, Grunt* was selected as one of *New York Times* Outstanding Books of the Year, 1971, *The Star-Spangled Banner,* 1973, and *Bored, Nothing to Do,* 1978; New York Academy of Science's Children's Science Book Award, 1972, for *Gobble, Growl, Grunt;* Christopher Award, and chosen one of *New York Times* Best Illustrated Children's Books of the Year, both 1977, Caldecott Medal, and Lewis Carroll Shelf Award, both 1978, International Board on Books for Young People Honor List, 1980, American Book Award finalist for paperback picturebook, 1982, all for *Noah's Ark;* Little Archer Award from the University of Wisconsin-Oshkosh, 1978; Christopher Award, and American Book Award finalist for children's hardcover nonfiction, both 1980, and Mass Media Award from the Conference of Christians and Jews, all for *People;* University of Southern Mississippi Silver Medallion, 1984, in recognition of his distinguished career as an author/illustrator of books for children.

WRITINGS—All self-illustrated; all published by Doubleday, except as noted: *The Fox Went Out on a Chilly Night: An Old Song* (ALA Notable Book; *Horn Book* honor list; Junior Literary Guild selection), 1961; *Of Dikes and Windmills,* 1970; *The Erie Canal* (Junior Literary Guild selection), 1970; *Gobble, Growl, Grunt* (Junior Literary Guild selection), 1971; *Crash! Bang! Boom!* (Junior Literary Guild selection), 1972; *Fast-Slow, High-Low: A Book of Opposites* (Junior Literary

PETER SPIER

Guild selection), 1972; *The Star-Spangled Banner* (Junior Literary Guild selection), 1973; *Tin Lizzie,* 1975; *Noah's Ark* (*Horn Book* honor list), 1977, published in England as *The Great Flood,* World's Work, 1978; *Bored—Nothing to Do!,* 1978; *Oh, Were They Ever Happy!* (ALA Notable Book), 1978, published in England as *Nothing Like a Fresh Coat of Paint,* World's Work, 1981; *The Legend of New Amsterdam,* 1979.

People, 1980; *The Pet Store,* 1981; *My School,* 1981; *The Fire House,* 1981; *The Food Market,* 1981; *The Toy Shop,* 1981; *Bill's Service Station,* 1981, published in England as *Bill's Garage,* Collins, 1981; *Rain* (ALA Notable Book), 1982; *Peter Spier's Christmas!,* 1983; *Peter Spier's Little Bible Storybooks,* 1983; *Peter Spier's Little Cats,* 1984; *Peter Spier's Little Dogs,* 1984; *Peter Spier's Little Ducks,* 1984; *Peter Spier's Little Rabbits,* 1984; (reteller) *The Book of Jonah,* 1985; *Dreams,* 1986; *Peter Spier's Advent Calendar,* 1987; *We the People: The Story of the U.S. Constitution,* 1987.

"Mother Goose Library" series: *London Bridge Is Falling Down!* (ALA Notable Book; *Horn Book* honor list; Junior Literary Guild selection), Doubleday, 1967; *To Market! To Market!,* Doubleday, 1967; *Hurrah, We're Outward Bound!,* Doubleday, 1968; *And So My Garden Grows,* Doubleday, 1969. Contributor to *Reader's Digest* and to Time/Life Books.

Illustrator: Nikolai Gogol, *Mantel,* [Holland], 1946; P. Bakker, *Logboek van de Gratias* (title means "Logbook of the Gratias"), Elsevier, 1948; E. Elias, *Op Reis Met Prins Bernhard* (title means "On a Journey with Prince Bernhard"), Bezige Bij, 1951; Steussy, *Straten Schrijven Historie* (title means "Street Names with History"), Schoonderbeek, 1951; Elmer Reynolds, *Thunder Hill,* Doubleday, 1953; Louis Untermeyer, *Adventurers All,* Golden Press, 1953; Ruth Langland Holberg, *Tam Morgan, the Liveliest Girl in Salem,* Doubleday, 1953; Margaret G. Otto, *Cocoa,* Holt, 1953; H. J. Berkhard, *Won-*

In order to form a more perfect Union.... ■ (From *We the People: The Story of the U.S. Constitution* by Peter Spier. Illustrated by the author.)

ders of the World, Simon & Schuster, 1953; Frieda K. Brown, *Last Hurdle,* Crowell, 1953; Marjorie Vetter, *Cargo for Jennifer,* Longmans, 1954; Frances H. Burnett, *Little Lord Fauntleroy,* Doubleday, 1954; Mark Twain (pseudonym of Samuel L. Clemens), *Prince and the Pauper,* Doubleday, 1954.

(With Emil Lowenstein) Paul Friedlander and Joseph Brooks, *Italy,* Simon & Schuster, 1955; Michel Rouzé, *Mystery of Mont Saint-Michel,* translated by George Libaire, Holt, 1955; Vera A. Amrein, *Cabin for the Mary Christmas,* Harcourt, 1955; "Science and Living in Today's World" series, Volumes 6, 7, and 8, Doubleday, 1955-56; Joy Anderson, *Hippolyte: Crab King,* Harcourt, 1956; Jennie Darlington and Jane McIlvaine, *My Antarctic Honeymoon: A Year at the Bottom of the World,* Doubleday, 1956; Phyllis Krasilovsky, *The Cow Who Fell in the Canal* (Junior Literary Guild selection), Doubleday, 1957; Margaret Hubbard, *Boss Chombale,* Crowell, 1957; *England,* Ginn, 1957; Ruth Strang and others, *Teenage Tales,* Volume 4, Heath, 1957; Margaret B. Boni, *Favorite Christmas Carols: Fifty-nine Yuletide Songs Both Old and New,* arranged by Norman Lloyd, Simon & Schuster, 1957; Mary Mapes Dodge, *Hans Brinker; or, the Silver Skates,* Scribner,

1958; Jessica Reynolds, *Jessica's Journal,* Holt, 1958; Douglas Angus, *Lions Fed the Tigers,* Houghton, 1958; Kenneth Dodson, *Hector the Stowaway Dog: A True Story,* Little, Brown, 1958; Elizabeth Fairholme and Pamela Powell, *Esmeralda Ahoy!,* Doubleday, 1959; Ann Frank, *Works of Ann Frank,* Doubleday, 1959; *Betty Crocker's Guide to Easy Entertaining,* Golden Press, 1959; Richard Watkins, *Mystery of Willet,* T. Nelson, 1959; Frances Carpenter, *Wonder Tales of Ships and Seas,* Doubleday, 1959.

John L. Strohm, *Golden Garden Guide: A Practical Handbook of Gardening and Outdoor Living,* Golden Press, 1960; Ardo Flakkeberg, *The Sea Broke Through,* Knopf, 1960; Elinor Parker, editor, *One Hundred More Story Poems,* Crowell, 1960; J. L. Strohm, *Golden Guide to Lawns, Shrubs, and Trees,* Golden Press, 1961; Lavinia Davis, *Island City: Adventures in Old New York* (Junior Literary Guild selection), Doubleday, 1961; George H. Grant, *Boy Overboard!,* Little, Brown, 1961; Dola De Jong, *The Level Land,* Scribner, 1961; J. L. Strohm and others, *Golden Guide to Flowers: Annuals, Perennials, Bulbs, and a Special Section on Roses,* Golden Press, 1962; Margaretha Shemin, *The Little Riders,* Coward, 1963; C. W.

(From *The Star-Spangled Banner* by Peter Spier. Illustrated by the author.)

Ceram (pseudonym of Kurt Marek), *Archaeology,* Odyssey, 1964; Jan de Hartog, *Sailing Ship,* Odyssey, 1964; K. Marek, *The History of the Theater,* Odyssey, 1964; R. Butterfield, *Ancient Rome,* Odyssey, 1964.

M. Valmarana, *Architecture,* Odyssey, 1965; Anthony West, *Elizabethan England,* Odyssey, 1965; Donald D. MacMillan, *Great Furniture Styles, 1660-1830,* Odyssey, 1965; *World of Michelangelo,* Time-Life, 1966; E. Parker, editor, *Here and There: One Hundred Poems about Places,* Crowell, 1967; *Animals You Will Never Forget,* Reader's Digest, 1969; M. Shemin, *Empty Moat,* Coward, 1969; T. R. Reese, *Frederica: Colonial Fort and Town,* United States National Park Service, 1969.

Golden Book Encyclopedia, Volume 1, Golden Press, 1970; *Traveler's Tale of Tikal,* National Geographic, 1975; Elmer Bendiner, *Virgin Diplomats,* Knopf, 1975; Peter Lippman, *Trucks, Trucks, Trucks,* Doubleday, 1984. Contributor of illustrations to *Ford Almanac,* 1956-72.

ADAPTATIONS: "The Cow Who Fell in the Canal" (cassette; sound filmstrip), Weston Woods, 1965, (feature film), 1970; "The Fox Went Out on a Chilly Night" (cassette; sound filmstrip), Weston Woods, 1965; "London Bridge Is Falling Down" (feature film), Weston Woods, 1969, (cassette; sound filmstrip), 1971; "The Erie Canal" (cassette; sound filmstrip), Weston Woods, 1974, (feature film), 1976; "The Star-Spangled Banner" (feature film; cassette; filmstrip with cassette), Weston Woods, 1975; "Oh, Were They Ever Happy!" (filmstrip with cassette), Random House; "Noah's Ark" (cassette; filmstrip with cassette), Weston Woods.

SIDELIGHTS: **Born June 6, 1927,** in Amsterdam, Netherlands. "I grew up in Broek-in-Waterland, a small village known as the birthplace of Hans Brinker, who, of course, is the hero of the novel by Mary Mapes Dodge. Most people living in Broek-in-Waterland have never heard of the American book.

"My brother, sister and I went to school in Amsterdam. From our house we would walk to the tram, and during the winter,

skate. The train was an ancient swaying vehicle filled with the smoke of cigars and clay pipes and with fishermen from the village of Volendam who wore huge wooden shoes and baggy pants, what most Americans tend to think of as the Dutch national costume. They were taking their catch to market—herring and smoked eel were stacked in baskets in the aisles. An unforgettable aroma! After the tram ride, we took a ferry. How I loved to be on the water in the early morning! Back on another tram and a short walk to our school. We never lacked for plausible excuses for being late!

"My father was a famous journalistic artist and political cartoonist. In the days before the 35mm camera, artists were sent to cover mining disasters, airplane crashes, court trials, and other events. After the invention of the 35mm, however, my father did less reportorial and more cartooning and philosophical drawings.

"I grew up in an intellectual milieu. Books were very important, and, needless to say, because of my father's profession, we were very 'up' on current events. We went to the theatre and concerts often, which I very much enjoyed. I can honestly say that my father's fame posed no problems for us. In town, we were given the best tables in restaurants and free theatre tickets and so on, but in Broek-in-Waterland, a small farming village, we were just another village family.

"We lived on the water in a house built in 1746 with boats passing quite close to our windows. I cannot remember a time when I was not making things, mostly in clay and plasticine. I sculpted horses, people, and sometimes entire villages and towns. But I didn't decide to make art my profession until I was eighteen. Most of the people in my family were lawyers, and I considered a career in law as well. I also showed interest in architecture, publishing, and in becoming a naval officer. After the Gymnasium—the European version of high school, based on the classical Latin school—I enrolled in the Royal Academy of Art in Amsterdam. There I took classes in drawing, etching and graphics.

(From *Crash! Bang! Boom!* by Peter Spier. Illustrated by the author.)

"I joined the navy after art school, where I spent three and a half years. I liked the service a lot and almost signed on for a couple of decades. The discipline, the ships, the water, the people—everything about it pleased me. I loved to travel and was happy to spend part of the time in South America and the West Indies. But my yen for publishing wouldn't let go.

"I went to work for _Elsevier's Weekblad,_ then the largest Dutch weekly newspaper. My first year was spent in Paris, which was wonderful. The next year I was transferred to Houston, Texas. Culture shock! I stayed there about a year then came to New York as a freelance.

"My first illustration in the States was a book about goats. Little did I know that all those hours of drawing goats as a kid would pay off! My first picture book, which I did not write was _The Cow Who Fell in the Canal._ I illustrated about fifty books before I started writing my own. In picture books, the burden of proof, so to speak, lies with the illustrations. Now, I only illustrate books that I have written.

"Writing and drawing are two of the same art forms. What you say in the text, you no longer have to say in the pictures and vice versa. The ideal picture book doesn't need any text. I realize that this doesn't apply to all picture books. Some stories need to be told in words as well as in pictures. I did a _Noah's Ark_ without text, but then everyone knows the story. And besides, the events in the story are sequential and clear-cut, so that it can be followed by those not familiar with the tale. For _Jonah. . . . ,_ I needed text. The tale is well known but the story more complex and difficult.

"For _Jonah. . ._ I translated the Dutch equivalent of the English King James version of the Bible. The original Dutch translations, done in the 17th century, have in common majestic cadences and exquisite sonorities. Using the Dutch original

(From _Dreams_ by Peter Spier. Illustrated by the author.)

made it feel more like my own. The border of the opening spread is derived from a Babylonian design commonly used in architectural ornamentation. The research for this book was half the fun. I acquired books on Assyrian art and design of the Biblical period—a feast for the eye!'' [Based on an interview by Marguerite Feitlowitz for *Something about the Author*.¹]

Spier won the prestigious Caldecott Medal in 1978 for *Noah's Ark*. ''It seems to be a hallowed tradition to call recipients of both the Newbery and Caldecott Medals out of bed in the middle of the night or at best in the very early hours of the morning. I suppose this is calculated to add to the dramatic effect, and in my case this was most certainly true: The phone rang at 4:30 Chicago time, and I picked up the receiver with trembling hands and pounding heart. The first thing that came to my mind was: 'My parents' house is on fire,' or at least someone near and dear had just died. It was therefore an immense relief to hear that *Noah's Ark* had just been given the Caldecott.

''Since that memorable morning, I. . .had five months to figure out that whole early-calling tradition carefully. It may have nothing to do with the dramatic effect after all and may be intended as a loving kindness. A safety measure, if you will. Picture this: Someone hearing that he or she had won during the day might easily suffer cardiac arrest from understandable amazement, joy, and excitement. By cleverly calling in the dark of night, the committee makes sure they catch you where you should be in case something fatal occurs—in your bed!

''A few days after being called in January, my wife and I were again called out of a deep sleep. 'Aha!' I thought. 'Won again! And with what foresight on behalf of the committee: This time they are giving it to me sight unseen for my next book, which is still at the printer's!' I was wrong, of course, for a raw voice asked if he was speaking to the fifth precinct. It is apparent that the whole thing must have gone a little to my head!

''In accordance with the instructions I received, my wife and I made our children swear not to tell a soul, and they didn't,

(From *The Erie Canal* [folk songs]. Illustrated by Peter Spier.)

although it subsequently became clear that the news had somehow leaked out in other quarters. That same day, on a plane to Chicago, I sat next to an editor I knew. The conversation went as follows:

"*The editor:* 'Where are you going?'

"*Me:* 'To Chicago.'

"*She:* 'I see. Why?'

"*Me, thinking quickly:* 'Oh, on some Doubleday business.'

"*She:* 'Is it secret?'

"*Me:* 'Yes.'

"*She:* 'Congratulations!'

"My contact with Randolph Caldecott, by the way, is of long standing. My father owned a collection of Caldecott's works, most of them first editions. I do not know whether I was showing early promise, but it seems that I took one of those valuable books—I was three years old—and with a red crayon expertly ruined each and every page of the book. I do not recall the spanking I was given, although my father assures me that it was fairly meted out. The story has a happy ending for me, though, for when I told him that *Noah* had won, he gave me his whole collection of Caldecott books.

"A successful book is not due to the effort of just one man but is the result of teamwork. An author-illustrator can create a most appealing book—but that same book then has to run a long and risky gauntlet before it finally staggers into your libraries! The editor—with the best of intentions—might make changes which could ruin the book. The company that makes the color separations could demolish the artwork. Inferior paper could undo all the considerable expense, time, and effort put into first-class film and outstanding offset plates. The printer in turn could ruin the sheets in countless different ways, and the bookbinder could do the same. And finally, the marketing, publicity, and advertising. These, too, can be done the right way or the wrong way.

"With *Noah's Ark* all went well from the beginning. . . .

"One of the questions I am often asked is: 'Why did you decide to do *Noah's Ark*?' The answer is simple: Because I have wanted to retell the story for years. The final catalyst was the seventeenth-century Dutch poem by Jacob Revius, which has the faith and, above all, the childlike simplicity which I found moving and inspiring. It was obviously not an original idea, and I went to our library to look at Bowker's *Books in Print* to find out precisely how unoriginal it actually was. There were over twenty *Noah's* in print. The library owned seven different versions, and when I tried to have a look at them I found that they were nearly always taken out on loan. So I bought all the versions I could get hold of to see what other artists had done with Noah. Some were good, others were less so. But I found that virtually all the books had the same slant; the Flood was invariably depicted as a joyous, sun-filled Caribbean cruise: happy flood, happy Noah (wearing a sailor's cap), happy beasts. No drownings, nothing to indicate God's wrath. It was difficult even to recognize the Bible text in any of those books, and it was not what I had in mind at all. A few books were a bit more sombre and followed the Bible closely, without adding any unexpected sidelights or intimate glimpses. None of them showed Noah shoveling manure or even hinted at the stench and the mess inside. It was then that I knew that there was room for one more *Noah's Ark*.

"When working on the layout of the book, not in sketches yet but with written notes, I had the ark floating away and the waters rising higher and higher, the animals that remained behind standing knee-deep, then waist-deep in the water—as I later showed in the book. The next page showed hundreds of drowned animals awash in the waves, some with their heads down, others with their legs sticking up in the air, with small creatures and birds having saved themselves on the floating carcasses. It was certainly dramatic. But it was to be a book for small children, and I decided that it went too far in its grisliness and left that part out.

"I always find it difficult to determine where that invisible line, the border between good taste and bad, runs. Between the believable and the unbelievable. Between the acceptable and the unacceptable. Between the grim and the gruesome. Between the necessary and the superfluous. But the pieces fell slowly into their proper places, and today it seems to me as if the book created itself and I was the ever-present and interested observer.

"Whenever I finish a new book, I show it to my children to hear their reaction. In *Noah's* case it was encouraging. They said, 'It's all right.' That was the highest praise I could expect. This is not always the case. When I showed them . . . *Oh, Were They Ever Happy* . . . they told me that it was 'kidstuff' (which of course it is supposed to be!) and, adding insult to injury, asked if it was really necessary to put *our* name on the cover?" [Peter Spier, "Caldecott Award Acceptance," *Horn Book,* August, 1978.[2]]

Spier's working process remains consistent from book to book. "Over the years, I have refined my techniques and learned some new tricks, but basically, it goes like this: I get a basic idea and refer to *Books in Print* to make sure that the book hasn't been done. Since I spend about six months on a book, I must feel certain that my idea is viable, otherwise, it just isn't worth half a year of my life. I then divide the story into parts which would roughly correspond to pages and do a dummy in which the entire story is roughed out. I include sketches and notes for illustrations. I send the dummy to my publisher and when I get the go-ahead, spend the next six weeks on research. For my book about the Erie Canal, I drove the full length of the Canal twice. It's important to know what I'm looking for at this stage. That's the purpose of the notes I make on my dummy. Of course, there are always marvellous surprises—a strangely-shaped tree, perhaps, overhanging an old fence, or unexpected animals. I do these sketches fast, in pencil, with color notes in the margins.

"I put my sketches together at home, usually in pencil. It is a far more willing tool than pen and the fact that it doesn't yield as well-defined a line as pen can be circumvented in production. The printer can use a fine-line developer which

Suppose the dog should run away,
My fair lady.

■(From *London Bridge Is Falling Down!* Illustrated by Peter Spier).

over-exposes the picture, resulting in a heavier line. I always work same size; that way, I am reasonably certain that everything I've put into the drawing will be there after it's printed.

"After the line drawings are done, they are photographed in what is called 'fugitive blue,' a misnomer since the lines tend to show up a little. A positive and a negative are made. The negative, of course, is used to make the plate. I do my coloring in Windsor & Newton watercolors on the 'blue,' which is then returned to the printer for color separations. These are just three-color separations, which means that we have just three colors plus black to make all the shades we need. After the separations are done, I get first proofs. Looking at first proofs is an aging experience. During the interval that the work is at the printer's, the drawings take on qualities of unearthly beauty in my mind. So it can be a shock coming to terms with reality! On first proofs, one can make only small corrections. By the time you get final proofs, you're better prepared about what to expect. One must be vigilant with regard to color, particularly in the three-color process. You learn to stay away from certain hues—oranges, grays and certain greens, for example. It can be very frustrating when a tree painted such a lovely shade of green in Windsor & Newton turns up reddish. I'll

ask the printer to turn down the red fount, which he does, with the result that all the faces on the following page come up yellow—there are many adjustments and compromises along the way. I am integrally involved in every phase of production. I do my own mechanicals, spec type, paste-up, work with the printer and handle foreign rights."[1]

Aiming for authenticity in his work can become a trap, as it was in his fieldwork for *The Erie Canal*. "I was sketching a stately old gingerbread house standing beside the overgrown towpath and an old canal lock. 'Used to be the Canal Hotel,' remarked an old fellow watching the drawing. 'Grand place . . . chandeliers : . . a long bar . . . lots of lovely girls. . . .' Only half listening, I kept working on the picture, which took half a day to perfect. When I showed it to the Erie Canal museum curator, he cried, "You can't use that! Canal *Hotel*? Ha! It was a whorehouse!

"Sidestepping such bloopers, trying to give a children's book a long and happy life by not dating it with illustrations showing trendy mini- or maxiskirts, autos sporting fins and other ephemera—these are tricky enough gambits at home, but nothing to what I encounter abroad. Since most of my books are

(From *Bored—Nothing to Do!* by Peter Spier. Illustrated by the author.)

published in foreign countries, I travel to book fairs whenever it is necessary, and some sessions are illuminating but sometimes dismaying.

"'Only the very wealthy live in a home like this one—and they would never paint it themselves,' declared the German publisher when he saw the perfectly ordinary, middle-class house pictured in *Oh, Were They Ever Happy!*

"In another book, a frog appeared in a pet store. '*Mais non,* Monsieur Spier,' insisted the French publisher. '*Impossible!* The frog belongs in the food market.

"The most monumental examples of how easy it is to go wrong occurred at the Bologna Children's Book Fair in 1979, when I took the *People* dummy to present to potential co-producers. On the cover I had drawn a traditional Japanese couple in kimonos and elevated wooden sandals, the lady wearing an obi and holding a dainty parasol. She was also carrying an infant in a sling on her back. When the first Japanese publisher visited the Doubleday booth, he stared at the cover, stared at me, bowed gravely and departed without a word. That happened a few more times. Then Tom Mori, the

Japanese agent, dropped by. After a glance at the picture, he said the baby had to go. 'Really,' he said, tapping the couple. 'Wedding dress! Wedding dress! They're in their wedding dress!' There is now a blank spot behind the bride.

"Later, two quiet gentlemen with flowing beards and equally flowing white robes came by to study the dummy. One was from Tripoli, the other from Damascus. 'Are there Arabs in the book?' they asked. There were, indeed; and the two men inspected each and every picture without finding fault—until they arrived at the spread showing 45 styles of writing from around the globe.

"The visitors' interest deepened and so did their agitation while they pored over the five types of Arabic script I had copied from an old but eminent European encyclopedia.

"The Arabs became increasingly confused, turning the dummy now this way, now that. They shook their heads, clucked, conferred in whispers and frowned. Finally they announced that all my Arabic was upside down. I was extremely grateful, of course, and lost no time making the corrections. I also lost no time reaching for that encyclopedia when I got home. Yes.

Hard work!

(From *Noah's Ark*, translated from the Dutch by Peter Spier. Illustrated by Peter Spier.)

There was the Arabic, upside down, in a reference that has been an admired fountain of knowledge for over 150 years.

"Flying home . . . from Bologna, I sat next to a German traveler who asked what I did for a living. I was all set to rave about the fascinations of my work, the thrills of a book fair, an event he should not pass up the chance of attending. But I never got started. *He* began to wax lyrical about *his* business, selling women's underwear.

"'I'm on my way to a trade show on the West Coast in America. Every manufacturer will be there. Ach! You *must* see, one day. *Herrlich! Fabelhaft!* Let me tell you, when you walk around those exhibits, *die Büstenhälter lachen Einem an!'*—the brassieres are smiling at you!'' [Peter Spier, "The Frog Belongs in the Food Market: And Other Perils of an Illustrator," *Publishers Weekly,* July 25, 1980.[3]]

We the People is a book about the Constitution in three parts. "The first is historical, with emphasis on the Constitutional Congresses of 1787. The last part is dedicated to "The Bill of Rights." The bulk consists of an illustrated version of the Preamble, which of course, begins, 'We the People.' The opening spread is made up of illustrations of all types of work—how those jobs are performed today and how they were done in 1787. There are also professions today which didn't exist then, and vice versa. The second spread, which emphasizes the fact that the Constitution exists to protect the rights of *all*

people is comprised of drawings of many, many folks—rich, poor, city dwellers, country dwellers, old, young, representatives of every race and most every ethnicity. As with all of my books, I did a lot of research. I made several trips to Washington, D.C. where the Bicentennial Committee went out of its way to be helpful."

When he is not working, Spier likes to build model ships. "I do these from scratch, of course. I work to scale—one quarter-inch to the foot—which means that most of my models are one to three feet long. I have done many Dutch seagoing vessels, as well as British cruisers and other ships. All told I have done between thirty and forty models. One of my neighbors just cut down his pear tree and I plan to sneak over there, retrieve the remains and use the wood for my next series of models!

"I also love to sail. Right now I don't have a boat, so we charter. The Chesapeake and Long Island Sound are great sailing. We've made a few trips from Long Island to Martha's Vineyard, which is lovely."

Spier also spends a lot of time with books. "History is my passion. I just re-read Churchill's history of World War II. Another favorite is Gibbon's *The Decline and Fall of the Roman Empire.* Gibbon is an entity unto himself—a genius." Among authors and artists who do books for children, Spier

Or their legs all dangling down-o, down-o, down-o. ■ (From *The Fox Went Out on a Chilly Night: An Old Song.* Illustrated by Peter Spier.)

(From *Rain* by Peter Spier. Illustrated by the author.)

particularly appreciates Brinton Turkle whose ''Obadiah books are masterpieces'' and Anno who is ''world-class and timeless.''[1]

''There is something special about books. Most things in history, no matter how ghastly or cruel, are forgotten in the end, but people still talk with special horror about the burning of the Alexandrian Library and about book-burning by dictators or during the Inquisition. Murders are forgotten, but the eradication of ideas, of books, is not.''[2]

Spier's advice for aspiring writers and artists is: ''Bear in mind that luck plays a role in everyone's career. Sometimes it's a matter of 'being there at the right time.' Also remember that quality books outlast inferior ones. It may take decades, even centuries, but it is so, nonetheless. Set high standards for yourself. You'll never regret it.''[1]

As an author/illustrator of books for young children, he added, ''Remember, . . . writing a book is a one-man business. No

man can do it for you. And remember, too, that a good book is always child-like—a poor one, childish.'' [''Peter Spier,'' *Juvenile Miscellany,* 1974.[4]]

Spier's works have been published in twenty-four languages, including Japanese and Chinese.

FOR MORE INFORMATION SEE: Bertha M. Miller and others, compilers, *Illustrators of Children's Books: 1946-1956,* Horn Book, 1958; Lee Kingman and others, compilers, *Illustrators of Children's Books: 1957-1966,* Horn Book, 1968; Joan Hess Michel, ''The Illustrations of Peter Spier,'' *American Artist,* October, 1969; Lee Bennett Hopkins, *Books Are by People,* Citation, 1969; *Horn Book,* October, 1970, August, 1978; *New York Times Book Review,* January 23, 1972; *Junior Literary Guild Catalogue,* March, 1972, September, 1972; Doris de Montreville and Donna Hill, editors, *Third Book of Junior Authors,* H. W. Wilson, 1972; Bernard M.

A nice shade of green! Covers well! ■ (From *Oh, Were They Ever Happy!* by Peter Spier. Illustrated by the author.)

Skolsky, "An Illustrator Shows How," *New York Times*, April 8, 1973; "Cover Artist," *Wilson Library Bulletin*, October, 1974; Martha E. Ward and Dorothy A. Marquardt, *Illustrators of Books for Young People*, 2nd edition, Scarecrow, 1975; L. Kingman and others, compilers, *Illustrators of Children's Books: 1967-1976*, Horn Book, 1978; Peter Spier, "The Frog Belongs in the Food Market: And Other Perils of an Illustrator," *Publishers Weekly*, July 25, 1980; "Quotes for Writers," *Writer*, August, 1982; Jim Roginski, compiler, *Newbery and Caldecott Medalists and Honor Book Winners*, Libraries Unlimited, 1982; L. Kingman, editor, *Newbery and Caldecott Medal Books: 1976-1985*, Horn Book, 1986.

Collections: de Grummond Collection at the University of Southern Mississippi; Kerlan Collection at the University of Minnesota; Port Washington Public Library, New York.

What are you able to build with your blocks?
Castles and palaces, temples and docks.
Rain may keep raining, and others go roam,
But I can be happy and building at home.

Let the sofa be mountains, the carpet be sea,
There I'll establish a city for me:
A kirk and a mill and a palace beside,
And a harbor as well where my vessels may ride.
                              —Robert Louis Stevenson

STAHL, Ben(jamin Albert) 1910-1987

OBITUARY NOTICE—See sketch in *SATA* Volume 5: Born September 7, 1910, in Chicago, Ill.; died of cancer, October 19, 1987, in Sarasota, Fla. Artist, illustrator, educator, and author. Stahl's award-winning artwork appeared in the *Saturday Evening Post* and other national magazines for more than fifty years. He illustrated C. S. Forrester's popular "Hornblower" serials, some limited editions of classic novels, and many books for children, including Marilyn Sach's *A Pocket Full of Seeds*, selected for the American Institute of Graphic Arts Children's Book Show in 1973. Stahl was also author of *The Secret of the Red Skull* and the self-illustrated *Blackbeard's Ghost*, which won the Sequoyah Award in 1969 and was adapted for film by Walt Disney Productions. A painter whose work was exhibited at the Chicago Institute of Art as well as other major galleries and museums around the world, Stahl co-founded the Famous Artists Schools in 1949 with *Post* colleague Norman Rockwell and other artists. Aside from painting and illustrating, he developed and wrote "Journey into Art with Ben Stahl," an educational series for television, and taught painting at a number of art schools. In 1979 Stahl was elected to the Society of Illustrators Hall of Fame.

FOR MORE INFORMATION SEE: The Illustrator in America: The Decade 1940-50, Reinhold, 1966; *Illustrators of Children's Books: 1957-1966*, Horn Book, 1968; *Illustrators of Books for Young People*, Scarecrow, 1975; *Contemporary Au-*

thors, Volumes 29-32, revised, Gale, 1978; *Who's Who in American Art,* Bowker, 1985. Obituaries: *New York Times,* October 24, 1987; *Washington Post,* October 26, 1987; *Los Angeles Times,* October 28, 1987.

TAYLOR, Herb(ert Norman, Jr.) 1942-1987

OBITUARY NOTICE—See sketch in *SATA* Volume 22: Born June 11, 1942, in Brooklyn, N.Y.; died in a plane crash, July 14, 1987, near Lincolnville, Me. Diver, photographer, publisher, and author. An underwater explorer and photographer since 1961, Taylor wrote on marine subjects and photography, including *The Lobster: Its Life Cycle,* which was named one of the best science books for children by the New York Academy of Science in 1975, *The Joy of Snorkeling, The Sport Diving Catalog,* and *Underwater with Nikonos and Nikon Systems.* He also contributed articles to a number of newspapers and magazines and served as editor of the *Encyclopedia of Practical Photography.* In 1980 Taylor and his wife founded a publishing firm, the Photographic Book Company.

FOR MORE INFORMATION SEE: Contemporary Authors, Volumes 97-100, Gale, 1981; *Macmillan Biographical Encyclopedia of Photographic Artists and Innovators,* Macmillan, 1983. Obituaries: *New York Times,* July 18, 1987; *Publishers Weekly,* July 31, 1987.

TAYLOR, Theodore 1921-

PERSONAL: Born June 23, 1921, in Statesville, N.C., son of Edward Riley (a molder) and Elnora (Langhans) Taylor; married Gweneth Goodwin, October 25, 1946 (divorced, 1977); married Flora Gray Schoenleber (a library clerk), April 18, 1981; children: (first marriage) Mark, Wendy, Michael. *Education:* Attended U.S. Merchant Marine Academy, Kings Point, N.Y., 1942-43, and Columbia University, 1948; studied at American Theatre Wing, 1947-49. *Politics:* Republican. *Religion:* Protestant. *Home:* 1856 Catalina St., Laguna Beach, Calif. 92615. *Agent:* Gloria Loomis, Watkins Loomis Agency, Inc., 150 East 35th St., Suite 530, New York, N.Y. 10016.

CAREER: Evening Star, Portsmouth, Va., cub reporter, 1934-39, sports editor, 1941-42; *Washington Daily News,* Washington, D.C., copyboy, 1940-41; National Broadcasting Co. Radio, New York City, sportswriter, 1942; *Sunset News,* Bluefield, W. Va., sports editor, 1946-47; New York University, New York City, assistant director of public relations, 1947-48; *Orlando Sentinel Star,* Orlando, Fla., reporter, 1949-50; Paramount Pictures, Hollywood, Calif., publicist, 1955-56; Perlberg-Seaton Productions, Hollywood, story editor and associate producer, 1956-61; free-lance press agent for Hollywood studios, 1961-68; full-time writer, 1961—. Producer and director of documentary films. *Military service:* U.S. Merchant Marine, 1942-44; U.S. Naval Reserve, active duty, 1944-46, 1950-55, became lieutenant. *Member:* Academy of Motion Picture Arts and Sciences, Writers Guild, Society of Children's Book Writers, Authors League of America, Mystery Writers of America.

AWARDS, HONORS: Commonwealth Club of California Silver Medal, 1969, Jane Addams Children's Book Award from Women's International League for Peace and Freedom, Lewis Carroll Shelf Award, Southern California Council on Literature for Children and Young People Notable Book Award,

Woodward Park School Annual Book Award, and Best Book Award from University of California, Irvine, all 1970, all for *The Cay; Battle in the Arctic Seas* was selected one of *New York Times* Outstanding Books of the Year, 1976; Spur Award, Best Western for Young People category from Western Writers of America, and Commonwealth Club of California Silver Medal for the best juvenile book by a California author, both 1977, both for *A Shepherd Watches, A Shepherd Sings;* Award from the Southern California Council on Literature for Children and Young People, 1977, for his total body of work; George G. Stone Center for Children's Books Recognition of Merit Award, 1980, for "Hatteras Banks" trilogy (Teetoncey stories); Young Reader Medal from the California Reading Association, 1984, for *The Trouble with Tuck;* Jefferson Cup Honor Book from the Virginia Library Association, 1987, for *Walking up a Rainbow.*

WRITINGS—Juvenile: *People Who Make Movies,* Doubleday, 1967; *The Cay* (ALA Notable Book; *Horn Book* honor list), Doubleday, 1969; *The Children's War,* Doubleday, 1971; *Air Raid—Pearl Harbor! The Story of December 7, 1941* (illustrated by W. T. Mars), Crowell, 1971; *Rebellion Town: Williamsburg, 1776* (illustrated by Richard Cuffari), Crowell, 1973; *The Maldonado Miracle,* Doubleday, 1973; *Teetoncey* (illustrated by R. Cuffari), Doubleday, 1974; *Teetoncey and Ben O'Neal* (illustrated by R. Cuffari), Doubleday, 1975; *Battle in the Arctic Seas: The Story of Convoy PQ 17* (Junior Literary Guild selection; illustrated by Robert A. Parker), Crowell, 1976; *The Odyssey of Ben O'Neal* (illustrated by R. Cuffari), Doubleday, 1977; (with Louis Irigaray) *A Shepherd Watches, A Shepherd Sings,* Doubleday, 1977; *The Trouble with Tuck,* Doubleday, 1981; *The Battle of Midway Island* (illustrated by

THEODORE TAYLOR

Andrew Glass), Avon, 1981; *H.M.S. Hood Versus Bismarck: The Battleship Battle* (illustrated by A. Glass), Avon, 1982; *Battle in the English Channel* (illustrated by A. Glass), Avon, 1983; *Sweet Friday Island*, Scholastic, 1984; *Rocket Island*, Avon, 1984; *Walking up a Rainbow*, Delacorte, 1986; *The Hostage*, Delacorte, 1988.

Adult: *The Magnificent Mitscher* (biography), Norton, 1954; *Fire on the Beaches*, Norton, 1958; *The Body Trade*, Fawcett, 1967; (with Robert Houghton) *Special Unit Senator: An Investigation of the Assassination of Senator Robert F. Kennedy*, Random House, 1970; (with Kreskin) *The Amazing World of Kreskin*, Random House, 1974; *Jule: The Story of Composer Jule Styne*, Random House, 1979; (with Tippi Hedren) *The Cats of Shambala*, Simon & Schuster, 1985; *The Stalker*, D. I. Fine, 1987.

Author of television play "Tom Threepersons," TV Mystery Theatre, 1964, of screenplays "Night without End," 1959, "Showdown," Universal, 1973, and "The Hold-Up," of a television play for children, "Sunshine, the Whale," 1974, and of seventeen documentary films. Contributor of short stories and novelettes to magazines, including *Redbook*, *Argosy*, *McCall's*, *Ladies Home Journal*, and *Saturday Evening Post*.

WORK IN PROGRESS: Screenplay of *The Stalker*, for Charles Fries Productions; *For Fear of Lions and Tigers*, a young adult suspense novel; *Mocki Jumbi Got Killed*, an adult novel set in the Caribbean.

(Jacket illustration by Richard Cuffari from *The Odyssey of Ben O'Neal* by Theodore Taylor. Illustrated by Richard Cuffari.)

(Jacket illustration by Saul Lambert from *The Maldonado Miracle* by Theodore Taylor, his novel about an illegal alien—a twelve-year-old boy.)

ADAPTATIONS: "The Cay" (motion picture), starring James Earle Jones, NBC-TV, October 21, 1974, (filmstrip), Pied Piper Productions, 1975; "The Trouble with Tuck" (filmstrip), Pied Piper Productions, 1986.

SIDELIGHTS: "On **June 23, 1921,** I was born in Statesville, North Carolina, last of six children of Edward Riley Taylor and Elnora Alma Langhans: four sisters and a brother, Edward, who had died of pneumonia two years previously, at the age of two. My mother was then in her early forties and I suppose I was spoiled by my sisters, especially Mary, the only one usually home when I was small. The others, Naoma, Eleanor, and Louise were off working; married.

"Statesville, in the heart of the Piedmont area of North Carolina, red-earth flatlands before the western rises of the Blue Ridges, had about five thousand inhabitants when I was born. County seat of Iredell, it was centered in an agriculture economy, mainly: cotton, tobacco, corn, some orchards; truck farms. There was a brickyard and a foundry, where my father worked; knitting mills provided most of the jobs. It was a nice, God-fearing Waspish town of the upper South.

"I'm told that I was very shy as a child, the kind that clung to Mother's skirt. And in certain situations I remain shy to this day, preferring to circulate with people I know well; slow to develop new friendships.

"I have a foggy memory of a boxy little white clapboard house with a peanut field beside it and my father's first car. He only had two in his lifetime. This must have been 1924 or 1925. He went to work, saying it needed fixing. When he came home, I said, 'I ficked it.' I had, indeed, breaking all the glass. Headlights, windshield, instrument panel. He was so stunned I didn't get punished.

"My father, though of absolute English descent, swore he was an Irishman and certainly had that temperament; never finished grade school. He went to work in a Pittsburgh foundry when he was barely twelve and became a molder, black-sheep of a moderately well-to-do family. He was an argumentative man; the highest wage he ever made in his life was in the fifty-dollar-a-week range.

"There were periods, especially during the Depression of the late 1920s and early 1930s, when I would not see him for months. He was a blue-collar workingman's working man and became involved in the International Workers of the World, 'the Wobblies,' left-wing labor organization, in the 1920s. When I was only four or five I remember him coming home one night bloodied and bruised, results of tangling with police during a strike.

"My mother was so different that we children (when I was a little older) could never understand how these two people got together and got married. She, delicate and fragile; he, stocky and muscular. Mother, reciting poetry; father, talking about the 'working man' endlessly. She'd wanted to be an actress and had taken part in school plays and Little Theatre; had won contests in elocution and would sometimes emote in the kitchen, acting out a part. She was so gentle and creative; he was so ungentle and so uncreative.

"Somewhat afraid of my father and his Irish temper, I worshipped my mother except for her religiosity. Sunday school each and every Sunday, then to church, then to vespers; then to Wednesday-night prayer meetings. My father, who was Roman Catholic, did not attend. I pumped the organ for services at a church in Tennessee for a while, sitting behind it and almost going to sleep during the sermons. Later on, I realized that the church, Lutheran always, was Mother's solace and her strength. She desperately needed it.

"The first stories that I recall were mainly Bible stories from a thick, illustrated children's version. Action was what I liked— David slaying Goliath; Samson and Delilah; Samson pulling down the Philistine temple. Mother read them to me countless times. I still have the book, published in 1922, and I still prefer action stories, both to read and to write.

"My next to oldest sister, Eleanor, had married a Britisher and lived in London. So from England came fat books with a

He pulled himself half out of the water, clinging to the overturned hull. ■ (From *Teetoncey* by Theodore Taylor. Illustrated by Richard Cuffari.)

different look and feel and, of course, English characters. The *Pip and Squeak Annuals* and the *BoPeep Bumper Books* were my favorites. I still have them, too. I was a dreamer when a child, and had a good imagination then, much better than now.''

Books were an extension of ''imaginary'' adventures. Taylor would go home with at least five—all adventure tales—from the public library. ''Though Mother had read to me likely from the age of two, and I was reading on my own at about five, my personal library card came along at the age of eight. One did not need to be twenty-one and have a bank account to check out books from the Statesville Public Library. By the time we left town, about a year later, I was bringing home books that made her cringe, good church lady that she was, yet there was no censorship practiced. In addition to all the *Tom Swifts* and 'Huck Finns' and L. Frank Baums, I remember lugging in adult mysteries and detective stories. I read both *Frankenstein* and *Dracula* about then. Heady stuff.

''I never was a very good student and my memories of Mulberry Street School and Davie Avenue School are more of endurance than anything else. Fascinated with World War I (there were a few army trucks of that vintage in town), I spent a lot of time drawing Fokkers and Spads and Sopwith Pups and Scouts in aerial battles; looping artillery fire into the Flan-

(Cover illustration from *Battle in the English Channel* by Theodore Taylor.)

ders trenches. When I should have been listening to the teacher I filled sheets of paper with war scenes: 'Dory,' of *The Children's War,* my least successful book.

''But it was after school and during the hot Piedmont summer that I excelled in the practice of freedom, a brand of which is not known to many of today's children of six or seven. With one or another of young friends, or, quite often, by myself, I roamed fields and muddy creeks and other interesting places around and about town: the abandoned headquarters of the volunteer cavalry, soon to burn down; the old brickyard, the strong-smelling building where chewing tobacco had once been manufactured; numerous drain pipes and other places of mystery.

''The unwitting accomplice was my mother. I do not remember, at this age of seven and upward, her ever asking, 'Where are you going?' She trusted in God that I'd always be safe. I had remarkable freedom for a kid curious about most things.''

Taylor's four older sisters were also a great childhood influence. One lived in England; another in New York; another was a schoolteacher. The youngest sister, who still lived at home, introduced him to Ernest Hemingway when Taylor was about eleven years old.

Early 1930s. ''Money was indeed a very big problem for millions of people the next two or three years, the depths of the Depression, and I went about trying to solve it my own way. I began raising greens to sell to the markets and got a route for the Greensboro morning paper. The latter was delivered to the front of the Vance Hotel at five in the morning by the first bus through from Greensboro. It did not occur to me until years later that there was anything exceptional about a boy just shy of ten getting up at four-thirty to walk, not bicycle, to the Vance, pick up sixty-odd newspapers; deliver them by seven; come home, have breakfast and go off to school.

''I sold candy by the box, buying it wholesale; picked up scrap metal to sell at the local junkyard. I wasn't alone in these endeavors and I'm not the least sorry that I went through them. My father and mother would have taken the rack rather than apply for welfare, which didn't exist, anyway. We never missed a meal though some nights we had fried apples for dinner. The apples were picked from the tree next door, with permission.

''About then into my life came Napoleon, a little black-and-white mongrel, auspices of Mary whose Chevrolet agency employer had a litter to give away. Nappy began my long love affair with dogs and many of the books I've written have canine characters in them, notably the *Teetoncey* trilogy, with 'Boo Dog'; 'Tuck' in *The Trouble with Tuck;* 'Rufus' in *Walking up a Rainbow.* Nappy had beagle, terrier, and some other breed mixed in.

''In early 1934, my father got his first job in six years, a molder's helper at the Norfolk Navy Yard, in Portsmouth, Virginia, salary about twenty-five a week. He summoned us to Portsmouth after school was over. I'd never been so excited. Another state; a town near water, near ships. I'd read a lot about the sea and ships. My father had a real job, at last. Mother and I sat up all night on the train to Portsmouth, talking most of it.

''Portsmouth sits on the banks of the Elizabeth River, opposite Norfolk, a navy town then and now, and a few miles outside on the southeast corner was Cradock, built in 1918 to house blue-collar workers of World War I. Cradock and the downstairs rooms of one of those war-built houses was our destination by streetcar. Nappy had ridden in the baggage car in a

SOON TO BE A PRIME TIME TV SPECIAL

The Trouble With Tuck

THEODORE TAYLOR

(Jacket illustration by Charles Santore from *The Trouble with Tuck* by Theodore Taylor.)

crate and was now in my lap as we bucked and pitched our way the three miles to a new life.

"We passed the fences of the sprawling Navy Yard that Sunday morning and I could see in the distance the great ships that were tied up there. Somewhere in me is a considerable dollop of salt, from an unknown past, perhaps a great-great-great-grandfather sailing out of Hamburg or Bremen, and I had a hankering for the water long before we moved to Virginia. I remember asking my father that day if we could have a boat. He said, Yes, without having the slightest idea where that wherewithal would come from. He was like that.

"The north boundary of Cradock was Paradise Creek, a muddy, shallow, winding estuary that smelled like anything but paradise at low tide. It was inhabited by herons, gudgeons, and crabs. I was to spend many days on it. The streetcar clicked across the wooden bridge over the creek and then we were in the little town named after a British admiral killed in the late big war, the war to end all wars.

"Cradock was, and is, a unique place, laid out with a street plan shaped like an anchor. It was one of the first communities in America designed for self-containment, historically significant as the first planned shopping center in America. Around Afton Square, modeled after towns in New England, were

grocery stores, a drugstore, barbershop, fish market, bakery, cleaners, a community hall. Auto traffic entered from the opposite end of the streetcar tracks, from George Washington Highway, through two brick gate posts. One had the feeling of going on to a campus or military reservation. On Afton Square was a bandstand and a big cannon. Afton Square could have served as backdrop for one of Norman Rockwell's *Saturday Evening Post* covers.

"There was a friendliness to the village from the moment we walked up from the streetcar line to our temporary quarters. My father had selected Cradock because it was a 'working man' place and he felt at home there. The man we rented from was also employed at the shipyard.

"A few days after arrival I had my thirteenth birthday and looked forward to entering high school in the fall with a freshman class of around seventy. Cradock High, serving a town of around two thousand, was in a one-story brick building in a T-shape, with elementary grades occupying the wings. In reality, Cradock High was a small and insignificant rural school, yet I now marvel at the quality of teaching there. My English teacher, *Miss* Caroline Hardy, she of the eagle and cool eyes, and faint smile, an aloof, regal 'spinster' lady, encouraged me to write once she saw I was serious about it. I owe much to her. The ill-paid teachers of that day had the respect and sup-

An hour passes and the distress signals become less frequent. ■ (From *Battle in the Arctic Seas: The Story of Convoy PQ17* by Theodore Taylor. Illustrated by Robert Andrew Parker.)

(Jacket illustration by Milton Glaser from *The Cay* by Theodore Taylor.)

port of the community and I cannot remember a bad one. Neither can I remember a single student who could not read.

"Until school began I explored. I highly recommend exploration to young and would-be writers. I followed the Norfolk and Western tracks down to the river, often hopping the slow coaljacks for a ride, to watch the small freighters that chugged down the Elizabeth toward North Carolina on the inland waterway; to see tankers unloading on the South Norfolk side. I followed the streetcar track on foot into Portsmouth and explored the waterfront, spending hours at the Isaac Fass fishing docks watching the boats unload. I watched the side-wheeler ferries, still coal-burners, plying the mile or so across to Norfolk. There was an all-encompassing excitement to this waterfront activity, so different from the flatlands of the Piedmont, and I was caught up in it.

"In bed, at night, when the wind was blowing westward I could hear ship's whistles, the tooting of tugboats, from the Elizabeth. I imagined what types of ships were doing it; where they were going. I was, for reasons unknown, more interested in the merchant ships than in the naval vessels at the Yard. Plums of the China Sea and Java and Sumatra kept dancing through my head.

"Eventually, I plucked chickens and bicycle-delivered for the cleaner on Afton Square to earn enough to buy a ten-dollar rowboat, carting it down to Paradise Creek on a little wagon. I crabbed from it, for home consumption, during the next three summers. Steamed crabs, blues.

"Because of the way I looked, all skin and bones, though of average height, and the way I talked, 'Carolina hick,' they said. I was nicknamed 'Hayseed' within a few weeks after school started. I had come from the redneck interior of North Carolina and there was a little more sophistication here in Tidewater, Virginia. Whatever, 'Hayseed' stuck with me until I graduated. Mostly, it was said in a warm and nonderogatory way.

"That late fall I saw the Atlantic Ocean for the first time in my life, an unforgettable thrill. The parents of a boy I'd met at school asked if I wanted to go along to Cape Henry, forty miles or so east of Norfolk. I wasn't aware of it but the Jamestown settlers had first touched shore there in 1607. I couldn't wait to go. The day was sunny and chilly and there stretched the blue ocean. England on the other side of it. I remember that Sunday afternoon so clearly—a Coast Guard surfboat from the nearby Cape Henry Lighthouse station riding the breakers as the crew practiced, their long oars sweeping waves. Barefoot, I waded along the edge of the cold water, finding a horseshoe crab shell, taking it home. Later, I used that visual of the drilling surfboat crew in the *Teetoncey* trilogy."

1934. Began writing at the age of thirteen as a cub reporter for the Portsmouth, Virginia *Evening Star,* covering high school sports events. He was paid fifty cents a week for his weekly sports column—his first professional money. "Never had I thought about writing of any sort. And, to my knowledge, I had no talent for it. But I was certainly willing to gamble that

(From the movie "Showdown," starring Dean Martin, Susan Clark, and Rock Hudson. Copyright © 1973 by Universal Pictures.)

I could put a story together. My father, with his new wealth of a steady job, managed to come up with five dollars for a secondhand L. C. Smith and I was on my way via the hunt-and-peck system which I use to this day.

"I remember studying the sports pages the *Star* and the larger *Norfolk Virginian-Pilot, just to see how the stories were written,* then placing them down by the typewriter for constant referral. That is, in fact, a good way to learn how to write. Copy good writers.

"After laboring all morning and up to midafternoon on the page and a half, I nervously rode the streetcar to Portsmouth clutching my first story, mentally and probably physically crossing fingers that it would be accepted. One David P. Glazer, in his early twenties, though he seemed older, was sports editor of the *Star,* and 'Pete' took a long look at my work through thick-lensed glasses. His copy pencil then said more than words. Over the next three years Pete Glazer was my patient teacher and fifty years later we remain in touch. In reviewing my first book, an adult biography, in 1954, Pete said, 'Ted Taylor was the rawest recruit we ever had. . . .'

"The *Star,* located near the waterfront, by the Seaboard Railway station, with police headquarters and the jail just down the street, a courtroom occupying the second floor of the old building, *smelled* like an old-fashioned, non-air-conditioned newspaper office. Noisy presses sixty or seventy feet from the newsroom, the strong odor of ink, the huge rolls of paper, hot lead from the typesetting machines, combined to make an acrid perfume. I'll never forget how the *Star* smelled.

"The staff was small: managing editor, city editor, Pete, as sports editor, and a part-time society editor. Everyone did double duty as general assignment reporters, even the managing editor, a little dynamo of man. It was the perfect learning institution for me and I lingered around each time after delivering my copy, listening to newsroom conversations about sports and crime and politics; life in general, life on the seamy side and beneath it, the side that most often gets into newspaper print. The *Star* and another paper, a fast-paced metropolitan tabloid, were to be my college, my seamy-side university, my graduate schools. I've often regretted I didn't attend college. City rooms were the substitutes, newsmen were the teachers."

1939. Graduated from Cradock High School, a year later than his class because of an inability to pass freshman math. "I took it over and over but simply could not conquer it; therefore, I had no required algebra credit. Straight A's in English and history, B's in most other subjects, I was totally defeated by mathematics and am not much better a half century later. . . . The officials allowed me to graduate, without a math credit. The principal said, simply, 'I give up.'

"Sister Mary then footed most of the bill for me to attend Fork Union Military Academy, in Virginia, just to obtain the necessary math credit. I received a partial scholarship by covering the school's athletic events for the *Washington Post,* doing exactly what I'd done at Cradock High. I finally earned the math credit but never used it. I entered the so-called 'college of hard knocks.'"

(From the movie "The Cay," starring James Earl Jones. Presented on NBC-TV, October 21, 1974.)

1940-1941. Worked as a copyboy for the *Washington Daily News* in Washington, D.C. "A metropolitan newspaper! A Washington paper! Abode of the blessed, the Elysian fields to which most reporters longed to go, and there I was happily answering to the yell of 'copy' or 'boy,' tearing off AP and UP stories from the teletype machine; filling pastepots, going out for coffee to please the big city reporters and editors who were getting out four or five editions a day."

Spring, 1941. Returned to Cradock and the Portsmouth *Evening Star.* "With war news coming off the teletypes each hour, England struggling against Nazi Germany, unsettling days, came a letter from first mentor Pete Glazer, saying he was going into the navy rather than be drafted into the army. Would I be interested in returning to Portsmouth as sports editor of the *Star?* I practically dashed to the pay phone down in the stairwell. I was two months from turning nineteen.

"Greeted warmly by Pete and other members of the *Star,* I was welcomed as if there'd just been a long pause before I came back to the good smells and coziness of the small-town paper. I was at home here; knew the town, knew the people. Pete gave me a short course in headline writing, selection of type and other responsibilities of an editor. Then off he went into the navy; off I went into running a one-man sports department. For variety, I also worked general news—courts, accidents, sometimes the police beat—fine training for a young reporter. To save on lunch, though my salary was now eighteen a week, I attended the local Kiwanis, Lion, and Rotary luncheon meetings, reporting on what their noon speakers had to say."

1942. When the United States entered World War II, Taylor joined the merchant marines. "Over the next seventeen months, I served as a deck cadet and then an able-bodied seaman aboard a gasoline tanker in the Atlantic and Pacific areas, a freighter in the European theater, then obtained a third-mate's license, sailing for a trip each on two other ships.

"Returning to the United States in the fall of 1944, I found out I'd been called up by the navy as a cargo officer and soon reported as an ensign, USNR, to the USS *Draco,* a cargo attack vessel in the Pacific. Following the Japanese surrender, I heard about Operation Crossroads, the nuclear experiment at Bikini Atoll, and volunteered for duty out there. I wanted to see the bomb go off. Unfortunately, but typically, my ship, the USS *Sumner,* was ordered home before the big blast."

October 25, 1946. Married Gweneth Goodwin. The couple had two sons and a daughter.

1947-1950. After a brief stint as sports editor of a newspaper in Bluefield, West Virginia, Taylor moved to New York City, where he attended playwriting classes at the American Theatre Wing and short-story classes at Columbia University and worked in public relations at New York University. "I knew I wanted to write. I didn't know exactly *what* I wanted to write. My strong suit was reportorial, nonfiction, so I tried that, selling a short piece to *Look* magazine, thrilled by the check for twenty-five dollars. I then wrote several dozen short stories, none of which sold. I'm not even sure I have them anymore. Back to nonfiction, I sold three or four travel pieces.

"My wife wasn't exactly enthused about this way to making a living, or even augment it—few wives are—but I was restless again and a few months after son Mark was born up came the stakes. I got a job with the *Orlando Sentinel-Star* as its 'space' reporter, keeping an eye on activity at the new space center at Cape Canaveral. I had a tiny office in Cocoa and sent my copy to Orlando by bus.

"I covered the first suborbital shot, a Bumper, converted German V-2 rocket, from Cape Canaveral, little understanding that in twelve years John Glenn would circle the earth in Mercury capsule *Friendship 7.* Perhaps for the same reason I couldn't pass freshman math. I'm not equipped to write futuristic themes, science fiction, even fantasy. I've tried the latter, meeting with unanimous rejection. It's good to know limitations."

1954. First book, a biography entitled *The Magnificent Mitscher* was published. At the time of publication, Taylor was on active duty with the U.S. Naval Reserve. "Having added a daughter, Wendy, to the family, we were down in the Caribbean by the time *Mitscher* was published. I'd served a short tour on the cruiser *Newport News* and was now public information officer for the Caribbean Sea Frontier, aide to the admiral, who also headed up the naval district centered at the Naval Air Station, San Juan, Puerto Rico. I'd sailed the Caribbean in the war, going in and out of the oil ports of Aruba and Curacao. Now there was a chance to explore the islands a bit more. A hurricane relief mission got me to Grenada long before the trouble there; to little-known Carriacou and Barbados. Another hurricane mission got me to Haiti. Saint Thomas and Saint Croix were quick hops over on one of the district's C-45s. I sponged up background and atmosphere, little knowing that *The Cay* was fourteen years up the path.

"But I had already decided on my next book, *Fire on the Beaches,* the story of the ships that fled from German submarines along the East Coast during the war, ships like the Cities Service tanker, SS *Annibal,* the one I'd served on."

1955. Moved to California where he worked in Hollywood for the next thirteen years as a publicist, story editor, associate producer and free-lance press agent. "Before becoming story editor and assistant to producer William Perlberg and director George Seaton, I did a screenplay for them, my first, and then spent almost a year in Europe on 'The Counterfeit Traitor,' a distinguished film starring [William] Holden and Lilli Palmer. *Fire on the Beaches* had been published to good reviews in April, 1958, but I was deeply involved in the film business then and didn't have a book in mind.

"Son Michael was born the year after we finished 'Traitor' and I decided to depart Hollywood and do documentary films, moving sixty miles down coast to Laguna Beach. Immediately, I found myself back in Europe shooting a travelogue for Lufthansa German Airlines. Over the next nine years I made documentaries all over the world, affording a lot of travel, many of them 'behind-scenes' films for TV, associated with various feature films.

"Between shooting and editing the documentaries, and some free-lance press agentry for Columbia and Twentieth Century-Fox, assignments lasting three or four months, I kept busy at the typewriter, mixing magazine fiction with nonfiction, selling action-adventure stories to such as *Argosy, Stag,* and *Male,* and similar others, up-graded publications from the old Street and Smith pulp days of the thirties. But I also sold to *McCall's, Redbook,* and the *Saturday Evening Post.* A *Redbook* novelette of the early 1960s became *The Maldonado Miracle,* a children's book of the 1970s. I often take a half-dozen years before the idea is transformed into a book."

1967. First children's book published. "After devoting more than an exciting year to Robert Wise's 'The Sand Pebbles,' a Steve McQueen-Richard Attenborough film shot mostly in Taiwan and Hong Kong, marvelous experience in exotic locales, I decided to try a book for young readers. My own children were interested in how motion pictures were made

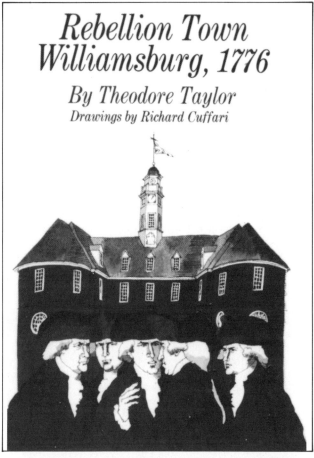

(Jacket illustration by Richard Cuffari from *Rebellion Town: Williamsburg, 1776* by Theodore Taylor.)

and I thought others might be, too. *People Who Make Movies* was quickly sold to Doubleday and I was astonished some two years later, after the book began circulating in the schools, to receive mail from young readers. More than three thousand responded to that book, most seeking Hollywood careers. I was amazed. In writing for adults, I'd probably received a dozen letters.

"After finishing a horrible Frank Sinatra film in Miami, and hearing Dr. Martin Luther King singing spirituals in the lobby of a hotel, I decided to go ahead with the long-brewing story of the boy on the life raft in the Caribbean. A few days after returning home from Florida, I rolled fresh paper into the typewriter. Three weeks later *The Cay* was completed and the printed version is little different from the first draft. By far it was the quickest and easiest book I've ever written, yet twelve years of occasional thought had gone into the work. I'm convinced that my subconscious or 'unconscious' does much of the writing for me. How else do I have half, or even well-formed, thoughts in the morning?

"The reviews were uniformly excellent, many awards came along, and I was surprisingly launched as a writer of children's books. But *The Cay* soon came under attack as a 'racist' book, a charge which I believe is untrue. A climate had been created and the early, and principal, attacks came from the Interracial Council on Children's Books. Later, *The Cay* was banned in many public libraries as a result of pressure from the Interracial Council. Five years after I received the Jane Addams Book Award I was requested to return it. The Jane Addams group succumbed to Council pressure."

The Cay won over eleven literary awards, including the Lewis Carroll Shelf Award, and was an NBC Bell Telephone Special starring James Earl Jones, in the fall of 1974. "I believe that had it been written by a black writer there wouldn't have been more than a ripple of dissent. *The Cay* is *not* racist, in my firm belief, and the character of Timothy, the old black man, modeled after a real person and several composites, is 'heroic' and not a stereotype. Would the critics have had him speak Brooklynese instead of Creole? Nonsense!"

1973. Began the *Teetoncey* trilogy, a work which Taylor favored. It's background was the Hatteras Banks of Virginia, a locale that he was especially fond of during his teenage years. "The Banks were less than a hundred miles from Cradock. They were wild then. No bridges over the inlets, only sand trails from Kitty Hawk on south. Many of the inbred people, descendants of shipwreck survivors, still spoke in Elizabethan dialect and some of the cottages, built with shipwreck timbers, were surrounded by whalebone fences. There were bones of ships that dated to the 1700s. Fascinated with these people and their history I visited the Banks four times as an adult and finally, after much research help from the University of North Carolina, I began the *Teetoncey* trilogy. The characters were drawn from real-life, as they are in all my books. I stress that I don't have a very good imagination, I'm still basically a reporter, finding it easier to work from real-life models.

"Continuing to mix children's books with the adult themes, I wrote a book with The Amazing Kreskin, the mentalist, learning something about ESP and mental trickery; I ghosted one about hyperactive children with a San Francisco doctor, which

(From the filmstrip adaptation of Taylor's novel *The Trouble with Tuck*. Produced by Pied Piper Productions, 1986.)

reached best-seller lists; ghosted another for comedian Jerry Lewis, which didn't. Meanwhile, I turned out three nonfiction juveniles for Crowell on war subjects: one notable one, *Air Raid: Pearl Harbor*, drawn directly from *Tora! Tora! Tora!* research. That one got a *Life* magazine review and I still don't understand how and why, I'm grateful. Dedicated to Christopher Robin Taylor, a good literary name, first grandchild, son of Mark, *Air Raid: Pearl Harbor* seems to be a favorite of twelve-year-old boys. I've been getting fan mail from that age and sex for seventeen years.

"During this period I also screenplayed a western, 'Showdown,' for Universal, starring Rock Hudson and Dean Martin. It seemed that I went from one project to another with very little time between. My New York agent, Gloria Loomis, has always seen to it that my table is filled."

1977. Marriage ended. "Writers do not have a very good track record for prolonged union but this one had lasted thirty-one stormy years. Not long after my wife had sent her papers to the court I was on the beach with two big dogs, in early morning. This has been a 6:30 A.M. routine for many years. Largely uninhabited except for birds and a few joggers, the dawn beach is a place for both exercise and thought. I often work out the first paragraphs of the day while walking along the tidelines.

"This particular morning, the youngest of the two dogs, Burney, originally owned by Michael, youngest son, normally a peaceful mixed breed, decided to attack a burly black dog owned by a widow. I'm so glad he did. His teeth were fateful. I pulled Burney off before he was annihilated and then, in the afternoon, called the lady to apologize. I'm not one to sit home very long and a date was soon arranged, for dinner and a movie. I hadn't 'dated' in thirty-one years and neither had Flora McLellan Schoenleber. We were married in April, 1981.

"As a former children's library clerk, though she indeed served as *The* librarian at three elementary schools, Flora has a deep interest in children's books and we exchange ideas. She remembers titles and plots and writers of books I've never read. Handy to have your own librarian at home. We share research on most of the books and she takes care of the business side as well.

"We live in a tree-hidden board-and-batten house three blocks from the ocean, close enough to hear breakers slam the sands on some nights. The house cannot be seen from the street because of all the trees and there's a sign in the winding driveway, 'The House in the Woods.' My office is situated, with large glass windows, so that I'm completely surrounded by trees."

1982. Travelled around the world on an island-hopping trip that included visits to Sri Lanka, the Seychelles and Bahrain. Taylor tries to take one foreign trip each year with his wife.

Besides travel, Taylor enjoys walking the beach. He works on his various writing projects—often working on two or three novels at once—from his office every day. "Long ago I learned about discipline and have no trouble going to my office about eight-thirty each morning. With a half-hour off for lunch, I work until four or four-thirty; sometimes five. I do this seven days a week except during football season, September to Super Bowl Sunday. During this grunt-grind period on the gridiron, I work only five days weekly—*without guilt*. Otherwise, I feel enormous guilt if I don't work. Precious hours going to waste."

FOR MORE INFORMATION SEE: New York Times Book Review, June 26, 1969, July 11, 1971, November 15, 1981;

Saturday Review, June 28, 1969, August 21, 1971; *Top of the News,* November, 1971, April, 1975; Doris de Montreville and Elizabeth D. Crawford, editors, *Fourth Book of Junior Authors and Illustrators,* H. W. Wilson, 1978; D. L. Kirkpatrick, editor, *Twentieth-Century Children's Writers,* St. Martin's, 1978, 2nd edition, 1983; *Washington Post,* May 26, 1979; Dorothy A. Marquardt and Martha E. Ward, *Authors of Books for Young People,* supplement to the 2nd edition, Scarecrow, 1979.

Collections: Kerlan Collection at the University of Minnesota.

TERBAN, Marvin   1940-

PERSONAL: Born April 28, 1940, in Chelsea, Mass.; son of Edward S. (a meat cutter) and Sally (a housewife, maiden name, Gillette) Terban; married Karen Youngman (a special education teacher), June 20, 1965; children: David, Jennifer. *Education:* Tufts University, B.A., 1961; Columbia University, M.F.A., 1963. *Home:* New York, N.Y. *Office:* c/o Clarion Books, 52 Vanderbilt Ave., New York, N.Y. 10017.

CAREER: Columbia Grammar and Preparatory School, New York, N.Y., teacher, 1963—; Cejwin Camps, Port Jervis, N.Y., director of children's plays, summers, 1977—. Worked in media and children's education at CBS Learning Center and a public television station. Actor in local community theater productions and amateur and student movies.

WRITINGS—Juvenile; all illustrated by Giulio Maestro, except as noted; all published by Clarion: *Eight Ate: A Feast of Homonym Riddles,* 1982; *In a Pickle and Other Funny Idioms,* 1983; *I Think I Thought: And Other Tricky Verbs,* 1984; *Too Hot to Hoot: Funny Palindrome Riddles,* 1985; *Your Foot's*

MARVIN TERBAN

(From "Body Parts" in *Mad as a Wet Hen! And Other Funny Idioms* by Marvin Terban. Illustrated by Giulio Maestro.)

on My Feet! And Other Tricky Nouns, 1986; *Mad as a Wet Hen and Other Funny Idioms*, 1987; *Guppies in Tuxedos, Funny Eponyms*, 1988; *The Dove Dove, Funny Homograph Riddles* (illustrated by Tom Huffman), 1988; *Superdupers! Fun Words*, 1989.

SIDELIGHTS: "I was born the youngest child, a son with two older sisters. I married a youngest child, a daughter with two older brothers. According to an article on what makes good marriages in a recent woman's magazine, that's the best combination. It must be. Karen and I have been happily married for almost twenty-three years. We even wrote two books together (classroom ideas for teachers published by Macmillan). My wife and I are both teachers. She teaches learning disabled students in a public school; I teach fifth- and sixth-grade English in a private school. Our schools are located very close to where we live because we both hate commuting. I'm three minutes from work. Karen has the longer commute, seven minutes. Both our children, David and Jennifer, are students at the school where I teach. For the past two years Jennifer has been a student in my English class. She has me for a teacher forty minutes a day (and for a father twenty-three hours, twenty minutes). At first she didn't know what to call me in school, Mr. Terban or Dad. She solved the problem by calling me Mr. Dad.

"During the summer I direct plays at Cejwin Camps in Port Jervis, New York. My wife is the nature counselor and both David and Jennifer are campers. They live in their own bunks; my wife and I live in ours. Jennifer and David have often appeared in plays directed by me, but they get their parts solely on their acting and singing talents, nothing else. David is over six feet tall and a great basketball player. Jennifer is shorter and loves tending all her animals.

"I first became interested in writing books for young people as a teacher. Many of my word play books for Clarion began as teaching games in my classroom or with my children. I do an enormous amount of research for my books both at my school library and in the public libraries. I have fifteen dictionaries on a shelf over my desk along with many other reference books. I used to write my books in longhand on yellow paper and then type them out. Now I do all my writing on a computer. David and Jennifer loved playing and working on my computer so much, I had to buy them computers of their own.

"I'm proud of my word play books for Clarion because I think that they help children use the English language better. English is a very complicated language; it has so many exceptions and peculiarities. I hope that my books on homonyms, homographs, idioms, etc., will help children unconfuse the language for themselves. I recently got a letter from China. They're using my word play books to teach English to college students! They must find English just as tricky as we do in America.

"In addition to writing and teaching, and being Karen's husband and David and Jennifer's father, I started (in my spare time!) a tutoring service to help eleventh and twelfth graders prepare for the tests to get into college. And I love to act in shows. I belong to a local community theater company, and whenever I can, I perform. I love to act and more recently sing in shows. I've been in 'South Pacific,' 'Show Boat' and 'Fiddler on the Roof.' I had to paste on a false beard so often for parts in shows that a few years ago I grew a real one. Then

I got a part in a movie and the director made me shave off my beard! It was only a minute on the screen ('Radio Days,' directed by Woody Allen), but I had great fun shooting the scene and didn't mind losing my beard because the next day I started growing it right back.

"For the future, I hope to continue teaching, tutoring, acting, and, of course, writing. Maybe some other interests will interest me too, so I'll try to find time for them."

TIERNEY, Frank M.   1930-

PERSONAL: Born August 2, 1930, in Ottawa, Canada; son of Frank (a mechanic) and Mary (a housewife; maiden name, Brennan) Tierney; married Audrey C. Gardner (a housewife), May 17, 1952; children: Susan, Steven, Frank, David, Dana, Catherine, Kerry. *Education:* University of Montreal, Ottawa, B.A., 1959, M.A., 1961; University of Ottawa, Ph.D., 1969. *Home:* 8 Mohawk Crescent, Ottawa, Ontario K2H 7G6, Canada. *Office:* University of Ottawa, Ottawa, Ontario K1N 6N5, Canada.

CAREER: R. L. Crain Ltd., Ottawa, Canada, sales manager, 1950-1965; University of Ottawa, Ottawa, Canada, English professor, 1965-84, department chairman, 1984—.

WRITINGS—Juvenile; "Silly Sally" series; all published by Borealis: *Silly Sally and the Picnic with the Porpoises* (illustrated by Ann Crook), 1973; *. . . and the Snowman* (illustrated by Derry G. Timleck), 1975; *. . . and the Golden Pail* (illustrated by Wendy Irvine), 1977; *. . . and the Little Pumpkin* (illustrated by W. Irvine), 1978; *. . . the Tire and Mrs. Corrigan* (illustrated by W. Irvine), 1979; *. . . and the Moon-Baker* (illustrated by Lucy Yuzyk), 1981; *. . . and Captain G. Rumpy* (illustrated by Aida Hudson), 1988.

Other: *Come Climb a Mountain and Other Poems,* University of Ottawa Press, 1970; *The Birch and Other Poems,* Borealis, 1971; *Fire-Cloud and Other Poems,* Borealis, 1972; *Beams of Love,* Borealis, 1973; *The Way It Stands* (illustrated by Douglas A. Fales), Borealis, 1974; *The Lilac Tree and Other Poems,* Borealis, 1988.

Editor; for adults: (With Stephen M. Gill) *Poets of the Capital,* Borealis, 1974; Desmond Pacey, *Waken Lords and Ladies Gay: Selected Stories of Desmond Percy,* University of Ottawa Press, 1974; Charles Sangster, *Norland Echoes and Other Poems and Lyrics,* Tecumseh, 1976; Charles Sangster, *Angel Guest and Other Poems and Lyrics,* Tecumseh, 1978; (with Glenn Clever) *Poets of the Capitol—II,* Borealis, 1978; Charles Sangster, *Hesperus and Other Poems and Lyrics,* Tecumseh, 1979; (with introduction) Isabella Valancy Crawford, *The Halton Boys,* Borealis, 1979; (with introduction) *The Crawford Symposium,* University of Ottawa Press, 1979; C. Sangster, *St. Lawrence and the Saguenay and Other Poems,* Tecumseh, 1984; (with introduction) *The Thomas Chandler Haliburton Symposium,* University of Ottawa Press, 1985; *The Poetry of Charles Sangster,* Tecumseh, 1988.

WORK IN PROGRESS: Nineteenth Century Canadian Narrative Poems, for Tecumseh.

SIDELIGHTS: "My stories are told to my children spontaneously, created as the story is told. It begins with whatever universal image or situation comes to mind as I sit with the children and let the imagination take over. The 'told' story is written immediately following the telling without changing any word or aspect of it."

P. L. TRAVERS

TRAVERS, P(amela) L(yndon)   1906-

PERSONAL: Born August 9, 1906, in Queensland, Australia; daughter of Robert and Margaret (Goff) Travers. *Education:* Privately educated. *Religion:* Anglican. *Home:* Chelsea, London, England. *Address:* c/o William Collins Sons Ltd., 8 Grafton St., London W1X 3LA, England. *Agent:* David Higham Associates Ltd., 5-8 Lower John Street, London W1R 4HA, England.

CAREER: Writer, journalist, dancer, and actress in Australia and England; full-time writer in England, 1930—. Writer-in-residence, Radcliffe College, Cambridge, Mass., 1965-66, Smith College, Northampton, Mass., 1966-67, and Scripps College, Claremont, Calif., 1970. *Member:* Cosmopolitan Club. *Awards, honors:* Nene Award from the Hawaii Association of School Librarians and the Hawaii Library Association, 1965, for *Mary Poppins; Friend Monkey* was chosen one of Child Study Association of America's Children's Books of the Year, 1971, and *About the Sleeping Beauty,* 1975; Order of the British Empire, 1977; honorary doctorate, Chatham College, 1978.

WRITINGS—Juvenile, except as noted: *Mary Poppins* (illustrated by Mary Shepard), Reynal & Hitchcock, 1934, Harcourt, 1962, revised edition, 1981; *Mary Poppins Comes Back* (illustrated by M. Shepard), Reynal & Hitchcock, 1935 (previous two titles appeared in one volume, *Mary Poppins* and *Mary Poppins Comes Back* (illustrated by M. Shepard), Reynal & Hitchcock, 1937, Harcourt, 1963); *Moscow Excursion* (adult), Reynal & Hitchcock, 1935; *Happy Ever After* (illustrated by M. Shepard), Reynal & Hitchcock, 1940; *I Go by Sea, I Go by Land* (illustrated by Gertrude Hermes), Harper, 1941, new edition, Norton, 1964; *Aunt Sass* (adult), Reynal & Hitchcock, 1941; *Ah Wong* (adult), privately printed (New York), 1943; *Mary Poppins Opens the Door* (ALA Notable Book; illustrated by M. Shepard and Agnes Sims), Reynal & Hitchcock, 1943,

Harcourt, 1962; *Johnny Delaney* (adult), privately printed, 1944; *Mary Poppins in the Park* (illustrated by M. Shepard), Harcourt, 1952, new edition, 1980; *The Fox at the Manger* (illustrated by Thomas Bewick), Norton, 1962; *Mary Poppins from A to Z* (illustrated by M. Shepard), Harcourt, 1962.

In Search of the Hero: The Continuing Relevance of Myth and Fairy Tale (adult), Scripps College (Claremont, Calif.), 1970; *Friend Monkey,* Harcourt, 1971; (translator with Ruth Lewinnek) Karlfried Dürckheim Montmartin, *The Way of Transformation: Daily Life as a Spiritual Exercise,* Allen & Unwin, 1971; *George Ivanovitch Gurdjieff* (adult), Traditional Studies Press (Toronto), 1973; *About the Sleeping Beauty* (illustrated by Charles Keeping), McGraw, 1975; (with Maurice Moore-Betty) *Mary Poppins in the Kitchen: A Cookery Book with a Story* (illustrated by M. Shepard), Harcourt, 1975; *The Complete Mary Poppins* (illustrated by M. Shepard and Agnes Sims), four volumes, Harcourt, 1976; *Two Pairs of Shoes* (folktales; illustrated by Leo Dillon and Diane Dillon), Viking, 1980; *Mary Poppins in Cherry Tree Lane* (illustrated by M. Shepard), Delacorte, 1982.

Contributor to *Cricket's Choice,* Open Court, 1974; also contributor to recording "Cricket and Other Friends." Consulting editor, Parabola.

ADAPTATIONS: "Mary Poppins" (dramatization written by Sara Spencer), Children's Theatre Press, c. 1940; "Mary Poppins" (motion picture), starring Julie Andrews, Walt Disney Productions, 1963, (videocassette), 1964; "Mary Poppins" (record or cassette; teacher's guide), Walt Disney Educational Media, 1976.

Records and cassettes; all produced by Caedmon: "Mary Poppins," "Mary Poppins Comes Back," "Mary Poppins Opens the Door," "Mary Poppins and the Banks Family," "Mary Poppins from A-Z," "Mary Poppins: Balloons and Balloons."

SIDELIGHTS: **1906.** "I was born well into this century in Queensland, Australia, just where the coast faces the Great Barrier Reef; and my childhood, in a house overlooking sweeping fields of sugar cane, was full of the reef's tokens—shells, palm fans, sprays of coral. My earliest memory is of walking through the green forests of the cane, as if through a jungle, and of making nests—which I hoped a bird would inhabit—between the juicy stalks. I chewed cane, when it was ripe, as modern children chew gum.

"It was here that I began to write poems and stories, at an early age and always in secret, for such activities were neither welcomed nor encouraged by my busy extroverted family. And this, I think, is the most sensible way to treat the budding artist. Praise him, show his efforts to the world, and you have taken something from him that he will never get again, his secret, his unselfconsciousness." [Stanley J. Kunitz and Howard Haycraft, editors, *Junior Book of Authors,* H. W. Wilson, 1951.']

(From the movie "Mary Poppins," starring Dick Van Dyke and Julie Andrews. Produced by Walt Disney Productions, 1964.)

(From *The Fox at the Manger* by P. L. Travers. Wood engraving by Thomas Bewick.)

"I lived a life that was at once new and old. The country was new and the land itself very old—the oldest in the world, geologists say, and in spite of all the brash pioneering atmosphere that still existed, even a child could sense the antiquity of it. We had also strong family traditions; we couldn't escape them, caught as we were between the horns of an Irish father and a mother of Scottish and Irish descent.

"It was simple, not rich, not centered at all around possessions or the search for status symbols. It seems to me that there were few *things* of any kind—furniture, of course, clothes and food, all the modest necessities. But of toys, and personal treasures, very few. If we wanted them we had to invent them, not by parental edict but from necessity. And there were very few books: Dickens and Scott, of course, Shakespeare, Tennyson, and some of the Irish poets. I ate my way through these like a bookworm not because of any highbrow leanings but simply because they were books. But for the children who, as far as I can remember, were seldom specially catered for, it was the grownup world that was important. There was a modest hodge-podge of good and bad: Beatrix Potter, simple—even babyish—comics, an odd book that nobody else seems ever to have heard of called *The Wallypug of Why*, Ethel Turner's stories, *Alice*, Kingsley's *Heroes*.

"Then, too, we had something that no child could find today, not anywhere in the world. We had penny books. You could buy a fairy tale for a penny—that's how their lore went into me." [P. L. Travers, "Only Connect," in *The Openhearted Audience: Ten Authors Talk about Writing for Children*, edited by Virginia Haviland, Library of Congress, 1980.[2]]

Buying penny books ". . . was a marvelous experience that a child can't have now: whenever we went to the little township, we would go to the little all-purpose shop holding a penny in our hand, and that penny brought in front of one an agonizing choice, because there were penny books, real paper books they were, little thin books, and the green covered ones were fairy tales and the blue and red ones were Buffalo Bill, and I would ponder with my penny in my hand. I'm so sorry now that I don't have those books. Naturally they were thrown away, as you'd throw away a comic nowadays." [Neil Philip, "The Writer and the Nanny Who Never Explain," *Times Educational Supplement*, June 11, 1982.[3]]

"I had a great affection for a book I found on my father's shelf called *Twelve Deathbed Scenes*. I read it so often that I knew it by heart, each death being more lugubrious and more edifying than the one before it. I used to long to die, on condition, of course, that I came alive again the next minute, to see if I, too, could pass away with equal misery and grandeur. I wonder about the author of that book. Nobody in his lifetime could possibly have told him that he was a writer for children. He would not have made such a claim himself. Yet, in a sense, he was writing for children since one loving reader 10 years of age was keeping his memory green.

"It was the same with my mother's novels. Every afternoon, when she took her siesta, I would slip into her room, avidly read for half an hour and sneak away just as she was waking. Those books fascinated me, not because they were so interesting but because they were so dull. They dealt exclusively with one subject, which seemed to be a kind of loving. But love to me was what the sea is to a fish; something you swim in while you are going about the important affairs of life. The characters were all stationary figures; like waxworks, they never did anything, never went anywhere, never played games as far as I could see, no teeth were ever brushed, no one was reminded to wash his hands, and if they ever went to bed it was not explicitly stated; or else they went to bed willingly but surreptitiously, often with dire unspecified results and amid

"Gently, please, gently!" she warned, as they crowded about her. "This is a baby, not a battleship!" ■ (From *Mary Poppins Comes Back* by P. L. Travers. Illustrated by Mary Shepard.)

general disapprobation. I looked forward to those stolen half-hours as, I suppose, a drunkard does to a drinking bout—not so much with pleasure as a kind of enthrallment. I was ensnared, as a snake is by a snakecharmer, by such a distorted view of life. But what of the authors? Did they, as they poured out their hearts with so much zest, see themselves as writers for children? Surely not. Yet for one child—indeed they were.

"And . . . the Bible . . . fascinated me, perhaps because there was an air about it as of something forbidden. I spurned the gutted children's version and went looking for enormous terrible facts. Tellings, anyway, are always diminishments. They present the lively plot of the story but omit the curious splendors—beheaded drunk in the pavilions; Jezebel eaten by dogs at the wall; the Beast that was, is not, yet is; harlots, unicorns. Don't think that I understood it—how could I? But the Bible's trumpets breached my inner walls and the potent brew came swirling in to mix with fairy tales and myths and whatever stuff was in me." [P. L. Travers, "I Never Wrote for Children," *New York Times Magazine,* July 2, 1978.⁴]

Travers grew up enthralled with fairy tales, myths and legends, which later had an enormous influence on her own writing. "Are there thirteen Wise Women at every christening? I think it very likely.

"I shall never know which good lady it was who, at my own christening, gave me the everlasting gift, spotless amid all spotted joys, of love for the fairy tale. It began in me quite early, before there was any separation between myself and the world. Eve's apple had not yet been eaten; every bird had an emperor to sing to and any passing ant or beetle might be a prince in disguise.

"This undifferentiated world is common to all children. They may never have heard of the fairy tales but still be on easy terms with myth.

"Skipping games, street songs, lullabies, all carry the stories in them. But far above these, as a source of myth, are the half-heard scraps of gossip, from parent to parent, neighbour to neighbour as they whisper across a fence. A hint, a carefully garbled disclosure, a silencing finger at the lip, and the tales, like rain clouds, gather. It could almost be said that a listening child has no need to read the tales. A keen ear and the power to dissemble—he must not *seem* to be listening—are all that is required. By putting two and two together—fragments of talk and his own logic—he will fashion the themes for himself.

"For me, the nods and becks of my mother's friends, walking under parasols or presiding over tinkling tea-tables, were preparatory exercises to my study of the myths. The scandals, the tight corners, the flights into the face of fate! When eventually I read of Zeus visiting Danaë in a shower of gold, Perseus encountering the Gorgon, or the hair-breadth escapes of the Argonauts, such adventures caused me no surprise. I had heard their modern parallels over tea and caraway cake." [P. L. Travers, *About the Sleeping Beauty,* McGraw, 1975.⁵]

Travers spent her childhood in Queensland and Sydney, but home for her was England and Ireland. "My father was an Irishman, and like all Irishmen lived not in the place where he was standing but back in the hills of Ireland—he lived there in his own mind."³

Ireland and "the sorrows of the 'most distressful country' got into me very early—how could it help doing so with my father's nostalgia for it continually feeding the imagination? My body ran about in the Southern sunlight but my inner world

Travers, at the time of *Mary Poppins*'s original publication.

had subtler colors, the grays and snows of England where Little Joe swept all the crossings and the numberless greens of Ireland which seemed to be inhabited solely by poets plucking harps, heroes lordlily [sic] cutting off each other's heads, and veiled ladies sitting on the ground keening.

"I think, perhaps, if there was any special virtue in my upbringing, it lay in the fact that my parents, both of them, were very allusive talkers. Neither of them ever read anything that didn't very quickly come out in conversation and from there pass into the family idiom. If my father discovered a poem he liked, even a piece of doggerel, it would presently be, as it were, on the breakfast table. Many a phrase, as ordinary to me then as the daily porridge, began its life, as I later learned, as a quotation from a poem or snatch from a ballad."²

From her father, Travers learned about Ireland; from her mother, she learned to live comfortably in the world of imagination. ". . . My mother would play *any* game; she'd quickly jump to a game, as I do, with a child. And one day I said to her: 'Mother, you be the mistress and I'll sit in the kitchen and come when you ring the bell and say "Yes, ma'am?"' But something in her didn't want to play that game—she'd be a leopard, a turkey, Rumpelstiltskin, but not someone giving orders—not mistress and maid. Something sensitive and delicate and loving in her rejected it.

"Alongside our house grew a great field of weeds. . . . It had masses of leaves on the outside, but when they fell down and dried up, they became the material for a nest inside the stems. And I used to nest there, thinking I was a bird. About six I was, and while I knew I was a child, I also knew that I was a bird. And I'd sit there brooding—it seemed like hours—my arms tightly clasped around me. And the others would say, 'She can't come, she's *laying*,' just as you might say of a blackbird, 'She's brooding.' Then my mother would come and undo my limbs—this knotted little body that was busy in its nest. 'I have told you once,' she would say, 'and I've told you twice—no laying at lunchtime.' She never said: 'No laying!' She never said: 'You're not a bird!' She never thought: 'Oh, my God, she must see a psychiatrist—my child thinks she's a wren or a kiwi!''' [Jonathan Cott, *Pipers at the Gates of Dawn: The Wisdom of Children's Literature*, Random House, 1983.⁶]

"My father who died when I was very young—my first great sorrow—was a poet *manqué,* in a way, a mixture of melancholy and gaiety. He was a wonderful *earth* for a child.

"My father never explained anything to us. Mary Poppins never explains anything. I don't think explaining helps anything." ["Mary Poppins," *New Yorker*, November 20, 1962.⁷]

Travers had a maternal great aunt Christina, who was later the subject of *Aunt Sass.* It was to her home in New South Wales that Travers went with her mother and two younger sisters upon the death of their father. She was seven and a half. "[Aunt Sass'] reaction to suffering and sorrow was direct and complete. Inarticulate in words, she was richly articulate when it came to deeds. When my Father died suddenly, leaving a nursery full of young children, she travelled seven hundred miles through scorching sub-tropical country to my Mother, that beloved niece whom she herself had brought up from babyhood.

Out of the glowing core of light emerged a curious figure. ■ (From *Mary Poppins Opens the Door* by P. L. Travers. Illustrated by Mary Shepard and Agnes Sims.)

"'Meg!' she said. It was all she knew how to say but I saw her face as the two women tenderly embraced. The little chestnut head went down on the gaunt square shoulder. Above it bent the sparse grey head and the face ravaged with sorrow and compassion. In the cool shadowy hall, smelling of sunlight and flowers, that look of hers told me what perhaps I already knew—that in the face of death there is nothing to be said. Perhaps, indeed, there is nothing to be said about anything.

"'You and the children will come to me!' She shook herself and gave the order like a sergeant on parade. And my mother merely nodded obediently and began to pack. A week later we were all in Aunt Sass's front hall." [P. L. Travers, *Aunt Sass,* Reynal & Hitchcock, 1941.⁸]

Aunt Sass died years later, at age ninety-four. "When I heard of it, I thought to myself 'Some day, in spite of her, I shall commit the "disrespectful vulgarity" of putting Aunt Sass in a book.'

"And then it occurred to me that this had already been done, though unconsciously and without intent. We write more than we know we are writing. We do not guess at the roots that made our fruit. I suddenly realised that there *is* a book through which Aunt Sass, stern and tender, secret and proud, anonymous and loving, stalks with her silent feet.

"You will find her occasionally in the pages of *Mary Poppins.*"⁸

The family's financial outlook was grim, and, after the death of Travers' father, she "... was brought up ... with everybody saying, 'What are you going to do when you grow up to help your mother?' I think that's very cruel of grown-ups and it used to sadden me sometimes. I used to think, Am I only going to grow up to help my mother?" [Michelle Field, "Reminiscing with P. L. Travers," *Publishers Weekly*, March 21, 1986.⁹]

She was not the only one helping her mother. There were a few servants, among them a family cook. "I was ten when I first met him. The place was a sugar plantation in the tropics of Australia, and the day juts out like a promontory from the level lands of memory. It is linked with another important occasion, the day when Sam Foo dropped the pan of boiling fat on his foot. That, too, was something to remember. For it meant the end of tapioca pudding.

"But I must begin at the beginning. At that time it was customary to have Chinese cooks on the plantations, and for a year we had suffered from the ministrations of Sam Foo. We never knew whether he thought white children really throve on an almost daily diet of tapioca or whether he was just plain lazy. Whichever it was, justice was at last meted out to him. An invisible avenging angel tipped the pan sideways one day and the next thing we knew Sam Foo, recumbent on a stretcher, was being carried through the cane fields to an ambulance. Amid general acclamation he departed, shrieking with anguish.

"But the loss of a cook in those outlying parts is fun only for the children. The cane was ready for cutting and not a man could be spared from the fields. The lubras (aboriginal women) shied away from the cookstove as though its flames were the tongues of the devil. That left only our mother and Kate Clancy, the Irish nurse—both of them as temperamental, as far as cooking went, as any Hollywood star. After a succession of meals cooked by them it was possible to think of Sam Foo with kindness—even nostalgia.

"Then one day, apparently out of nowhere, Ah Wong walked in. He was thin, where Sam had been fat; he was old and wrinkled where Sam had been young and moon-faced. Sam had waddled; Ah Wong had a light tripping step that was almost a run. But the distinctions did not end there. The most wonderful difference was that from under Ah Wong's hat there swung, long and black and shiny, a pigtail. Sam Foo had been short-haired, a modern Chinese. But here was a Chinese out of a fairy story.

"Thus it was that Ah Wong walked into our lives and hearts. Within a week he had become the center of the household, the small, high-powered dynamo that set us all in motion. For Ah Wong did not merely cook for the family. It soon became apparent that he owned the family. He darted like lightning about the house, dusting, making beds, sweeping and polishing. Ornaments and furniture were reshuffled and arranged according to Ah Wong's taste, and his tidiness in our sprawling, untidy house was very like a miracle." [P. L. Travers, "Ah Wong," *Mademoiselle,* November, 1943.[10]] Ah Wong was discharged when the family moved.

"I can't remember a time when I didn't write, but then, I never called it 'writing.' It never seemed important in that sense. I thought of it more as listening, then putting down what I had heard. Nobody in my family called it writing; in fact, nobody was very pleased or proud. I feel that was rather a good thing for me because I was never made to feel that I was anything special.

"Actually, I had two loves when I was a child. Writing seemed to me a part of daily life, but my real love was the stage. I began writing poems when I was very young and told stories to the rest of the children in my family, but that was just like breathing. The things I really wanted to do were all connected with the theater, and in my boarding school I used to write the school plays and act in them and produce them.

"Then one day a real director happened to attend my school, and he said, 'I want a child who will play in my production of *A Midsummer Night's Dream* and she must be small and round and have a good voice.

"So he watched me running across the playground and said, 'That one will do.' So that was my first real part, that of Bottom, when I was about ten.

"This director offered to take me and train me for the stage, but this was quite impossible in my kind of family at that time—shocking, in fact—so I had to wait until I grew up before I returned to the stage." [Roy Newquist, editor, *Conversations,* Rand McNally, 1967.[11]]

As a teenager, however, she found employment first as an actress and then as a writer. "... I began in Shakespearean companies, playing all sorts of parts and gaining all sorts of experience, much against my family's wishes. All this time I was writing. Then, while I was still touring, I happened to meet a young man who was a journalist on a newspaper and I showed him an article. (Very shyly; I didn't think much of it.) He brought this to his editor who sent for me and said, 'Have you any more pieces like this?' and I said, 'No, I haven't, but I could do some more.' He said, 'All you can do I will buy and I will give you five pounds for each of them.'

"Then it occurred to me to try to do something with my poems, so I showed these to a rather good literary paper and they were taken, too. I never set out to be a writer, but after these blushes of success there was nothing else I could do."[11]

She was given the job of interviewing a boat captain whose cargo was old Chinese men returning to China after a lifetime

of working in Australia. "My heart thumped. Here was I, on my first assignment. My own name was shouting to me from all the books that eventually would result from it. And there was the *Santa Lucia,* a grimy, battered ship crouching against the wharf, her furled sails gray with wind and water. But I saw, as I came up the gangway, that her decks were white and every strip of metal twinkled in the sun."[10]

Among these men was Ah Wong. "He was lying in one of the lower bunks, his pigtail dangling to the floor. His black eyes stared from his yellow face. He was just the same—frailer, of course, a shrunken image of the old Ah Wong, but the same in essence. He smiled at me and I took his yellow hands in mine as we gazed at each other. Once again there was nothing to be said because there was so much to say.

"Happiness filled me.

"I was flooded with a tide of life all the richer for coming straight from death. Infinite with experience, the world opened before me, itself borne upon that living stream. And I knew that Ah Wong was flooded with it, too. Like all those who are very young I had made the mistake of thinking that there are separate rivers of life and death. Now I knew that there is only one tide, whole and indivisible. The same flood that was flinging me into life was taking Ah Wong home...."[10]

"... I saved money, deciding quite secretly that I would save enough money by my writing and by the acting I was doing at the same time, to go to England. And I did. I came to England with ten pounds in my pocket—two five pound notes, one of which was immediately stolen by someone. So there I

She was sitting bolt upright against the tree....And above her, from a flowering branch, the parrot umbrella dangled. ■ (From *Mary Poppins in the Park* by P. L. Travers. Illustrated by Mary Shepard.)

was, fresh in England with five pounds to my name. I had to get a job immediately, and luck was with me, for I picked up a journalistic job. It paid enough to keep me going, and I went on with my own writing, tackling comparatively challenging articles and poems which were soon being published in the English papers.

"I then decided that I would like to go to see my father's people in Ireland. . . . A great contemporary of W. B. Yeats was the poet AE [George William Russell], a poet and editor, actually. I wrote to AE, having been brought up on him and Yeats by my father, and sent him a poem, but without a covering letter. I was rather proud in those days; I wanted the poem to stand on its own feet. I sent a stamped envelope for its return, but shortly I got back a check for two guineas. Two guineas was quite a lot then, but I was more thrilled by the letter that came from AE saying, 'I accept your poem. If you have any more, I'm pretty sure I will accept those. I have a strong suspicion that you are Irish; if you are, and if you are ever coming to Ireland, will you come to see me?' He was wonderful to young people.

"So I went to Ireland and saw AE in his wonderful great room in [Merrion] Square, the room he had painted with all sorts of mythological figures. He talked to me about literature and made all sorts of suggestions regarding my work and said, 'I know you're going on now, to stay with your uncle in the south of Ireland. On your way back to London come and see me again.' Well, I stayed with my family and met all my Irish people and on the way back I thought, 'Oh, so great a man, I can't disturb him; I'm sure he was only being polite.' I was too shy to knock at his door again, so I went on back to London without seeing him.

"A few days later I got a letter from him and he said, 'By this time you should be back in London, and I believe you just bypassed me. I'm coming to London and I will come to see you.' In a few days he stood at my door with all his books under his arm, signed and dedicated, and a friendship began which became a very great thing in my life."[11]

Through her friendship with AE, Travers became acquainted with another Irish author, William Butler Yeats. On one occasion, her admiration for Yeats led her to bring him a huge armful of rowan branches from the Isle of Innisfree. ". . . I carried the great branches to Yeats's house in Merrion Square and stood there, with my hair like rats' tails, my tattered branches equally ratlike, looking like Birnam come to Dunsinane and wishing I was dead. I prayed, as I rang the bell, that Yeats would not open the door himself, but my prayer went unheard.

"For an articulate man to be struck dumb is, you can imagine, rare. But struck dumb he was at the sight of me. In shame, I heard him cry a name into the dark beyond of the house and saw him hurriedly escape upstairs. Then the name came forward in human shape and took me gently, as though I were ill or lost or witless, down to the basement kitchen. There I was warmed and dried and given cocoa; the dreadful branches were taken away. I felt like someone who had died and was now contentedly on the other side, certain that nothing more could happen. In this dreamlike state, I was gathering myself to go—out the back way if possible—never to be seen again. But a maid came bustling kindly in and said—as though to someone still alive!—'The master will see you now.' I was horrified. This was the last straw. 'What for?' I wanted to know. 'Ah, then, you'll see. He has his ways.'

"And so, up the stairs—or the seven-story mountain—I went and there he was in his room with the blue curtains.

"'My canary has laid an egg!' he said and joyously led me to the cages by the window. From there we went round the room together, I getting better every minute and he telling me which of his books he liked and how, when he got an idea for a poem—There was long momentous pause, here. He was always the bard, always filling the role of poet, not play-acting but knowing well the role's requirements and giving them their due. He never came into a room, he *entered* it; walking around his study was a ceremonial peregrination, wonderful to witness. 'When I get an idea for a poem,' he went on, oracularly, 'I take down one of my own books and read it and then I go on from there.' Moses explaining his tablets couldn't have moved me more. And so, serenely, we came to the end of the pilgrimage and I was just about to bid him good-bye when I noticed on his desk a vase of water and in it one sprig of fruiting rowan. I glanced at him distrustfully. 'Was he teaching me a lesson?' I wondered, for at that age one cannot accept to be taught. But he wasn't; I knew it by the look on his face. He would do nothing so banal. He was not trying to enlighten me and so I was enlightened and found a connection in the process. It needed only a sprig, said the lesson. And I learned, also, something about writing. The secret is to say less than you need. You don't want a forest, a leaf will do.

"These men . . . had aristocratic minds. For them, the world was not fragmented. An idea did not suddenly grow, like Topsy, all alone and separate. For them, all things had antecedents, and long family trees. They saw nothing shameful or silly in myths and fairy stories, nor did they shovel them out of sight in some cupboard marked Only for Children. They were always willing to concede that there were more things in heaven and earth than philosophy dreamed of. They allowed for the unknown. And, as you can imagine, I took great heart from this."[2]

Wrote *Mary Poppins* while recovering from an illness. At the time, Travers was living in England writing for AE's literary weekly, *The Irish Statesmen*, and for English magazines. She wrote her famous book from an old thatched manor house, ". . . built before 1066, which is a great date in England—so it was built before even William the Conqueror came.

"It was thatched with straw, and the walls, between the skeleton of old oak beams, were made of wattle and daub. You mix earth with water—that's the daub part—and the wattle part is very thin slits of fine wood that you plaster the daub over, in between the big oak beams. The fireplace was huge; you could have put a bed in it. And the thatch came down over the eaves—you know, like an old-fashioned sunbonnet. It sat there, quiet and upright and solid on the ground. When strong winds blew, the other, newer, younger houses would shiver and tremble; but this little old house with its strong beams hadn't even a quiver.

"So, you see, that was where I wrote the first *Mary Poppins*. It was called 'The Pound House.'" ["Some Friends of Mary Poppins," *McCall's,* May, 1966.[12]]

"I think that the idea of Mary Poppins has been blowing in and out of me, like a curtain at a window, all my life. My sister assures me that I told her stories of Mary Poppins when we were very small children. In *my* memory, however, the chief character in those stories was a magical white horse; and the monsoon rain . . . was his hoofs thundering on the broad tin roof of the house. On the other hand, in *The Three Little Foxes,* which I have had since I was seven, I . . . found, scrawled inside the hard cover, the bold, strong name, 'M. Poppins.' How it got there I do not know. Was it, perhaps, her book, not mine? When I tell children about this, they have no doubts

Listen now to the story of Ayaz, the Treasurer and trusted friend of the great King, Mahmoud. ∎
(From "The Sandals of Ayaz" in *Two Pairs of Shoes,* retold by P. L. Travers. Illustrated by Leo and Diane Dillon.)

whatever. 'It belonged to Mary Poppins, of course. She left it for you when she went away.'

''This ability to know things for certain is what I most love in children; and one of the underlying assumptions in *Mary Poppins* is that the young know more than grown-ups do. Think of the Park Keeper, for instance, and the way he greets each unusual fact with his puzzled, despairing cry—'I never heard of such a thing, not even when I was a boy.' The word 'even' tells us much—that children live wide open to wonder, a wonder that fades away as they grow.

''Then, too, all children understand in the same way no matter how different their heredity. When a boy from the rice fields of Japan and a girl from the coconut palms of Trinidad ask the same questions as children ask in Ohio or London, one cannot but feel that the young everywhere are just one large fraternity.

''Well, but how does one create books for this huge like-minded family? What is the secret of writing for children? Here is another popular question, and for this, thank goodness, I have an answer. The secret is *not* to write for children. If you aim at a particular audience you are sure to be lost at the start. For whom, then? Well, Beatrix Potter put it in a Squirrel Nutkin nutshell, 'I write,' she said, 'to please myself.''' [P. L. Travers, ''Where Did She Come From? Why Did She Go?,'' *Saturday Evening Post,* November 7, 1964.[13]]

''I used to put people off by saying, 'I'm not sure how I came to think of Mary Poppins.'

All night long the wind and the rain went roaring through the jungle. ■ (Jacket illustration by Charles Keeping from *Friend Monkey* by P. L. Travers.)

''I think the only possible answer, even now, must be put this way: Henrik Willem Van Loon became a friend; I can't remember how I met him, but I remember once when he invited me to luncheon, and during luncheon he was busy drawing some elephants for me on the back of a menu. He always drew things on the backs of menus. Anyway, he was drawing elephants and I said, 'You know, people are always asking me how I came to think of Mary Poppins and I just don't know. I don't know how to answer them.' And he went on drawing with his head down. He was silent for a moment and then he shrugged his shoulders and said, 'Doesn't interest me; doesn't interest me at all.'

''After having been asked about Mary Poppins by so many people, I was a bit peeved and said, 'Not at all?' Van Loon said, 'No, not at all. What interests me is how Mary Poppins came to think of you,' and he handed me a little drawing of dancing elephants. Suddenly something came clear to me, and this belief has stayed with me ever since. Perhaps ideas go hunting for people, for writers. You see, I never felt that Mary Poppins had very much to do with me. I've never been able to puff out my chest and swagger and say, 'I did this.' I've never felt any pride of possession.

''While we're on this subject, when children ask me, 'Where did you get that idea?' I throw the question back to them by saying, 'Where does anybody get an idea? Where do you get an idea that you want candy, a new penknife, that you'd like to go for a walk or see a particular friend?' And they always say that they don't know where those ideas come from.

''Well, I don't know where ideas come from either; I never know where I get an idea for a poem or a story. I have the attitude, the feeling, I had as a child: It is not so much inventing as listening. I think that Mary Poppins just fell into me at a time when I was particularly open, and I'm grateful that she did.''[11]

During the same year (1934), Travers visited Russia and wrote *Moscow Excursion,* an account of a state-regulated tour she took. But she was soon back in Ireland, at the death bed of AE. She wrote some of his last letters for him and was with him when he died in 1935. ''It was AE who showed me how to look at and learn from one's own writing. 'Popkins,' he said once—he always called her just plain Popkins, whether deliberately mistaking the name or not, I never knew, his humor was always subtle—'Popkins, had she lived in another age, in the old times to which she certainly belongs, would undoubtedly have had long golden tresses, a wreath of flowers in one hand, and perhaps a spear in the other. Her eyes would have been like the sea, her nose comely, and on her feet winged sandals. But, this being Kali Yuga, as the Hindus call it—in our terms, the Iron Age—she comes in the habiliments most suited to it.'

''Well, golden tresses and all that pretty paraphernalia didn't interest me; she could only be as she *was.* But that AE could really know so much about it astonished me, that he should guess at her antecedents and genealogy when I hadn't thought of them myself—it put me on my mettle. I began to *read* the book. But it was only after many years that I realized what he meant, that she had come out of the same world as the fairy tales.''[2]

''He was always quoting the *Bhagavad Gita,* the *Mahabharata,* the great things that he believed in. And although I was not then deliberately going towards them, I have since, and have understood much more of what he was then saying to me than I did at the time.''[3]

". . . AE was a great soul. And his death was an enormous event for me because I was there all the days of his dying; being with him much during his earlier sickness, but also during his last days, I watched a great man doing his own dying . . . something that comes to not very many. His death was the epitome of his life.

"He never set out to teach . . . but I learned from him continually, very much by osmosis. I took it in like sunlight and rain, as a plant does, and only much later did it become a kind of teaching for me. For instance, he taught me that true poverty means not being without the comfortable bed, the easy chair, the whole loaf—but being able to dispense with them at any moment—not being *attached* to things."[6]

1941-1943. Travers went to the United States at the request of the British Ministry of Education, and to escape the dangers of World War II. "I lived with the Indians, or I lived on the reservations, for two summers. . . . John Collier, who was then the Administrator for Indian Affairs, was a great friend of mine and he saw that I was very homesick for England but couldn't go back over those mineswept waters. And he said, 'I'll tell you what I'll do for you. I'll send you to live with the Indians.' 'That's mockery,' I replied, 'What good will that do me?' He said, 'You'll see.'

"I'd never been out West and I went to stay on the Navaho reservation at Administration House which is at Window Rock beyond Gallup. Collier had sent a letter to the members of the committee at Administration House and asked them to take me about so that I could see the land and meet the Indians. They very kindly did. Fortunately, I was able to ride and I was equipped with jeans and boots and a western saddle. Then I saw that the Indian women wore big, wide, flounced Spanish skirts with little velvet jackets. And I, who didn't like trousers very much, said I must have one of those. So they made me a flounced skirt and a velvet jacket, and I rode with the Indians. It was wonderful the way they turned towards me when, instead of being an Eastern dude, I put on their skirt.

"One day the head of Administration House asked me if I would give a talk to the Indians. And I said, 'How could I talk to them, these ancient people? It is they who could tell me things.' He said, 'Try.' So they came into what I suppose was a clubhouse, a big place with a stage, and I stood on the stage and the place was full of Indians. I told them about England, because she was at war then, and all that was happening. I said that for me England was the place 'Where the Sun Rises' because, you see, England is east of where I was. I said, 'Over large water.' And I told them about the children who were being evacuated from the cities and some of the experiences of the children. I put it as mythologically as I could, just very simple sayings.

"At the end there was dead silence. I turned to the man who had introduced me and said, 'I'm sorry. I failed, I haven't got across.' And he said, 'You wait. You don't know them as well as I do.' And every Indian in that big hall came up and took me silently by the hand, one after another. That was their way of expressing feeling with me.

". . . The Indians in the Pueblo tribe gave me an Indian name and they said I must never reveal it. Every Indian has a secret name as well as his public name. This moved me very much because I have a strong feeling about names, that names are a part of a person, a very private thing to each one. I'm always amazed at the way Christian names are seized upon in America as if by right instead of as something to be given. One of the fairy tales, 'Rumplestiltskin,' deals with the extraordinary pri-

(From *Mary Poppins* by P. L. Travers. Illustrated by Mary Shepard.)

vacy and inward nature of the name. It's always been a big taboo in the fairy tales and in myth that you do not name a person. Many primitive people do not like you to speak and praise a child to its face, for instance, and they will make a cross or sign against evil when you do that, even in Ireland sometimes." ["The Art of Fiction LXXIII: P. L. Travers," *Paris Review*, winter, 1982.[14]]

The desire to protect her anonymity was essential to Travers, who since *Mary Poppins*, has signed herself solely with her initials. "You know C. S. Lewis, whom I greatly admire, said: 'There's no such thing as creative writing.' I've always agreed with that and always refuse to teach it when given the opportunity. He said: 'There is, in fact, only one Creator and we mix.' That's our function, to mix the elements He has given us. See how wonderfully anonymous leaves us? You can't say, '*I* did this; this gross matrix of flesh and blood and sinews and nerves did this.' What nonsense! I'm given these things to make a pattern out of. Something gave it to me.

"I've always loved the idea of the craftsman, the anonymous man. For instance, I've always wanted my books to be called the work of Anon, because Anon is my favorite literary character. If you look through an anthology of poems that go from the far past into the present time, you'll see that all the poems signed 'Anon' have a very specific flavor that is one flavor all the way through the centuries. I think, perhaps arrogantly, of myself as 'Anon.' I would like to think that *Mary Poppins* and the other books could be called back to make that change. But I suppose it's too late for that.

Ceremoniously clad, in top hat, black jacket and striped trousers, he was crawling about on hands and knees.... ■ (From *Mary Poppins in Cherry Tree Lane* by P. L. Travers. Illustrated by Mary Shepard.)

"You know, in America, everybody thinks there's an answer to every question. They're always saying, 'But why and how?' They always think there is a solution. There is a great fortitude in that and a great sense of optimism. In Europe, we are so old that we know there are certain things to which there is not an answer. And you will remember, in this regard, that Mary Poppins' chief characteristic, apart from her tremendous vanity, is that she never explains. I often wonder why people write and ask me to explain this and that. I'll write back and say that Mary Poppins didn't explain, so neither can I or neither will I. So many people ask me, 'Where does she go?' Well, I say, if the book hasn't said that, then it's up to you to find out. I'm not going to write footnotes to *Mary Poppins*. That would be absolutely presumptuous, and at the same time it would be assuming that I know. It's the fact that she's unknown that's so intriguing to readers."[14]

"I don't think authors are all that important. It's the book and the characters that matter. I like to be anonymous and faraway. If people think mostly about Mary Poppins, then they can forget me, and I can go on writing, hidden away in my private life."[12]

"I'm rather shy of publicity; it pulls me out of my socket. It makes me feel disjointed, so I've felt that if I just used initials nobody would know whether I was a man or a woman, a dog or a tiger. I could hide from view, like a bat on the underside of a branch. I thought too, that if I signed myself as a woman, people would feel that the *Mary Poppins* books were sentimental books, and this was the last thing I wanted. Few people wondered what Milne's A. A. stood for, or Yeats' W. B. Yet everybody wants to plunge into my secret world and find out what those two initials mean. They mean simply, 'Don't come in. Stay out!'"[11]

"Have you noticed what I write at the end of all my books? That should tell you everything." The sentence is *AD MAJORAM GLORIA DEO*. [Janet Watts, "A Walk Down Cherry Tree Lane," *Observer*, April 11, 1982.[15]]

Despite her desire for anonymity, Travers enjoys hearing from readers. "After the third *Mary Poppins* you will remember that she goes away for good. There are five *Mary Poppins* books, but the last two are supposed to have taken place while she was down there visiting the Banks family. Well, after the third one a little boy wrote me a very touching letter. It began: 'Madum: I have just finished reading *Mary Poppins Opens the Door*. She has gone away. Did you know? You are awful. You shouldn't have done that. You have made the children cry.' A marvelous letter, really, because there was such praise in that reproach. So I wrote back, 'I'm not surprised that you cried. I cried bitterly. My typewriter was rained with tears when I was writing it.'

"I wonder if writers would go on writing if they didn't hear from people. It's the only tangible proof you have that they're reading and enjoying your work."[11]

1963. The film version of *Mary Poppins* was produced by Walt Disney. In the same year, Travers posed for a statue of Mary Poppins to be built in Central Park. "When I first saw the film I had an emotional shock. I don't quite know where it sprang from. I was deeply disturbed and had to ask myself, 'Am I so identified with Mary Poppins?' Well, I know myself *not* to be identified with her; I don't feel that she is me or part of me. I don't feel that I invented her. She's one of those joys that do fly and brush you as they pass. So I don't feel that was what disturbed me. I think I was disturbed at seeing it so externalized, so oversimplified, so generalized. Not vulgar-

ized, really; it isn't exactly that. The movie hasn't simplicity; it has simplification. I think that *Mary Poppins* needs a subtle reader, in many respects, to grasp all its implications, and I understand that these cannot be translated in terms of the film.

"I went out to Hollywood probably, oh, bound to a promise made to myself, if you like, that I would feel that the book hadn't got onto the screen. I was intellectually prepared for a jar, but even so it was a shock—and I don't mean a shock of disappointment. Parts of the film, those that refer to the human family, are not exactly like my story, but it seems to me that the dramatic shape that the Disney writers have made is viable. Yet I can't understand why—with five books of imaginative ideas to choose from—the writers or the director should have had to introduce a quite different sort of fantasy, a fantasy on a totally new level.

"The film, to me, falls into two halves, and the halves don't entirely blend. I'm not saying that I'm against the film; it's charmingly acted. Julie Andrews gives a beautifully understated performance; she's very great indeed. And there is a lovely performance by an English actor, David Tomlinson, in the part of the papa, that pleased me. The little children are very good, too.

"I'm bound to say that Mr. Disney has been faithful in all of his promises to me. He agreed to my suggestion that it should be put into the Edwardian period. I wanted that because I thought that if it were to be a timeless tale, it could not have a contemporary look. It would soon seem old-fashioned, but a period would be recognized as a period a hundred years from now. It would still be Edwardian and retain its freshness. Anyway, Mr. Disney agreed to this and faithfully carried out his promise. He also agreed that there should be no love affair for Mary Poppins. I knew this would be difficult for him because most musical comedies thrive on love affairs, but he was faithful in this matter, too.

"However, I don't think it was at all necessary to increase the fantasy. The whole point of *Mary Poppins* is the fact that she's a down-to-earth and very solid person, serious and even commonplace, and it's from this character that the fantastic things spring. To my point of view the fantastic things must be rooted in something that's of an everyday nature. But in the film there are long sequences of pop tunes in which the human figures mix with the cartoon characters. I know that Mr. Disney is essentially a cartoonist and that one of his cherished dreams is to mix human and cartoon characters to create a new art form. I think many people like this, but I feel that it rather breaks the film in two, that it would be even funnier and more like *Mary Poppins* if the cartooned figures, such as the dancing penguins and the racehorses, had been real. There's a scene where Mary Poppins rides a race with cartooned racehorses and says to one of the riders, 'Will you let me by, please?' and of course they let her by because she is Mary Poppins. Imagine if they had used real horses and real riders, how much funnier it would have been. The incongruity would have been immense.

"At the same time, in spite of the introduction of what, to me, are extraneous measures, I think there is enough of the spirit of Mary Poppins in the film to persuade people to want to know more about her by reading the books. The film is splendid in its own right and deserves the success it is having, yet I hope, in the end, that its effect will be to bring more people to the books."[11] Travers used some of her profits from the film version to set up the Cherry Tree Trust, a foundation for children.

1970-1976. Lived in New York City for six years, during which time, she wrote *Friend Monkey* (1971) and *Mary Poppins in the Kitchen.* ''*Friend Monkey* came about as a result of long brooding on the idea of Hanuman, the monkey lord of the Hindu myths, who would never do anything by halves. When I was well-started on the book, the manuscript, by an unfortunate accident, disappeared; it couldn't be found anywhere. But after a long period of disappointment I eventually began again, and in fourteen months there he was!

''One's favorite book is like the new baby in a family. It needs one more; it is nearest to newness. So I suppose at this moment, in 1972, *Friend Monkey* comes first, since he was only born on November 3, 1971. There are bits in all my books

that have favorite moments for me. But ask me again in five years time, I'll know more about it then.'' [Lee Bennett Hopkins, editor, *More Books By More People: Interviews with Sixty-five Authors of Books for Children,* Citation Press, 1974.[16]]

''I'd like it so much to be done as a film—but certainly not as a cartoon, for you must show the sorrow and the grief and the endless love that is in Monkey . . . it never fails. He brings disaster in his train until the very end. . . . You know, I didn't realize that Professor McWhirter wasn't a bad guy until that very end, I had no idea! It came upon me as a shock—in a garden in Virginia—and I lifted up my hands and said, 'To have given me such an idea, how marvelous, where could I have got it from?' He was *not* a villain, after all, but the

A record album cover featuring songs from "Mary Poppins." Produced by Pickwick International, Inc. in 1971.

rescuer. Perhaps, in a sense, the villain is always the rescuer, the one who throws the story forward, like the Wicked Fairy in the Sleeping Beauty story.

". . . I'm so grateful to D. H. Lawrence—I've quoted this again and again, and think he should be canonized for saying that there's the truth of truth as well as the truth of fact. You see, everybody sees Professor McWhirter collecting and stealing the animals—that's the truth of fact—but they don't know till the end of the story that he's taking them to the secret islands in order to protect them. That's the truth of truth.''[6]

Returned to London in 1976, where she lived in a small period house in Chelsea furnished with Japanese screens and the allegorical ''10 Oxherding Pictures'' by a Chinese Zen master.

1981. Wrote a revised edition of *Mary Poppins* when it was removed from the San Francisco libraries at the request of a ''minority'' group. ''The Irish have an expression: 'Ah, my grief!' It means 'the pity of things.' The objections had been made to the chapter 'Bad Tuesday' where Mary Poppins goes to the four points of the compass. She meets a mandarin in the East, an Indian in the West, an Eskimo in the North, and blacks in the South who speak in a picaninny language. What I find strange is that, while my critics claim to have children's best interests in mind, children themselves have never objected to the book. In fact, they love it. That was certainly the case when I was asked to speak to an affectionate crowd of children at a library in Port-of-Spain in Trinidad. On another occasion, when a white teacher friend of mine explained how she felt uncomfortable reading the picaninny dialect to her young students, I asked her, 'And are the black children affronted?' 'Not at all,' she replied, 'it appeared they loved it.' 'Minorities' is not a word in my vocabulary. And I wonder, sometimes, how much disservice is done children by some individuals who occasionally offer, with good intentions, to serve as their spokesmen. Nonetheless, I have rewritten the offending chapter, and in the revised edition I have substituted a Panda, Dolphin, Polar Bear, and Macaw. I have done so not as an apology for anything I have written. The reason is much more simple: I do not wish to see Mary Poppins tucked away in a closet. Aside from this issue, there is something else you should remember. I never wrote my books especially for children.

''When I sat down to write *Mary Poppins* or any of the other books, I did not know children would read them. I'm sure there must be a field of 'children's literature'—I hear about it so often—but sometimes I wonder if it isn't a label created by publishers and booksellers who also have the impossible presumption to put on books such notes as 'from five to seven' or 'from nine to twelve.' How can they know when a book will appeal to such and such an age?

''If you look at other so-called children's authors, you'll see they never wrote directly for children. Though Lewis Carroll dedicated his book to Alice, I feel it was an afterthought once the whole was already committed to paper. . . . And I think the same can be said of Milne or Tolkien or Laura Ingalls Wilder.

''I certainly had no specific child in mind when I wrote *Mary Poppins*. How could I? If I were writing for the Japanese child who reads it in a land without staircases, how could I have written of a nanny that slides up the bannister? If I were writing for the African child who reads the book in Swahili, how could I have written of umbrellas for a child who has never seen or used one?

''But I suppose if there is something in my books that appeals to children, it is the result of my not having to go *back* to my childhood; I can, as it were, turn *aside* and consult it (James Joyce once wrote, 'My childhood bends beside me'). If we're completely honest, not sentimental or nostalgic, we have no idea where childhood ends and maturity begins. It is one unending thread, not a life chopped up into sections out of touch with one another.''[13]

It is this ''unending thread'' that binds together Travers' view of a woman's life. ''I've said several times that I think women's liberation is, in a way, an aspect of realizing the Divine Mother. Not that I think women's libbers are Divine Mothers. Far from it. But I think the feminine principle, which we could say the Divine Mother embodies, is rising. All I want is that they don't use the feminine principle in order to turn themselves into men. We have all that we need as women. We just don't recognize it, some of us.

''I am happily a woman. Nothing in me resents it. All of me accepts it and always has. Mind you, I haven't suffered. I haven't been in a profession where women are paid less than men. Nothing has been hard for me as a woman. But I sympathize with women who want to live themselves to the full. But I don't think you can do that by being a Madison Avenue executive or president of a woman's bank. All those things I've never wanted.

''Women belong in myth. We have to think of the ideas of yin and yang. So I feel we're really sitting, if we only knew,

We rode horses called Marcus and Mayflower and the music grew louder and the World's Fair went spinning round us. ■ (From *I Go by Sea, I Go by Land* by P. L. Travers. Illustrated by Gertrude Hermes.)

exactly where we ought to be, where the Divine Mother sits. If we don't know this is so, then it isn't so."[14]

"Or it may be that you will categorize all this as 'old wives' tales.' But I am one who believes in old wives' tales and that it is the proper function of old wives to tell tales. Old wives have the best stories in the world, and long memories. Why should we treat them with contempt? The tales have to be told in order that we may understand that in the long run, whatever it may be, every man must become the hero of his own story; his own fairy tale, if you like, a real fairy tale.

"The fairy tales also tell us a great deal about women—or, perhaps about woman and her role in life, the triple role of maiden, mother, and crone. Each of us, of course, begins as a maiden and whether she becomes a physical mother or not makes no difference, the role of mother is the next step, the flowering of the bud. Last of all comes the grandmother— again, not the physical grandmother, but the stage where the flower withers into seed pod. To become a crone, it seems to me, is the last great hope of woman, supremely worth achieving. An old woman who remembers, who has gathered up all the threads of life and sits by the fire with her hands in her lap—not doing anything anymore—what a marvelous thing! This is what it is to become wise. There you sit in your rocking chair as in the fairy tales—I hope I shall, anyway—aware of all you have learned and garnered and having it available in case the young ones want it. You will not force it on them, but simply tell it. That's what the crones—all those good and bad fairies—are doing in the tales."[2]

"The great sorrow in my childhood is the fact that my grandmothers had passed on before I was born. And don't forget, childhood is a sorrowful time; people think it's so wonderful, the best years of life, but they're wrong. Childhood is sorrowful or at least it was sorrowful before it became so cushioned. Even now, children don't have money; everybody who is adult is right and they are wrong; they don't know that the minor disasters in their lives will have an ending in fact and in memory. They are like an occupied country with the adults being the occupiers. But to get back to grandmothers: I was always wanting somebody who could tell me the answers—who I was, why was I born, how did I get born? Ordinary childhood questions, but important ones. I wanted the important answers, but the grown-ups around me were disappointing in their answers and I came to the conclusion that they didn't know, either. I used to feel, 'Oh, if I only had a grandmother, she would know all these things.' This is why I think grandmothers are so very useful. They ought to be able to be there in the background, waiting for children's questions such as I asked. They are the carriers of tradition, and we lose them at our peril. They are carrying the thread. A child sees where he comes from and gathers, to some extent, an idea of where he is going."[11]

Mary Poppins has been translated into twenty-five languages, and sales of the book have run into the millions.

HOBBIES AND OTHER INTERESTS: Gardening.

FOR MORE INFORMATION SEE: P. L. Travers, "Children Are Tough," *Woman's Home Companion*, June, 1942; P. L. Travers, "Ah Wong," *Mademoiselle*, November, 1943; *New Republic*, December 25, 1944; *Good Housekeeping*, February, 1945, April, 1948, November, 1950; Elizabeth Rider Montgomery, *The Story behind Modern Books*, Dodd, 1949; Stanley J. Kunitz and Howard Haycraft, editors, *Junior Book of Authors*, H. W. Wilson, 2nd edition, 1951; "P. L. Travers: Bulletin from Chelsea," *New York Herald Tribune Book Re-*

view, October 12, 1952; P. L. Travers, "Christmas Books-I: My Childhood Bends Beside Me," *New Statesman and Nation*, November 29, 1952; S. J. Kunitz, editor, *Twentieth Century Authors*, H. W. Wilson, 1955.

New Yorker, October 20, 1962; *Christian Science Monitor*, June 4, 1963, July 31, 1963, November 18, 1968; *New York Herald Tribune*, July 7, 1963, September 20, 1964; *New York Times*, August 11, 1963, October 4, 1966, October 15, 1966, November 12, 1975, January 3, 1977; *Saturday Review*, August 22, 1964, November 7, 1964; *New York Daily News*, September 6, 1964; *New York Journal American*, November 4, 1964, June 2, 1965; P. L. Travers, "Where Did She Come From? Why Did She Go?," *Saturday Evening Post*, November 7, 1964; *Observer*, December 13, 1964, April 11, 1982; Nora Ephron, "Mary Poppins' Confidante," *New York Post*, October 14, 1965; Roger Lancelyn Green, *Tellers of Tales*, F. Watts, 1965; "Elusive Mary Poppins Author Expansive for Children's Audience," *Library Journal*, March 15, 1966; "Some Friends of Mary Poppins," *McCall's*, May, 1966; Joseph Roddy, "A Visit with the Real Mary Poppins," *Look*, December 13, 1966; *New York Times Magazine*, December 25, 1966, July 2, 1978, June 3, 1979; "The Cup of Sorrow in Every Woman's Life," *Ladies' Home Journal*, February, 1967; *Quarterly Journal of the Library of Congress*, October, 1967; Roy Newquist, *Conversations*, Rand McNally, 1967; Brian Doyle, *The Who's Who of Children's Literature*, Schocken Books, 1968; Eleanor Cameron, *The Green and Burning Tree*, Atlantic-Little, Brown, 1969; Norah Smaridge, *Famous Modern Storytellers for Young People*, Dodd, 1969.

"Travers Trust," *Observer Review*, December 20, 1970; *New York Times Book Review*, November 7, 1971, May 7, 1972, November 15, 1975; *Publishers Weekly*, December 13, 1971; *Time*, December 27, 1971; Martha E. Ward and Dorothy A. Marquardt, *Authors of Books for Young People*, 2nd edition, Scarecrow, 1971; *Horn Book*, February, 1972; Lee Bennett Hopkins, *More Books by More People*, Citation, 1974; *Women's Wear Daily*, November 5, 1975; P. L. Travers, "Give the Kid a Bible, for Instance," *Esquire*, March, 1976; *Children's Literature Review*, Volume II, Gale, 1976; *Times Literary Supplement*, July 5, 1977; D. L. Kirkpatrick, editor, *Twentieth-Century Children's Writers*, St. Martin's, 1978, new edition, 1982.

Virginia Haviland, editor, *The Openhearted Audience: Ten Authors Talk about Writing for Children*, Library of Congress, 1980; Nancy Mills, "Mary Poppins Rides Winds of Change," *Los Angeles Times*, December 20, 1981; Jonathan Cott, *Pipers at the Gates of Dawn: The Wisdom of Children's Literature*, Random House, 1981; "The Writer and the Nanny Who Never Explain," *Times Educational Supplement*, June 11, 1982; *Parabola*, Volume VII, number 2, 1982, Volume VIII, number 1, 1983; *Paris Review*, winter, 1982; Francelia Butler and Richard Rotert, editors, *Reflections on Literature for Children*, Library Professional Publications, 1984; Michele Field, "Reminiscing with P. L. Travers," *Publishers Weekly*, March 21, 1986.

VAN KAMPEN, Vlasta 1943-

PERSONAL: Born August 22, 1943, in Belleville, Ontario, Canada; daughter of Frank (a mechanical engineer) and Muriel (a homemaker; maiden name, Bowman) Rabel; married Jan Van Kampen (a graphic designer), June 4, 1964; children: Dimitri, Saskia. *Education:* Ontario College of Art, diploma in design and illustration (with honors), 1966; attended Gerrit

VLASTA VAN KAMPEN

Rietveld Akademie, Amsterdam, Holland, 1967-68. *Home and office:* 206 Glenview Ave., Toronto, Ontario M4R 1R3, Canada.

CAREER: Illustrator, 1967—. Commissioned by Parks Canada to do eight paintings for Kouchibouquac National Park, 1985. *Awards, honors:* Canada Council Children's Literature Prize for Best Illustrated Children's Book, 1983, for *ABC, 123*.

WRITINGS—Self-illustrated: *ABC, 123: The Canadian Alphabet and Counting Book,* Hurtig, 1982.

Illustrator: Muriel Whitaker, editor, *Great Canadian Animal Stories,* Hurtig, 1978; M. Whitaker, editor, *Great Canadian Adventure Stories,* Hurtig, 1979; M. Whitaker, editor, *Stories from the Canadian North,* Hurtig, 1980; M. Whitaker, *The Princess, the Hockey Player, Magic and Ghosts: Canadian Stories for Children,* Hurtig, 1981; Kathy Corrigan, *Emily Umily,* Annick Press, 1984; Dorothy Joan Harris, *Four Seasons for Toby,* Scholastic-TAB, 1987; D. J. Harris, *Racing Stripes for William,* Three Trees Press, 1987; Patricia Quinlan, *My Dad Takes Care of Me,* Annick Press, 1987.

Also illustrator of ten books for Natural Science Company of Canada, 1970-75, and "The New Schoolteacher" (filmstrip), National Filmboard of Canada, 1985.

WORK IN PROGRESS: Illustrations for a story in poetry entitled *Hours of Animals,* introducing the young child to time telling; story concept and illustrations for a picture book about the survival of a city cat when left alone in the country for a week, based on a true experience with our own cat; story concept and illustrations in collaboration with a musician/composer for a picture book about the different instruments and how they make up an orchestra.

SIDELIGHTS: "I have always had a pencil in my hand and I cannot remember not being interested in drawing or creating things with my hands. I started drawing my own cut-out dolls and designing their clothes when I was in third grade. I remember vividly winter recesses spent in the basement lunch room in the small country school that I attended. Crouching in front of the benches lining the four walls, I had paper, pencils, crayons and scissors strewn out around me and I hap-

pily drew and snipped through many recesses and lunch hours. Soon I started to sew and design my own clothes and clothes for my dress-me-doll (an old fashioned version of the Barbie doll). I was lucky to have had a very big bedroom to house all of my projects. I then started to create rooms full of furniture for my dolls. These were made from interesting box shapes (covered in fabric or painted) and anything that my mother had lying about. My mother has always had a sewing room where just about anything could be found and it was this room that inspired many of my projects.

"When I entered high school I was bused into Belleville, a town twenty miles away, so I became a commuter at age fourteen. At the high school I lost no time discovering the art department and took as my option course, one to two hours of art per week. I also joined the art club which was responsible for all the posters and decorations for any school activity. The most exciting project each year was the annual school formal dance. We would easily spend up to a month every day after school and evenings (as the date drew nearer) designing, drawing, cutting out, pasting and hanging the most intricate decorations. I am proud to say that our high school always had the best decorations and that I was part of the enthusiastic group that put it all together.

"I entered the Ontario College of Art in Toronto in 1962 with great trepidation. I was far from home living on my own in a rooming house with several other girls. It was a great change from a small village to a giant city. I was homesick and scared. There was so much talent at the college and it was a very intimidating new environment. The slickness of the presentations made by the city educated students overwhelmed me. I worked very hard to overcome all my fears and finished my fourth year as an honours student—also winning a scholarship to study in the Netherlands.

"It was at the Gerrit Rietveld Akademie in Amsterdam that I became interested in children's book illustration. During my year at the college I produced a book of fables by La Fontaine in which I set the type (by hand), executed woodcuts for eight illustrations, printed and bound the entire book. I made eight books all in different colour combinations and printed on different papers experimenting with paper textures. It was a wonderful learning experience. During my year in Holland I learned to speak Dutch fluently and now correspond in Dutch with my husband's family there.

"When I returned to Canada, I was determined to make illustration my career. I have been very lucky because I have been able to combine quite happily for my family a career as an illustrator, a mother of two children and a wife. My family has been very supportive. The children have always been a great source of inspiration for many illustrations and stories for my books. I always listen to their suggestions, comments and ideas because, after all, I am designing and illustrating for children.

"Today there is a lot of competition in the field of children's book illustration and as a result the artist can become overwhelmed and frustrated. I hope to be able to always push these things aside and continue doing the thing I love most in life, designing and illustrating children's books."

HOBBIES AND OTHER INTERESTS: Reading, listening to music, sewing, knitting, designing household articles and clothing, collecting old interesting bottles and plates, camping in wildlife parks. "Recently acquired a log cabin in a picturesque valley as a family retreat from the city. Plan to use this new environment as a source of inspiration for future work and as a place to think fresh thoughts."

WATSON, Jane Werner 1915-
(A. N. Bedford, Annie North Bedford, Monica Hill, W. K. Jasner, Elsa Ruth Nast, Elsa Jane Werner, Jane Werner)

PERSONAL: Born July 11, 1915, in Fond du Lac, Wis.; daughter of Henry Charles (a physician) and Elsa (Nast) Werner; married Earnest Charles Watson (a professor), October 6, 1954 (died December 5, 1970). *Education:* University of Wisconsin, B.A., 1936. *Home:* 166 Eucalyptus Hill Circle, Santa Barbara, Calif. 93103.

CAREER: South Side Junior High School, Sheboygan, Wis., teacher of English and social science, 1936-37; Time-Life, Chicago, Ill., clerk, 1937; Whitman Publishing Co., Racine, Wis., editorial assistant, 1938-42; Artists and Writers Guild, New York, N.Y., editor and staff writer, 1942-54; free-lance writer, 1954—; Santa Barbara Community College, Continuing Education Division, Santa Barbara, Calif., part-time instructor in creative writing and cultural geography, 1966—. Trustee, Santa Barbara Museum of Art; member of board of trustees, Santa Barbara Public Library; member of Santa Barbara County Library Advisory Committee; honorary member of board of directors, Santa Barbara Friends of the Library; member of board of directors, Planned Parenthood of Santa Barbara County; member of board, University of Wisconsin; member of Art Council, Elvehjem Museum of Art, Madison, Wis. *Member:* Authors Guild, Authors League of America.

AWARDS, HONORS: Junior Book Award from the Boys' Clubs of America, 1954, for *The Golden Geography;* named Woman of the Year in Literature by the *Los Angeles Times,* 1958; Best Book for Neo-Literates in Hindi Award from the Government of India, 1964, for *Aab hom azad hung; Rama of the Golden Age* and *Castles in Spain* were both chosen one of Child Study Association of America's Children's Books of the Year, 1971; L.H.D., University of Wisconsin, 1975; Outstanding Science Books for Children Award from the National Science Teachers Association and the Children's Book Council, 1975, for *Whales: Friendly Dolphins and Mighty Giants of the Sea,* and 1981, for *Deserts of the World.*

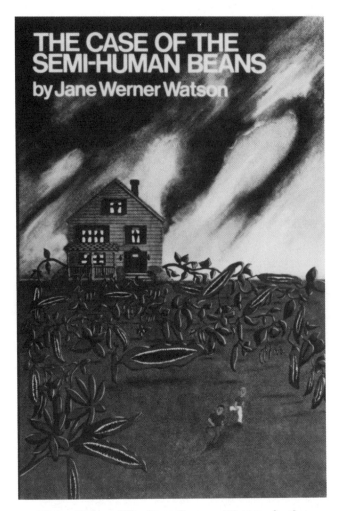

My mother says Mrs. Boggs' beans set the tone for the whole summer. ■ (Jacket illustration by Salem Krieger from *The Case of the Semi-Human Beans* by Jane Werner Watson.)

JANE WERNER WATSON

WRITINGS—All juvenile; under name Jane Werner Watson, except where noted: (With Bertha Morris Parker) *The Everyday Atom* (illustrated by James Teason), Row, Peterson, 1959; (adapter) *Man in Flight* (based on the Walt Disney film; illustrated by Nino Carbe), L. W. Singer, 1959; *The Seaver Story,* Pomona College, 1960; *Aab hom azad hung* (title means "Now We Are Free"), [India], 1964; (with David K. Todd) *Rescue!* (illustrated by Wayne K. Blickenstaff), Xerox, 1976; *Living Together in Tomorrow's World: A Challenging Preview of Future Developments in Community Living, Transportation, and Communication,* Abelard, 1976; *Conservation of Energy,* F. Watts, 1978; *Alternate Energy Sources,* F. Watts, 1979; *The Case of the Semi-Human Beans,* Coward, 1979; *The First Americans: Tribes of North America* (illustrated by Troy Howell), Pantheon, 1980; *The Mystery of the Gold Ring* (illustrated by Alfred Perry), Xerox, 1980; *The Volga,* Wayland, 1980; *This Year at Christmas,* W. K. Jasner Enterprises, 1980; *Deserts of the World: Future Threat or Promise?,* Philomel, 1981; *The Case of the Vanishing Space Ship,* Coward, 1982.

Published by Simon & Schuster, except where noted: (Editor) P. L. Travers, *Stories from Mary Poppins,* 1952; *The Golden History of the World* (illustrated by Cornelius De Witt), 1955; *Heroes of the Bible* (illustrated by Rachel Taft and Marjorie Hartwell), 1955; (under pseudonym Elsa J. Werner) *Houses* (illustrated by Tibor Gergely), 1955; *Our World: A Beginner's*

Introduction to Geography (illustrated by William Sayles), 1955; *Smokey, the Bear* (illustrated by Richard Scarry), 1955; *The True Story of Smokey the Bear* (illustrated by Feodor Rojankovsky), 1955.

(Adapter) *The Iliad* [*and*] *The Odyssey: The Heroic Story of the Trojan War* [*and*] *The Fabulous Adventures of Odysseus* (illustrated by Alice Provensen and Martin Provensen), 1956; *My Little Golden Book about God* (illustrated by Eloise Wilkin), 1956, new edition published as *My First Book about God*, 1957; (adapter) Lincoln Barnett and others, *The World We Live In*, 1956 (Watson was not associated with earlier edition); *How to Tell Time* (illustrated by Eleanor Dart), 1957; *Walt Disney's Sleeping Beauty* (based on the film "Sleeping Beauty"), 1957; *Wonders of Nature* (illustrated by E. Wilkin), 1957, published as *Wonders of Nature: A Child's First Book about Our Wonderful World*, 1958, revised edition published as *My Big Book of the Outdoors*, Golden Press, 1983; *A Catholic Child's Book about God* (illustrated by E. Wilkin), 1958; *A Giant Little Golden Book about Plants and Animals* (illustrated by Ted Chaiko), 1958; *A Giant Little Golden Book of Birds* (illustrated by E. Wilkin), 1958, reissued, Golden Press, 1977.

Published by Golden Press: *The World of Science: Scientists at Work Today in Many Challenging Fields* (illustrated with photographs by Wilson Hole, McPherson Hole, and others), 1958; (adapter) *The World's Great Religions*, 1958; *Birds* (illustrated by E. Wilkin), 1958; *This World of Ours* (illustrated by E. Wilkin), 1959; *Dinosaurs* (illustrated by William Ruth-erford), 1959; (with the staff of Walt Disney Studios) *Walt Disney's People and Places* (based on the film series "People and Places"), 1959; (adapter) *Walt Disney's True-Life Adventures: Nature's Half-Acre, Bear Country, Seal Island*, 1959.

The Giant Golden Book of Dinosaurs and Other Prehistoric Reptiles (illustrated by Rudolph F. Zallinger), 1960, published as *Dinosaurs*, 1962; *The Lion's Paw: A Tale of African Animals* (illustrated by Gustaf Tenggren), 1960; *The Sciences of Mankind: Social Scientists at Work Today in Many Challenging Fields* (charts and drawings by Campbell Grant), 1960; (with Kenneth S. Norris) *The Whale Hunt* (illustrated by Claude Humbert), 1960; *Animal Dictionary* (illustrated by F. Rojankovsky), 1960; (editor) Dorothy Agnes Bennett, *The New Golden Encyclopedia* (illustrated by Cornelius De Witt), revised edition, 1963; *My First Golden Encyclopedia* (sixteen books; illustrated by William Dugan), 1965, revised edition published in one volume, 1969, also published as *My First Golden Learning Library* (four volumes), 1965; (with K. S. Norris) *The Happy Little Whale* (illustrated by T. Gergely), 1968.

Toward a Better Environment for Our World Tomorrow (illustrated by David Klein), 1973; *Stories from Nature* (illustrated by Gerda Muller), 1973; *Whales: Friendly Dolphins and Mighty Giants of the Sea* (illustrated by Richard Amundsen), 1975; (with Sol Chaneles) *The Golden Book of the Mysterious* (illustrated by Alan Lee), 1976; *Disney's Numbers Are Fun*, 1977; *Where Jesus Lived*, 1977; *Whales* (illustrated by Rod Ruth), 1978.

Then she fed them bread and jam and milk. ■ (From *Tanya and the Geese* by Jane Werner Watson. Illustrated by June Goldsborough.)

"Living in Today's World" series; all published by Garrard: *India: Old Land, New Nation* (illustrated by Shanti Dave and others), 1966; *Iran: Crossroads of Caravans* (illustrated by Parviz Kalantari and others), 1966; *Ethiopia: Mountain Kingdom* (illustrated by Afework Tekle and others), 1966; *Thailand: Rice Bowl of Asia* (illustrated by Payut Ngaokrachang), 1966; *Nigeria: Republic of a Hundred Kings* (illustrated by Vincent Amaefunah and others), 1967; *Peru: Land Astride the Andes* (illustrated by Gilberto Bueno and others), 1967; *Egypt: Child of the Nile* (illustrated by Samiha Hassanein and others), 1967; *Greece: Land of Golden Light* (illustrated by Spyros Vasiliou), 1967; (with Clara Louise Grant) *Mexico: Land of the Plumed Serpent* (illustrated by Ernest Alvarez and others), 1968; *Canada: Giant Nation of the North* (illustrated by Aileen T. Richardson and William J. Wheeler), 1968; *Japan: Islands of the Rising Sun* (illustrated by Taro Kurotani), 1968; (with Leonora Curtin Paloheimo) *Finland: Champion of Independence,* 1969.

The Indus: South Asia's Highway of History (maps by Henri Fluchère), 1970; (reteller) *Rama of the Golden Age: An Epic of India* (illustrated by Paul Frame), 1971; *The Niger: Africa's River of Mystery* (maps by H. Fluchère), 1971; (editor) Washington Irving, *Castles in Spain: From the "Alhambra"* (illustrated by Vincent Colabella), 1971; *The Volga: Russia's River of the Five Seas* (map by Edward Malsberg), 1972; *The Mysterious Gold and Purple Box* (illustrated by Cary [variant of Louis F. Cary]), 1972; *Dance to a Happy Song* (illustrated by Cary), 1973; *The Soviet Union: Land of Many Peoples,* 1973; *India Celebrates!* (illustrated by Susan Andersen), 1974; *Tanya and the Geese* (illustrated by June Goldsborough), 1974; *A*

Parade of Soviet Holidays (illustrated by Ben Stahl), 1974; *The People's Republic of China: Red Star of the East,* 1976.

All written with Robert E. Switzer and J. Cotter Hirschberg; published by Golden Press, except as noted: *Sometimes I'm Afraid* (illustrated by Hilde Hoffmann), 1971, new edition (illustrated by Irene Trivas), Crown, 1986; *Sometimes I Get Angry* (illustrated by Hilde Hoffmann), 1971, new edition (illustrated by I. Trivas), Crown, 1986; *My Friend the Babysitter* (illustrated by Hilde Hoffmann), 1971; *Look at Me Now!* (illustrated by Hilde Hoffmann), 1971; *My Body: How It Works* (illustrated by Hilde Hoffmann), 1972; *My Friend the Dentist* (illustrated by Hilde Hoffmann), 1972, revised edition (illustrated by Cat Smith), Crown, 1987; *My Friend the Doctor* (illustrated by Hilde Hoffmann), 1972, revised edition (illustrated by C. Smith), Crown, 1987; *Sometimes I'm Jealous* (illustrated by Hilde Hoffmann), 1972, new edition (illustrated by I. Trivas), Crown, 1986; *Sometimes a Family Has to Move,* Crown, 1988; *Sometimes a Family Has to Split Up,* Crown, 1988.

Under name Jane Werner, except as noted; published by Simon & Schuster, except as noted: *Noah's Ark* (illustrated by T. Gergely), Grosset, 1943; *A Child's Book of Bible Stories: From the Garden of Eden to the Promised Land* (illustrated by Masha [pseudonym of Marie Stern]), Random House, 1944.

(Editor) *Wings of the Morning: A Child's Own Treasury of Bible Sayings* (illustrated by Decie Merwin), Grosset, 1946; (editor under name Elsa Jane Werner) *The Golden Bible: From the King James Version of the Old Testament* (illustrated by

These boats on the Indus River do not look very different from the boats of Chandragupta's day. ■ (From *The Indus: South Asia's Highway of History* by Jane Werner Watson. Photograph by Rene Burri, Magnum.)

F. Rojankovsky), 1946 (published in England as *The Golden Book of Bible Stories from the Old Testament,* Publicity, 1953); (editor) *The Golden Book of Poetry* (illustrated by Gertrude Elliot), 1947, abridged edition, 1949; *Joseph and His Brethren* (illustrated by Polly Jackson), Grosset, 1947; *The Little Golden Book of Hymns* (illustrated by Corinne Malvern), 1947; (editor) *The Golden Book of Nursery Tales* (illustrated by T. Gergely), 1948, published as *Nursery Tales,* Golden Press, 1963; (editor) *The Golden Mother Goose* (illustrated by A. Provensen and M. Provensen), 1948, published as *The Giant Golden Mother Goose,* Golden Press, 1963; *Good Morning and Good Night* (illustrated by E. Wilkin), 1948; *Mr. Noah and His Family* (illustrated by A. Provensen and M. Provensen), 1948; *Christopher Bunny, and Other Animal Stories* (illustrated by R. Scarry), 1949; *The Fuzzy Duckling* (illustrated by A. Provensen and M. Provensen), 1949; *The Golden Book of Words: How They Look and What They Tell* (illustrated by C. De Witt), 1949, published as *The Golden Picture Book of Words: How They Look and What They Tell,* 1954.

Chatterly Squirrel, and Other Animal Stories (illustrated by J. P. Miller), 1950; *The Marvelous Merry-Go-Round* (illustrated by J. P. Miller), 1950; *Pets for Peter* (illustrated by Aurelius Battaglia), 1950; (editor) *The Tall Book of Make-Believe* (illustrated by Garth Williams), Harper, 1950, reissued, 1980; *Albert's Zoo: A Stencil Book* (illustrated by R. Scarry), 1951; (editor) *The Giant Golden Book of Elves and Fairies with Assorted Pixies, Mermaids, Brownies, Witches, and Leprechauns* (illustrated by G. Williams), 1951; *The Christmas Story* (illustrated by E. Wilkin), 1952; *The Golden Geography: A Child's Introduction to the World* (illustrated by C. De Witt), 1952, revised edition, Golden Press, 1964; *Animal Friends* (illustrated by G. Williams), 1953; (reteller) *Bible Stories of Boys and Girls* (illustrated by R. Taft and M. Hartwell), 1953; (editor under name Elsa Jane Werner) *The Golden Bible for Children: The New Testament* (illustrated by A. Provensen and M. Provensen), 1953 (published in England as *The Golden Book of Stories from the New Testament,* Publicity, 1954); *The Golden Book of Trains* (illustrated by Robert Sherman), 1953; *The Little Golden Christmas Manger,* (illustrated by Steffie Lerch), 1953; *Uncle Mistletoe* (illustrated by C. Malvern), 1953; (reteller) *First Bible Stories* (illustrated by E. Wilkin), 1954; *The Giant Golden History of the World,* Golden Press, 1954; (reteller) Wilhelm Grimm and Jacob Grimm, *Twelve Dancing Princesses* (illustrated by Sheilah Beckett), 1954.

(Editor under name Elsa Jane Werner, with Charles Hartman) *A Catholic Child's Bible,* Volume I: *Stories from the Old Testament* (illustrated by F. Rojankovsky), Volume II: *The New Testament* (illustrated by A. Provensen and M. Provensen), 1958, published in one volume as *The Holy Bible,* Guild Press, 1960; *The Big Golden Book of Poetry,* Golden Press, 1974.

Under name Jane Werner; books based on Walt Disney films; illustrations adapted from pictures by the Walt Disney Studio; published by Simon & Schuster, except as noted: *Walt Disney's Mickey Mouse's Picnic,* 1950; ... *Cinderella,* 1950; ... *Cinderella's Friends,* 1950; ... *Donald Duck's Toy Train,* 1950; *Mad Hatter's Tea Party: From Walt Disney's Alice in Wonderland,* 1951; *Walt Disney's Alice in Wonderland Finds the Garden of Live Flowers,* 1951; ... *Alice in Wonderland Meets the White Rabbit,* 1951; ... *Grandpa Bunny,* 1951; (with Campbell Grant) ... *Snow White and the Seven Dwarfs,* 1952; (with the staff of Walt Disney Studios) ... *Living Desert,* 1954; (with the staff of Walt Disney Studios) ... *Vanishing Prairie,* 1955; ... *Bunny Book,* Golden Press, 1972.

Under pseudonym A. N. Bedford: *Roy Rogers and the New Cowboy* (illustrated by Hans Helweg and Mel Crawford), Simon & Schuster, 1953.

Under pseudonym Annie North Bedford; published by Simon & Schuster, except as noted: *The Jolly Barnyard* (illustrated by T. Gergely), 1950; *Susie's New Stove: The Little Chef's Cookbook* (illustrated by C. Malvern), 1950; *Bugs Bunny and the Indians,* 1951; *Bugs Bunny's Book,* 1951; (adapter) *Frosty the Snowman* (illustrated by C. Malvern), 1951, reissued, Golden Books, 1985; *Bugs Bunny Gets a Job,* 1952.

Under pseudonym Annie North Bedford; books based on Walt Disney films; illustrations adapted from pictures by the Walt Disney Studio; published by Simon & Schuster, except as noted: *Walt Disney's Donald Duck's Adventure,* 1950; ... *Noah's Ark,* 1952; ... *Peter Pan and the Indians,* 1952; ... *Peter Pan and Wendy,* 1952; ... *Pluto Pup Goes to Sea,* 1952; ... *Seven Dwarfs Find a House,* 1952; ... *The Ugly Duckling,* 1952; *Donald Duck and the Witch,* 1953; (editor) *Walt Disney's Mickey Mouse Birthday Book,* 1953; ... *Mickey Mouse Goes Christmas Shopping,* 1953; ... *Story Book of Peter Pan* (illustrated by C. Grant), 1953, new edition, Golden Press, 1969; ... *Chip 'n' Dale at the Zoo,* 1954; ... *Disneyland on the Air,* 1955; ... *Dumbo,* 1955; ... *Little Man of Disneyland,* 1955; ... *Robin Hood,* 1955; ... *Donald Duck and the Mouseketeers,* 1956; ... *Donald Duck, Prize Driver,* 1956; ... *Goofy, Movie Star,* 1956; ... *Jiminy Cricket, Fire Fighter,* 1956; ... *Mickey Mouse and the Missing Mouseketeers,* 1956; ... *Mickey Mouse Flies the Christmas Mail,* 1956; ... *Perri and Her Friends,* 1956; ... *Donald Duck Treasury* (anthology), Golden Press, 1960; *Walt Disney Presents "The Jungle Book,"* Golden Press, 1967; *Walt Disney Presents "Legends of America"* (illustrated by M. Crawford), Golden Press, 1969.

Under pseudonym Monica Hill; published by Simon & Schuster: *Dale Evans and the Lost Gold Mine* (illustrated by M. Crawford), 1954; *Rin Tin Tin and Rusty* (illustrated by M. Crawford), 1955; *Gene Autry and the Champion* (illustrated by Frank Bolle), 1956; *Lassie Shows the Way* (illustrated by Lee Ames), 1956; *Rin Tin Tin and the Lost Indian* (illustrated by Hamilton Greene), 1956; *The Life and Legend of Wyatt Earp* (illustrated by M. Crawford), 1958.

Under pseudonym W. K. Jasner: *Which Is the Witch?* (illustrated by Victoria Chess), Pantheon, 1979; *Witch's Shop,* Xerox Education Publications, 1979.

Under pseudonym Elsa Ruth Nast; published by Simon & Schuster, except as noted: *A Woods Story* (illustrated by Masha), Harper, 1946; *A Farm Story* (illustrated by Masha), Harper, 1946; (compiler) *Little Steps: Children's Poems of Thanks* (illustrated by Pelagie Doane), Grosset, 1947; *Our Puppy* (illustrated by F. Rojankovsky), 1948; *The Magic Wish, and Other Johnny and Jane Stories* (illustrated by C. Malvern), 1949; *How to Have a Happy Birthday: A Party Cut-Out Book* (illustrated by Retta Worcester), 1952; *Tex and His Toys* (illustrated by C. Malvern), 1952; *Fun with Decals* (illustrated by C. Malvern), 1953.

Also author of eleven beginning readers on Indian subjects, Rajkamal Prakashan (Delhi).

ADAPTATIONS: "Dance to a Happy Song" (cassette); "The First Americans" (cassette), Random House.

SIDELIGHTS: Born **July 11, 1915** in Fond du Lac, Wisconsin, the daughter of a psychiatrist. "What was different about my growing up was that for much of my childhood we lived at

I don't mean to be bad,

I just want you to see
how great it is
to be me,
me,
ME!

(From *Sometimes I Get Angry* by Jane Werner Watson, Robert E. Switzer, and J. Cotter Hirschberg. Illustrated by Irene Trivas.)

the various psychiatric hospitals my father was in charge of. From the time I was two until I was eight, we lived at a special hospital for young people who were then called, 'feeble-minded.' These mentally retarded young people were our friends; we knew them very well, and some of them even worked in our house. Living so close to them gave us a different point of view, from most children, about people who are disadvantaged.

"My mother was an extremely congenial, merry, warm-hearted person who always helped others in need. A trained nurse, she often looked after ailing relatives whom she freely invited into our house. She was also very artistic, and enjoyed writing verse and drawing.

"I was three at the end of World War I, and vaguely remember visiting my grandmother on Armistice Day. One of her neighbors took us downtown to watch the parade and my aunt was one of six young women holding a huge American flag which people threw money at.

"At four, I was ready for school. But we lived outside a very small village where there weren't any kindergartens. My older sister was away at class all day and that left me with nobody to play with. Rather than isolate me, my parents sent me to school for one year with the 'children,' as we called them, who were patients in the hospital. I learned to recognize letters and pick out headlines in newspapers. When I was five, my parents didn't think there was much point in my going to the hospital school any longer so they obtained permission to send me to first grade. I attended the small village school where teachers were trained for the rural schools in the two surrounding counties. There were only three pupils: two little boys, and me. After several weeks, the teacher, a friend of the family, asked my parents for permission to give me second grade-level work. Apparently, I had been forming bad study habits at the age of five! As a consequence, I started third grade when I was six, and continued along at this advanced pace without difficulty until I hit my teens. Then I felt a bit out of place socially. I was much younger than my classmates and it didn't help matters that we lived out of town at the hospital.

"Later we moved to another hospital for World War I veterans with mental difficulties. Some of them were in rather good shape and were allowed 'ground parole,' which meant they could move around the beautiful grounds that included a lot of lake shore where, as children, we would join them to ice fish. They were good companions; I think they enjoyed having children around.

"I always read a great deal. Then one year, at my regular eye examination, the doctor discovered that my myopia had rapidly progressed and he advised that I give up reading for six months. I was stricken; I went home and wept until my mother reminded me that crying wouldn't help my eyes. I had to tell my teachers that I wouldn't be able to read for the rest of the year, and this made me feel a bit important. The teachers weren't alarmed; I was getting along well enough in my studies that I could afford to coast for awhile. I genuinely didn't read anything more than a newspaper headline all through that period; it was quite a strain. But my vision did stabilize.

"My early interest in writing was stimulated by *John Martin's Book*, a magazine my sister and I started receiving when I was five. Largely created and designed by one man, this illustrated magazine (a forerunner of *Highlights for Children*) featured serials, short stories, poems, and a comic 'manners' page. I particularly liked the ongoing tales of 'Uncle Joe,' whose marvelous travel adventures left their mark on me. So much did I enjoy *John Martin's Book*, I decided at seven that I would like to write for children when I grew up.

"At nine, I changed my mind and decided that I would go into law, then politics, and become the first woman president of the United States around 1952. I gave up the presidency at eleven when I became stage struck. In those days, there were many stock theater companies around the country. I'm not quite sure how I managed to get to the Saturday matinee every week on twenty-five cents allowance, but I did.

"One of my numerous aunts knew a young woman in the local stock company. This actress came to our house for dinner several times and invited us backstage after a performance to meet the cast. This fueled my fantasy.

"I later acted in high school plays. The University of Wisconsin High School was small, but wonderful. Most of the teachers also taught at the University, so we had marvelous instruction. Long after I graduated, the high school became inadequate for the University's practice-teaching needs, and was closed.

"I learned Latin and German. Most of my friends took French, but my family background was German so it seemed a more sensible course of study. I suppose there was also an unconscious motivation. You see, my parents were second and third generation Americans but spoke German fluently; they had attended bilingual schools in Wisconsin, which had a large German population. They never spoke German at home, *except* before Christmas, when in our presence they would cryptically discuss our gifts. As a result, German was a rather magical language to us."

Attended University of Wisconsin. "Inspired by my father's humanitarian work, I wanted to major in psychology. Unfortunately, psychology did not seem a very promising field for a bachelor degree. Those were the depression years; my father's hospital had already closed down due to insufficient funding, and I knew that rather than pursue graduate studies, I would have to get a job. I took an English major and settled on the typical field for a girl: teaching. My first year out of college I taught English and social science at South Side Junior High School in Sheboygan, Wisconsin. I knew nothing about discipline, and junior high is not a very civilized age. Many of the boys were much taller than me; I was barely twenty, and some of them were sixteen. I started having migraines; all in all, it was not a great year.

"The next fall in **1937** I went to Chicago to look for a job. My first day out, to the shock of the cousin I was staying with, I found one. It was the end of the Depression and everyone had been having such a hard time getting or keeping work that my cousin thought it improper that I should go out looking one morning and arrive at the end of the day with a decent job—a clerical position in the circulation department of Time-Life, which had its printing done in a Chicago plant.

"I lived in what was laughingly known as a 'girls club,' a brownstone rooming house on Michigan Avenue, a block from the marvelous Drake Hotel, a very nice section of Chicago. Every day, I took the bus down Michigan Avenue to the South Side. Chicago was a lively cultural center, but of course, at nineteen dollars a week, you don't have access to a great deal of culture. A friend and I used to change buses each evening at the Chicago Art Institute. If we got out of work very promptly, we'd have just enough time to rush in for a quick browse before our bus connection. I became extremely well-acquainted with the first few yards of the main floor.

"While I was in Chicago, my father wrote to a friend, president of a printing company in Wisconsin, to ask if he knew anyone in Chicago who might employ me in a publishing firm. He did not, but asked my father if I would be interested in coming back to Wisconsin to work in his editorial department in Racine. I was loath to go. I thought it *dreadful* to get a job because your father knew the president of the company. My mother said, 'Don't worry, they won't keep you if you don't do well!' But I thought that would be even worse! Finally, I did go to Racine for an interview with the man in charge of the editorial department. I don't think he was too impressed but, as the president had sent me in, he hired me.

"After the holidays, I moved to Racine and began my work with the Western Printing and Lithographing Company which, at the time, published in its Whitman Publishing branch, popular books sold in dime and variety stores. After a few weeks, my boss handed me a recently acquired manuscript and told me to make a dummy. I knew nothing about layout and consequently cut up the original manuscript! I eventually learned layouts, typeface selection, paste-ups, copy editing, captions—you name it! Then I began writing some of Whitman's 'Better Little Books' at the rate of two and three a week. It was my first professional and disciplined writing."

1942. "Men were rapidly being swept off into the army. Western had a very small office in New York where they put together 'packages' for major publishers. They would buy manuscripts, hire out the illustrations, and print the books. Before the books went to print, they would sell the 'package' to a major publisher like Little-Brown, Random House, or Doubleday.

"The two young men in the editorial department were both being drafted, so I was asked if I would like to transfer to the New York office. I was of two minds: I am not a big city person, and my family was not enthusiastic about the distance. My brother was in the Air Force (he was a bomber pilot who died in the war), and my family would have preferred to have me close to home. Finally, however, I decided to take the job.

"My first day there I was assigned a desk. The two men I was to replace were still in the office and a little resistant to my presence. 'My goodness,' I said, 'there's no typewriter here. . . .' The younger of the two, who has remained a very good friend, replied, 'Oh, don't ask for a typewriter. They'll expect you to use it.'

"I did get a typewriter and immediately began a variety of writing. My first task was to rewrite a manuscript which was to be sold to Harper. They had liked the illustrations, but not the story. I was to take the pictures and write a new story to go with them. Harper published it and, although it was not an earth-shaking success, it was satisfying to see my first book in print. Next I rewrote another illustrated manuscript for Doubleday, a history of decisive battles in which new warfare techniques had been introduced."

Watson was one of the original group of editors who worked on the famous Golden Books series originated by Western Publishing in collaboration with Simon & Schuster. "The Golden Books series was just in the process of establishing itself; the first twelve books were at the printers when I arrived in the New York office. The original Golden Books were forty-two pages, all in color, with a color dust jacket, and were sold for just twenty-five cents. What made their low price possible was that Western Printing had an unusually large paper quotient. They had always printed a great many commercial sales catalogues, but during the war peacetime production was cut off. While many other publishers were short of paper because their quotas had been adjusted to their previous year's use,

Western was able to utilize some of its unusually large paper quota for Golden Books.

"Golden Books were a completely new offering in children's books. They had more variety and substance than the books Western had previously published in its own Whitman line. They were well written and well illustrated and, most of all, affordable to large numbers of people. In addition, Simon & Schuster had an imaginative merchandising man. Because of his marketing savvy, Golden Book racks were set up in almost every drugstore, supermarket and variety store in the country.

"At editorial meetings, we planned the Golden Book series up to two years in advance. We tried to strike a balance between factual titles, stories, nonsense books, and Disney titles.

"Western, in those days, had an exclusive franchise with Disney to publish all their books. Disney had begun making animated feature films about the same time I started working with Whitman in Racine, so I was familiar with Disney material. I wrote the Golden Books based on most of the Disney films, continuing even after I moved to California.

"In **1943,** the first of the Giant Golden Books was published. As we moved into the larger format our little editorial group decided it would be sensible to do a basic series of reference books in the Giant Golden Book size. Our idea was that every family should be able to own a Golden Book Encyclopedia and Picture Dictionary, for example. I worked on *The Golden Bible* and *The Golden Geography,* two other titles planned for this family reference shelf.

"After the war the two men I had replaced returned to work and I was sent to California. There I worked in a small office, largely on Disney material and movie rights. In the two years I was there, I developed a close working relationship with Disney Studios. As the Golden Book series grew, the men decided there was room for me back in the New York office. I returned, but made frequent trips to Beverly Hills to keep in touch with Disney material.

"In the early 1950s, Georges Duplaix, head of the Simon & Schuster side of the Golden Book operation, went to Greece and came back very excited about it. He wanted to publish a Golden Book version of the *Iliad* and the *Odyssey,* and asked me to do the adaptation. I wasn't very enthusiastic; I didn't see how we could cut the two classics down enough to fit into one Giant Golden Book. 'Oh, you've simply got to go to Greece,' said Georges. 'I know once you've seen it, you will want to do the book.' I told him I could think of just two reasons against going, and they were both financial. 'That is the reasoning of an old man,' said Georges. Not being able to bear that comparison, I went.

"I joined a cruise ship which, before it went to Greece, offered a one week side trip from Cairo to Jerusalem, Baghdad, Babylon, Damascus, Palmyra, Baalbek, and Beirut. I was interested in ancient history, so I decided to be extravagant and take this one week tour before heading for Greek waters.

"We were a very small group, sixteen altogether. One of the sixteen was a very shy bachelor professor from the California Institute of Technology, whom I found very congenial. I did go on to Greece to work on the book, returned briefly to New York and then went to Scotland, where we were married. The group at the office presented me with a very special book called "Little Golden Jane," illustrated by a wide and distinguished sampling of Golden Book illustrators. I treasure it."

(From *The Volga: Russia's River of the Five Seas* by Jane Werner Watson. Photograph courtesy of FPG.)

1954. Moved to Pasadena, California with her husband, Earnest Watson, a physics professor and dean of the faculty at California Institute of Technology. "We finished up the last of Earnest's sabbatical, visiting the Middle East and the Mediterranean. In Spain, Earnest contracted blood poisoning. While he was in bed in the hotel we began to plan a book for young people, intended to introduce them to the latest developments in scientific research. The first Sputnik had just gone up, and everybody was saying things like, 'Oh, the Russians are so far ahead of us in education; our children are hopelessly disinterested in science.' When Golden Press expressed an interest in the project, Earnest approached the men in charge of various research divisions at Cal Tech for help. Each division head was to choose four current projects, the most important in his field of geology, biology, physics, chemistry, mathematics, astronomy, and engineering. Earnest then set up interviews for me with the men in charge of these projects. As he was dean of the faculty, they couldn't very well decline. I wrote up what I understood about each project. I had a very limited scientific background, but the scientists at Cal Tech were excellent teachers. I finished the manuscript in one year, and spent most of the next year lining up the illustrations and photographs. The book, *The World of Science,* did extremely well, selling hundreds of thousands of copies in many languages.

"Aside from the vast world of scientific research, Earnest introduced me to foreign travel. In 1960, we traveled to India,

where he served as the science attaché to the United States Embassy. It was he who located an Indian publisher, Rajkamal Prakashan in Delhi, who expressed interest in our idea of starting an experimental line of picture books for beginning readers. We had discovered there were very few children's books in India, and particularly few with good illustration. I wrote eleven of the first twelve books, which were planned for beginning literates—children or adults—because there were many adults in India who were just learning or who wanted to learn to read. Some of the books were factual; the rest were little stories, which I had written about life in various regions of India. Earnest and I had been collecting Indian paintings, both ancient and contemporary, and so we invited some of the young painters we had met to do the illustration.

"There are fifteen official languages in India, and many dialects among those. The Indian publisher had planned to print the illustrations and leave space to drop in the text in the various languages. We approached the Ministry of Education with our project and the man in charge expressed interest in printing 35,000 copies of each of our first twelve books. The government was to translate the books and try them out in various regions around the country. At that time, there was no national publishing company in India; regional publishers produced books in their areas which were distributed in local bookstore outlets. Our project was therefore quite revolutionary in concept. Unfortunately, directly after we left India in

Before the Communist era, China had little industry. ■ (From *The People's Republic of China: Red Star of the East* by Jane Werner Watson. Photograph by Michael J. O'Neill.)

1962, the Chinese came in over the northeast boundaries and all the money that had been allocated to our project was spent on defense rather than on education. The series was dropped by the government, but the Delhi publishers did subsequently arrange for publication of the books in five of the fifteen regional languages.

"Back in the United States, it occurred to me that it would be nice for some of these young artists to have their work published in America. I put together some of the stories I had written for the Indian series with some background material and my own photographs and sent it to Garrard Publishing. The project in India thus led to my Garrard series, 'Living in Today's World,' on behalf of which Earnest and I traveled extensively."

Watson conducted original research for each book. "We went at least twice to every country in the series. When we were ready to compile the illustrations, we usually returned to locate illustrators there. All the books were anchored in personal experience, and we tried very hard to present each country from the point of view of the people concerned, rather than that of an outside observer. We felt very strongly that we did not want to pose as the haughty Americans, looking down at a 'strange' culture, seeing only the differences.

"We generally traveled by ourselves. Often we had a car and driver and in some countries, like Japan, we were assigned a local guide. As an example of how our personal experiences contributed to the writing of the books, our Japanese guide on the northern island of Hokkaido gave me background for a story which went into my book *Japan: Islands of the Rising Sun*. Apparently among the great experiences of his life were the week-long school excursions he made during his school years. He spoke of these trips with such enthusiasm that I wrote a little story about a school excursion, making it as personal as possible. In the story, as in the real tale, the boy's mother fixes him a knapsack full of things he might need for the journey. At first, the boy thinks this is ridiculous, even embarassing. But along the way, he finds a use for everything his sage mother had packed."

Watson has recently completed a book for young people on population control. "When we were living in Pasadena, I often attended the Women's Faculty Club meetings. One of the first speakers I heard was a Cal Tech professor of economics who was interested in world population and the problems it posed. I had never thought much about world population, and was very impressed by his lecture. Several years later, when we moved to Santa Barbara, Planned Parenthood was just beginning to organize locally and I was invited to be on the board. I am now finishing my sixth three-year term there. Partly because of what I had seen and experienced in India, I have become increasingly concerned about what the growth of population has done to resources in various parts of the world. The cutting of the rain forests, which are irreplaceable, the spread of deserts from over grazing, the destruction of farmland through careless soil erosion, the disappearance of fish through over fishing—all of this deeply concerns me. In every area, it seems, we are acting as very poor stewards of the earth. It is important to get these ecological concepts across to young people so that they will have a value system on which to base their judgments *before* they become politically aware.

Bushmen of the Kalahari desert fill ostrich-shell containers from underground water sources....
■ (From *Deserts of the World: Future Threat or Promise?* by Jane Werner Watson. Photograph courtesy of The American Museum of Natural History.)

"I am also concerned about the serious drug problem in this country. It is quite tragic that children don't feel they can be stimulated or thrilled except by artificial means. As far as democracy is concerned, we can't afford to bring up a large proportion of our young people to feel completely disinfranchised. Many feel they have no place or social system, and have no hope for the future. What has fostered this sense of hopelessness? I don't have any one answer. Perhaps the Vietnam War, an immoral war, disillusioned many people. But it is also the price of affluence—too much has come too early for many young people. They lack a sense of commitment and shared social responsibility. Urbanization, which has stranded so many youths in pockets of poverty must also contribute to the malaise of young people who have no prospects of jobs or betterment through education.''

Watson still travels abroad once a year, focusing on various cultural areas and religions—information she shares through adult education courses (slide talks) in Santa Barbara. She also teaches creative writing through Santa Barbara Community College's Continuing Education Program. "Cultures are not nationally defined and I don't really have one favorite. Perhaps the most profound effect of all my travel has been the great broadening of my religious beliefs. I do believe in God, that is, a force behind the universe, and I am also convinced there is such a thing as a 'soul,' which relates to other 'souls' on a different basis than our mental and physical relationship to the world. But I cannot imagine a force of universal scale really caring whether one worships on Sunday, or Friday, or Tuesday! Religious intolerance is, I feel, perhaps one of our most tragic human flaws.''

—*Based on an interview by Rachel Koenig*

HOBBIES AND OTHER INTERESTS: Archaeology, ancient history, photography, collecting Indian miniature paintings, travel, needlepoint to own designs.

WILKIN, Eloise (Burns)   1904-1987

OBITUARY NOTICE—See sketch in *SATA* Volume 49: Born March 30, 1904, in Rochester, N.Y.; died of cardiac arrest following surgery for cancer, October 4, 1987. Illustrator of children's books. Wilkin, who studied illustration at Rochester Institute of Technology, began her career in New York City shortly after graduation and subsequently illustrated over one hundred books for children. She won a *New York Herald Tribune* Spring Book Festival Award for her illustrations in Irmengarde Eberle's *A Good House for a Mouse*, 1940, and Maud Hart Lovelace's *The Tune Is in the Tree*, 1950. Wilkin's self-illustrated writings include *The Baby Book, My Good Morning Book,* and *Rock-A-Bye Baby: Nursery Songs and Cradle Games. Eloise Wilkin's Book of Poems*, scheduled for posthumous publication, contains poetry by her daughter, Deborah Springett. During her long career, Wilkin also collaborated on more than twenty books with her sister, Esther.

FOR MORE INFORMATION SEE—Obituaries: *Democrat and Chronicle* (Rochester, N.Y.), October 7, 1987; *School Library Journal*, January, 1988.

Ah! what would the world be to us
    If the children were no more?
We should dread the desert behind us
    Worse than the dark before.
        —Henry Wadsworth Longfellow

WILLIAMS, Brian (Peter)   1943-

PERSONAL: Born October 7, 1943, in London, England; son of Llewellyn Roy (a clerk) and Margaret (a clerk; maiden name, Lawdham) Williams; married Brenda Hope Clarke (an editor), February 2, 1980. *Education:* University of Birmingham, England, B.A. (with honours), 1965. *Politics:* Democrat. *Religion:* Christian. *Home:* 259 Woolwich Rd., Upper Abbey Wood, London SE2 OAR, England.

CAREER: Hanley High School, and Brownhills High School, England, English teacher, 1965-67; *Encyclopaedia Britannica*, London, England, editor, 1968-85, *Children's Britannica*, editor, 1976-85; free-lance writer, 1985—. Editorial consultant to the new international edition of *Children's Britannica*, 1985-87.

WRITINGS: Aircraft (juvenile; illustrated by John Bishop and others), Sampson Low, 1974, new edition, Warwick, 1982; *Inventions and Discoveries* (illustrated by Nigel Chamberlain and others), F. Watts (London), 1978, Warwick, 1979; *War and Weapons* (juvenile; illustrated by John Berry and others), Ward Lock, 1978, revised edition, Random House, 1987; *Under the Sea* (illustrated by Graham Allen and others), Ward Lock, 1978, published in the United States as *Exploring under the Sea*, F. Watts, 1979; *First Picture Encyclopedia* (illustrated by Roy Coombs and others), Ward Lock, 1979, Scholastic, 1981; *Secrets of the Sea* (juvenile; illustrated by G. Allen and others), F. Watts (London), 1979, Rourke, 1981; *Come to Russia* (juvenile; illustrated by Mike Atkinson and others), Warwick, 1979; *Genghis Khan* (illustrated by Francis Phillips and Doug Post), Ward, Lock, 1979; *Joan of Arc* (juvenile; illustrated by Roger Payne), Ward, Lock, 1979, Rourke, 1981; *Napoleon Bonaparte* (juvenile; illustrated by Michael Lynn and others), Ward, Lock, 1979, Rourke, 1981; *Conquerors of Everest* (juvenile; illustrated by N. Chamberlain and F. Phillips), Ward, Lock, 1979, Rourke, 1981.

The Wonder Book of Battles (juvenile), Ward, Lock, 1981, 2nd edition published as *Battles*, Kingfisher, 1985, published in the United States as *The Great Book of Battles*, Rourke, 1981; (with others) *Book of Transport*, Ward Lock, 1981; *Ships and Other Seacraft*, Piper Books, 1983, F. Watts, 1984; (with Lyn Williamson) *Picture Encyclopaedia of Our World*, Kingfisher Books, 1984; *George Washington*, Chivers Press, 1988; *Winston Churchill*, Chivers Press, 1988; *1001 Wonders of Science*, Grisewood & Dempsey, 1988; *Twenty Names in Space Exploration*, Wayland, 1988.

SIDELIGHTS: "Born in London, I moved to the industrial north midlands of England at the age of twelve. After the domesticated greenness of the Home Counties (the suburban areas around London), the industrial landscape of North Staffordshire, home of Britain's pottery industry and also an important coal-mining region, was an eye-opener. It made me more aware not only of the effect that the Industrial Revolution had on the British landscape, but also of the great changes it brought about in social habits—and this fascination has remained with me.

"I have written ever since I can remember. Television did not arrive in our household (I was an only child) until I was in my early teens. Until then, it was books—when I wasn't playing soccer (a sporting love that is still strong; and has to be since for my whole life practically I have followed one of the less famous and certainly less successful London-based soccer teams, Fulham). To follow Fulham you need faith, hope and love, and a sense of humour too!

BRIAN WILLIAMS

"My father and a teacher who taught me when I was aged nine or so had an important influence on my life; it was the teacher who first suggested that I might find a career in writing.

"After school, I went on to study for an English degree at the University of Birmingham. Again, I think I enjoyed the soccer and the social life at least as much as the academic work, into which I probably put less than all my endeavours! Still, I got a degree, and met some interesting people: including (then on the teaching staff) Richard Hoggart, David Lodge and Malcolm Bradbury.

"By one of those accidents which so often seem to determine the path of our lives, I spent some time teaching in school, before answering an ad in a newspaper and finding myself back in London (which I'd known as a child), learning to be an editor and finding out that there is a lot more to writing than putting pen to paper at a great pace. The presentation of facts is obviously one of my prime concerns, since I spend quite a lot of my time working with encyclopaedias and other information books. One of my firmest beliefs about information-presentation is that: a) you must know your reader, and b) you should always give him/her just a little more—to stretch the mind, challenge the imagination. Combining fact with fiction works well with young readers who still have that instinctive feeling for narrative that probably held people around smoky fires in prehistoric times. Now it's television, but the stories are less gripping!

"I met my wife, Brenda Clarke, while we were both working for Britannica in London. We now work together as free-lance writers and editors. Book-work gives all manner of satisfactions; you can derive as much pleasure from a paragraph as

from a hundred pages. That's another facet of fact-book making: to be concise makes it so much easier for the reader. A wise old history teacher at school once told me: 'Remember, it's not what you put in that matters, it's what you leave out.'''

HOBBIES AND OTHER INTERESTS: Sports, gardening, looking at birds and other animals, visiting historic and interesting places, aeroplanes, especially old ones.

WINSTON, Clara 1921-1983

PERSONAL: Born December 6, 1921, in New York, N.Y.; died of leukemia, November 7, 1983, in Northampton, Mass.; married Richard Winston (a biographer and translator; died, December 22, 1979); children: Krishna Winston-Billingsley, Justina Winston Gregory. *Education:* Attended Brooklyn College.

CAREER: Professional translator in collaboration with husband; novelist. *Awards, honors:* Guggenheim fellowship, 1962; American Translators Association Alexander Gold Medal, 1966; P.E.N. Translation Prize, 1971, for *The Letters of Thomas Mann 1889-1955;* American Book Award for Translation, 1978, for *In the Deserts of This Earth;* International Board on Books for Young People Translator's Honor List, 1980, for *The Magic Stone.*

WRITINGS: The Closest Kin There Is, Harcourt, 1952; *The Hours Together,* Lippincott, 1961; *Painting for the Show,* Constable, 1969; (with husband, Richard Winston) *Notre-Dame de Paris,* Newsweek, 1971; (with R. Winston) *Daily Life in the Middle Ages,* American Heritage Publishing, 1975.

Translator: Maurice Messegue, *The Way to Natural Health and Beauty,* Macmillan, 1974.

Translations in collaboration with R. Winston: H. E. Jacob, *Six Thousand Years of Bread,* Doubleday, 1944; Herman Rauschning, *Time of Delirium,* Appleton, 1946; Theodor Plievier, *Stalingrad,* Appleton, 1946; Hans Bernd Gisevius, *To the Bitter End,* Houghton, 1947; Rene Fulop-Miller, *Sing, Brat, Sing,* Holt, 1949.

R. Fulop-Miller, *The Web,* Abelard, 1950; H. E. Jacob, *Joseph Haydn,* Rinehart, 1950; Jurgen Thorwald, *The Triumph of Surgery,* Pantheon, 1950; Walter Mehring, *The Lost Library,* Bobbs-Merrill, 1951; Margot Benary-Isbert, *The Ark,* Harcourt, 1953; M. Benary-Isbert, *Rowan Farm,* Harcourt, 1954; M. Benary-Isbert, *The Shooting Star,* Harcourt, 1954; Johanna Moosdorf, *Flight to Africa,* Harcourt, 1954.

Konrad Adenauer, *Word Indivisible,* Harper, 1955; Viktor E. Frankl, *The Doctor and the Soul,* Knopf, .1955; R. Fulop-Miller, *The Night of Time,* Bobbs-Merrill, 1955; Kaethe Kollwitz, *Diary and Letters,* Regnery, 1955; M. Benary-Isbert, *The Wicked Enchantment,* Harcourt, 1955; M. Benary-Isbert, *Castle on the Border,* Harcourt, 1956; Luise Rinser, *Nina,* Regnery, 1956; Henry Winterfeld, *Detectives in Togas* (illustrated by Charlotte Kleinert), Harcourt, 1956; Jacques Carton, *La Belle Sorel,* Ives Washburn, 1956; C. W. Ceram, *The Secret of the Hittites,* Knopf, 1956; Hannah Arendt, *Rahel Varnhagen: The Life of a Jewish Woman,* East & West Library, 1957; C. W. Ceram, *The March of Archaeology,* Knopf, 1958; Heimito von Doderer, *The Demons,* Knopf, 1958; Josef Pieper, *Happiness and Contemplation,* Pantheon, 1958; L. Rinser, *Rings of Glass,* Regnery, 1958; J. Thorwald, *The Century of the Surgeon,* Pantheon, 1959; Ethelbert Stauffer, *Jesus and*

His Story, Knopf, 1959; Erich Schenk, *Mozart and His Times,* Knopf, 1959; Friedrich Duerrenmatt, *The Pledge,* Knopf, 1959; Thomas Mann, *Last Essays,* Knopf, 1959; J. Pieper, *Prudence,* Pantheon, 1959; M. Benary-Isbert, *The Long Way Home,* Harcourt, 1959.

F. Duerrenmatt, *Traps,* Knopf, 1960; R. Fulop-Miller, *The Silver Bacchanal,* Atheneum, 1960; T. Mann, *Letters to Paul Amann,* Wesleyan University Press, 1960; J. Pieper, *Scholasticism,* Pantheon, 1960; T. Mann, *The Story of a Novel: The Genesis of Dr. Faustus,* Knopf, 1961; Erich Maria Remarque, *Heaven Has No Favorites,* Harcourt, 1961; J. Thorwald, *The Dismissal,* Pantheon, 1961; Hans Sahl, *The Few and the Many,* Harcourt, 1962; Felix Klee, *Paul Klee,* Braziller, 1962; Walter Nigg, *The Heretics,* Knopf, 1962; Ernst Benz, *The Eastern Orthodox Church,* Doubleday, 1963; H. E. Jacob, *Felix Mendelssohn and His Times,* Prentice-Hall, 1963; Carl G. Jung, *Memories, Dreams, Reflections,* Pantheon, 1963; J. Pieper, *Belief and Faith: A Philosophical Tract,* Harcourt, 1963; H. von Doderer, *Every Man a Murderer,* Knopf, 1964; Martin Gregor-Dellin, *The Lamp Post,* Knopf, 1964; Rolf Hochhuth, *The Deputy,* Grove, 1964; J. Pieper, *Enthusiasm and Divine Madness,* Harcourt, 1964.

E. Benz, *Buddhism or Communism,* Doubleday, 1965; C. W. Ceram, *Archaeology of the Cinema,* Harcourt, 1965; F. Duerrenmatt, *Once a Greek,* Knopf, 1965; J. Pieper, *In Tune with the World,* Harcourt, 1965; J. Thorwald, *The Century of the Detective,* Harcourt, 1965; Herbert Wendt, *The Red, White and Black Continent,* Doubleday, 1966; Uwe Johnson, *Two Views,* Harcourt, 1966; Gunnel Linde, *The White Stone,* Harcourt, 1966; Karl Loewenstein, *Max Weber's Political Ideas in the Perspective of Our Time,* University of Massachusetts Press, 1966; M. Benary-Isbert, *Blue Mystery,* Harcourt, 1967; Hermann Hesse, *The Glass Bead Game,* Holt, 1969.

"You poor little thing," the field mouse said, for she was a kindly old soul, "come into my warm house and eat with me." ■ (From *Thumbeline* by Hans Christian Andersen. Illustrated by Lisbeth Zwerger. Translated from the Danish by Richard and Clara Winston.)

H. Hesse, *Klingsor's Last Summer*, Farrar, Strauss, 1970; Albert Speer, *Inside the Third Reich*, Macmillan, 1970; C. W. Ceram, *The First American*, Harcourt, 1971; *The Letters of Thomas Mann 1889-1955*, Knopf, 1971; J. Thorwald, *The Patients*, Harcourt, 1972; Simon Wiesenthal, *Sails of Hope: The Secret Mission of Christopher Columbus*, Macmillan, 1973; Erich Kahler, *The Inward Turn of Narrative*, Princeton University Press, 1973; Hans Georg Wunderlich, *The Secret of Crete*, Macmillan, 1974; Joachim C. Fest, *Hitler*, Harcourt, 1974; Jozsef Cardinal Mindszenty, *Memoirs*, Macmillan, 1974.

J. Thorwald, *The Illusion*, Harcourt, 1975; *An Exceptional Friendship: The Correspondence of Thomas Mann and Erich Kahler*, Cornell University Press, 1975; A. Speer, *Inside the Walls of Spandau*, Macmillan, 1976; Uwe George, *In the Deserts of This Earth*, Harcourt, 1977; Leonie Kooiker (pseudonym of Johanna M. Kooyker-Romijn), *The Magic Stone* (illustrated by Carl Hollander), Morrow, 1978; Hans Joachim Schadlish, *Approximations*, Harcourt, 1979; Hans Christian Andersen, *Thumbeline* (illustrated by Lisbeth Zwerger), Morrow, 1980; T. Mann, *Diaries, 1918-1939*, Abrams, 1982; Albert Schweitzer, *Albert Schweitzer* (illustrated by Etienne Delessert), Creative Education, 1985. Also translator of Franz Kafka's *Letters to Friends, Family, Publishers*, Schocken Books; Thomas Bernhard's *Gargoyles;* J. Pieper's *Guide to Thomas Aquinas;* and many others.

SIDELIGHTS: Winston was born in a back room of a second-hand bookshop in New York City. She was more influenced by a bookish family atmosphere than by formal education, and by sixteen, was already writing poetry. For the next six years Winston wrote and published poetry and then began writing prose.

She is, however, best remembered for the numerous translations she did with her husband, Richard. Together they translated more than 150 books including the works of Thomas Mann, Franz Kafka, Albert Speer, Hermann Hesse, and other German writers, winning numerous awards for their translations, including the American Book Award in 1978 for their translation of George's *In the Deserts of This Earth*. About their work together, Winston once remarked: "We worked on everything from the sublime to the ridiculous with little hope of payment.

"You need stamina. You begin a book and it goes on and on; you don't always admire it, but you have to be careful about every detail." [C. Gerald Fraser, "Richard Winston, 62, Translator of Books from German, Is Dead," *New York Times Biographical Service*, January, 1980.[1]]

Winston claimed that by working together, they were able to avoid the usual loneliness associated with the job. "The book becomes more alive because we are both engaged in it. We talked about it while working on it. We were both giving full attention to it."[1]

Their collaboration ended with the death of Richard on December 22, 1979. Clara Winston continued their work until her death on November 7, 1983. At the time, she was working with her daughter Krishna on a translation of a book by Goethe.

FOR MORE INFORMATION SEE: Library Journal, February 15, 1952; *Observer Review*, November 16, 1969, June 21, 1970, November 20, 1970, December 11, 1970; *New York Times*, August 24, 1970, November 27, 1970; *Newsweek*, August 31, 1970, March 8, 1971; *Nation*, September 14, 1970; *Listener*, December 31, 1970; *Antioch Review*, fall/winter, 1970-71, spring, 1971; *Bookseller*, January 16, 1971, March 27,

1971; *Time*, February 22, 1971; *Saturday Review*, February 27, 1971; *Books and Bookmen*, February, 1971; *Christian Science Monitor*, March 25, 1971; *Best Sellers*, April 15, 1971.

Obituaries: *New York Times*, November 10, 1983.

WINSTON, Richard   1917-1979

PERSONAL: Born July 21, 1917, in New York, N.Y.; died of pulmonary cancer, December 22, 1979, in Brattleboro, Vt.; married Clara (a professional translator and a novelist; died, November 7, 1983); children: Krishna Winston-Billingsley, Justina Winston Gregory.

CAREER: Professional translator for thirty-six years, working chiefly from the German, but also doing translations from four other European languages; biographer, lecturer, and reviewer. *Awards, honors:* American Translators Association Alexander Gold Medal, 1966; P.E.N. Translation Prize, 1971, for *The Letters of Thomas Mann 1889-1955;* Guggenheim fellowship, 1971; American Book Award for Translation, 1978, for *In the Deserts of This Earth;* International Board on Books for Young People Translator's Honor List, 1980, for *The Magic Stone*.

WRITINGS: Charlemagne: From the Hammer to the Cross, Bobbs-Merrill, 1954; *Thomas Becket*, Knopf, 1967; (with wife, Clara Winston) *Notre-Dame de Paris*, Newsweek, 1971; (with C. Winston) *Daily Life in the Middle Ages*, American Heritage Publishing, 1975; *Thomas Mann: The Making of an Artist*, Knopf, 1981.

Translator: Valeriu Marou, *Ancient on Power: The Life and Times of Machiavelli*, Farrar & Rinehart, 1939; Theodor Reik, *From Thirty Years with Freud*, Farrar & Rinehart, 1940.

Translations in collaboration with C. Winston: H. E. Jacob, *Six Thousand Years of Bread*, Doubleday, 1944; Herman Rauschning, *Time of Delirium*, Appleton, 1946; Theodor Plievier, *Stalingrad*, Appleton, 1946; Hans Bernd Gisevius, *To the Bitter End*, Houghton, 1947; Rene Fulop-Miller, *Sing, Brat, Sing*, Holt, 1949.

R. Fulop-Miller, *The Web*, Abelard, 1950; H. E. Jacob, *Joseph Haydn*, Rinehart, 1950; Jurgen Thorwald, *The Triumph of Surgery*, Pantheon, 1950; Walter Mehring, *The Lost Library*, Bobbs-Merrill, 1951; Margot Benary-Isbert, *The Ark*, Harcourt, 1953; M. Benary-Isbert, *Rowan Farm*, Harcourt, 1954; M. Benary-Isbert, *The Shooting Star*, Harcourt, 1954; Johanna Moosdorf, *Flight to Africa*, Harcourt, 1954.

Konrad Adenauer, *World Indivisible*, Harper, 1955; Viktor E. Frankl, *The Doctor and the Soul*, Knopf, 1955; R. Fulop-Miller, *The Night of Time*, Bobbs-Merrill, 1955; Kaethe Kollwitz, *Diary and Letters*, Regnery, 1955; M. Benary-Isbert, *The Wicked Enchantment*, Harcourt, 1955; M. Benary-Isbert, *Castle on the Border*, Harcourt, 1956; Luise Rinser, *Nina*, Regnery, 1956; Henry Winterfeld, *Detectives in Togas* (illustrated by Charlotte Kleinert), Harcourt, 1956; Jacques Carton, *La Belle Sorel*, Ives Washburn, 1956; C. W. Ceram, *The Secret of the Hittites*, Knopf, 1956; Hannah Arendt, *Rahel Varnhagen: The Life of a Jewish Woman* East & West Library, 1957; C. W. Ceram, *The March of Archaeology*, Knopf, 1958; Heimito von Doderer, *The Demons*, Knopf, 1958; Josef Pieper, *Happiness and Contemplation*, Pantheon, 1958; L. Rinser, *Rings of Glass*, Regnery, 1958; J. Thorwald, *The Century of the Surgeon*, Pantheon, 1959; Ethelbert Stauffer, *Jesus and His Story*, Knopf, 1959; Erich Schenk, *Mozart and His Times*,

Knopf, 1959; Friedrich Duerrenmatt, *The Pledge,* Knopf, 1959; Thomas Mann, *Last Essays,* Knopf, 1959; M. Benary-Isbert, *The Long Way Home,* Harcourt, 1959; J. Pieper, *Prudence,* Pantheon, 1959.

F. Duerrenmatt, *Traps,* Knopf, 1960; R. Fulop-Miller, *The Silver Bacchanal,* Atheneum, 1960; T. Mann, *Letters to Paul Amann,* Wesleyan University Press, 1960; J. Pieper, *Scholasticism,* Pantheon, 1960; T. Mann, *The Story of a Novel: The Genesis of Dr. Faustus,* Knopf, 1961; Erich Maria Remarque, *Heaven Has No Favorites,* Harcourt, 1961; J. Thorwald, *The Dismissal,* Pantheon, 1961; Hans Sahl, *The Few and the Many,* Harcourt, 1962; Felix Klee, *Paul Klee,* Braziller, 1962; Walter Nigg, *The Heretics,* Knopf, 1962; Ernst Benz, *The Eastern Orthodox Church,* Doubleday, 1963; H. E. Jacob, *Felix Mendelssohn and His Times,* Prentice-Hall, 1963; Carl G. Jung, *Memories, Dreams, Reflections,* Pantheon, 1963; J. Pieper, *Belief and Faith: A Philosophical Tract,* Harcourt, 1963; H. von Doderer, *Every Man a Murderer,* Knopf, 1964; Martin Gregor-Dellin, *The Lamp Post,* Knopf, 1964; Rolf Hochhuth, *The Deputy,* Grove, 1964; J. Pieper, *Enthusiasm and Divine Madness,* Harcourt, 1964.

E. Benz, *Buddhism or Communism,* Doubleday, 1965; C. W. Ceram, *Archaeology of the Cinema,* Harcourt, 1965; F. Duerrenmatt, *Once a Greek,* Knopf, 1965; J. Pieper, *In Tune with the World,* Harcourt, 1965; J. Thorwald, *The Century of the Detective,* Harcourt, 1965; Herbert Wendt, *The Red, White and Black Continent,* Doubleday, 1966; Uwe Johnson, *Two Views,* Harcourt, 1966; Gunnel Linde, *The White Stone,* Harcourt, 1966; Karl Loewenstein, *Max Weber's Political Ideas in the Perspective of Our Time,* University of Massachusetts Press, 1966; M. Benary-Isbert, *Blue Mystery,* Harcourt, 1967; Hermann Hesse, *The Glass Bead Game,* Holt, 1969.

(From *Thumbeline* by Hans Christian Andersen. Illustrated by Lisbeth Zwerger. Translated from the Danish by Richard and Clara Winston.)

H. Hesse, *Klingsor's Last Summer,* Farrar, Strauss, 1970; Albert Speer, *Inside the Third Reich,* Macmillan, 1970; C. W. Ceram, *The First American,* Harcourt, 1971; *The Letters of Thomas Mann 1889-1955,* Knopf, 1971; J. Thorwald, *The Patients,* Harcourt, 1972; Simon Wiesenthal, *Sails of Hope: The Secret Mission of Christopher Columbus,* Macmillan, 1973; Erich Kahler, *The Inward Turn of Narrative,* Princeton University Press, 1973; Hans Georg Wunderlich, *The Secret of Crete,* Macmillan, 1974; Joachim C. Fest, *Hitler,* Harcourt, 1974; Jozsef Cardinal Mindszenty, *Memoirs,* Macmillan, 1974.

J. Thorwald, *The Illusion,* Harcourt, 1975; *An Exceptional Friendship: The Correspondence of Thomas Mann and Erich Kahler,* Cornell University Press, 1975; A. Speer, *Inside the Walls of Spandau,* Macmillan, 1976; Uwe George, *In the Deserts of This Earth,* Harcourt, 1977; Leonie Kooiker (pseudonym of Johanna M. Kooyker-Romijn), *The Magic Stone* (illustrated by Carl Hollander), Morrow, 1978; Hans Joachim Schadlish, *Approximations,* Harcourt, 1979; Hans Christian Andersen, *Thumbeline* (illustrated by Lisbeth Zwerger), Morrow, 1980; T. Mann, *Diaries, 1918-1939,* Abrams, 1982; Albert Schweitzer, *Albert Schweitzer* (illustrated by Etienne Delessert), Creative Education, 1985. Also translator of Franz Kafka's *Letters to Friends, Family, Publishers,* Schocken Books; Thomas Bernhard's *Gargoyles;* J. Pieper's *Guide to Thomas Aquinas;* and many others.

SIDELIGHTS: Richard Winston was born, raised, and educated in New York City, and first began translating books for German exiles who lived there in the late 1930s. He became interested in the German language at Brooklyn College, and from the onset of his career as a translator, German was his primary interest.

In partnership with his wife, Clara, he translated the work of Thomas Mann, Martin Buber, Hermann Hesse, Franz Kafka, Albert Speer, as well as other prominent literary figures. In all, they translated over 150 major books and many smaller works, working principally at turning German prose into English, although they also translated Dutch, French, Norwegian, Swedish and Danish. "Every translator makes his way through thickets of words, across the barriers of national psychologies, toward this ideal. He falls into all kinds of traps on the way, and he is likely to make a fool of himself. But if he has the artist's passion for perfection, he keeps trying anyhow.

"This sounds rather melodramatic in connection with the lowly translator. But translators do have a passion for perfection, and translation at its best is an art. When it reaches greatness, as it occasionally does, the qualities that make it great are both as obvious and as indefinable as greatness in any art. As with everything else, it is more often run-of-the-mill than either terribly bad or very good. And as with any other art, it is more rewarding to talk about craft and craftsmen than to consider the higher theory.

"I am sometimes asked to work over translations done by amateurs. At such times I am always impressed afresh by the importance of technique. Amateur translations have a dispiriting sameness about them. Inevitably they strain for literalness; they try to convey the sense of every slightest particle in the original. Yet all the subtler modulations of the original are missing. The translation reads like a piece of music that rocks unimaginatively back and forth between tonic and dominant. The sentences lack rhythm entirely or have a movement quite foreign to English. Of the living emotion in the original you find only fossil remains.

"These amateur translations may have been done by persons who have an intimate knowledge of the foreign language, lit-

erature and culture. Some are done by writers who are good or even gifted stylists at their own writing. Yet a good English style and knowledge of the other language are only the minimum equipment for the translator. So much more is involved in translation than the substitution of equivalent words. Ideally, the translator should combine the abilities of both writer and editor—although if he is too much of a writer he will balk at the self-denial that good translation demands. . . .

"Every language, every writer and every book pose their own special problems for the translator. That is, every work to be translated has three kinds of peculiarity. Intellectually or intuitively, the translator has to assess these qualities and then reproduce them in English.

"In translating from the German, for example, we must always be on our guard against sentimentality and overemphasis. The German language itself allows greater leeway for these qualities than does English. The translator has to impose some of the notorious Anglo-Saxon restraint upon the German text, or the translation will sound grotesque. . . .

"Another major problem of translation from the German is clarification of the thought. Nietzsche wrote that the Germans have a fondness for everything 'crepuscular, misty and obscure.' This lack of verbal definiteness has advantages; German can achieve emotional and musical effects that can hardly be put into English. There is no question here of the 'superiority' or 'inferiority' of one language in respect to another. They are simply different, and the translator must take their differences into account. Where the German is general, the translator must often make his English specific.

"French, on the other hand, is justly famous for its clarity. English lies somewhere in between French and German. To turn French successfully into natural English the translator may find he has to blur slightly the lucidity of French prose. . . . For French clarity is largely due to the liberal use of distinguishing adjectives. If German is a language of nouns, French is a language of adjectives. When French prose is translated literally into English, the effect is 'overwriting.' The translator has to recast sentences, using other parts of speech in place of adjectives." [Richard Winston, "The Craft of Translation," *American Scholar,* Volume 19, number 1, winter, 1949-50.[1]]

Over the thirty-six years the Winstons were professional translators, they gained the reputation of being the foremost German translators in the United States. Among the awards that they received were the P.E.N. Translation Prize and a National Book Award for translation. Winston believed that " . . . successful transmutation of thought and emotion from one language to another is both a technique and, ultimately, a mystery. How a translator earns his living is another mystery. . . .

"The fact is that they don't make a living. How could they? The translator's fee for even the hardest kind of translation, abstruse technical stuff like philosophy, rarely exceeds ten dollars a thousand words. The cheapest pulp magazines and the smallest trade journals pay more than that for their material. In this age, when every intellectual can hope that some day he will be rewarded far beyond his merits, the translator is without that comforting illusion. He knows he'll always live on Grub Street.

" . . . Certainly translation is no profession for those who are bent on security. Nor is it a profession for those seeking even modest recognition. Acclaim for a translation . . . is very rare. It is the usual thing for translations not to be noticed at all. Unless they are really atrocious, they are taken for granted.

"Yet there must be some compensations, or no one would stick to so unrewarding an occupation. What are they?

"This is a question I have asked myself many times. Part of the answer is the satisfaction of working as a free lance, of not being tied to routine. (This is a specious lure.) Another part, perhaps, is that translation is the creative process within a fixed framework. Possibly the translator's creative satisfaction is like the actor's, whose lines are already written.

"I was never sure. Then one day I read what Justin O'Brien, the translator of Gide, had said to an interviewer. Quite inadvertently he had touched the heart of the matter. How often I had had the same feeling! I realized that fulfilment for the translator lies in his identification with the writer.

"'Sometimes,' O'Brien had said of Gide's *Journals,* 'I feel as though I had written them myself.'"[1]

Winston's literary career was cut short by his death in 1979, while he was writing a biography of Thomas Mann, according to his wife, Clara, who noted: " . . . Dick would jokingly tell friends that he expected to spend the rest of his life on the biography. He was cheerful, sustaining his faith in the project even when not directly at work on it. For often time had to be set aside for the translation that was our livelihood. Thomas Mann had also done his writing amidst much other business.

"Dick was troubled, though, in his last year, by how slowly reading went. It was age, he supposed; he was now two years over the line of sixty, though such chronology seemed scarcely to matter. There was no lapse in his vitality or his confidence that he could do what he meant to. In a rainy spell in mid-August he caught some kind of cold, began to cough. It seemed only a summer flu, but it hung on and there was a good deal of pain. By the end of September it was diagnosed as cancer of the lungs. So common a phrase, so hard to comprehend. Chemotherapy was begun; and though the doctors warned that it could only be palliative, they suggested that if it worked at all, it might give him six to nine months.

"The treatment seemed to work well. Dick reasoned that with his sound constitution and his will, he could extend the period long enough to finish the book, which now of course would have to be far more summary. But perhaps it would be more vivid that way. He was even glad of having such a good reason to let other responsibilities go, to practice a singlemindedness that had normally seemed too great a luxury.

"He lay upstairs in his sunny room and went on with the reading of *The Magic Mountain,* which he was now attacking 'with a pencil,' as Thomas Mann would have said. I would find him smiling with pleasure. He even sat at his desk and continued smoothly, with seeming imperturbability, from the previous section. He outlined to me where he was going. In his writing he had reached the point of *Death in Venice,* which was the place to deal with a delicate, perhaps crucial, biographical question. Of course it was, like much else in Thomas Mann's life, ambiguous. But Dick thought he could put the matter in perspective, for he had evidence from all the periods in Mann's life that had to be balanced. But he was never to muster these arguments. The medical promises, which had also been ambiguous, were suddenly withdrawn, and we were left with our own special cause for tears—'Those clear drops flowing in such bitter abundance every hour of the day all over our world.'" [Clara Winston, "Afterword," *Thomas Mann: The Making of an Artist,* by Richard Winston, Knopf, 1981.[2]]

FOR MORE INFORMATION SEE: Richard Winston, "The Craft of Translation," *American Scholar,* winter, 1949-50; *Observer Review,* November 16, 1969, June 21, 1970, November 20, 1970, December 11, 1970; *New York Times,* August 24, 1970, November 27, 1970; *Newsweek,* August 31, 1970, March 8, 1971; *Nation,* September 14, 1970; *Listener,* December 31, 1970; *Antioch Review,* fall/winter, 1970-71, spring, 1971; *Bookseller,* January 16, 1971, March 27, 1971; *Time,* February 22, 1971; *Saturday Review,* February 27, 1971; *Books and Bookmen,* February, 1971; *Christian Science Monitor,* March 25, 1971; *Best Sellers,* April 15, 1971.

Obituaries: *New York Times,* January 5, 1980.

Cumulative Indexes

Character Index

The following index lists selected characters from books and other media created by the authors and illustrators who appear in *Something about the Author (SATA)* and in its companion series, *Yesterday's Authors of Books for Children* (noted below as *YABC*). This index is intended to help readers locate a *SATA* (or *YABC*) entry when they know the name of a character but not the name of its creator.

In this limited space it would be impossible to cite every character; yet there is no final authority that might determine the ''most important'' characters. (Several hundred important characters might be taken from Dickens alone, for example.) Therefore, the *SATA* editors have used their best judgment in selecting those characters that are most likely to interest *SATA* users. Realizing that some favorite character may not appear in this index, the editors invite all users, and librarians in particular, to suggest additional names, thereby helping to build a uniquely useful research tool for young people.

Each entry in this index gives the character's name followed by a ''*See*'' reference to the character's creator and the *SATA* (or *YABC*) volume number in which the creator's bio-bibliographical sketch can be found. If a character's name is not part of the title of the work in which the character appears, the title of the work is also listed below the character's name in this index. Character names are given in non-inverted form. For example: ''Bartholomew Cubbins'' is listed in the B's; ''Captain Nemo'' is listed in the C's.

Character Index

Illustrations Index

(In the following index, the number of the volume in which an illustrator's work appears is given *before* the colon, and the page on which it appears is given *after* the colon. For example, a drawing by Adams, Adrienne appears in Volume 2 on page 6, another drawing by her appears in Volume 3 on page 80, another drawing in Volume 8 on page 1, and another drawing in Volume 15 on page 107.)

YABC

Index citations including this abbreviation refer to listings appearing in *Yesterday's Authors of Books for Children,* also published by the Gale Research Company, which covers authors who died prior to 1960.

Author Index

The following index gives the number of the volume in which an author's biographical sketch, Brief Entry, or Obituary appears.

This index includes references to all entries in the following series, which are also published by Gale Research Company.

YABC—*Yesterday's Authors of Books for Children: Facts and Pictures about Authors and Illustrators of Books for Young People from Early Times to 1960,* Volumes 1-2

CLR—*Children's Literature Review: Excerpts from Reviews, Criticism, and Commentary on Books for Children,* Volumes 1-15

SAAS—*Something about the Author Autobiography Series,* Volumes 1-7